PENGUIN

THE PENGUIN BOOK OF RUSSIAN POETRY

ROBERT CHANDLER has translated Sappho and Guillaume Apollinaire for Everyman's Poetry. His translations from Russian include Alexander Pushkin's *Dubrovsky* and *The Captain's Daughter*, Nikolay Leskov's *Lady Macbeth of Mtsensk* and Vasily Grossman's *Life and Fate*, *Everything Flows* and *The Road*. With his wife Elizabeth and other colleagues he has co-translated numerous works by Andrey Platonov; *Soul* won the 2004 American Association of Teachers of Slavic and East European Languages award for best translation from a Slavonic language, as did his translation of *The Railway* (2006) by the contemporary Uzbek novelist Hamid Ismailov. His *Russian Short Stories from Pushkin to Buida* and *Russian Magic Tales from Pushkin to Platonov* are published in Penguin Classics.

BORIS DRALYUK holds a PhD in Slavic Languages and Literatures from UCLA and is a Lecturer in Russian at the University of St Andrews. His work has appeared in the *Times Literary Supplement*, *The New Yorker*, *World Literature Today* and other journals. He is the translator of Lev Tolstoy's *How Much Land Does a Man Need* (2010), *A Slap in the Face: Four Russian Futurist Manifestos* (2013), Anton Chekhov's *Little Trilogy* (2014), Isaac Babel's *Red Cavalry* (2014); co-translator of Polina Barskova's *The Zoo in Winter: Selected Poems* (2011) and Dariusz Sośnicki's *The World Shared: Poems* (2014); and author of the monograph *Western Crime Fiction Goes East: The Russian Pinkerton Craze 1907–1934* (2012). He received first prize in the 2011 Compass Translation Award competition and, with Irina Mashinski, first prize in the 2012 Joseph Brodsky/Stephen Spender Translation Prize competition.

IRINA MASHINSKI is a bilingual poet, the author of nine books of poetry and translations. Her most recent collections are *Volk* (Wolf, 2009) and *Ophelia i masterok* (Ophelia and the Trowel, 2013). Irina Mashinski's work has been translated into several languages and has appeared in *Poetry International*, *Fulcrum*, *Zeek*, *The London Magazine* and other literary journals and anthologies, both in Russia and abroad. She is the co-founder (with the late Oleg Woolf) and editor of the StoSvet literary project, which includes the literary journals *Cardinal Points* (in English) and *Storony Sveta* (in Russian). She has received several literary awards, most recently first prize in the 2012 Joseph Brodsky/Stephen Spender Translation Prize competition (with Boris Dralyuk). Irina Mashinski holds a PhD in Physical Geography from Lomonosov Moscow State University and an MFA in Poetry from New England College.

The Penguin Book of Russian Poetry

Edited by
ROBERT CHANDLER, BORIS DRALYUK
and IRINA MASHINSKI

with introductory notes to the individual poets by
ROBERT CHANDLER and BORIS DRALYUK

PENGUIN BOOKS

PENGUIN CLASSICS

UK | USA | Canada | Ireland | Australia
India | New Zealand | South Africa

Penguin Books is part of the Penguin Random House group of companies
whose addresses can be found at global.penguinrandomhouse.com.

Penguin
Random House
UK

These translations first published in book form in Penguin Classics 2015

014

This publication was effected under the auspices of the Mikhail Prokhorov Foundation
TRANSCRIPT Programme to Support Translations of Russian Literature.

Mikhail
Prokhorov
Fund

transcript

Supporting
the translation
of Russian
literature

Published with the support of the Institute for Literary Translation, Russia

ИНСТИТУТ ПЕРЕВОДА

AD VERBUM

This book has been selected to receive financial assistance from English PEN's 'PEN Translates!' programme, supported by Arts Council England. English PEN exists to promote literature and our understanding of it, to uphold writers' freedoms around the world, to campaign against the persecution and imprisonment of writers for stating their views, and to promote the friendly cooperation of writers and the free exchange of ideas. www.englishpen.org

ENGLISH PEN

ARTS COUNCIL ENGLAND

Supported using public funding by
ARTS COUNCIL
ENGLAND

Set in 10.25/12.25pt Adobe Sabon
Typeset by Jouve (UK), Milton Keynes
Printed in Great Britain by Clays Ltd, Elcograf S.p.A.

ISBN: 978-0-141-19830-9

www.greenpenguin.co.uk

MIX
Paper from
responsible sources
FSC® C018179
FSC
www.fsc.org

Penguin Random House is committed to a sustainable future for our business, our readers and our planet. This book is made from Forest Stewardship Council® certified paper.

Contents

3
ALEXANDER PUSHKIN

4
AFTER PUSHKIN

5
THE TWENTIETH CENTURY

6
THREE MORE RECENT POETS

7
FOUR POEMS BY NON-RUSSIANS

Chronology

1380 Battle of Kulikovo. The power of Muscovy begins to grow; that of the Mongols to wane.

1652 Patriarch Nikon's reforms to Orthodox rituals bring about a major schism.

1682 Archpriest Avvakum, the chief opponent of these reforms, is burnt to death.

1703 Peter the Great founds St Petersburg.

1799 Birth of Alexander Pushkin.

1812 Napoleon captures Moscow but is forced to retreat.

1825 Decembrist Revolt: an unsuccessful coup by liberal members of the aristocracy. Tsar Nicholas I comes to the throne.

1833 Pushkin publishes *Eugene Onegin*.

1837 Pushkin is killed in a duel.

1840 Publication of Lermontov's *A Hero of Our Time*.

1841 Lermontov is killed in a duel.

1842 Publication of Gogol's *Dead Souls* and 'The Greatcoat'.

1853–6 The Crimean War, which ends in Russia's defeat.

1861 Emancipation of the serfs.

1865–9 Publication of Tolstoy's *War and Peace*.

1879–80 Publication of Dostoevsky's *The Brothers Karamazov*.

1881 Alexander II assassinated by members of the terrorist Narodnaya Volya (People's Will) organization.

1891 Beginning of construction of Trans-Siberian Railway.

1905 Russia is defeated in a war with Japan. The '1905 Revolution' is defused by liberal reforms. Russia becomes, in principle, a constitutional monarchy.

1910 Tolstoy's funeral is attended by several thousand people.

1914 First World War begins. Sankt-Peterburg (St Petersburg) is given the more Russian name of Petrograd.
1916 Murder of Rasputin, a self-styled 'holy man' who exercised a malign influence on the Tsar and his family.
1917 Nicholas II abdicates after the February Revolution. Workers' soviets (i.e., councils) are set up in Petrograd and Moscow. Lenin and his Bolshevik Party seize power in October.
1918–21 Russian Civil War. After 1919: emigration of much of the upper and middle class, including Bunin, Nabokov, Teffi and Georgy Ivanov.
1921 Alexander Blok dies on 7 August. Nikolay Gumilyov is executed on 25 August.
1922 Official establishment of the Union of Soviet Socialist Republics (USSR).
1924 Death of Lenin. Petrograd is renamed Leningrad. Stalin begins to assume power.
1925 Sergey Yesenin commits suicide.
1929 Collectivization of agriculture begins.
1930 Vladimir Mayakovsky commits suicide.
1932 Foundation of Union of Soviet Writers.
1933 Nobel Prize for Literature awarded to Bunin.
1934 First congress of Union of Soviet Writers. First arrest of Osip Mandelstam.
1934–39 The purges: a million people are shot and several million sent to the Gulag.
1939 Stalin–Hitler pact. Beginning of Second World War.
1941 Hitler invades the USSR. Leningrad is blockaded and Moscow threatened.
1945 End of Second World War.
1946 Control over the arts is tightened. Akhmatova and Zoshchenko are expelled from the Writers' Union. Platonov's 'The Return' is fiercely criticized.
1953 Death of Stalin. Khrushchev begins to seize power.
1956 Khrushchev denounces Stalin at twentieth Party Congress. Varlam Shalamov returns to Moscow, one of several millions released from the camps. Start of more liberal period known as 'The Thaw'.

1958 Pressured by the Soviet authorities, Pasternak declines the Nobel Prize for Literature.

1962 Publication of Solzhenitsyn's *One Day in the Life of Ivan Denisovich*.

1964 Khrushchev is replaced by a triumvirate of Brezhnev, Kosygin and Gromyko. Brezhnev soon becomes the unchallenged leader, and remains so until his death in 1982. The Brezhnev era is often called 'the time of stagnation'.

1974 Solzhenitsyn deported after publication in the West of *The Gulag Archipelago*.

1985 Gorbachev comes to power. Beginning of period of reform known as *perestroika* ('restructuring'); the next few years see the first publication in Russia of works by Grossman, Kharms, Nabokov, Platonov, Shalamov, Solzhenitsyn and others.

1987 Joseph Brodsky receives the Nobel Prize for Literature.

1991 Yeltsin becomes President of the Russian Federation. The USSR breaks up.

Introduction

A friend – a well-read poet and editor – once told me how astonished he had been to discover, many years after first reading him, that Mayakovsky – the Poet of the Russian Revolution – always wrote in rhyme and metre. My friend does not know Russian and all the translations he had seen were in free verse. And he had taken it for granted that a revolutionary poet would want to be free of the constraints of traditional form . . . Russian poetry, however, has developed differently from the poetry of most other European countries.

In the development of a culture, as in the life of an individual, poetry comes before prose. In the life of a country, the oral epic comes before the novel; in the life of an individual, nursery rhymes come before stories. And poetry arises from many sources. Lyric poetry springs from prayers, charms and magic spells; narrative poetry from the need to preserve important myths in a memorable form.

In most of Europe the invention of print made it seem less important that a work of literature be easy to commit to memory. The decline of a magical or religious worldview also did much to encourage the rise of prose and the decline of poetry. Russia, however, has never seen the full emergence of a rational and secular culture – the official ethos of the Soviet era, though avowedly secular, was supremely *irrational* – and poetry has, throughout most of the last two hundred years and in most social milieus, retained its importance. Almost all Russians see Pushkin, rather than Tolstoy or Dostoevsky, as their greatest writer. Akhmatova, Mandelstam, Pasternak and Tsvetaeva are loved at least as passionately as Bulgakov, Nabokov, Platonov, Sholokhov and Zoshchenko.

In the late eighteenth and early nineteenth centuries poetry's pre-eminence was unchallenged. There was no prose fiction as important as the work of Derzhavin, Krylov or the poets of the 'Golden Age' – that is, Pushkin and his contemporaries. Only for a single brief period – the second half of the nineteenth century – did poetry become secondary to prose. The serfs were liberated in 1861. The Trans-Siberian Railway was built in the 1890s. A Russian middle class was coming into being, and the novel, at least for a while, seemed better able than poetry to answer its political and social concerns. Early twentieth-century Europe, however, saw a general collapse of belief in reason and progress. In Russia this was more sudden, and more complete, than in most other countries. The realistic novel now seemed oddly unreal. Poetry again became dominant, and most of the poets of this 'Silver Age' held to a magical view of the world. A poet's business was to listen to the music of other worlds – not to interpret this world. Most of the poetry of Alexander Blok and his fellow Symbolists is incantatory; rhyme and rhythm draw still more attention to themselves than in the work of earlier poets.

During the Soviet period poetry became even more dominant. Even the Bolshevik political leaders had a magical belief in the power of the word. They found it difficult to bring into being the new world they had promised; it was easier simply to proclaim its existence through speeches and slogans. As for poetry, it remained unapologetically itself, insisting on the formal features that distinguish it from prose. Mayakovsky wrote 'agit-prop' slogans; it was crucial, of course, that these be memorable, and so, like most Russian poets before and after him, he used strong metres and prominent rhymes – both for these and for more complex poems.

As for such poets as Osip Mandelstam, Anna Akhmatova and others disaffected with the new reality, they were soon living in what Akhmatova called a 'pre-Gutenberg' age. They could no longer publish their own poems and it was dangerous to write them down. Akhmatova's confidante, Lydia Chukovskaya

(1907–96), has described how writers would memorize one another's works. Akhmatova would write out a poem on a scrap of paper, a visitor would read it and Akhmatova would burn the paper. 'It was like a ritual,' Chukovskaya says. 'Hands, matches, an ashtray. A ritual beautiful and bitter.'[1] Mandelstam died in a prison camp in 1938. Had his handling of rhyme, metre and other formal devices been less perfect, his widow might have been unable to preserve his work in her memory and much might have been lost.

Russian poetry has been forced, again and again, to return to its oral origins. This is especially evident with regard to the Gulag. There are many accounts of how people survived, and helped their fellow-prisoners to survive, through reciting poetry. The poet and ethnographer Nina Gagen-Torn has written how, in 1937, she and a cellmate were between them able to recite most of Nikolay Nekrasov's *Russian Women*, a poem of at least two thousand lines about two aristocratic women, who, in 1826, chose to follow their husbands – participants in the failed Decembrist Revolt – to exile in Siberia. Ten years later, imprisoned for a second time, Gagen-Torn recited Blok, Pushkin, Nekrasov, Mandelstam, Gumilyov and Tyutchev. Every day her cellmates would ask her to recite more. Afterwards it was (in her words) 'as if someone had cleaned the dust from the window with a damp sponge – everybody's eyes now seemed clearer'. Gagen-Torn goes on to reflect on the role of rhythm: 'The shamans knew that rhythm gives one power over spirits. He who had power over rhythm in the magic dance would become a shaman, an intermediary between spirits and people; he who lacked this power would fly head over heels into madness. Poetry, like the shaman's bells, leads people into the spaces of "the seventh sky".'[2]

The greatest of all works about the Gulag is Varlam Shalamov's *Kolyma Tales*, a long cycle of stories set in Kolyma, a vast area in the far north-east of the Soviet Union. Through most of the Stalin era this was, in effect, a mini-State run by the secret police, the NKVD. 'Athenian Nights', one of the *Kolyma Tales*, begins with a discussion of what the Renaissance humanist Thomas More saw as the four essential human needs – for food and sex, and to be able to urinate and defecate. Shalamov adds a fifth essential requirement: poetry. He goes on to describe a series of late-evening meetings, during his last, relatively tolerable, years in the Gulag between 1949 and 1951. When he was on night duty in a camp hospital, he and two other medical assistants – all still prisoners – regularly spent two or three hours together, sharing all the poetry they could recall. Remarkably, the 'anthology' they compiled during these 'Athenian Nights' included an early version of Akhmatova's 'Poem without a Hero', a long work not published in the Soviet Union until the late 1980s; one of the prisoners, a former scriptwriter, had been sent a copy by a friend.[3] *The Kolyma Notebooks*, Shalamov's five poem-cycles from these years, almost constitute a short anthology of world literature in themselves. There are poems not only about all the most important Russian poets, but also about Homer, Dante, Shakespeare, Victor Hugo and the *Song of Roland*. In one poem Shalamov describes himself as constructing another *Inferno* 'out of thin air', with no tools but a pencil and notebook. It seems he owed his survival, at least in part, to his creative power, to the command of rhythm that, as Gagen-Torn tells us, gave him 'power over spirits'.

Even during the post-Stalin decades poetry retained an importance in Russia that is hard for Westerners to imagine. Poems by Boris Slutsky circulated anonymously, as oral folklore. In the 1960s and 1970s both poets and singer-songwriters performed to huge and enthusiastic audiences in Soviet football stadiums. In a world governed by official lies, poetry was seen as a truth to live by. And a poem's formal integrity – its being able to stand on its own poetic feet and thus stay in a person's memory – seemed to many, including Joseph Brodsky, to be linked to its ethical integrity.

There is a clear need for a new anthology of Russian poetry in translation. Nineteenth-century Russian poetry remains a closed book to the English and American reader. Tyutchev and Fet are barely known even by name; Lermontov is recognized only as a prose writer; and people carry on lazily repeating that Pushkin is untranslatable (in spite of the late Stanley Mitchell's outstanding recent version of *Eugene Onegin*). As for the twentieth century, the idea that there are *four* great Russian poets of the era – Akhmatova, Mandelstam, Pasternak and Tsvetaeva – has gone too long unquestioned. There is a pleasing symmetry about this picture of Russian poetry being represented by two men and two women – two from Moscow and two from St Petersburg; two who survived the Stalin era and two who died young – but this does not justify the neglect of other poets of equal stature. It is a joy to be able to bring to the Anglophone reader substantial selections from such great and original poets as Georgy Ivanov and Varlam Shalamov.

Like all anthologists, we have had to omit much that is important. In the end, lack of space meant we could not include folk poetry or any of the fine poetry written for children. I would especially have liked to introduce readers to the children's poetry of Korney Chukovsky (1882–1969), both because of its intrinsic merit and because I admire Chukovsky – a true 'man of letters' who wrote well about the art of translation and who consistently used his public standing to help authors persecuted by the regime.

The nineteenth-century poets Anna Bunina (1774–1829) and Karolina Pavlova (1807–93) have also been omitted. They are important in literary history, not least because they meant a lot to some of the great Russian women poets of the twentieth century, but we have chosen *not* to include poets merely because of their historical significance. We also decided to omit Konstantin Balmont and Vyacheslav Ivanov, despite their major role in the development of Russian Symbolism.

We have included only three of the many good Soviet war poets. Our most serious omission is Alexander Tvardovsky (1910–71), whose verse narrative *Vasily Tyorkin* (1941–5) is said to have made a real contribution to the morale of the Red Army. *Tyorkin* is funny and at least relatively truthful. Its effect, however, is cumulative and no extract seemed interesting enough on its own.

We are sorry to be including only a few poems by Innokenty Annensky, possibly the greatest of the Russian Symbolists. Alexander Blok is more popular, but Annensky is subtler, more surprising. Sadly, this very subtlety defeated our attempts at translation – and our aim has been to include only translations that work as poems in English. The number of pages given to a poet does not always reflect our estimate of his or her importance.

Several large anthologies of contemporary Russian poetry in English translation have appeared in the last fifteen years, but less attention has been given to poetry from earlier periods and so we originally meant to conclude with Joseph Brodsky. In the end, though, we added a few examples of work by more recent poets. Elena Shvarts is here because her last poems have been so beautifully translated by Sasha Dugdale. Dmitry Prigov is here because we wanted to call attention to his mock addresses to the Soviet people. Strictly speaking, these are not poems at all, but they are witty, courageous and graceful. And Marina Boroditskaya's wise and tender reproach to Shakespeare's Cordelia is of obvious interest to an English-language readership.

Russia and Russian literature have long fascinated poets in the West, many of whom have written about such figures as Mandelstam and Mayakovsky. This book ends with a few lesser-known poems about Russia by non-Russians; we hope this additional perspective will prove valuable.

It is hard to predict which poems one will be able to translate and which not. There is no single correct approach to translation; translation is an art, and there is more than one way to go about it. In my own attempts to bring a given poem to life in English, I have at times tried anything from the freest of free verse to the strictest of strict forms. Nevertheless, my inclination is to favour translations that use metre and rhyme – or at least hint at them – when the original uses metre and rhyme. Form, I believe, matters.

My most important guides have been my two Russian-American co-editors Boris Dralyuk and Irina Mashinski. Both are poets in their own right, and both have a broad and deep knowledge of Russian poetry. Boris was only eight when he emigrated to the United States in 1991; unlike either Irina or myself, he is truly bilingual. Irina also emigrated in 1991, but, being older, she retains a clear memory of the last decades of the Soviet Union and of how important poetry was in that world.

Another guide has been Dimitri Obolensky, whose earlier *Penguin Book of Russian Verse* I have turned to many times since I first started learning Russian forty-five years ago. I have often had to buy new copies of this fine bilingual anthology, either because my own copy has fallen apart from constant use or because I have felt obliged to give it away. During my first visit to the Soviet Union in 1970 my Intourist guide, entranced by her first sight of Osip Mandelstam's poems, begged me to leave her my copy at the end of our trip; I, of course, agreed. I have also learned a lot from *While People still Weep over Poems* by the late Vladimir Kornilov. Kornilov writes with clarity and conviction, and his stories of his own meetings with individual poets are illuminating.

About a fifth of the translations are listed as my own, though Boris Dralyuk has helped me with most of them.* I have included translations (some already published, some new) by around fifty other translators. Among those who have contributed most are Peter France, Alexander Levitsky, Anatoly Liberman and Antony Wood; all have been a joy to work with. My thanks go, above all, to my two co-editors, and also to my wife Elizabeth, to whom I have read aloud nearly every word of this book, often many times. Working with all three of them has greatly enriched my understanding of Russian poetry.

We thank the GB-Russia Society, the Institute of Translation (Moscow), PEN and the Mikhail Prokhorov Foundation for their financial support.

This anthology is dedicated to the memory of two friends and colleagues who did not live to see its completion: Stanley Mitchell (1932–2011), translator of the definitive English *Eugene Onegin*), and Oleg Woolf (1954–2011), poet and founder of the *StoSvet* literary project.

R. C.

* All unattributed translations in the introductory notes are by Robert Chandler.

The Penguin Book of Russian Poetry

I
THE EIGHTEENTH CENTURY

Gavrila Derzhavin (1743–1816)

Gavrila Derzhavin was born in Kazan, the son of a poor country squire who died when Derzhavin was eleven years old. After receiving some formal education in Kazan, the young Derzhavin went to St Petersburg and enlisted as a private in the Guards. He served in the ranks until 1772, distinguished himself as a junior officer during the Pugachov Rebellion, left the Army in 1777 as a lieutenant colonel, then rose to high governmental office. In 1802 Alexander I appointed him Minister of Justice, only to dismiss him a year later. After 'the most illustrious, if rocky, administrative career of any great Russian writer',[1] Derzhavin spent most of his remaining years at Zvanka, his country estate near Novgorod.

Though often seen as a classicist, Derzhavin is closer in spirit to the baroque. He largely ignored the conventional system of genres and his odes contain both humour and realistic detail. One of his odes to Catherine the Great (1729–96), for example, includes a passage about a lady searching for lice in the hair of her husband, a courtier. Alexander Pushkin famously wrote that 'his genius thought in Tatar and knew no Russian grammar for want of time'.[2] This may tell us more about Pushkin's youthful irreverence than about Derzhavin himself, but there is no doubt that much of Derzhavin's verse is deliberately cacophonous – part of the reason it now seems so modern. Among the many poets who have acknowledged his influence are Tyutchev, Fet, Nekrasov, Mandelstam, Tsvetaeva and Brodsky.

Derzhavin considered his most important poem to be 'God', the first poem he published under his own name; it was translated into several languages (including Mandarin and Japanese) during his lifetime, and was widely discussed throughout Europe. Many nineteenth-century Russians knew this poem by heart, and Fyodor Dostoevsky has Dmitry Karamazov quote from it repeatedly.

In his *History of Russian Literature* D. S. Mirsky refers to Derzhavin as 'a barbarian', but he also speaks of the 'wonderful sweetness and melodiousness' of such late poems as 'Life at Zvanka', which he sees as inspired 'by an enormous love of life in all its forms'. In Mirsky's view, Derzhavin is the only Russian poet to have struck such a note 'of joyous, sturdy, sane sensuality of a green old age'.

The poet Vladislav Khodasevich published a fine biography of Derzhavin in 1931. An exile, and conscious of his own marginal status in the public world, Khodasevich envied Derzhavin his ability to combine the roles of statesman and poet.

In 1815 Derzhavin sat in on the exams of the first intake of students at the elite lycée at Tsarskoye Selo. When the young Alexander Pushkin recited a poem about the lycée, Derzhavin wept with emotion, recognizing Pushkin as a successor. Twenty years later, Pushkin based the figure of Petrusha Grinyov, the hero of *The Captain's Daughter*, at least in part on Derzhavin.

God

O Thou, in universe so boundless,
alive in planets as they swarm
within eternal flow, yet timeless,
unseen, you reign in triune form!
Thy single Spirit all comprises,
from no abode or cause arises,
keeps paths that Reason never trod,
pervades, incarnate, all that's living,
embracing, keeping and fulfilling,
to Thee we give the name of GOD!

To put the ocean depths to measure,
to sum the sands, the planet's rays,
a lofty mind might want at leisure –
but knows no rule for Thee, nor scales!
Nor can the spirits brought to seeing,
born from Thy light into their being,
trace the enigmas of Thy ways:
our thought, with daring, space traverses,
approaching Thee, in Thee disperses, –
a blink in the Abyss – no trace.

Thou didst call forth great Chaos's presence
from out the timeless, formless deep,
and then didst found Eternal essence,
before the Ages born in Thee:
within Thyself didst Thou engender
Thy selfsame radiance's splendour,
Thou art that Light whence flows light's beam.
Thine ageless Word from the beginning
unfolded all, for aye conceiving,
Thou wast, Thou art and Thou shalt be!

The chain of Being Thou comprisest,
and dost sustain it, give it breath;
End and Beginning Thou combinest,
dost Life bestow in Thee through death.
As sparks disperse, surge upward, flying,
so suns are born from Thee, undying;
as on those cold, clear winter's days
when specks of hoarfrost glisten, shimmer,
gyrate and whirl – from chasms' glimmer
so Stars cast at Thy feet bright rays.

Those billions of lumens flaming
flow through the measureless expanse,
they govern laws, enforce Thy bidding,
they pour forth life in gleaming dance.

Yet all those lampions thus blazing,
those scarlet heaps with crystal glazing,
or rolling mounds of golden waves,
all ethers in their conflagration,
each world aflame in its own station –
to Thee – they are as night to day.

A drop of water in the ocean:
such is Creation in Thy sight.
What sets the Cosmos into motion?
And what – before Thee – what am I?
Should I count worlds, afloat by billions
in heaven's seas on unseen pinions,
and multiply them hundredfold,
then dare compare to Thee their measure,
they'd form a blot for quick erasure:
and so, before Thee, I am Naught.

Before Thee, Naught! – And yet Thy brightness
shines forth through me by Thy good grace;
Thou formest in me Thine own likeness,
as in a drop Sol finds its trace.
But Naught? – Yet Life in me is calling,
uplifts me in an upward soaring
beyond the clouds my course to chart;
in search of Thee my Spirit wanders,
it reasons, contemplates and ponders:
I am – assuredly, Thou art!

Thou art! Thus claim the laws of Nature,
this Truth my heart has erstwhile known,
it gives my mind the strength to venture:
Thou art! – No naught, my Self I own!
Made part of universal order,
and set, meseems, not on its border,
but in Creation's central site,
whence crowned Thou Earth with creatures living,
with light celestial spirits filling,
and linked through me their chain of life.

I bind all worlds Thou hast created,
creation's top and crown am I,
to be Life's centre I am fated,
where mortal borders on Divine.
My body sinks to endless slumber,
and yet my mind commands the thunder,
a king – a slave – a worm – a god!
I am most marvellously fashioned,
yet, whence came I? I cannot fathom:
myself could not this self have wrought.

Thy creature am I, O Creator!
Thy wisdom shaped me, gave me form,
blest Giver, Life's Originator,
O Soul of mine own soul – my Lord!
to Thy Truth was it necessary
for my immortal soul to carry
its life, unscathed, o'er Death's abyss,
my spirit should don mortal cover,
so that I might return, O Father,
through death to Thine immortal bliss.

Ungraspable, beyond all knowledge,
my feeble fancy's listless flight
can never capture, I acknowledge,
the merest shadow of Thy light;
but hast Thou need of exaltation?
No mortal's pale imagination
could craft a song fit for Thine ears,
but must instead – to Thee aspiring,
Thy boundless variance admiring –
pour forth, before Thee, grateful tears.

(1784)*
Alexander Levitsky

* Dates of poems are included, except when unknown

To Rulers and Judges[3]

To judge the gods of Earth in council
arisen is the Most High God:
How long, quoth He, how long your counsel
will spare the wicked and corrupt?

You must uphold the Law's just ordinance,
display no favours to the strong,
leave not the widows nor the orphans
without defence or help for long.

Your charge: help Innocence recover,
give shelter to all those in pain;
defend the powerless from Power,
the poor deliver from their chains.

They hear not; though they know, they see not!
Their gaze is veiled by bribery;
the wicked shake the Earth, the Sea-bed,
and Falsehood makes the Heavens reel.

Ye Kings! I deemed you gods almighty,
with none to give your word the lie,
yet you are passionate and flighty,
you are but mortal – as am I.

As autumn leaf drops earthward, crumbled,
so shall you plummet from on high;
and you shall perish, as the humbled
poor slave you rule shall surely die!

Arise, ye Ruler of the righteous!
Give ear unto the men of worth.
Come judge the wicked and the spiteful,
and Thou alone be King of Earth!

(1780–87)

Alexander Levitsky

On the Death of Prince Meshchersky[4]

Metallic clangour! Tongue of time!
Your fatal voice oppresses me;
your groans call me insistently,
call me and speed me to the grave.
Scarcely the light of day I see
and death already grinds her teeth;
like lightning flashes her scythe gleams
and cuts my days like stalks of wheat.

Nothing escapes the fatal claws,
no creature can avoid her stroke;
monarch and slave are food for worms,
the elements devour our tombs;
time gapes and wears away our fame;
as rivers pour into the seas,
eternity eats our days and years;
kingdoms are swallowed in death's jaws.

On the abyss's edge we slide
and soon will plunge head first; our life
is given us with our death – and we,
when we are born, begin to die.
Without an ounce of pity, death
strikes all things, brings to nothing stars,
and suns are quenched by her cold breath –
destroyer of the universe.

Only we mortals think that we
shall never die, eternity
is ours – but no, death like a thief
creeps up on us and steals our life.
Alas! where least we fear her, she
is soonest there to strike us down,
more swiftly than the thunderbolts
that smash the proud peaks in a storm.

Meshchersky, son of luxury
and happy ease, where have you gone?
Leaving the shores of life behind
you wander through death's distant land.
Your dust is here, but not your soul.
Where is it now? – There. – Where is there?
We do not know, we weep and wail:
'Woe to us, born to live on earth!'

Where pleasures, love and happiness
shone brightest, in health's golden glow,
now the blood freezes in the veins
and sorrow agitates the soul.
Where once a feast was spread, there stands
a coffin, and where singers graced
the party, funeral dirges sound
and pale death looks in every face.

She looks in every face, at kings
for whom the world's a narrow space;
looks at the men of wealth, whose gold
and silver ruled our mortal race;
looks at the beauties of the world,
looks at the proud, exalted mind,
looks at the dreaded men of war
and whets the edge of her sharp scythe.

Death that makes nature quake with dread!
today we are gods, tomorrow dust,
creatures of poverty and pride,
today hope fondly flatters us,
tomorrow – man, where are you now?
Your hours have barely fled away
into the pit of chaos, your time
fades like a dream at the new day.

So like a dream of sweet delight
my youthful years have gone. No more
does beauty tempt me as it did,
nor is my spirit stirred by joy,
my mind is not so free to roam,
I am less easy with my fate:
the thirst for honours tears my soul,
I hear the urgent call of fame.

But manhood, too, will pass away,
and fame and the desire for fame;
the pull of riches will be tamed
and all the passions' urgent flame
will pass, will pass, all in their turn.
You dreams of happiness, leave me,
unreal and fleeting as you are.
I stand before eternity.

Tomorrow or today to die,
Perfilyev, that is our destiny –
why grieve then and torment yourself?
Your mortal friend eternally
could not have lived. Life is a gift
that will not last. So rest your soul
in peace, with your pure spirit bless
the stroke that fate now lays on us.

(1779)

Peter France

from *The Waterfall*[5]

A mount sifts diamonds in rows,
down from the heights, four cliffs cascading;
a pearl and silver chasm below
churns water up in massy braiding;
a blue hill looms within the spray;
the roar resounds from far away.

It roars; amidst the deep pine thickets
diffuses, blending with the brush;
athwart the brook, a swift ray quickens;
'neath shifting vaults of trees, kept hushed,
the waves roll slowly, weighed by sleeping,
their course in milky surges keeping.

In dark, dense thickets by the verge
deep mounds of greyish spume are foaming,
the wind bears hammer-blows, the whirr
of saws, the bellows' hollow groaning:
O Waterfall! Your dread abyss
devours all in depthless mist! . . .

When, wind-struck, do the pine trees creak? –
you tear asunder their tall stand.
Does thunder split the mountain peak? –
you grind all stones to finest sand.
Does ice-floe dare to bind your waters? –
to glassy dust it's crushed in torrents.

(1794)

Alexander Levitsky and Martha Kitchen

Monument[6]

I have built myself a monument, miraculous, eternal,
stronger than metal, higher than pyramids;
whirlwind and thunder will not overthrow it;
it will not be destroyed by flying years.

So! I shall not all die; my greater part,
fleeing corruption, will survive my death,
my fame will grow and spread and never fade
as long as Slavs are honoured in this world.

My name will run from the White to the Black Sea,
where Volga, Don, Neva and Ural flow;
those people's songs will guard my memory,
how from an unknown birth I became known

for being the first to dare in sprightly verse
to tell all Russia of Felitsa's[7] worth,
the first to talk of God in simple words
and with a smile to speak the truth to tsars.

O Muse! Be rightly proud of your exploits.
If any scorn you, scorn them in your turn,
and with a free unhurried hand exalt
this brow with immortality's new dawn.

(1795)

Peter France

from *To Eugene: Life at Zvanka*

Blest is that man who least depends on other men,
whose life is free from debt and from capricious striving,
who goeth not to court for praise, or gold to lend;
    and shuns all vanities conniving!

Why venture to Petropolis, if uncompelled,
change space for closeness, liberty for locks and latches,
live weighed with luxury and wealth, their siren spell,
endure the gentry's quizzing glances?

Can such a life compare with golden freedom here,
with Zvanka's solitude, with Zvanka's rest and quiet?
Abundance, health, sweet concord with my wife – and peace
to round my days – these I require. [. . .]

I see my doves with grains of wheat well fed,
then watch them as they wheel their flight above the waters,
I view the many-coloured songbirds, warbling in their nests,
and fowl which cloak the mead like snowfall.

Nearby, I hearken to the shepherd's horn; aloft –
I hear a snipe; afar – the heath-cock's muffled drum call;
below – the nightingale; now oriole peals forth,
now horses neigh, now cattle bellow.

As swallow on the roof begins her chirr, then scent
of Manchu tea or Levant coffee wafting, prompts me,
I take my place at table – the gossip starts at once:
of dreams we talk, of town and country,

or of the feats ascribed to those great men of yore
whose portraits shine from golden frames upon the panels,
preserving thus their days of fame – now kept as lore –
while sprucing up my drawing-chamber,

in which same room, at morning or at even,
I read the *Herald*, save the broadsheets for tomorrow,
I revel in our Russia's might: each man – a hero,
commanding general – Suvorov!

In which, before the mistress, for the guests to praise,
they bring the divers fustians, homespuns, textiles, weavings,
and patterned samples of embroidered napkins, lace,
of floor-cloths woven in the evenings.

I see there, from the barns and hives, the cotes and ponds,
rich gold in butter and in honeycombs on tree limbs,
in berries – royal purple, on mushrooms – velvet down,
and silver, in the bream atremble;

where, in the clinic having seen those ill or bruised,
our surgeon comes, reporting of their health and sickness,
then orders up their diet: for some it's bread and gruel,
for others wait his herbal mixtures;

where also sometimes on the tally stick or beads
a bearded elder or fat miser from the village,
sums up the treasury, the grain, provisions, deeds,
and smiles – a trickster's roguish grimace;

and where, from time to time, young artisans will flock
to show their efforts, limned on canvas or on beech-planks,
and some receive a coin or other for their work,
mayhap a half a rouble, each one.

And where, to chase off sleepiness before we sup,
we – sometimes with great vigour for the games, and ardour –
take up the cards, play faro or at whist, set up
for kopek forfeits, never rendered.

From thence I come into the Muses' sacred grove,
with Horace, Pindar, feasting with Olympians,
I raise my song to monarchs, friends, to realms above,
or tune my lyre to rustic paean. [. . .]

The while, a crowd of peasant children gathers round:
for any of my thoughts they hardly make their visit,
but rather that each one may have a pretzel or a roll,
    and learn their master's not a skinflint.[8]

And now my scribe must comb my botched and blotted page,
as shepherd combs his sheep for burdocks and for thistles,
to smooth the fleece – though no great thoughts do there engage –
    yet pebbles in their foil may glister.

When noon has struck, the servants rush to dress the board;
the mistress leads our troop of guests to sit at table.
And to my gaze the varied dishes there award
    a patterned garden, neatly angled.

The crimson ham, green sorrel soup with yolks of gold,
the rose-gold pie, the cheese that's white, the crayfish scarlet,
the caviar, deep amber, black, the pike's stripes bold,
    its feather blue – delight the eyesight.

Delight the eye and joy to every sense impart;
though not with glut or spices brought from foreign harbours,
but with their pure and wholesome Russian heart:
    provisions native, fresh and healthful. [. . .]

Yet holiday or not, I often take my leave
to sit alone, atop the span of newel railing,
my grey head bending to the *gusli*'s[9] tunes at eve,
    I soar in cherished dreamworlds, sailing –

what nimble thoughts do not then brim my sleep-drowned
    mind?
I see how all Time's dreams are swiftly flying,
the days roll on, the years, the roar of seas and wind,
    and all the Zephyrs' gentle sighing. [. . .]

And thus from night to night the brightest stars now blur;
what is this paltry life? My lyre is clay and mortal!
Alas! The dust of my remains shall be dispersed
from off this world by wings of Saturn.

This house shall fall to ruin, its orchard blighted, bare,
and no one shall recall the very name of Zvanka;
from hollow yet shall flash the barn owl's flame-green stare,
and smoke will smoulder from the hovel. [. . .]

or mayhap not, Evgene! – your pen may rouse and warn
our heirs from sleep, in that metropolis due northward;
and whisper to the trav'ller, like a distant storm:
'Here dwelt God's bard – Felitsa's prophet.'

(pub. 1808)

Alexander Levitsky

On Transience[10]

Time's river in its rushing course
carries away all human things,
drowns in oblivion's abyss
peoples and kingdoms and their kings.

And if the trumpet or the lyre
should rescue something, small or great,
eternity will gulp it down
and it will share the common fate.

(July 1816, written on a slate a few days or
perhaps only hours before Derzhavin's death)

Peter France

Ivan Krylov (1769–1844)

Ivan Andreyevich Krylov was born in Moscow. His father, an army officer, died in 1779, leaving the family destitute. In response, Krylov was quick to embark on a professional literary career; aged fourteen he sold his first comedy to a publisher and used the proceeds to buy volumes of Molière, Racine and Boileau. His father had been an avid reader.

Krylov's first volume of twenty-three fables, mostly imitations of La Fontaine, was published in 1809. It won him immediate acclaim and he was elected a member of the Russian Academy of Sciences as early as 1811. Krylov went on adding to this collection over the years and the final edition, published shortly before his death, contained 197 fables. Most of the later fables treat subjects drawn from Russian life, often inspired by topical events. Krylov also worked at the Imperial Public Library, eventually as head of the Russian Books Department – an undemanding job that allowed him plenty of time to write.

Krylov's work is remarkable for its wit, for its linguistic energy and for a musicality perhaps linked to his being a gifted violinist; throughout his life he performed both as a soloist and, alongside the best-known musicians of the day, in quartets. His language is elegant, yet vigorous; many of his most famous lines draw equally on the peasant proverb and the salon epigram. With his deep understanding of human foibles, Krylov can also be seen as a founder of Russian realism.

The following translations are by Gordon Pirie. Most stay close to the original, but some are free. 'The Donkey and the Nightingale' is more than three times longer than the original. Whether it can be called a translation is debatable, but there is no doubt about its brilliance, and it would surely have delighted Krylov – whose adaptations of Aesop and La Fontaine exhibit a similar verve and freedom.

The Donkey and the Nightingale

A donkey saw a nightingale
sitting, by day, up in a tree.
She looked so insignificant and frail,
he wondered, was this really she
whose night-time song, he'd often heard,
could not be matched by any other bird
for sweetness and variety?
'Madam,' said he,
'I know it's not your favourite hour,
but since, somehow,
I've always missed your music up to now,
do me a favour, show your power,
display your virtuosity!
Then I shall know, for sure, whether your song
is all that it's made out to be.'
She didn't keep him waiting long,
but graciously unlocked her throat,
and out the notes came, sweet and strong.
It wasn't something got by rote
and mindlessly repeated, like 'Cuckoo!'
It was the same song as she always sang,
But every time she made it new;
and this time she began
in playful mood, as if to tease
the other inmates of the wood with calls
to mimic them, such as the 'Chink!
Chink!' of the chaffinch, wide-spaced intervals
they'd never manage (spanned by her with ease),
and sudden runs and jumps that made you think
of fingers skipping nimbly over keys
or dancing among strings; then changed her tone
and dwindled to a muted, soft
and melancholy strain
that seemed to come from further off,
as if the bird herself had flown

to some dense gloomy thicket to complain;
then, as a flash-stream rises after rain
until it overflows
its banks and makes a flood,
so all at once her music rose
to such a rapid, urgent throbbing
as seemed to come almost too close
for comfort – like pulsing in the blood,
or someone loved, beside you, sobbing
as much for joy as pain.
But what's the good of trying to explain
the music of the nightingale –
you're bound to fail!
Song without words,
it spoke of what no words could tell,
and cast a spell
on all the other birds.
The wind dropped, and the grazing flocks and herds
lay down and listened too.
The shepherds stood entranced,
and now and then, as men who knew
the power of music to beguile
long hours of lonely watching, glanced
at one another with a smile.
She ceased.
The donkey, who had stood there looking down
and listening with a frown
of concentration, brow all creased,
now gave his verdict on her voice:
'Yes, that was quite a pleasant ditty –
but it's a pity
that you've not met our cock.
He makes a really splendid noise
when he stands on the dunghill, crowing loud
and clear to all his flock!
You ought to take a lesson or two
from him.' To argue would have done no good;
and anyhow, she was too proud.

In scorn the little songster bowed
her head, and off she flew
to make her music in another wood.

A donkey's ears are large and long,
but he's no connoisseur of song.

(II, 23)
Gordon Pirie

The Geese Going to Market

Geese prize their dignity,
and hate to have it ruffled; so, to be
driven along a public road
to market by a peasant
armed with a goad –
a great long stick
to prod you when your progress isn't quick
enough – is really most unpleasant.
The peasant didn't think of that:
Christmas was coming, and his geese were fat.
With jabs and prods, and now and then a curse,
he drove them down the road pell-mell,
eager to have not birds to sell,
but money in his purse.
Now I don't blame the man for this
(Men do things infinitely worse
to one another, I'm afraid,
when there's a profit to be made).
But those poor geese, they took it much amiss,
and thus addressed a passer-by
who seemed to view them with a pitying eye:
'Sir, did you ever see
unhappier geese than we?
Look how this peasant's treating us!
But then he's just an ignorant fellow,

and obviously doesn't know
that we're no ordinary geese,
but come of ancient Roman stock,
and trace our ancestry, unbroken, back
to that illustrious flock
that saved the Eternal City from the sack.'
'I see,'
replied the passer-by,
'So you've a longish pedigree . . .'
'Why yes! Our forefathers, you know . . .' 'All right!
All right! I've heard the story
of how they raised the alarm at night;
but that can hardly qualify
a modern goose for glory.
You'll have to find a better claim
to honour, than your forebears' fame.
More to the point would be to know
what you yourselves have ever done
that's been of use to anyone.
What's that you say? Nothing to show?
Well then, you silly geese,
you'd better leave your ancestors in peace!
They've had whatever fame's their due;
and as for you,
in spite of all your boasting,
I'd say you're only fit for roasting!'

To make the moral plain
would only irritate the geese again,
so I'll refrain.

(III, 15)
Gordon Pirie

The Fly and the Travellers

One hot July, about midday,
while from a burning, cloudless sky
the sun looked down, and with his fiery eye
turned fields of cut grass into hay;
while panting flocks and herds
took shelter in what little shade
was left them, and the birds,
for all the noise they made,
could well have flown away;
four sturdy horses, pulling with a will,
had dragged a big coach half way up a hill.
The coach was laden, and the roof piled high
with trunk and hamper, chest, and bag, and poke –
the copious luggage of the gentlefolk
inside. The wheels – for this was long before
the days when roads were tarred –
sank deep into the summer dust,
which made the going doubly hard.
No wonder that the team of four,
sweating and straining fit to burst,
slowed down, and would have dearly liked to stop
and rest before they reached the top.
But this was not to be allowed. Down came
the coachman from his seat, and set about
The luckless horses with a wicked knout,
while from the other side a servant did the same.
In vain – the team could go no faster.
So out from inside clambered master,
mistress, son and daughter, governess
and tutor, chambermaid – the lot!
With seven passengers the less,
the team would surely quicken to a trot.
But no – their weight was small
compared to their impediments;
and soon the pace had dwindled to a crawl,

when who should happen to come by,
but a busy little buzzing fly,
who thought that Providence had surely sent her
to help those plodding horses climb the hill.
In any case, she'd try her skill.
So down she comes, and buzzes round their eyes
And ears and noses. They, well used to flies,
pay no attention, so she tries
some other likely places:
she settles on the shaft, the traces,
she even gets astride the coachman's nose;
and when he sneezes, off she goes
to see what all those passengers are at.
The servants, deep in idle chat,
she finds are lagging far behind;
delighted to be unconfined,
the children gambol with the dog, or chase
a butterfly; my lady's walking
with governess and tutor, quietly talking;
unmindful of his proper place,
the master's wandered off into the shade
to look for mushrooms with the chambermaid –
all very fine
(and here her tone changed to a plaintive whine),
but this was not the time
to look for mushrooms, with a hill to climb!
While thus the insect fussed around,
The patient horses, flogged and fagged
almost beyond endurance, dragged
the coach up to the top, and stood on level ground.
'There now!' exclaimed the fly,
'we've made it to the crest!
Well, that was quite a strain!
And now you're on the flat again,
I'll say goodbye.
I reckon I've deserved a good long rest!'

A lot of people, like this fly,
poke fingers into every pie,
and never guess you're not delighted
to see them, though they weren't invited.

(III, 17)
Gordon Pirie

The Hind and the Hermit

A hind had lost her fawn before
her dugs were dry, and wandered, sore,
disconsolate, forlorn,
until she found,
lying abandoned on the ground,
two wolf cubs, newly born,
and suckled them, as if they were her own.
A local hermit, wonderstruck,
cried: 'Foolish creature! Why give suck
to those?
Wolves are your foes!
The day may come when, fully grown,
without a pang,
they'll tear your tender flesh with claw and fang!'
'You may be right,' replied the hind.
'Perhaps they will be so unkind
but I don't mind.
To give them suck, and see them grow,
these are the only needs I know;
and fear of what may come behind
is nothing, to the joy of doing so.'

Unused, unshared,
abundance is a burden.
Doing good should make us glad,
and virtue not require a guerdon.

(III, 19)
Gordon Pirie

The Kite and the Butterfly

A kite – the kind held by a string –
was sailing in the sky,
and looking down, observed a butterfly.
From such a height, its lowly fluttering
seemed hardly flight at all.
'I say!' the insect heard it call.
'Just look at me, riding so high
that I can hardly see you! I dare say
you can't help envying the way
I spurn the ground, and wishing you could do the same.'
'Far from it!' came
the prompt reply;
'for whereas you just dance attendance
on someone else's idle pleasure,
I fly in perfect independence;
and that's a blessing beyond measure.'

(IV, 4)
Gordon Pirie

The Lion's Share

Once, long ago, the poets say,
a wolf, a dog, a lion and a fox agreed
to pool their cunning, strength and speed,
and share, in equal portions, any prey
that came their way.
The fox, by cunning or good luck,
managed to catch a buck,
and called the other three to join the feast.
The wolf came, and the dog. Last, but not least,
the lion came, and counting on his claws,
said: 'There are four of us, so by the laws

of mathematics, I suggest
we split the carcass into four' –
and did so. Then, placing the best
bit firmly underneath his royal paw,
he said: 'This piece is due to me
by right of sovereignty.'
How could the others disagree?
And given his absolute supremacy
in feats of strength and bravery,
how could they fail to find it fair
when portions two and three should also be
included in the lion's share?
Then, tail a-twitch and eyes a-glare,
'As for the fourth,' he said,
'don't any of you dare
to touch it, or I'll strike you dead!'

(IV, 16)
Gordon Pirie

The Peasants and the River

One year, when local streams in spate
had done their best to devastate
their lands, the peasants sought redress
for all the damage and the mess
by sending off an embassy
to that great river, mistress of the plain,
to whom those lesser streams were tributary.
And there was plenty to complain about!
That autumn, after heavy rain,
the streams had burst their banks and sallied out
over the fields where, like a barbarous horde of water,
looking for battle,
eager for slaughter,
they'd flooded farms, uprooted winter corn,

and carried off unnumbered sheep and cattle,
leaving the homesteads barren and forlorn.
The river, on the other hand,
(so they'd been led to understand)
wandered sedately through the land,
bordered by stately country seats,
with here and there a thriving town,
while up and down
her placid waters, to and from the sea,
plied barges, fishing boats and paddle-steamers;
and never, in living memory,
had she been guilty of such misdemeanours.
So, hopefully,
they thought,
she'd call those lesser streams to order,
making them keep within their borders
as they ought.
But when they came up close, and gazed
at that great mass of water rushing past,
the peasants stood amazed,
aghast,
to see a number
of the precious things they'd lost
come floating by them, pitched and tossed
about like so much old, discarded lumber.
They watched them dwindle out of sight,
then shook their heads and turned
for home. Clearly, they might
have spared their journey. Still, one thing they'd learned:

where great men profit from the small man's crime,
to seek redress is just a waste of time.

(IV, 18)
Gordon Pirie

The Prodigal and the Swallow

A young man once inherited
a rich estate.
He was a likely lad, but a bit mad,
and sudden affluence went to his head.
He lived it up, at such a rate,
with eating, drinking, gambling, party-giving,
that soon he'd squandered all he had
in riotous living,
and found himself with nothing he could call
his own, except a good thick coat.
Now, had this been the month of May,
his coat, too, would have gone the way
of all the rest. But it was March, and snow still lay
deep in the streets, so he was glad
to draw it tightly round his throat
and keep the cold at bay.
But as he walked the streets one day,
he saw a swallow flying past
on long black pointed wing,
and thought: 'Ah! Spring's here at last!
No need for coats! I'll sell it! Why not?'
Why not, indeed – except that he forgot
One swallow doesn't make a spring.
Coatless now, the foolish rake
soon found he'd made a rash mistake.
After a brief, beguiling thaw,
Jack Frost came cracking down once more,
patterning every window pane,
and turning slush to ice again.
From every chimney stack, the smoke
stood straight up in the frosty air, and spoke
of indoor comforts. Weeping for the cold,
and desperate for the coat he'd sold,
our young man plodded down the street
with frozen hands and frozen feet

and nowhere warm to go.
And suddenly, there on the snow,
he saw the little harbinger of spring.
With drooping head and trailing wing,
she looked as though she'd fly no more.
He stared at her, and said
(though no one heard it for
the noise his teeth made, chattering in his head):
'Deceiving bird, you're very nearly dead!
And here am I, at Death's door too,
for having put my trust in you!'

(VII, 4)
Gordon Pirie

The Pig under the Oak Tree

A pig, let out to forage in a wood,
snuffled her way to where an oak tree stood
and found
an autumn scattering
of acorns round it on the ground –
good food for pigs, tasty and fattening.
She ate as many as she could,
lay down under the tree, and slept;
then, waking full of energy,
began to root about,
adept
at digging with her pointed snout.
'That doesn't do the oak tree any good,'
remarked a crow
perched on a branch, watching these antics down below.
'If you expose the roots like that,
the summer drought
will dry them out,
and then the tree will die.'
'Who cares?' replied the pig. 'Not I!

Maybe you birds think differently,
but I don't fly,
so this old tree's no use to me,
and might as well be lying flat
as poking up there in the sky.
Now acorns – they're another matter.
They're good to eat, and make me fatter!'
At that, the oak
rustled and spoke:
'Ungrateful creature! Why,
you've only got to lift your snout, to see
those acorns you're so fond of, growing on me!'

(VII, 7)
Gordon Pirie

The Sheep with Shaggy Fleeces

The lion found he couldn't stand
the sight of sheep with shaggy fleeces.
He could have killed the whole lot, out of hand;
but to exterminate a species
on grounds so slight,
he knew would not be right:
it wasn't for that sort of thing
he'd been appointed king.
But there it was, the awkward fact
that though he didn't mind
sheep of the usual kind,
with fleeces tidy and compact,
to see a shaggy one, whose coat hung loose,
as like as not all dagged with dirt,
and flapping like a ragged skirt –
that drove him up the wall.
So, desperate for an excuse
to do away with them, he called
the bear and fox, and having sworn them both

to secrecy, told how he'd come to loathe
the very sight of shaggy sheep.
'Sire,' growled the bear, straightforward and obtuse,
'you mustn't lose a moment's sleep
on that account. Exterminate
the lot! I wouldn't hesitate
to have them all put down!'
Seeing the lion frown,
the fox, who understood
much better how to gauge his master's mood,
cried: 'God forbid a king so good
should persecute the innocent!
How could Your Majesty consent
to shed their guiltless blood?
Allow me to propose a scheme
which, though less drastic and extreme,
may well prove more expedient.
Let certain favoured pastures be assigned
solely to sheep of this offensive kind;
and since we've no shepherds to spare,
give that job to the wolves. Under their care,
somehow, I think you'll find that by and by
those shaggy sheep will simply disappear.
In any case, it's worth a try,
and leaves the royal reputation clear.'
The lion liked the fox's plan,
and gave his orders. Others ran
to execute them. By and by
those shaggy sheep were in such short supply
that he could wander through the fields all day
and never meet one in his way.
What did his other subjects have to say?
The wolves, of course, were held to blame,
and not a word was said against the king's good name.

(VII, 27)
Gordon Pirie

The Lion, the Chamois and the Fox

Through bush and brake a lion chased
a chamois. Fleet of foot though she might be,
he gained upon her steadily.
Uphill and down, the chamois raced,
but soon the lion was so close at heel
that he felt certain of his meal.
A gully cut across their path, narrow
and sheer. The chamois jumped, and like an arrow
she flew across the deep divide.
The lion stopped. What should he do?
A fox was standing by,
and cried, 'My Lord, shall it be said that you
were beaten by a chamois? Why,
you'll do it easily!
Wide though the gap may be,
you've jumped much wider ones, as I,
your servant and your friend, can testify.'
Spurred by this flattering speech,
the lion made a desperate leap to reach
the other side. He failed,
and falling, perished on the rocks
below. What did the fox
do then? He neither wept nor wailed,
but picked his way
discreetly down to where the lion lay.
And finding that his Majesty
had no more use for flattery
or any other service, then and there
began to celebrate
his funeral in state:
he tucked into the good red meat
(it proved a rich and royal treat),
And in a week or so, the bones were bare.

(VIII, 2)
Gordon Pirie

2
AROUND PUSHKIN

Vasily Zhukovsky (1783–1852)

The son of a small landowner and his Turkish housekeeper, Vasily Andreyevich Zhukovsky was born in a village in the province of Tula, then educated in Moscow. As a young man, he was encouraged by Nikolay Karamzin, the most eminent literary figure of the day.

Through his verse translations – many of them now seen as classics of Russian literature – Zhukovsky did much to bring the Romantic Movement to Russia. Aged nineteen, he published a free translation of Thomas Gray's 'Elegy Written in a Country Churchyard' that won him immediate fame. 'A poetic uncle' – as he himself put it – 'of both German and English devils and witches,' he went on to translate Virgil, Ovid, Goethe, Schiller and Byron; with the help of German cribs, he translated the whole of the *Odyssey* and episodes from the *Shahnameh* and the *Mahabharata*. He experimented with form and metre, using blank verse and unrhymed hexameters for many of his later translations. His translations are, on the whole, finer than his original work; he himself once said, 'Almost everything of mine is someone else's, or about someone else, and yet it is all my very own.'[1]

After the Napoleonic Wars Zhukovsky's work came to the attention of the Grand Duchess Alexandra Fyodorovna, the German-born wife of the heir to the throne, and she invited him to tutor her in Russian; many of his translations of Goethe began as language exercises. Later, he was appointed tutor to her son, Alexander. Zhukovsky was a moderate and enlightened liberal, and his influence on the young tsarevich (the future Tsar Alexander II) may have been, at least in part, responsible for the latter's decision to liberate the serfs in 1861.

Zhukovsky was a founder of Arzamas, a light-hearted society that promoted more modern and European-oriented literary values. The youngest member was the teenage Alexander Pushkin, who soon outshone Zhukovsky. Zhukovsky accepted this with remarkable grace; when, in 1820, Pushkin published his mock-epic *Ruslan and Lyudmila*, Zhukovsky sent him his portrait inscribed with the words: 'To the victorious pupil from the vanquished teacher'. Throughout the next seventeen years, whenever Pushkin was in trouble with the authorities, Zhukovsky interceded on his behalf. He also tried to prevent Pushkin from fighting his last, fatal duel. After Pushkin's death, he edited his unpublished work, rewriting some of it to meet the demands of the censors. The concept of a 'Pushkin Pleiade' – a Golden Age of Russian poetry centred on Pushkin – is largely the creation of Zhukovsky and his fellow-poet Prince Vyazemsky; both did all they could to promote Pushkin's posthumous reputation.[2] Until Pushkin's death, it was Zhukovsky himself who was seen as the central literary figure of the age.

Zhukovsky travelled widely, meeting and corresponding with such figures as Goethe and the landscape painter Caspar David Friedrich. In 1839 he accompanied Tsarevich Alexander on a journey through western Europe. While in England, Zhukovsky visited the churchyard at Stoke Poges and re-read Gray's 'Elegy' there; on his return to Russia, he retranslated the poem, this time more literally. In 1841, he retired from court; and in 1852 he died in Baden-Baden.

The first poem in this brief selection, a free translation of a German song, is probably addressed to Maria Protasova – the daughter of one of Zhukovsky's half-sisters. Zhukovsky was in love with her for many years; their affair seems to have been passionate but unfulfilled. The second poem is also addressed to Protasova; the title is the date of their last meeting. The last poem is about the death of Pushkin.

To Her

Where's there a name for you?
No mortal's art has the power
to express your charm.

Nor are there lyres for you!
Songs? Not to be trusted –
the echo of a belated rumour.

If they had ears for the heart,
every one of my senses
would be a hymn to you.

I carry your life's charm,
this pure, holy image,
like a mystery in my heart.

All I can do is love;
only eternity can speak
the love you inspire.

(1811)
Robert Chandler

9 March 1823

You stood before me
so still and quiet.
Your gaze was languid
and full of feeling.
It summoned memories
of days so lovely . . .
It was the last
such day you gave me.

Now you have vanished,
a quiet angel;
your grave is peaceful,
as calm as Eden!
There rest all earthly
recollections,
There rest all holy
thoughts of heaven.

Heavenly stars,
quiet night!

(1823)
Boris Dralyuk

*

Still he lay without moving, as if, after some difficult
task, he had folded his arms. Head quietly bowed, I stood
still for a long time, looking attentively into the dead man's
eyes. These eyes were closed. Nevertheless, I could
see on that face I knew so well a look I had never
glimpsed there before. It was not inspiration's flame,
nor did it seem like the blade of his wit. No, what I could
see there,
wrapped round his face, was thought, some deep, high
thought.
Vision, some vision, I thought, must have come to him. And I
wanted to ask, 'What is it? What do you see?'

(1837)
Robert Chandler

Konstantin Batyushkov (1787–1855)

Konstantin Nikolayevich Batyushkov's parents belonged to the old nobility. His mother died when he was seven, after two years of mental illness. Batyushkov studied in St Petersburg, then worked for the Ministry of Education. There he became friends with the poet Nikolay Gnedich, who was working on his translation of the *Iliad* – the first into Russian.

Batyushkov took part in several campaigns of the Napoleonic Wars, and worked briefly, along with Gnedich and Krylov, at the Imperial Public Library. In 1817 he attended meetings of the St Petersburg literary society Arzamas. From early 1819, he served as a diplomat in Naples. He is often seen as an Italophile, but what he loved was the Roman past – Pompeii, Baiae – not the Italy of his own time.

In 1820, after long bouts of depression, Batyushkov began to suffer from paranoia. In 1824 he made three attempts at suicide. Zhukovsky persuaded the Tsar to send him to Germany for treatment at state expense, but this did not help. In 1833 Batyushkov was released from service and granted a life pension. In 1855 he died from typhus.

Along with Zhukovsky, Batyushkov did much – both through his own poems and through his translations – to create a more fluent poetic language; among the poets he translated or adapted are Tibullus, Horace, Parny, Petrarch, Ariosto and Tasso. Batyushkov's later poems were important to Osip Mandelstam, who in 1932 wrote of him: 'No one commands such curves of sound, / never was there such speech of waves.'[3] The finest of these poems are the 'Imitations of the Ancients' composed shortly before he went mad. He published almost nothing after 1822.

To My Friends

Here is my book of verse,
which may perhaps be precious to my friends.
A kindly spirit tells me
that in this maze of words and rhymes
art is in short supply:
but friends will find my feelings here,
the story of my passions,
delusions of my mind and heart;
cares, worries, sorrows of my earlier years,
and light-winged pleasures;
how I would fall, then rise again,
then vanish from the world,
then trust my little boat to fate.
And, in a word, my friends will find
the diaries of a carefree poet here,
and having found them, say:
'Our friend was often credulous,
fickle in love, in poetry eccentric,
but he was always true to friendship;
he wearied no one with his poems
(a wonder on Parnassus!)
He lived just as he wrote . . .
Not well, not badly!'

(1815)

Peter France

*

You wake, O Baiae, from your tomb
with the appearance of Aurora's rays,
but crimson dawn will not return
the radiance of bygone days,

will not bring back the cool of sanctuaries
where swarms of beauties played,
and never will your columns of porphyry
rise from the depths beneath blue waves.

(1819)
Boris Dralyuk

from *Imitations of the Ancients*

1.

Life without death's not life. What is it then? A bowl
with a drop of honey in a sea of wormwood.
Magnificent the ocean! Tsar of the azure desert,
O sun, you are a wonder amid heaven's wonders!
And there is so much beauty on the earth!
Yet all is counterfeit and pointless silver.
Weep, mortal, weep! Your earthly fortune
is in the hands of ruthless Nemesis.

2.

Mountains can feel the pull of music;
the camel is attentive to love's tune,
groaning beneath his load; you see the rose
blush deeper red than blood at songs
of nightingales in valleys of the Yemen . . .
And you, my beauty . . . I don't understand.

3.

Look how the cypress, like our steppe, is barren –
but always fresh and green.
Citizen, you can't bear fruit like the palm-tree?
Then imitate the cypress;
Alone, like it, and dignified and free.

4.

When a girl in agony is fading
 and her body is blue and chilled,
it is in vain love pours out flowers
 and amber; she must lie still,
pale as a lily of the fields,
 like a waxen form; and now
flowers cannot warm her cooling hands
 and perfume has no power.

[. . .]

6.

Do you want honey, son? – Never fear stings.
 The crown of victory? – Fight bravely!
Or is it pearls you long for? – Dive down deep
 into the crocodile waters.
Fear not! God loves the brave; they are his own.
He keeps for them honey, pearls, death . . . a crown.

(1821)

Peter France

*

Reader, have you not heard
of grey Melchisedech's last words?
 Man is born a slave,
 a slave goes to the grave –
and can he hope that death will say
why he walked through this lovely vale of tears,
suffered, complained, accepted, disappeared?

(1821)

Peter France

Prince Pyotr Vyazemsky (1792–1878)

Pyotr Andreyevich Vyazemsky's mother was Irish; his father belonged to one of the most ancient families of the Russian nobility. As a young man he fought at the Battle of Borodino in 1812. In 1820 he signed an unsuccessful petition to Tsar Alexander I to abolish serfdom. He continued to express his radical views in poems, private letters and conversations, and in 1821 he was dismissed from government service.

Vyazemsky and his wife Vera were Pushkin's closest friends. In his youth Vyazemsky was a champion of Romanticism, but his mature poetry is sober, even bleak. By his mid-forties he had outlived not only five of his own children but nearly all his literary contemporaries. In 1837, the year of Pushkin's death, he wrote:

> And if my life has seemed among the hardest
> and though my storeroom's stock of grain is small,
> what sense is there in hoping still for harvest
> when snow from winter clouds begins to fall?[4]

Vyazemsky is remembered for his correspondence, for his *Old Notebook* (a collection of brilliantly told anecdotes about literary life), and for a small number of poems in which (as Donald Rayfield writes) he 'found unforgettable metaphors for [his] and his homeland's moral ills'.[5] One of the best known of these, 'The Russian God', was written in 1828 but first published over twenty years later, during the Crimean War. To publish such an anti-patriotic poem at a time of war was bold – but Vyazemsky seems always to have been eager to court opposition. The Russian exile Alexander Herzen (1812–70) translated this poem into German for Karl Marx.

One of Vyazemsky's favourite metaphors is that of a dressing gown, standing for carefree indolence and perhaps for Russia herself. He wrote 'Farewell to a Dressing Gown' in

1817, when he was about to set out on government service to Warsaw; some sixty years later he wrote the poem beginning 'Life in old age'.

The Russian God

Do you need an explanation
what the Russian god can be?
Here's a rough approximation
as the thing appears to me.

God of snowstorms, god of potholes,
every wretched road you've trod,
coach-inns, cockroach haunts and rat holes,
that's him, that's your Russian god.

God of frostbite, god of famine,
beggars, cripples by the yard,
farms with no crops to examine,
that's him, that's your Russian god.

God of breasts and . . . all that's sagging,
swollen legs in bast shoes shod,
curds gone curdled, faces dragging,
that's him, that's your Russian god.

God of brandy, pickle vendors,
those who pawn what serfs they've got,
of old women of both genders,
that's him, that's your Russian god.

God of medals and of millions,
god of yard-sweepers unshod,
lords in sleighs with two postilions,
that's him, that's your Russian god.

Fools win grace, wise men be wary,
there he never spares the rod,
god of everything contrary,
that's him, that's your Russian god.

God of all that gets shipped in here,
unbecoming, senseless, odd,
god of mustard on your dinner,
that's him, that's your Russian god.

God of foreigners, whenever
they set foot on Russian sod,
god of Germans, now and ever,
that's him, that's your Russian god.[6]

(1828)

Alan Myers

from *Farewell to a Dressing Gown*

Farewell, my dressing gown! Friend of sweet leisure
and idleness, sharer of secret thoughts! [. . .]
With you I kept care at a distance, dreams
and visions soothed and comforted my heart,
and in the evening, sitting at my hearth,
where a bright stream of fire glowed red, the sleep
of idleness was stirred into new life
by eloquent reflection, and the shades
of bygone things awoke and crowded round
in the transparent darkness; or I flew
on wings of dream through the uncertain mists
and saw the future, leaping across the years
to live that distant life, and mixing up
truth and illusion, castles in the air.
Just as your easy folds set free my movements
from tailors' tyranny, my thoughts could roam
with equal freedom through the fields of air,

accompanied by memory and hope. [. . .]
How often, rising from the arms of sleep,
I went straight to my desk and found the Muse
greeting me with a story, an epistle,
or some invention, whispered in the night.
Fashion was foreign to her, and she loved
my homely style of reasoning, and my verse
flourished in freedom and simplicity;
I wrote light-heartedly; my smiles, my jokes
were never dashed by any hint of toil.

How pitiful the Muse's tepid servant
who doesn't know the dressing gown's enchantment!
Worshipping fashion, dressed up like a doll,
warmed by respectable enthusiasm,
he enters his study as he would a ballroom.
His flowers are rouge and powder; he dips his quill
in scented ink to sketch a madrigal. [. . .]
But *my* model
is Anacreon. Immortal idler,
Bacchus' and beauty's friend, he sang and drank,
believe me, in a dressing gown; the darling
of all the nymphs and muses, spoiled by them
and thinking only of enjoyment, he played
and won the crown of immortality.
I know too well I cannot share his fame
but I can equal him in idleness:
I love the joys of carefree life like him,
like him, I love the quiet dreams of leisure. [. . .]
My dressing gown, greet me as you once did
and welcome me to your embrace. [. . .]
Return to me the treasure of old blessings;
with passions spent, and with a quiet mind,
without a blush before my hidden judge,
give me the joy, alone with you, to find
the traces of my old self in my self.
In cold oppression kindle once more in me
my dwindled ardour for the muses' gifts,

and then my genius, freeing itself from chains,
will rouse again its slumbering inspiration.
And let my former life revive in me,
and, born again in the enchanted warmth
of sweetest dreams, allow me to forget
all that I saw when I was still awake.

(1817)
Peter France

*

Life in old age is like a worn-out gown.
I feel ashamed to wear it, loath to leave it.
We are old brothers, used to one another –
no skilful darns can make us slick and sleek.

As I have aged, just so my gown has aged.
My life's in tatters; so my gown's in tatters,
spattered with ink – and yet these inky stains
say more to me than any fine-spun patterns.

They are the offspring of my pen, to which
in days of brilliant joy or clouded sorrow
I trusted youthful mysteries and thoughts,
passed on my fantasies, confessed my story.

My life is scored and wrinkled too; complaints,
laments – all can be read in its bleak scars.
Traces of pain and sorrow can be seen there –
but these dark shadows have their rueful charms.

Shadows bear tales and memories. Our heart's
response to love still lives in death and loss.
The morning's freshness and the heat of noon
still live within our mind as darkness falls.

There still are moments when I love my life
with all its pains, its melancholy outcome.
Old veteran with a bullet-ridden cloak,
I treasure and respect my worn-out gown.

(1875–7)

Robert Chandler

Wilhelm Küchelbecker (1797–1846)

Born into the Baltic German nobility, Wilhelm Karlovich Küchelbecker attended the elite lycée at Tsarskoye Selo, where he became friends with Alexander Pushkin. After taking part in the Decembrist Revolt of 1825, he was sentenced to ten years of imprisonment, followed by exile. He died from tuberculosis in Tobolsk, Siberia.

Donald Rayfield refers to Küchelbecker's prison diaries as 'a gold mine'.[7] His best-known poem, 'The Fate of Russian Poets', commemorates Kondraty Ryleyev, hanged as a leader of the Decembrists; the poet and playwright Alexander Griboyedov, killed when a furious mob stormed the Russian Embassy in Tehran; and Pushkin and Lermontov, both killed in duels. It begins: 'Bitter is the fate of poets of all tribes, but Fate has punished Russia worst of all.'

The following, more unusual 'fragment', written after Küchelbecker had gone blind, also touches on this theme.

Fragment

Before death I have felt the dark of death;
I thought: like Ossian I shall lose my way
in mist by the grave's edge and blindly stare
from wild moors down through the dim precipice
of dawnless night and see no trees, no fields
of freedom, no soft grass, no azure skies,
and no sun rising like a miracle.
Yet with the soul's eye I shall see you, shades
of prophets, friends too soon flown out of sight,
and I shall hear the blessed poets' song
and know each voice and recognize each face.

(1845)

Peter France

Anton Delvig (1798–1831)

Baron Anton Antonovich Delvig studied in the Tsarskoye Selo lycée together with Pushkin, and the two became lasting friends; Delvig was also close to both Baratynsky and Vyazemsky.

Delvig's best work is vivid, deeply felt and more complex than is at first apparent. Donald Rayfield has described it as a pastiche of classical idylls that contains 'a fearsome anticipation of the irruption of reality into an artificial dream world'.[8]

Some of Delvig's imitations of folk songs were set to music by the Russian composer Mikhail Glinka. Between 1825 and 1831 Delvig edited *Northern Flowers*, an annual journal to which Pushkin was a regular contributor. In January 1830 Delvig and Pushkin founded the weekly *Literary Gazette*, but the authorities closed this down after eighteen months. Delvig's sudden death at the age of thirty-two affected Pushkin deeply; he wrote of it in a letter as 'the first death that made me weep'.[9] In 1832 Pushkin edited a final issue of *Northern Flowers*.

Russian Song

Nightingale, my nightingale,
sweet-voiced, loud-voiced nightingale!
Where are you flying to, oh where?
Where will you sing the whole night through?
Will some poor maiden just like me
hear you singing all night long,
never getting a moment's sleep,
lying drowning in her tears?
Fly away, my nightingale,
fly beyond the gates of earth,
fly beyond the dark blue sea –
you'll never find in any land,
in any village, any town,

a maiden as miserable as me.
See me here, a maid who wears
a precious pearl on her young breast,
see me here, a maid who wears
a fiery ring on her young hand,
see me here, a maid who bears
a darling boy in her young heart.
On a gloomy autumn day
the fine pearl faded on my breast,
on a frosty winter night
the ring was broken on my hand,
and now that spring is here,
my darling boy loves me no more.

(1825)
Peter France

The Poet's Lot

The Young Man:
Lovely! I'll read it again! All praise to your name, sweetest singer!
Marvellous how you have wrapped meaning in sonorous cloth!
Tell me whose garden it was where you breathed in the rich, vernal fragrance –
where did the murmuring brooks teach you the language of love?

The Genius of the Poet:
Where? I discovered the bard lying sick in his bed; he was poorer
even than aged Homer, sadder than Tasso in love.
But Camoëns was the same when I found him in a wild cavern;
so, too, Cervantes forgot sorrow and prison with me.

(1830)
Rawley Grau

Yevgeny Baratynsky (1800–44)

Yevgeny Abramovich Baratynsky was ten when his father, a lieutenant general, died. Five years later, Baratynsky was expelled for theft – probably merely a teenage prank – from the Corps des Pages, a military academy in St Petersburg. In 1819, three years after this disgrace, he joined the army as a private soldier. Stationed first in St Petersburg, then in nearby Finland, Baratynsky attended meetings of the literary society Arzamas, along with Delvig, Pushkin and Zhukovsky.

In 1825 he received a commission. He then married, left the army and settled on an estate near Moscow. In late 1843 he travelled to France. Baratynsky spent the winter in Paris, attending literary salons, where he read aloud French translations of his poems and met – among others – the poets Alphonse de Lamartine and Alfred de Vigny and the author and playwright Prosper Mérimée. In the spring of 1844 he died in Naples of a sudden illness.

'Baratynsky ranks with the very best of our poets,' Pushkin wrote in 1830. 'Here in Russia he is original in that he thinks. He would indeed be original anywhere, for he thinks in his own way, correctly and independently, while his feelings are strong and deep.'[10] In general, however, Baratynsky's poetry – especially his later work – was received coolly. D. S. Mirsky suggests that this is because he is 'a poet of thought' and 'this made him alien to his younger contemporaries and to all the later part of the century, which identified poetry with sentiment.'[11] Sadly, Baratynsky fared no better with those critics who believed they *did* value thought; his last collection, *Twilight* (1842), was attacked by the influential but dogmatic literary critic Vissarion Belinsky, who wrongly saw Baratynsky as an enemy of science and enlightenment.

Despite a brief revival of interest in him in the early twentieth century, it is only more recently that Baratynsky has achieved the 'place in the Russian Parnassus' that Pushkin had claimed for him. Osip Mandelstam acknowledged Baratynsky's influence. Nikolay Zabolotsky re-read him with passionate enthusiasm in spring 1941, during one of the more bearable periods of his six-year term in the camps, when he was working as a technical draughtsman. Shalamov writes of his own joy on rediscovering Baratynsky in similar circumstances (see page 387). And on being asked what first impelled him to write poetry, Joseph Brodsky replied that, in 1959, he had got stuck in Yakutsk because of bad weather: 'I remember walking around that awful city, and stopping in at a bookstore, and stumbling upon Baratynsky. There wasn't much else to read, and once I found this little book and read it through, I realized – this is what I had to do.'[12]

'Pushkin is irresistibly attractive, Baratynsky is probably more of an acquired taste,' writes Peter France, one of his translators. 'When I first started to read him, he wasn't exactly my type of poet – too bleak, too aloof. Yet [. . .] I found myself increasingly fascinated by Baratynsky's special tone, disillusioned but visionary, romantic in many of his impulses but preferring a cool classical approach to poetry, both the contemporary of Byron and the inheritor of the Russian eighteenth-century ode. [. . .] Of all European poets, Leopardi is the one who most reminds me of Baratynsky, with his blend of *noia* (a kind of Baudelairean spleen) and wounded idealism, and with the beautiful clarity and precision of his writing.'

Disillusionment

Don't tempt me with your tender ruses,
with the return of passion's blaze:
a disenchanted man refuses
inveiglements of former days!
My faith in faithfulness has faded,
my faith in love has passed its prime;
I won't indulge another time
in dreams degrading and degraded.
Let blind despair not increase,

the things that were, pray, do not mention,
and, caring friend! allow the patient
to doze in long, untroubled peace.
I sleep, and sweet is relaxation;
let bygone dreams be laid to rest:
you will awaken agitation,
not love, in my tormented breast.

(1821)
Anatoly Liberman

*

My talent is pitiful, my voice not loud,
but I am living; somewhere in the world
someone looks kindly on my life; far off
a distant fellow-man will read my words
and find my being; and, who knows, my soul
will raise an echo in his soul, and I
who found a friend in my own time,
will find a reader in posterity.

(1828)
Peter France

The Muse

I am not blinded by my Muse:
no one would call her a great beauty,
and seeing her, no throng of youths
would give her chase with wild entreaties.
It's not her gift or inclination
to woo with brilliant conversation,
exquisite dress or playful eyes;
and yet the world is struck at times
by the calm plainness of her speech,

by her uncommon countenance,
and then, in place of sharp reproach,
it honours her with casual praise.

(1829)
Boris Dralyuk

On the Death of Goethe

She has appeared, and he has closed his eagle eyes
in peace, our mighty ancient;
having accomplished all this world allows,
he fell asleep, unshaken.
And at this sacred grave let no one mourn
that now a great man's skull is home to worms.

He is extinguished! but he greeted all
that lives beneath the sun;
his heart responded to each living call
touching the heart of man;
on wings of thought he soared through earth and sky,
bounded by nothing but infinity.

His soul found food in sayings of the wise,
in art's inspired creations,
in dreams of happy future centuries,
in time-bequeathed traditions;
at will imagination carried him
to beggars' shacks and palaces of kings.

His life was consonant with nature's breath:
he knew the river's language,
he understood the grass beneath his feet,
the speaking forest's foliage;
the book of stars revealed its mysteries
to him, and the wild dialogue of the seas.

Humanity he knew, all human ways!
And if God bounds our minutes
of fleeting life to our terrestrial days,
and behind the gravestone's limits,
beyond the world's appearance, lies a void, –
his tomb still justifies the ways of God.

But if a life beyond the grave is ours,
this man of earth, now resting
having given back dust to dust, with sonorous power
responding to all questions,
will rise light-souled to the great light,
and nothing earthly will offend his sight.

(1832)
Peter France

Autumn

1.

September's here! The sun each morning wakes
        a little later, its rays are colder,
and in the shaky mirror of the lake
        it glitters tremulous and golden.
Grey vapour shrouds the hilltops, and the dew
        drenches the flat lands by the river;
the fretted oak trees cast a yellowing shade
        and the red leaves of aspen shiver;
the birds no longer overflow with life,
the forests and the skies have lost their voice.

2.

September's here! The evening of the year
        is now upon us. Frost at morning
already spreads its silver filigree
        over the fields and hills, and stormy
Aeolus will awaken from his sleep,

driving The flying dust before him,
the wood will toss and roar, its falling leaves
will strew the swampy valley bottom,
and clouds will rise to fill the heavenly dome,
and waters will grow dark in froth and foam.

3.

Farewell, farewell, you brilliant summer skies!
Farewell, farewell to nature's splendour!
The waters gleaming in their golden scales,
the woods with their enchanted murmur!
Oh happy dream of fleeting summer joys!
The woodmen's axes are disturbing
the echoes in the emaciated groves,
and all too soon the frozen river
will be a mirror for the misty oaks
and hills in their white covering of snow.

4.

And now the villagers will find the time
to gather in their hard-earned harvest;
hay in the valley is stacked up into piles,
and in the corn the sickle dances.
Over the furrows, once the grain is cleared,
sheaves in stooks stand high and gleaming,
or else they trundle past the empty field
on loaded carts wearily creaking.
The golden summits of the shining ricks
rise up around the peasants' huddled shacks.

5.

The village people celebrate the day!
The barns steam merrily, the clatter
of flails awakes the millstones from their sleep,
and noisily they turn and chatter.

Let the cold come! The farmer has saved up
supplies to last him through the winter:
his hut is warm, the bread, the salt, the cup
of beer make welcome all who enter;
without a care his family now can eat
the blessed fruit of work in summer's heat.

6.

And you, a labourer in the field of life,
when you too move into your autumn
and see the blessings of your earthly time
spread out abundantly before you;
when the rich acres ploughed by work and cares
display the profits of your labours,
rewarding you for all the weary years
and you can reap the precious harvest,
gathering the grain of long-considered thought,
tasting the fullness of our human lot –

7.

are *you* rich like the farmer who sowed
in hope? Like him, the seed you scattered
and you too cherished golden dreams that showed
you rich rewards far in the future . . .
Now you behold that day; greet it with pride
and count your painful acquisitions!
Alas, your passions, your dreams, your arduous road
are buried in scorn, and your condition
is the soul's irresistible disgrace,
the sting of disappointment on your face!

8.

Your day has risen; now you can clearly see
the arrogance, the gullibility
of youth, and you have plumbed the yawning sea
of people's madness and hypocrisy.

You, once enthusiasm's faithful friend,
ardently seeking fellow-feeling,
a king of brilliant vapours – in the end
you contemplate a sterile thicket
alone with misery, whose mortal groan
is barely muffled by your haughty soul.

9.

But if your indignation's potent cry,
or if a howl of urgent longing
should rise out of the heart's dark misery,
solemn and wild amid the thronging
young boys and girls at their capricious games,
their bones would shake in fear, the infant
would drop its toys and in the midst of play
set up a roar of pain, all gladness
would vanish from its face, humanity
would die in it before death set it free.

10.

Be open-handed then; invite them all
to join the feast, those splendid people!
Let them all take their places in the hall
around the gold-encrusted table!
What tasty titbits you can offer them!
What a display of dishes gleaming
so variously! But they all taste the same
and like the grave they make us tremble;
sit there alone, perform the funeral rites
for your soul's worldly, transient delights.

11.

Whatever illumination in years to come
may take possession of your fancy,
whatever the last vortex of your thoughts
and feelings may one day give birth to –

let your triumphant and sarcastic mind
        suppress your heart's vain tremors
and bridle the unprofitable wind
        of late laments. Then see the treasure
you will receive, the greatest gift of life,
experience, which binds the soul in ice.

12.

Or else, in a life-giving surge of grief,
        casting aside all earthly visions,
seeing their boundaries, and not far off,
        a golden land beyond the darkness,
a place of redress, with a heart renewed
        dreaming dreams of benediction,
and hearing those tumultuous voices tuned
        to hymns of reconciliation,
like harps whose over-lofty harmony
is unintelligible to your human ear,

13.

before a vindicated Providence
        you will bow down, humble and thankful,
with an unbounded hope and with the sense
        that you have reached some understanding –
but know, you never will communicate
        your vision to your fellow-mortals;
their frivolous souls will not appreciate
        true knowledge in society's bustle;
knowledge of mountain peaks or of the deeps
is not for earth, earth has no place for it.

14.

The hurricane goes hurtling through the void,
        the forest raises up its voice in anger,
the ocean foams and rages and its mad
        breakers explode against the shingle;

so sometimes the dull rabble's idle minds
are woken from their torpid slumber
by the crude voice of commonplace, that finds
a sonorous echo in their blether –
but there will be no echo for the word
that goes beyond the passions of the world.

15.

What if a star from heaven disappears
into the chasm of nothing, missing
its way, and never finds its place again;
another one replaces it unheeded.
One star the less is nothing to the earth,
our people are too hard of hearing
to spot the distant howling of its death
or see the brightness of a star appearing
new born amid the sisters of the sky
and greeting them with rapturous melody![13]

16.

Winter draws on, and over the bare earth
impotence stretches with a shiver,
and furrows overflow with golden ears,
and all the cornfields gaily glitter.
Life and death, want and wealth lie side by side –
all the variety of the year now vanished
is equalized beneath a snowy shroud
that hides it in indifferent sameness –
thus all things will appear to you henceforth,
but you will reap no harvest from the earth.

(1837)

Peter France

*

Thought, yet more thought! Poor artist of the word,
thought's priest! For you there can be no forgetting;
it's all here, here are people and the world
and death and life and truth without a veil.
Ah! chisel, cello, brush, happy the man
drawn to you by his senses, going no further.
He can drink freely at the world's great feast!
But in your presence, thought, in your sharp rays,
before your unsheathed sword, our life grows pale.

(1840)

Peter France

A Grumble

Bane of the gorgeous summer, meddlesome fly, why must you torture me, ducking and weaving, clinging to face and to fingers?
Who was it gave you that sting that has power to cut short at will
thought on its albatross wings or the burning kisses of love?
You make of the peaceable thinker, bred on the pleasures of Europe,
a barbarous Scythian warrior, thirsting for enemy blood.

(1841)

Peter France

from *Rhyme*

You, like the faithful dove, bring back
a green branch to the waiting ark
and place it in his eager hand;
you only with your echoing voice
give inspiration a human face
and bring his dream to land.

(1840–43)

Peter France

Nikolay Yazykov (1803–46)

Nikolay Mikhailovich Yazykov was born in Simbirsk (now Ulyanovsk) into an old family of minor aristocracy. His first poems were published in 1819. While studying at the University of Dorpat (now Tartu in Estonia), he became known for his poems in celebration of freedom and student merriment. In 1826, during the last of his summer vacations at the estate of Trigorskoye, he spent a great deal of time with Pushkin, then in exile on the neighbouring estate of Mikhailovskoye.

From 1829 Yazykov lived in Moscow. From 1838, in poor health, he spent much of his time in German spas and on the French and Italian rivieras. He grew close to Nikolay Gogol, who admired Yazykov and travelled with him to Venice and Rome.

Pushkin once joked that the Castalian fount from which Yazykov drank ran not with water but with champagne. The poem we have chosen evokes the first months of their friendship.

On the Death of Pushkin's Old Nurse

I'll track it down among graves of strangers,
the humble cross that marks the place
where, worn out by a life of labour
and the years' burden, your dust is laid.
You will live on in the remembrance
of my young days, my happy times,
and in the time-honoured traditions
that perpetuate our poets' lives.

There, where the woodland on the hillside
slopes steeply to the valley floor,
where you can see two lakes, a river
and meadows with a winding road;

where, hidden in its ancient garden,
the manor house, standing alone,
decays, a relic of the days when
Elizabeth was on the throne;[14]

there, full of youth and fancy free,
we three were living: the two singers
and Wulf, the glory of our table,
rich with a soldier's energy;
he had abandoned boyish pastimes
and set out on the path of war,
winning on the field of honour
distinction for his student heart.

That was the place – the flimsy paper
in patches on the wooden walls,
the messy unswept floor, two windows
and in between, a glass-paned door;
a bed tucked underneath the icons
and a few chairs, a table, new
provisions there of wine and victuals,
and standing by the table, you!

We banqueted. You weren't too timid
to share our feasts – from time to time
your tender dreams brought forth an image
from the first springtime of your life;
you liked to listen to our chorus,
the living sounds of foreign lands,
the ebb and flow of our discussions,
the merry clash of glass on glass.

Already night dims her bright candles,
on the horizon dawn burns red;
and you an age ago have told us
that it was time to go to bed.
But all in vain! The feast grows wilder

under the influence of Tokay.
Relax, sit down with us, old lady
and join us in our revelry!

And tell us now: don't you remember
that in the old days your young lords
and masters would spin out the evenings
into the night, just as we do?
Isn't that so? And yet, thank goodness,
the earth still turns. But times have changed
and everything is topsy-turvy,
more complicated day by day.

And as for us . . . Playful as childhood
and free as our unbridled youth,
wise with the wisdom of experience
and talkative as Veuve Clicquot,
you chattered with me all night long,
you captured my imagination,
and here is my commemoration
of fresh-picked flowers for your tomb.

I'll track it down among graves of strangers,
the humble cross that marks the place
where, worn out by a life of labour
and the years' burden, your dust is laid.
I'll stand before it, and remember
so much, and bow my grieving face,
and through a dream of sweet emotion
my soul will melt in tenderness.

(1830)
Peter France

3
ALEXANDER PUSHKIN
(1799–1837)

Born in Moscow, Alexander Sergeyevich Pushkin was brought up mainly by tutors and governesses. One of his great-grandfathers, Abram Gannibal (1696–1781), was an African slave who became a favourite and godson of Tsar Peter the Great. Like many aristocratic children of his time, Pushkin learned Russian from household serfs; until the Napoleonic Wars, the aristocracy still spoke French rather than Russian.

As an adolescent, Pushkin attended the new elite lycée at Tsarskoye Selo, outside St Petersburg. In his early twenties, because of his political poems, he was exiled – first to the south of Russia, then to Mikhailovskoye, his mother's family's estate in the north. Several of his friends took part in the Decembrist Revolt of 1825, but Pushkin did not – perhaps simply because his friends did not trust him to keep a secret. In 1826 Pushkin returned to St Petersburg, with Tsar Nicholas I promising to be his personal censor. During his last years Pushkin suffered many humiliations, including serious debts and worries about the fidelity of his young wife Natalya Goncharova. He was fatally wounded in a duel with Baron Georges d'Anthès, the Dutch Ambassador's adopted son, who was rumoured to be having an affair with Natalya.

Pushkin's position in Russian literature is similar to that of Goethe's in Germany. Not only is he Russia's greatest poet; he is also the author of the first major works in a variety of genres. As well as his masterpieces – the verse novel *Eugene Onegin* and the narrative poem *The Bronze Horseman* – Pushkin wrote one of the first important Russian dramas, *Boris Godunov*; the first great Russian historical novel, *The Captain's Daughter*;

and the greatest of all Russian short stories, *The Queen of Spades*. In his later work, Pushkin shows a remarkable ability to treat dark, difficult material (obsessive madness, insoluble personal and socio-political conflict) with clarity and grace. Unlike the writers of the French Enlightenment, he writes lucidly without being simplistic. And unlike many later writers he can evoke the most terrifying aspects of human nature without, even momentarily, losing his balance.

Russians have always seen Pushkin as embodying something uniquely precious. In a speech at the Petrograd House of Writers in 1921, on the eighty-fourth anniversary of Pushkin's death, Vladislav Khodasevich talked of how the 'Pushkinian sun' would soon be eclipsed. He concluded: 'Our desire to make the day of Pushkin's death a day of universal remembrance is, I think, partly prompted by this same premonition: we are coming to an agreement about how to call out to one another, by what name to hail one another in the impending darkness.'[1] Sixteen years later, on a train taking her towards the labour camps of Siberia, Yevgenia Ginzburg – as if responding to these words – recited from memory *Eugene Onegin*, *The Bronze Horseman* and many other works. A guard at one point demanded that she surrender her books; cursing furiously, he searched the entire freight car – but found nothing.[2]

Few people have written better about Pushkin than the writer and scholar Andrey Sinyavsky. In *Strolls with Pushkin* (a high-spirited book he composed in the late 1960s, in a labour camp, and sent out in instalments in letters to his wife) he declares, 'Pushkin is the golden mean of Russian literature. Having kicked Russian literature headlong into the future, he [. . .] now plays in it the role of an eternally flowering past to which it returns in order to become younger. The moment a new talent appears, there we see Pushkin with his prompts and crib notes – and generations to come, decades from now, will again find Pushkin standing behind them. If we take ourselves back in thought to far-off times, to the sources of our native tongue, there too we will find Pushkin – further back still, earlier still, on the eve of the first chronicles and songs. An archaic smile plays on his lips.'[3]

It is too often said that Pushkin is 'untranslatable'. The late Stanley Mitchell's translation of *Eugene Onegin* is one of the greatest of all verse translations into English. It deserves to be read in full; we have not included extracts. Sadly, Mitchell died before completing his translation of *The Bronze Horseman*; here we include his version of the Prologue and Antony Wood's new, equally fine version of the rest of the poem.

Prologue to *Ruslan and Lyudmila*

On the curved strand a green oak grows,
on the green oak a golden chain,
and on it round and round there goes
the cat of knowledge, night and day –
goes to the right and sings a ditty,
goes to the left, begins a tale.
Strange beings are there: there roams the *leshy*,[4]
a mermaid swings a fishy tail;
there on the paths untrod by humans
are footprints of unheard-of beasts;
a house on chicken's legs from romance
stands without windows, doors or gates;
there hill and dale are full of visions;
there as dawn comes, the waves are breaking
upon an empty, sandy shore,
and thirty champions come striding
out of the waters, noble, handsome,
and after them the ocean's lord;
there the prince charming as he passes
takes prisoner a fearsome tsar;
there in the clouds before the masses,
above the woods and seas, to war
a wizard leads a knight-at-arms;
a queen there sorrows in her chamber,
a grey wolf faithfully attends her;

there Baba Yaga's fearful mortar
comes rushing home with clash and clatter;
there golden Kashchey meets his fate . . .
All *Rus*'s magic lies in wait!
There too was I, and sipped the honey;
the green oak by the strand I saw;
beneath its shade the cat of knowledge
told me its tales. I can recall
just one of them, and over tea
I'll tell it to society.

(1820)
Peter France

Epigram[5]

Part Black Sea merchant, part milord,
a half-baked sage and halfwit fool,
a semi-scoundrel – but there's hope
his scoundrelhood may soon be full.

(1824)
Robert Chandler

*[6]

I cannot forget that hour:
you were leaving an alien country
for the shores of your distant home
and I stood there and wept:
my arms grew colder
as they tried to hold you back,
my tears implored you to prolong
the agony of parting.

But you, you tore your lips away
from that most bitter kiss,
calling me from the gloom of exile
to follow you home,
saying we will meet again
in the cool of an olive-grove,
beneath a sky of lasting blue –
in the kisses of love.

But in your homeland, where heaven's vault
shines an eternal blue,
where olive trees shadow the waters,
you fell asleep for the last time.
Your sufferings, your beauty
are now just ash and dust;
but the sweet kiss of our next tryst –
where is it now? You owe it me.

(1830)
Robert Chandler

*

The season's last flowers yield
more than those first in the field.
The thoughts they rouse, sharp, sweet,
have an incomparable power.
Likewise the parting hour
as against when we merely meet.

(1825)
Christopher Reid

To Vyazemsky

It seems the sea, that scourge of ages,
contrives your genius to inspire?
You laud upon your golden lyre
old Neptune's trident as he rages.

Don't waste your praise. These days you'll find
that sea and land have no division.
On any element mankind
is tyrant, traitor, or in prison.

(1826)
Alan Myers

The Prophet

I wandered in a lonely place;
my soul's great thirst tormented me –
and at a crossing of the ways
a six-winged seraph[7] came to me.
Like slumber, fingers light and wise
he laid upon my weary eyes:
and like an eagle's in amaze
they opened with all-seeing gaze.
My ears he touched – and noise and sound
poured into them from all around:
I heard the heavens in commotion,
and angel hosts' celestial flight,
and sea-beasts stirring in the ocean,
and vines' growth on the valley-side.
And to my lips he bent, tore out
my tongue, an idle, sinful thing;
with bloody hand, in my numb mouth
he placed a serpent's subtle sting.
And with his sword he clove my breast,

and took my trembling heart entire;
a coal alight with brilliant fire
into my opened breast he thrust.
In that lone place I lay as dead,
and God's voice called to me, and said:
'Prophet, arise, behold and hearken:
over the world, by sea and land,
go, and fulfil my will unshaken,
burn with my Word the heart of man.'

(1826)
Antony Wood

To Ivan Pushchin[8]

First friend, friend beyond price,
one morning I blessed fate
when sleigh bells, your sleigh bells
sang out and filled my lonely home
lost in its drifts of snow.

May my voice now, please God,
gladden your soul
in that same way
and lighten your exile
with light from our Lycée's clear day.

(1826)
Robert Chandler

Scene from Faust

at the seaside. Faust and Mephistopheles

FAUST

Demon, I'm bored.

MEPHISTOPHELES

What's to be done,
Faust? Man's not without limits, is he?
And to be bored, like it or not,
is every rational being's lot:
some are too idle, some too busy,
have too much or too little faith;
some find no joy, while some are dizzy
with it, enjoying themselves to death.
You yawn your lives out, till you fall
into the grave that yawns for all.
Why shouldn't you yawn too?

FAUST

The joke
is stale. Distraction's what I want,
so find me some.

MEPHISTOPHELES

Just be content
With reason's proof. Write in your book
this little album verse that goes:
Fastidium est quies – boredom
is nothing but the soul's repose.
I ask you, psychologist that I am,
(Ah, there's a science!) when indeed
were you *not* bored? Think. Was it when
you dozed to Virgil, and would need
birch on your backside to rouse again?
Or when with roses you would feed

those oh-so-willing girls' delights,
whose raucous orgies you would lead
through ardours of hung-over nights?
Or was it when you were engrossed
in lofty dreaming, and got lost
in murky depths of knowledge? Lord,
don't you recall, you were so bored,
that like a harlequin from the fire
you finally conjured me up entire?
A petty demon, I wriggled free,
endeavoured to cheer you, let you see
witches and spirits. And what for?
It only served to bore you more.
You yearned for fame, and now you've won it;
you wanted to fall in love – you've done it.
You've had from life what life can offer.
Have you been happy?

FAUST

Enough, you scoffer.
Don't make my secret sore spot fester.
In that deep knowledge nothing lives;
I curse the false light that it gives,
and as for fame, its random lustre
soon fades away. Senseless as dreams
are worldly honours. There is, it seems,
but one real blessing: the mingling of
two souls.

MEPHISTOPHELES

And the first tryst of love.
Right? Might I know – not to be rude –
to whom it is that you allude?
Not Gretchen?

FAUST

O vision of pure wonder!
O purest flame of love! There, there,

deep in the rustling shadows, under
the leaves, by waters' sweet rush, where,
my head resting on that tender
breast, my weariness took flight.
There I was happy . . .

MEPHISTOPHELES

Holy thunder,
you're dreaming, Faust, in broad daylight!
And a compliant recollection
flatters you in your self-deceit.
Was it not I whose diligent action
laid that beauty at your feet,
who, in the darkest midnight hour,
brought her to you? My labours done,
I was as tickled as anyone,
and revelled alone to see their flower:
you two together. I won't forget!
While your poor beauty, rapturous, let
her wits fall prey to her elation,
you, restless as ever, – nay, more so –
were buried deep in cogitation
(and you and I proved long ago
that boredom has its seed in thought).
My fine philosopher, you do know
what you were thinking then, do you not,
at a time when no one thinks at all?
Shall I tell you?

FAUST

Well, then, what? Do tell.

MEPHISTOPHELES

You thought: sweet angel of devotion!
I longed for you so avidly!
How cunningly I set in motion
a pure heart's girlish fantasy!
Her love's spontaneous, self-forgetful;

she gives herself in innocence . . .
Why does my heart, in recompense
feel its old tedium grow more hateful?
I look upon her now, poor thing,
a victim of my whim's compulsion,
with insurmountable revulsion.
So does a fool, unreckoning,
but bent on doing something evil,
for a trifle slit some beggar's throat,
then curses the poor ragged devil.
So on the beauty he has bought
the rake, enjoying her in haste,
now looks timidly shame-faced.
So, adding it all up, you might
see one conclusion to be drawn . . .

FAUST

You hellish creature, away, begone!
Don't let me catch you in my sight!

MEPHISTOPHELES

Please. Give me some little task:
you know I cannot part from you
unless I'm given work to do –
not to be idle is all I ask.

FAUST

What's that white spot on the water?

MEPHISTOPHELES

A Spanish three-master, clearing the sound,
fully laden, Holland-bound;
three hundred sordid souls aboard her,
two monkeys, chests of gold, a lot
of fine expensive chocolate,
and a fashionable malady
bestowed on your kind recently.

FAUST

Sink it.

MEPHISTOPHELES

Right away.

(*Vanishes*)

(1825)

Alan Shaw

*

City of splendour, city of poor,
spirit of grace and servitude,
heaven's vault of palest lime,
boredom, granite, bitter cold –
still I miss you rather, for
down your streets from time to time
one may spy a tiny foot,
one may glimpse a lock of gold.

(1828)

Antony Wood

*

I loved you – and maybe love
still smoulders in my heart;
but let my love not trouble
you or cause you any hurt.
I loved you but stayed silent,
timid, despairing, jealous;
I loved you truly – God grant
you such love from someone else.

(1829)

Robert Chandler

from *A Feast in Time of Plague*[9]

There is joy in battle,
poised on a chasm's edge,
and in black ocean's rage –
that whirl of darkening wind and wave –
in an Arabian sandstorm,
and in a breath of plague.

Within each breath of death
lives joy, lives secret joy
for mortal hearts, a pledge,
perhaps, of immortality,
and blessed is he who, storm-tossed,
can see and seize this joy.

(1830)
Robert Chandler

from *Mozart and Salieri*

(from Scene 1)

SALIERI
Justice, they say, does not exist on earth.
But justice won't be found in heaven either:
that's plain as any simple scale to me.
Born with a love of art, when as a child
I heard the lofty organ sound, I listened,
I listened and the sweet tears freely flowed.
Early in life I turned from vain amusements;
all studies that did not accord with music
I loathed, despised, rejected out of hand;
I gave myself to music. Hard as were
the earliest steps, and dull the earliest path,

I rose above reverses. Craftsmanship
I took to be the pedestal of art:
I made myself a craftsman, gave my fingers
obedient, arid virtuosity,
my ear precision. Killing sound, dissecting
music as if it were a corpse, I checked
all harmony by algebra. At last,
having achieved a mastery of theory,
I ventured on the rapture of creation.
I started to compose; in secrecy,
not dreaming yet of fame. And many a time,
when I had sat in silence in my cell
two days and more, forsaking sleep and food,
tasting the bliss and tears of inspiration,
I burned my work and watched indifferently
as my ideas, the sounds I had created
flared up and disappeared in wisps of smoke.
But what of that? For when the mighty Gluck
revealed to us his new, exciting secrets,
did I not put behind me all I knew,
all that I loved, believed so fervently?
Did I not follow promptly in his path,
as trustful as a traveller redirected
by someone he encounters on his way?
Through zealous, unremitting application
I gained a not inconsequential place
in art's infinity. Fame smiled on me;
I found the hearts of men in harmony
with my creations. I was satisfied,
enjoying my work, success and fame in peace,
as too the work and the success of friends,
my fellows in the wondrous art of music.
I knew no envy – never! – not when first
I heard the opening of *Iphigenia*,
not when Piccinni tamed Parisian ears.
Who could have ever called the proud Salieri
a wretched envier, a trampled serpent,

alive yet helpless, biting sand and dust?
No one! . . . But now – and *I* who say it – now
I envy – I profoundly envy. Heaven!
O where is justice when the sacred gift,
immortal genius, comes not in reward
for toil, devotion, prayer, self-sacrifice –
but shines instead inside a madcap's skull,
an idle reveller's? O Mozart, Mozart!

(1830)
Antony Wood

Epigraph to *The Queen of Spades*

In rainy weather
they gathered together
to play.
To double – redouble –
a stake was no trouble,
they say.
They did not find it hard
to entrust to a card
their pay,
So no day of rain
ever slipped by in vain,
they say.

(1833)
Robert Chandler

Autumn (A Fragment)

What then does not invade my drowsy mind?
Derzhavin

1.

October's here already; the grove already
is shaking from bare branches its last leaves;
the breath of autumn begins to ice the roadway,
the stream still rushes gurgling past the mill,
but the mill pond is frozen; my sporting neighbour
hurries off with his pack to the far fields.
The winter corn suffers his boisterous pleasure,
his yelping hounds disturb the forest's slumber.

2.

Now is my time. I bear no love for spring:
the floods, the mud, the stink – I feel unhealthy,
my blood ferments, longing chokes heart and mind.
Better harsh winter; *then* I can feel happy,
I love the snows, and then beneath the moon
the freedom of a sleigh ride, gliding swiftly,
a fresh-faced girl, wrapped in sable furs,
giving your hand a timid, passionate squeeze.

3.

And what a joy to race across the mirror
of frozen ponds with sharp steel on your feet!
And the excitement of those winter parties . . . !
But there's a limit; the snow goes on for weeks
and months, even a bear at length would suffer
from boredom. After all, we can't devote
a life to sleigh rides with these young Armidas
or moping by the stove behind sealed windows.

4.

Ah! gorgeous summer, I would love you, but
the heat, the dust, the flies and the mosquitoes!
You torture us; our souls, once rich, grow flat,
we suffer like the barren fields, drought-stricken,
just longing for some freshness, for a glass –
that one thought fills our minds. We miss old winter,
and having seen her off with cakes and wine,
with ice and ice-cream we recall her reign.

5.

People have harsh words for these days of autumn,
but, reader, they are dear to me, I love
their unassuming light, their quiet beauty.
Autumn attracts me like a neglected girl
among her sisters. And, to be quite honest,
she is the only season to my taste.
She has her good points; whimsically dreaming
and free from vanity, I find her charms appealing.

6.

How can I put it? She perhaps appeals
as sometimes a young sufferer from consumption
catches the eye. Unseen, her death awaits,
and without protest, quietly she sickens;
she cannot sense the yawning of the grave,
but life fades from the lips that still are smiling;
a rosy hue still plays around her eyes,
today she is alive, tomorrow dies.

7.

A mournful time of year! Its sad enchantment
flatters my vision with a parting grace –
I love the sumptuous glow of fading nature,
the forests clad in crimson and in gold,
the shady coolness and the wind's dull roaring,

the heavens all shrouded in a billowing mist
and the rare gleams of sun, the early hoarfrosts
and distant grey-beard winter's gloomy portents.

8.

Each autumn's coming makes me bloom anew;
my health is well served by the cold of Russia;
I feel a new love for the old routines,
sleep has its turn, and after it comes hunger;
the blood runs light and cheerful through the veins,
desires flock in – happy again, and youthful,
I'm full of life again – my organism
is like that (pardon my prosaicism).

9.

Tossing his mane, my steed carries his rider
over the open flatlands, and beneath
his flashing hooves he rouses up the echoes
in frozen valleys and cracks the ringing ice.
But then the short day fades, a fire blazes
in the forgotten hearth, now casting a bright flame,
now crumbling slowly, while I sit there reading
or give my drifting thoughts their hour of freedom.

10.

And I forget the world, in blissful peace
I am sweetly lulled by my imagination,
and poetry awakens in me then;
my soul, hard pressed by lyric agitation,
trembles, resounds and seeks as if in sleep
to surface finally in free expression –
and I receive a host of guests unseen,
old-time acquaintances, fruits of my dreams,

11.

and in my head thoughts spring into existence,
and rhymes dance out to meet them, and the hand
stretches towards the pen, the pen to paper,

and unimpeded verse comes pouring out.
So a ship, motionless in motionless water,
lies dreaming, then suddenly the sailors race
and climb aloft, wind swells the sails, the vessel
moves slowly out, bow cutting through billows,

12.

and sails away. Where shall *we* sail to . . . ?

(1833)
Peter France

*

It's time, my friend, it's time. We long for peace
of heart. But days chase days and every hour
gone by means one less hour to come. We live
our lives, dear friend, in hope of life, then die.
There is no happiness on earth, but peace
exists, and freedom too. Tired slave, I dream
of flight, of taking refuge in some far-
off home of quiet joys and honest labour.

(1834)
Robert Chandler

from *The Egyptian Nights*[10]

(An improvisation on the theme 'Cleopatra e i suoi amanti')[11]

The palace shines. Sweet melodies,
accompanied by flute and lyre,
and her sweet voice, and her bright eyes,
make light of dark, make night expire.

All hearts bow down towards her throne;
she is the queen whom all must court –
but then her own fair head sinks down
towards her golden cup in thought.

Flutes, lyres and voices – all goes dead.
A deepening silence fills the hall.
But when once more she lifts her head,
her words both frighten and enthrall:
'My love holds bliss, so I keep hearing.
If there is truth in what you claim,
blessed is he whose love has daring
enough to pay the price I name.
My contract binds all equally:
he who would claim me as his wife,
he who desires one night with me,
must for that night lay down his life.

'Once I lie on the bed of pleasure –
I swear by all the gods above –
I'll bring delight beyond all measure
yet be the meekest slave of love.
Hear me, O splendid Aphrodite,
and you, dread god who reigns below,
and you above, great Zeus almighty –
I swear: until the dawn's first glow
brightens the sky, I shall divine
each hidden wish of my lord's heart;
I'll set on fire, then soothe with wine;
I'll bare the mysteries of love's art.
But when the Eastern sky turns red,
when my lord feels the morning's breath,
soldiers will lead him from my bed
to meet the lasting kiss of death.'

All hearts rebel, and yet they all
remain enslaved by beauty's charm.
Uncertain murmurs fill the hall;

she listens with untroubled calm
and looks around with haughty pride,
thinking her suitors spurn her offer.
Then one emerges from the crowd;
two others follow quickly after.
Their steps are bold, their eyes are bright;
she rises to her feet to meet them.
The bargain's struck; each buys one night,
and when it's over, death will greet them.

The lovers' lots are blessed by priests
and dropped inside the fateful urn.
Then, watched in silence by the guests,
a lot is drawn. First comes the turn,
the gods decree, of gallant Flavius,
Flavius whose courage never wavers.
Such scorn in a mere woman's eyes
is more than Flavius can endure;
amazed by Cleopatra's gall,
this grey-haired veteran of war
now leaps to answer pleasure's call
as once he answered battle cries.
Criton comes next, a youthful sage
born in the groves of Epicure,
whose graceful verses sing the rage
evoked by Venus and Amor.
The third is like a glowing rose
whose petals dawn has coaxed apart,
a joy to both the eye and heart,
a youth whose name the centuries
have lost. The softest shadow lies
over his cheeks; love fills his eyes.
The passions raging in his breast
are like a still-closed book to him
and Cleopatra looks at him
with eyes surprised by tenderness.

(1828)

Robert Chandler

The Bronze Horseman:[12] *A Petersburg Tale*

Where desolate breakers rolled, stood *he*,
immersed in thought and prophecy;
and looked afar. A spacious river
flowed by before him; hurriedly
a poor boat strove in lone endeavour.
Upon the mossy, swampy shore
huts showed up blackly here and there,
the shelters of the wretched Finn;
and forest that no light came near,
where, through mist and gloom, a din
reverberated.
And he thought:
the Swedes we'll threaten with our labour.
We'll build a city here, a port,
to challenge our disdainful neighbour.
From nature we have this behest:
to strike a window on the West,
to guard our seaway like a treasure.
Upon the waves we've decked anew
we'll welcome every flag and crew,
and banquet with them at our leisure.

A hundred years have passed since then;
a northern city, young, a wonder,
has, from the forest and the fen,
risen in majesty and splendour.
Where Nature's stepson in the past,
the Finnish fisherman, had sought his
subsistence on the lowly coast,
casting his ancient net in waters
without a name, now there are scores
of buildings on enlivened shores,
creations of a crowded city,
palaces, towers, ships seeking berth
from every corner of the earth

at places by a wealthy jetty.
Here granite borders the Nevá[13]
and bridges hang above the river;
and dark green gardens lay a cover
upon each island near and far.
As the young capital unseats her,
old Moscow fades, no more prevails,
just as before a new tsaritsa
a dowager in purple pales.

I love you, miracle of Peter's,
your stern and graceful countenance,
the broad Nevá's imperious waters,
the granite blocks that line your banks,
the railings in cast-iron muster,
the melancholy of your nights,
transparent twilight, moonless lustre,
when, in my room, I use no lights
to write and read, when massed facades
and sleeping empty boulevards
are clear to see, and all afire
glitters the admiralty's spire,
and, not permitting night to smother
the golden skies, there rushes through
a new dawn to replace the other,
and night gets half-an-hour's due.
I love your cruel winter season,
the placid air and frosty bite,
the broad Nevá where sleighs are legion
and girlish cheeks are rosy bright,
the ballroom splendour, noise and chatter,
and, at the bachelors' carouse,
the wine cups with their foam and flutter
and blue-flamed punch that warms the house.
I love the warlike animation,
boy soldiers on the fields of Mars,
the repetitious decoration
of horse and infantry that pass

in balanced and proportioned pace,
the shreds of the triumphant banners,
the copper caps agleam with honours
shot through in battle's every place.
I love you, capital of Peter,
the smoke and thunder of your fort,
when the septentrial tsaritsa
has borne a son to give the court,
when news of victory is brought
and Russia once again rejoices
or, breaking blue ice by degrees,
the Nevá consigns it to the seas,
and thrills on sensing springlike voices.

Glory, city of Peter, stay
unyielding like the Russian land,
and let the elements at bay
submit to our pacific hand.
Let Finnish waves no more remember
their enmity and their arrest,
nor vain vindictiveness encumber
Peter the Great's eternal rest!

It was a terrible bequest,
still fresh in its commemoration.
There's nothing, friends, for me to add,
you'll learn it all from my narration.
The tale I tell you will be sad.

Stanley Mitchell[14]

Part One

Over murky Petrograd
breathed November cold and hard.
With thunderous waves the river Neva
struck against its stately railings,

cast about in restless flailings
like someone in a raging fever.
It was late and it was dark;
the rain beat down, became berserk,
the wind set up a dismal whine.
Our youthful hero chose this time
to visit friends and then come home:
Yevgeny we shall have his name . . .
It has a pleasant sound; besides,
my pen first knew it long ago.
His family name we need not know;
although it may be one that rides
high in the annals of our land,
thanks to the pen of Karamzin,[15]
now it has sunk to mere has-been,
forgotten by both low and grand.
Our hero does some kind of work,
lives in Kolomna, shuns the great,
and in his mind no memories lurk
of bygone days or of the dead.

Late coming home one night, Yevgeny
threw off his coat, and soon to bed.
But long he lay awake, for many
and rousing thoughts ran through his head . . .
That he was poor, that only work
could bring him independence, honour –
if only God would one day make
him sharper-witted, earn more money;
that some there were, well-fed, bone-lazy,
not clever – *their* life was so easy!
While it was two years altogether
that he had laboured. What foul weather,
he thought too; it had not abated –
with such a swiftly rising river
they'd take the bridges off the Neva;
and so he might be separated
from his Parasha for, who knew,

longer than a day or two.
Yevgeny, with a heartfelt sigh,
turns to poetic reverie:

Get married? Well . . . why not? He'll see.
It will be hard, he'll not deny;
however, he is young and strong,
there's nothing he'll refuse to try;
it certainly won't take him long –
he'll make a simple home one day,
and with Parasha as his wife
he will enjoy a peaceful life.
'A year, and I'll be on the way.
I'll have a post – Parasha, she to
take charge of household matters, see to
the children's upbringing . . . And so,
until the grave lays claim to us,
hand in hand through life we'll go;
our grandchildren will bury us.'

Thus he mused. And he was sad
that night; he wished the angry rain
would beat less madly on the pane,
the wailing of the wind would fade . . .
He closed his sleepy eyes at last.
The next he knew, the stormy night
had ended; came pale dawn . . . Aghast,
he saw the day.
With all its might
the River Neva all night long
had strained towards the open sea
against its savage adversary,
to prove, though, in the end, less strong . . .
Now people gathered all along
the riverside to see the night's
aftermath – the foaming heights.
The sea-winds blowing up the gulf
had checked the Neva's flow; it reared,
forced backwards, in a mighty huff,

and all the islands disappeared . . .
Soon the weather grew still worse,
the angry Neva roared and swelled
and like a cauldron seethed and swirled;
as if a captive beast let loose
fell on the city . . . Before it[16]
the people flee; soon none to see –
and now the waters suddenly
gush into cellars underground,
canals and hidden sluices sound –
behold Petropolis like Triton
appearing, waist-deep, to Poseidon.[17]

Siege! Assault! Malicious waves
swarm over windowsills like thieves.
Sterns of loose careering boats
smash through panes. Soaked street-stall boards,
pieces of houses, roofs and logs,
bundles of hoarded merchants' stocks,
the worldly goods of poverty,
coffins from the cemetery,
parts of bridges – helter-skelter
down the streets!
The people see
God's anger, and the penalty.
Nothing is left now: food and shelter!
Where have they gone?
At this dark time
the late tsar ruled with glory still.
Out on the balcony he came
and, troubled, spoke. 'It is God's will;
the elements no tsar can rule.'
In gloomy thought he sat; his eye
was fixed upon calamity,
each mighty square a rising pool
into which new rivers streamed.
Amongst it all the palace seemed
a hapless islet. But the Tsar

was soon to send his generals out
through streets and byways near and far
to brave the perils of the flood
and save the helpless from the foam,
or else from drowning in their home.

And on that day, on Peter's Square,
upon an elevated porch,
pride of a new-built mansion, where
a pair of marble lions stood watch,
each with raised paw, as if alive;
without a hat, arms crossed, astride
one of these poor Yevgeny sat,
fearfully pale, but not afraid
on his account. He did not hear
the greedy waves advancing near,
feel on his face the rain that lashed,
the squall that had removed his hat,
he did not feel his feet being splashed.
His desperate gaze was firmly set
upon a single spot, and there
like mountain summits, jet on jet
the furious waters clove the air –
the howling centre of the storm,
spewing debris in every form . . .
Out where, oh God! it was most rough,
very nearly on the gulf –
a fence, unpainted, and a willow,
an age-worn little house, a widow
with his Parasha, with his dream . . .
Or was this really all a dream,
can all our life be nothing worth,
a trick that heaven plays on earth?

Bewitched he sat, as if in fable,
as if he too were made of marble,
motionless. On every quarter
all he sees is water, water!

And high above the invaded land,
above the raging of the flood,
with back to him, and outstretched hand
in overmastering command,
the mounted bronzen idol stood.

Part Two

But now, well wearied by destruction,
the Neva rests its sated maw,
and having relished insurrection,
begins to settle down once more,
dropping its prey. A band of robbers
thus takes a village, slashes, clobbers,
smashes, wrecks and seizes; howls,
violence, terror, oaths and wails! . . .
The robbers tire; weighed down by spoils,
they fear pursuit and disappear,
with booty scattered in their rear.

The waters fell, the thoroughfares
opened again; Yevgeny hastened,
clinging to hope, but full of fears,
towards the river scarcely chastened.
Filled with the flush of victory,
the waves still boiled maliciously,
as if on top of smouldering fires,
capped still with foam from shore to shore;
the Neva breathed with heavy sighs,
spent as a steed returned from war.
Yevgeny looks about: he spies
a boat; at once his spirits rise;
he hails the boatman heaven-sent –
the boatman names a modest fee
and launches off audaciously
into the fearsome element.

The oarsman, skilled through many a year,
struggled with the turbulence;
and he was ready more than once,
with daring strokes, to disappear
between the billows deep and sheer –
at last he reached the shore.
Poor soul!
Down the street Yevgeny hastens,
seeking out familiar places
but recognizing none at all.
Dreadful sight! The street is shattered,
everything is strewn and battered:
the houses stand there crooked, many
collapsed, some vanished; unconcealed,
as upon a battlefield,
bodies lie around. Yevgeny,
tormented, trembling in his shoes,
utterly oblivious,
still hurries headlong to the place
where fate awaits him with its news,
like an unopened letter. Here –
the settlement, the gulf, he's near
the house . . . But what is this?
He stops.
Back he turns; retraces steps.
He looks . . . walks on . . . another look.
Here's where it was, the little nook,
and there's the willow. But the gate –
has it been torn off in the spate?
And where's the house? In deepest slough
round and round he walks and walks
and loudly to himself he talks –
suddenly he struck his brow
and laughed out loud.

Darkness lay deep
upon a city all in fear;
its people did not try to sleep,
the talk was ceaseless everywhere
of what had come to pass that day.

From tired, pale clouds the morning ray
shone on the silent capital
and found no traces of disaster,
the ill work crimson-covered.[18] All
was as before. The streets now free
saw no concern or sympathy.
Clerks, work-bound, left their night's abode;
the intrepid trader, undismayed,
opened his cellar robbed by flood,
hoping to win back losses made
from fellow traders. Many a boat
appeared from courtyards.
Count Khvostov,[19]
poet beloved of heaven above,
began to sing in timeless verse
the Neva settlements' distress.

But poor, my poor Yevgeny . . . He,
troubled, alas, in heart and mind,
could not withstand catastrophe.
The fury of the waters, wind
roared in his ears. He roamed aghast,
consumed by wordless thoughts of doom;
he was bedevilled by a dream.
Days, and soon a fortnight passed –
a month, and he did not go home.
When term was up, the landlord let
his empty niche to some poor poet.
Yevgeny did not come to fetch
his few belongings there. Poor wretch,
an alien to society,
he went about all day on foot,
and slept upon the embankment; food

was handed him in charity
at windowsills. His tattered clothing
rotted away on him; with loathing
malicious children plied their pebbles.
The coachman's whip would often find him –
he never looked ahead, behind him,
deaf with the noise of inner troubles.
And so his miserable span
was dragged out, neither beast nor man;
not an inhabitant of earth
and not a phantom from the dead,
not one and not the other . . .
Berth
one night he found to lay his head
above the Neva. Autumn breathed
its wind. Frustrated waters seethed
against the embankment, beat its steps
like a petitioner who raps
despairingly upon the door
of deaf officials of the law.
Rain began; Yevgeny woke.
Wind howled, and in the distant dark
a sentinel exchanged his call
with it . . . He started to recall
the horror that had passed. He rose,
and quickly walked about . . . and froze –
it was as if his end was nigh.
He stood beneath the columned arch
of that great mansion, on the porch
a pair of marble lions on watch,
each with raised paw, as if alive,
and on a palisaded rock
the bronzen idol, hand held high,
rode above him in the dark.

Yevgeny trembled. In his mind
all was dreadfully defined.
How could he not recognize
where he had seen the grim waves spill,

the waters in rebellion rise,
the lions, the square, while stark and still
he whose indomitable will
had raised a city from the sea
towered in bronze above it – *he*,
fearsome from the gloom below . . .
What thoughts are pressing on that brow!
Within him, what unbounded force!
What fire comes flashing from that horse!
Where, proud stallion, are you bound,
where will your hooves put down to ground?
Destiny's great lord and master!
Was it not exactly thus
your iron bridle reared up Russia
upon the brink of the abyss?

Around the idol's pedestal
the madman now began to pace;
his poor wild eyes saw face to face
the ruler over half the world.
His chest was tight. He pressed his brow
against cold railings; fire ran through
his heart, his blood was boiling over;
his gaze was visionless in mist.
Before the mighty image, sombre
he stood, and clenching teeth and fist –
as if possessed by some dark power –
'Miracle builder! – Right!' he hissed,
'Just you wait!' The awesome tsar,
it seemed to him, now turned his head,
in sudden rage began to glare . . .
Headlong across the empty square
he ran, behind him as he fled,
like rumbling thunder, hooves resounding
upon the shaken thoroughfare.
And after him, astride his bounding
steed, the Horseman, hand held high,
outstretched beneath the moonlit sky,

followed; and all night long, no matter
whither the poor madman bent
his steps, with heavy echoing clatter
after him the Horseman went.

Whenever next he chanced to pass
that way, his face was overtaken
by inner turmoil; he would press
his heart as if to ease its aching,
take off his threadbare cap; his gaze
he could not bring himself to raise;
he kept his distance.

Off the shore
a tiny islet can be seen.
There a fisherman will moor,
out fishing late, bring in his seine,
and cook his meagre supper; or
a clerk will of a Sunday row
to that place where no blade will grow.
The flood had borne there, in its sport,
an age-worn little house. Above
the waves, like some black bush, it stood.
Last spring, a wherry took it off,
empty and ruined. They discovered
my madman on its threshold; there
upon that spot his corpse was covered
and was committed to God's care.

(1833)
Antony Wood

Wedding Song[20]

from *The Captain's Daughter*

Our lovely apple tree
has no young shoots and no fine crown;
our lovely bride

has no dear father and no dear mother.
No one to dress her
in a wedding gown,
no one to bless her.

(1836)
Robert Chandler

*[21]

Exegi monumentum

I have built, though not in stone, a monument to myself;
the path that leads to it will not be overgrown;
indomitably, the summit of my monument rises
higher than Alexander's Column.[22]

Not all of me shall die – for in my sacred lyre
my soul shall outlive my dust, it shall escape decay –
in the sublunary world my fame shall be unending
as long as a single poet holds sway.

And word of me shall spread through all the Russian lands,
my name shall be pronounced in all its living tongues,
by proud Slav race and Finn, by Kalmyk on the steppe,
and by the far-flung tribe of Tungus.

Long will there be a place for me in people's hearts,
because in my harsh age I sang of Liberty,
because my lyre awoke warm-hearted sentiments
and asked, for the fallen, Charity.

Be, O my Muse, obedient to the will of God,
to praise and calumny in equal measure cool,
be not afraid of insult, seek no laurel-crown,
and do not argue with a fool.

(1836)
Antony Wood

4
AFTER PUSHKIN

Fyodor Tyutchev (1803–73)

Born into the old nobility, Fyodor Ivanovich Tyutchev spent most of his childhood in Moscow. A gifted tutor, a poet and translator who wrote under the name of Semyon Raich, endowed Tyutchev with a deep knowledge of both Russian and classical literature. Tyutchev published his first work, a free adapation of an epistle by Horace, when he was only fifteen.

After studying at Moscow University he took up a post at the Russian Embassy in Munich in 1822. Among his friends were the German philosopher Friedrich von Schelling and the poet Heinrich Heine, several of whose poems Tyutchev translated.

In Munich he fell in love with a woman who married another man, but in 1826 he married Eleonore Peterson. Five years later he began an affair with Ernestine von Dörnberg. Eleonore died in 1838 and Tyutchev married Ernestine, but his first wife's death affected him deeply and he wrote almost no poetry for ten years.

Tyutchev could have been a successful diplomat – except that he did not take his work at all seriously. In 1839 he was dismissed from his post for neglecting his duties. On returning to St Petersburg in 1844 he was reinstated in the Foreign Office. He became a senior censor in 1848 and chairman of the Foreign Censorship Committee in 1858.

In 1850 Tyutchev began an affair with Yelena Denisyeva, who became, in effect, another wife. Denisyeva died of tuberculosis in 1864, as did two of her children by Tyutchev the following year. In the early 1870s the deaths of his brother and a son and daughter from his marriage to Ernestine left Tyutchev deeply depressed. He died six months after suffering a severe stroke.

Nationalist in his views, Tyutchev lived much of his life abroad; he spoke French better than Russian and favoured French for everything except poetry, which he wrote in an archaic style similar to Derzhavin's. One of Russia's greatest nature poets, Tyutchev preferred to live not on his country estate but in St Petersburg. Though seemingly not a strong believer, he saw Orthodoxy as central to Russia's identity and the Tsar as God's representative on earth.

In his lifetime Tyutchev was best known for his nationalistic political poems. Most now seem tedious, but a few – like this second stanza of '14 December 1825' (the date of the Decembrist Revolt) – transcend their apparent subject:

O sacrifice to reckless thought,
it seems you must have hoped
your scanty blood had power enough
to melt the eternal Pole.
A puff of smoke, a silent flicker
upon the age-old ice –
and then a breath of iron winter
extinguished every trace.

Tyutchev's philosophical poems are structured around the oppositions between night and day, dream and reality, cosmos and chaos. They are imbued with a deep – and, despite the archaic diction, modern – sense of anxiety; the world of reason and cosmos seems terrifyingly fragile. The themes of his nature poems are conventional – blazing sunsets, snowy mountain peaks, etc. – but he presents these scenes from an unexpected point of view. The greatest of his poems are the love poems – above all, the 'Denisyeva cycle'. One of his most striking gifts is his ability not so much to bring opposites together as to allow them to coexist. The language of insomnia is alien to everyone, yet 'audible to everyone, like conscience'. His last love – for

Denisyeva – is both bliss *and* despair; in Russian, the two nouns are in perfect balance: *blazhenstvo i beznadezhnost'*.

Tyutchev took little care of his lyric poems, either losing them or not writing them down at all. In 1833 he lost or destroyed an unknown quantity of his work in a fire, including a translation of one act of Goethe's *Faust*, which he valued. In 1836 a selection of his lyrics was published in *Sovremennik* (*The Contemporary*), the literary journal founded by Pushkin. Tyutchev's first book of poems appeared in 1854 and his second in 1868. The novelist Ivan Turgenev edited the first book and Tyutchev gave him carte blanche to make changes that now seem unfortunate; most were 'corrections' of Tyutchev's bold infringements of metrical regularity.

Tyutchev's admirers included Dostoevsky and Tolstoy, as well as Nekrasov and Fet, but it was not until the end of the nineteenth century that he was generally recognized as one of the very greatest of Russian lyric poets. Osip Mandelstam, in a passage later cited approvingly by Shalamov, observed that a Russian poet should not have a copy of Tyutchev in his personal library – he should know all of Tyutchev by heart.[1]

De Profundis

When again the earth shall return to chaos,
and all that men have wrought
be hidden beneath the waters –
the waters will again reflect the face of God.

(1829)
John Cournos

Silentium

Be silent, hide away and let
your thoughts and longings rise and set
in the deep places of your heart.

Let dreams move silently as stars,
in wonder more than you can tell.
Let them fulfil you – and be still.

What heart can ever speak its mind?
How can some other understand
the hidden pole that turns your life?
A thought, once spoken, is a lie.
Don't cloud the water in your well;
drink from this wellspring – and be still.

Live in yourself. There is a whole
deep world of being in your soul,
burdened with mystery and thought.
The noise outside will snuff it out.
Day's clear light can break the spell.
Hear your own singing – and be still.

(1829–early 1830s)
Robert Chandler

*

I like the Lutheran service, calm and grave,
I like its ritual, solemn and severe;
the message of these bare and empty walls
I bow to, I revere.

But don't you see? Why surely you must know
that for the last time Faith is with us there.
She has not crossed the threshold yet to go,
but all is swept and bare.

She has not crossed the threshold on her way,
she has not gone for good, and closed the door.
But yet the hour has struck. Kneel down and pray,
for you will pray no more.

(1834)

Frances Cornford and Esther Polianowsky Salaman

*

Tears of humanity, tears of humanity,
flowing eternally early and late . . .
Flowing invisibly, flowing in secrecy,
ever abundantly, ever unceasingly –
flowing as rain flows with autumn finality
all through the night like a river in spate.

(Autumn 1849)

Peter Tempest

*

There is deep meaning in a parting:
fleeting love, eternal love –
love's but a dream, a dream's but a moment . . .
Today, tomorrow – awakening is imminent.
And you wake up, at last.

(6 August 1851)

Irina Mashinski

*

The sacred night has scaled the sky and rolled
the day of cheer, the day of graciousness
up and away like a great golden shroud:
a shroud, spread over an abyss.
The outer world is over like a vision,
as Man, a homeless orphan, takes his place
in naked helplessness to stand alone
before the big black of unfathomed space.

He is abandoned to his very self.
His mind is orphaned, thought is nullified.
He plummets through the fissure of his soul
with no support or limit from outside.
As all things of the living and the light
seem but a dream to him, a dream long past,
in the unsolved, the strange, the very night,
he feels a fateful heritage at last.

(1848–50)
A. Z. Foreman

*

Pray, do not say: 'His love for me has not diminished,
his feeling is as long as life . . .'
Oh no! Because of him my days are almost finished,
though his hand may shake – the hand that holds the knife.

Despondent or enraged, unhappy, sobbing, lonely,
in love with him, with jealousy insane,
I yearn, I do not live . . . I live by him, him only –
but oh! This life! . . . What agony, what pain!

He stints me of my air with all the miser's ardour . . .
To hated foes he would have more to give . . .
Oh yes, I still can breathe, though breath is coming harder,
I still can breathe, but cannot, cannot live.

(1850–51)
Anatoly Liberman

Last Love

Towards our end, as life runs out,
love is more troubled and more tender.
Fade not, fade not, departing light
of our last love, our farewell splendour.

Shadow overshadows half the sky;
far to the west the last rays wander.
Shine on, shine on, last light of day;
allow us still to watch and wonder.

What if our blood runs thinner, cooler?
This does not make the heart less tender.
Last love, last love, what can I call you?
Joy and despair, mortal surrender.

(1851–4)
Robert Chandler

*

How bare the countryside! What dearth.
How stark the hamlets' desolation . . .
Long-suffering country of my birth,
poor homeland of the Russian nation.

Never will the proud stranger's gaze
look deeper to perceive or guess
what hidden light there is that plays
and shimmers through your nakedness.

In servant's guise the King of Heaven,
beneath the cross in anguish bent,
has walked the length and breadth of Russia,
blessing her people as he went.

(1855)
Avril Pyman

*

In early autumn sweetly wistful,
there is a short but wondrous interim,
when days seem made as though of crystal,
with evenings luminously dim . . .

Without their tillers, empty fields look wider;
where sickles ravaged in the harvest's ebb,
a single thread left by a spider
still speaks of the unravelled web.

Warblers have gone, afraid of future shadows,
yet far away is winter's firstborn storm,
and heaven pours its azure, pure and warm,
on quietly resting fields and meadows . . .

(1857)
Anatoly Liberman

*[2]

You will not grasp her with your mind
or cover with a common label,
for Russia is one of a kind –
believe in her, if you are able . . .

(1866)
Anatoly Liberman

Russia is baffling to the mind,
not subject to the common measure;
her ways – of a peculiar kind . . .
One only can have *faith* in Russia.

Avril Pyman

*

Not in our power to foretell
what response our words will meet.
Fellow feeling, heaven's grace –
mysteries we can't predict.

(1869)
Robert Chandler

*

My brother, who has kept us both alive,
you, too, are gone! We all are going there:
I've reached a height for which I did not strive,
I stand alone – and all around is bare.

Shall I stand so alone a day, a year –
till all has died upon the piece of ground
on which I stand and through the darkness peer –
unconscious of myself and things around? . . .

Life leaves no trace – 'tis easy not to be!
What does it matter if I come or go?
Night will descend as it descends on me,
the wind will weep and bitter wormwood grow.

My days are few, my losses multiply –
the sparks of living life have ceased to burn;
'tis time to toe the fatal line, and I
stand by myself, just waiting for my turn.

(1870)
Anatoly Liberman

*

I am deprived of everything,
of health, of will, of air, of sleep.
A vengeful God has let me keep
just you – to keep me praying to Him.

(February 1873)
Donald Rayfield

Mikhail Lermontov (1814–41)

The only son of an army officer of partly Scottish descent, Mikhail Yuryevich Lermontov was raised by his paternal grandmother on her estate in central Russia; his mother died before he was three and he had little contact with his father. Lermontov's health was poor and he lived much of his childhood in the realm of his imagination, producing competent verse by the age of fifteen. He wrote 'The Angel', which usually opens selections of his work, when he was only seventeen. Typical of his early romanticism, the poem is about a soul unable to forget the songs of the angel who first carried her down to earth to be incarnated. It ends:

> And with a strange desire all her days
> she walked her worldly ways;
> for dull the melodies of earth she found
> after that heavenly sound.
>
> (trans. Frances Cornford)

Lermontov entered Moscow University in 1830, but left after only two years, possibly the consequence of a prank he had played on an esteemed professor. After enrolling at a military academy in St Petersburg, he became an officer in the Life Guard Hussars. Lermontov made his name with an eloquent poem accusing court circles of complicity in Pushkin's death; this led to his being exiled to the Caucasus. After returning to St Petersburg in 1838 Lermontov was exiled again in 1840 – this time for duelling with the son of the French Ambassador.

Lermontov was hailed as Pushkin's successor and their careers followed a similar pattern. Like Pushkin, he mastered many genres, writing not only lyric and satirical poems but also a verse drama, *The Masquerade*; a pastiche folk epic, *The Song of the Merchant Kalashnikov*; and two Byronic narratives set in the Caucasus, 'The Novice' and 'The Demon'. Like Pushkin, Lermontov moved from romanticism towards a subtle and psychologically informed realism. Like Pushkin, Lermontov turned increasingly to prose. His short novel *A Hero of Our Time* now seems surprisingly modern: there is no omniscient narrator and the hero is presented from several perspectives, both positive and negative. And like Pushkin, Lermontov died in a duel; he was just twenty-six.

Much of Lermontov's best work dates from his last two years, making his early death all the more tragic. Tolstoy admired Lermontov, identifying with him as a fellow officer who kept apart from the literary world; he spoke of 'Borodino', Lermontov's poem about the inconclusive battle fought a week before Napoleon entered Moscow in 1812, as the germ from which *War and Peace* developed. ('Borodino' won new popularity in 1941, as German armies – close to the centenary of Lermontov's death – neared Moscow.) Boris Pasternak dedicated *My Sister Life* (1917) to Lermontov, 'as if he were still there, not just alive but among the chance passers-by'.[3] And the translator and children's writer Samuil Marshak has recounted how, aged fourteen, he was asked by the composer Anatoly Lyadov if he loved Pushkin: 'I replied as most adolescents at the time would have replied: "I love Lermontov more!" Lyadov bent down towards me and said earnestly and affectionately, "Love Pushkin, dear child!" By this he did not in the least mean, "Stop loving Lermontov!" Lermontov captures our imagination at an early age and always retains his special place in our soul.'[4]

A Prophecy

A year will come – of Russia's blackest dread;
then will the crown fall from the royal head,
the throne of tsars will perish in the mud,
the food of many will be death and blood;
both wife and babe will vainly seek the law:
it will not shield the victims any more;
the putrid, rotting plague will mow and cut
and boldly walk the road from hut to hut;

in people's sight its pallid face will float,
and hunger's hand will clutch them by the throat;
a scarlet sea will send its bloody surge;
a mighty man will suddenly emerge:
you'll recognize the man, you'll feel
that he has come to use a knife of steel;
oh, dreadful day! Your call, your groan, your prayer
will only make him laugh at your despair;
and everything in his forbidding sight –
his brow, his cloak – will fill the land with fright.

(1830)
Anatoly Liberman

*

No, I'm not Byron, I'm unknown;
I am, like him, a chosen one,
an exile hounded by this world –
only I bear a Russian soul.
An early start, an early end –
little indeed will I complete;
within my heart, as in a sea,
lie shattered hopes – a sunken load.
Grim ocean, tell me, who can glean
your deepest secrets? Who can speak
my thoughts to the unheeding crowd?
I . . . God . . . or will they die unheard?

(1832)
Boris Dralyuk

The Sail[5]

White on the blue, the sail has gone,
  to vanish with the breeze;
what does the sailor seek alone
  in far-off seas?

His tackle tautens in the stress
  of favouring winds astir;
alas, he seeks not happiness,
  nor flies from her.

The sun is bright above; below,
  the ripples curve and crease;
he, rebel, craves a storm, as though
  in storm were peace.

(1832)

Frances Cornford and Esther Polianowsky Salaman

*

White sail out in the bay
  billowing in the wind.
Why sail so far away?
  Why leave so much behind?

Winds must play on the seas
  and masts creak in the wind.
Fortune is not what he seeks,
  nor what he's left behind.

A golden light still pours
  down onto deep blue seas;
this rebel, alas, seeks storms,
  as if in storm lies peace.

Robert Chandler

*

Lone sail against blue sea-mist:
  what is it seeking?
  what forsaking?

Wind, waves, and bending mast:
  not happiness . . .
  not happiness.

In beams of gold, on azure
  the rebel flees
  for stormy seas.

Antony Wood

Borodino

'Come tell me, was it all for nought
that Moscow burned, although we fought
  and would not yield?
Come, Uncle, tell the tale again
of how we fought with might and main,
and men remember, not in vain,
  our Borodino's field.'

'Yes, in our time the men were men,
and from the heat of battle then
  how few returned,
how few returned their fields to till!
Heroes – not lads like you – they still
fought on, but could not stay God's will,
  that Moscow burned.

'We beat retreat by day and night,
we fumed and waited for the fight;

the old men jeered:
"We'd better winter in the bogs,
and build up huts and bring in logs,
but never turn to face the Frogs,
and singe their beard."

'But then a noble stretch of ground
to build a great redoubt we found,
and there entrench.
All night we listened. Nought astir!
But when the dawn touched fir by fir
and lit the guns – why then, good sir,
we saw the French.

'I had my powder tightly rammed.
"I'll serve you now and you be damned,
my fine Mounseer!
No hope for you to lurk and crawl;
we'll stand against you like a wall;
and if needs must, we'll give our all
for Moscow, here!"

'For three whole days without a change
we only shot at distant range;
no use at all!
You heard men saying left and right,
it's time to buckle to and fight –
until across the fields the night
began to fall.

'I lay to sleep beside my gun,
but heard the cheer, till night was done,
the Frenchmen made.
Our men were quiet. One would sit
and mend his coat where it was slit,
or bite his long moustache and spit
and clean his blade.

'The very hour night was fled
our guns began to move ahead:
my God, the rattle!
Our officers were gallant then;
they served their tsar and loved their men,
they lie asleep in field or fen,
who led the battle.

'The colonel set our hearts astir:
"Moscow's behind. My lads, for her,
as all have heard,
our fathers fought with might and main.
Let's swear to die for her again!"
And there on Borodino's plain
we kept our word.

'That was a day. Towards our redoubt
we saw the Frenchmen gallop out
through smoky air,
dragoons as bright as on parade,
and blue hussars with golden braid,
and Uhlans – what a show they made!
they all were there.

'That was a day will never die:
the flags like spirits streaming by –
a fire ahead –
the clash of steel – the cannon's blast –
our arms too weak to slay at last:
but few the bullets were that passed
our wall of dead.

'That day the foemen learned aright
the way we Russian soldiers fight –
fierce hand-to-hand,
horses and men together laid,

and still the thundering cannonade;
our breasts were trembling, as it made
  tremble the land.

'Then darkness fell on hill and plain;
yet we were game to fight again
  when dawn was red,
till all at once the drums began,
and as they rolled the Frenchmen ran;
and we must reckon, man by man,
  our friends, the dead.

'Yes, in our time the men were men;
soldiers – not lads like you – were then
  heroes indeed!
Hard was the fate their courage earned;
not many from the field returned,
and never had our Moscow burned –
  but God decreed.'

(1837)

Frances Cornford and Esther Polianowsky Salaman

*

Though we have parted, on my breast
your likeness as of old I wear.
It brings my spirit joy and rest,
pale phantom of a happier year.
To other passions now I thrill,
yet cannot leave this love of mine.
A cast-down idol – god-like still,
a shrine abandoned, yet a shrine.

(1837)

Avril Pyman

Cossack Lullaby[6]

Sleep, my little one, sleep soundly;
  high above your head,
bright and clear the moon is shining,
  silver on your bed.
I shall tell you one more story,
  sing you one more song –
close your eyes and let sleep take you;
  sleep, my little one.

Splashing over stones and shingle,
  the Terek swirls below us,
while some Chechen hones his dagger,
  squatting by a boulder.
But your father's battle-hardened,
  he'll protect his son.
Sleep in peace and fear no stranger;
  sleep, my little one.

You'll grow up and, like your father,
  live a fighter's life;
sword in hand, you'll leap on horseback,
  glad to join the strife.
I'll embroider brilliant colours,
  golden as the sun –
silk to lay upon your saddle;
  sleep, my little one.

You will have a warrior's bearing
  and a Cossack soul.
I shall watch you leave the village;
  a wave – and off you go.
I shall know long nights of weeping;
  bitter tears will run.
Sleep, my angel, deeply, sweetly;
  sleep, my little one.

I'll know only fear and worry
  when you're out of sight;
all day long I will be praying,
  reading signs all night.
I shall dream you in strange countries,
  friendless and alone.
Sleep now, while you know no trouble;
  sleep, my little one.

Keep this icon I shall give you,
  keep it close at hand;
pray to it when darkness holds you
  in some distant land.
And when riding into battle,
  think of me, my son,
don't forget your grieving mother;
  sleep, my little one.

(1837–8)
Robert Chandler

*[7]

Farewell forever, unwashed Russia!
O land of slaves, of masters cruel!
And you, blue-uniformed oppressors!
And you, meek nation whom they rule!

Beyond the Caucasus' high ridges,
I may be safe from your viziers –
far from those eyes – unseen, all-seeing –
and far from their all-hearing ears.

(1841)
Guy Daniels, revised by Robert Chandler

*[8]

I go outside to find the way.
Through broken mist I glimpse a flinty path.
I am alone. This empty place hears God;
and stars converse with stars.

The heavens are a miracle
and pale blue sleep lies over all the earth.
What's wrong with me? Why does life seem so hard?
Do I still cherish hope? Or hurt?

No, no, I have no expectations.
I've said goodbye to my past joys and griefs.
Freedom and peace are all I wish for now;
I seek oblivion and sleep.

But not the cold sleep of the grave –
my dream is of a sweeter sleep that will
allow life's force to rest within a breast
that breathes, that still can rise and fall.

I wish a voice to sing all day
and night to me of love, and a dark tree,
an oak with spreading boughs, to still my sleep
with the green rustle of its leaves.

(1841)
Robert Chandler

My Country

I love my country, but with a strange love –
stronger than reason! . . .
Neither the fame that blood can buy,
nor the calm pride of confidence,

nor the time-honoured gifts of ignorant days
can stir my soul with dreams of happiness.
But what I love – for some strange reason –
is the cold silence of her plains,
the swaying branches of her endless forests,
her rivers as wide-spreading as the sea;
galloping in a cart on country tracks
and gazing slowly deep into the dark,
seeing on either side, longing for sleep,
the poor sad villages' bright windows.
I love the smoke of burning stubble,
the lines of carts crossing the steppe,
and in bright meadows, on a hill,
a pair of birches gleaming white.
I feel a pleasure few can share
seeing the barns piled high with grain,
the hut beneath a roof of thatch
with fretted shutters on the windows;
and on a dewy feast-day evening
I'll gaze till late into the night
at whistling dancers, stamping feet,
and hear the drunken peasants talk.

(1841)

Peter France

Dream

At blazing noon, in Dagestan's deep valley,
a bullet in my chest, dead still I lay,
as steam yet rose above my wound, I tallied
each drop of blood, as life now seeped away.

Alone I lay within a sandy hollow,
as jagged ledges teemed there, rising steep,
with sun-scorched peaks above me, burning yellow,
I too was scorched, yet slept a lifeless sleep.

I dreamt of lights upon an evening hour,
a lavish feast held in my native land,
and fair young maidens garlanded with flowers:
their talk of me was merry and off-hand.

But one of them, not joining their free chatter,
sat timidly apart, bemused, alone,
sunk in a dream, her soul by sadness shattered:
God only knows what made her so forlorn;

she dreamed of sand in Dagestan's deep valley,
a gorge in which a man she knew lay dead,
black steam still rose above the wound's scorched hollow,
as blood streamed down and cooled like molten lead.

(1841)
Alexander Levitsky

A. K. Tolstoy (1817–75)

A second cousin of Leo Tolstoy, Alexey Konstantinovich Tolstoy was a poet, novelist and playwright. His delicate love poems inspired many composers, including Tchaikovsky. Now, though, he is remembered mainly for his satirical *History of the Russian State* and for the parodic verses and maxims, in the voice of a complacent bureaucrat by the name of Kozma Prutkov, that he co-wrote with two of his cousins. Among the best known are:

Even an oyster has enemies.

The man wishing to dine too late risks dining next morning.

Only in government service do you learn truth.

In the depth of every breast lies its serpent.

A good cigar is like the globe: it turns for the contentment of man.

If you have a fountain, put a sock in it; even a fountain needs rest.

In Prutkov Tolstoy has created a memorable example of a man who thinks he has power over words but is in fact at their mercy, blind to the absurdity of the images his words conjure up.

Below we include an unusual poem in Tolstoy's own voice.

Wolves

When the streets empty out
and the singing dies down
and a white fog covers

the swamps and the town,
from the forests in silence
one after another
the wolves come out and go hunting.

Seven wolves walk on bravely;
in front of them walks
an eighth with white fur;
while bringing up the rear
is a ninth, who is lame:
with a heel that is bloody
he completes their mysterious procession.

Nothing frightens or scares them.
If they walk through the town
not a dog will bark at them,
while a man will not dare
even to breathe if he sees them.
He becomes pale with fear
and quietly utters a prayer.

The wolves circle the church
carefully all around;
into the parson's yard they enter,
with tails sweeping the ground;
near the tavern they listen
pricking their ears
for any words being said that are sinful.

All their eyes are like candles,
sharp as needles their teeth.
Go and take thirteen bullets,
with goat's fur plug them in,
and then fire at them bravely.
The white wolf will fall first;
after him, the rest will fall also.

When dawn comes and the townsmen
are awoken by the cock,
you will find nine old women
lying dead on the ground.
In front, a grey-haired one,
in back, a lame one,
all in blood . . . may the Lord be with us!

(1840s)

Ilya Bernstein

Afanasy Fet (1820–92)

His paternity remains uncertain, but we know that Fet was the child of a German woman by the name of Charlotta, who, in 1820, left her husband Johann Foeth and eloped to Russia with Afanasy Shenshin, a rich landowner. Charlotta married Shenshin in 1822 when her son was two years old. When he was fourteen it was decreed that the boy could not be considered one of the nobility and must bear the surname 'Fet' (a Russian version of Foeth) rather than 'Shenshin'. This humiliation – which Fet felt deeply – may have led, indirectly, to the death in 1850 of Maria Lazich, a young woman who was in love with Fet and whom he loved. This was probably suicide; she burned to death after dropping a match on her clothes. Fet had decided he was unable to marry her because her family, though landowners, were poor.

In 1844 Fet joined a cavalry regiment. His aim was to regain the title of nobleman. The authorities, however, kept upping the rank that granted entry to the nobility, so Fet was repeatedly frustrated. In 1857 he married, leaving the army the following year. From 1860 he lived the life of a country squire, taking pride in the management of his estates and publishing articles about agriculture. In 1873, after years of litigation, Fet was admitted to the nobility.

Leo Tolstoy was a neighbour and the two became close and lasting friends. Tolstoy, who had few friends among other writers, valued Fet's practical good sense as well as his ability to think with what Fet, in a letter to him, once called 'the heart's mind'.[9] Fet had a gift for healing quarrels and he once reconciled Tolstoy and Turgenev after a famous falling-out. Tolstoy was aware of Fet's greatness; in a letter written in 1857 he asked, 'And whence does this stout, genial officer get the incomprehensible lyric daring that is the mark of a great poet?'[10]

During the 1850s the poet and editor Nikolay Nekrasov regularly published Fet in his influential journal *The Contemporary*. During the 1860s, however, Nekrasov and other radicals attacked Fet as a reactionary. Perhaps because of this, or because he was enjoying the life of a country landowner, Fet wrote few poems during the 1860s and 1870s. During his final decade, however, he published four editions of a collection titled *Evening Lights*, adding more poems each time.

During his last years Fet also wrote 1,500 pages of memoirs. His many translations include several volumes of Schopenhauer, the whole of the *Aeneid* and of Goethe's *Faust*, Shakespeare's *Julius Caesar*, the complete works of Horace, and selections of Ovid, Propertius, Catullus, Martial, Juvenal, Heine and Adam Mickiewicz.

A champion of pure poetry at a time when prose was dominant and writers were expected to be politically committed, Fet was an important influence on the next generation of poets, especially on Innokenty Annensky and Alexander Blok. Tchaikovsky called Fet 'a poet-musician'. Fet himself wrote that 'a lyrical poem is like a rosebud: the tighter folded, the more beauty and fragrance it contains.'[11] He also once said that Turgenev had 'expected [him] to write a poem one day in which the final couplet would have to be conveyed by a silent stirring of one's lips'.[12]

There is much in common between Fet and Emily Dickinson. Boris Dralyuk writes, 'The appropriate word, I suppose, is insight, as opposed to prophetic vision; their revelations are small-scale, intensely private, but this makes them all the more ravishing. And Fet's poems composed entirely of nouns reflect something like the fragmentary, dynamic impressionism that Dickinson achieves with her dashes. By excluding so much, by focusing on only a few essential details, Dickinson creates a thrilling impression both of airiness and of vivid sensuality. This is just what I find in Fet. Both poets were at odds with their time, and both turned inward; regardless of what it was that isolated them, they have their isolation in common. A familiarity with Dickinson's phrasing, with her idiosyncratic ellipticism, helped us find a voice for Fet in English.'

The peculiar place of Fet and Dickinson in the Romantic tradition is epitomized in their shared love of insects. Whereas earlier Romantics favoured eagles and mountain peaks, Fet and Dickinson focus on humbler creatures in their own gardens: gnats, flies, bees, moths, beetles, cicadas, glow-worms and butterflies. A well-known early poem by Pushkin is about a captive eagle, a symbol of the persecuted poet. Fet's more modest equivalent is a plea made by a butterfly to a boy with a butterfly net; the butterfly begs to be allowed to enjoy its one day of life.

Fet influenced not only subsequent Russian poetry but also theatre and the novel. Chekhov's debt to Fet's modesty, and to his impressionism, is obvious. And Rayfield has written, 'Without always being aware of it, the readers of the great Russian novel were imbibing the poets whom the writers of novels had read. Tyutchev's last love poems, riddled with guilt, and Fet's late poetry, in the grip of Schopenhauerian despair, underpin Tolstoy's *Anna Karenina* and Turgenev's *Smoke*.'[13]

Spring

I come again with greetings new,
  to tell you day is well begun;
to say the leaves are fresh with dew
  and dappled in the early sun;

to tell you how the forest stirs
  in every branch of every brake,
and what an April thirst is hers,
  with every whistling bird awake;

to say, as yesterday, once more,
  with love as passionate and true,
my heart is ready as before
  for serving happiness and you;

to tell how over every thing
  delight is blowing on the air –
I know not yet what I shall sing;
  I only know the song is there.

(1843)

Frances Cornford and Esther Polianowsky Salaman

*

Billowing dust
so far away.
On horse, on foot?
Hard to say . . .

There! Galloping
on a swift steed . . .
O far-flung friend,
remember me!

(1843)
Robert Chandler

The Aerial City

At the peep o day in the lift forgether
bonnie cloods like a steepled toun,
wi mony a dome like a bubble o gowd
and white roofs and white waas blinterin doun.

O yon is my ain white city –
or I came to the earth I bade there!
abune the derk warld quhile it sleeps
in the reid lift skinklan fair.

waas blinterin walls gleaming *or . . . bade* Before . . . lived there
quhile while *reid lift skinklan* red sky glittering

But it hauds awa to the North,
sails saftly, saftly, and high –
and a voice is fain that I'd join it –
but gies me nae wings to try.

(1846)
Hugh MacDiarmid

*

Look, outside my window the vine is spreading so fast it
almost blocks out the light. Dark, picturesque green now
covers up half of the panes. And amidst the foliage a bunch of
seemingly carefully-placed grapes has started to turn
yellow . . . Hands off, sweetest! Why this rage for destruction?
If one plump little white hand should be seen to steal
into the yard for a bunch of grapes, the neighbours will waste no
time in declaring: *she* must have been in his room.

(1847)
Robert Chandler

Whispers

Whispers, timid breathing,
trills of a nightingale,
the silver and the shiver
of a sleepy rill.

Pale light and nighttime shadows,
shadows without end,
all the magic transformations
of eyes and lips and brows.

In smoky clouds, a rose's purple,
the shine of amber beads,
and the kisses, and the tears,
and the dawn, the dawn!

(1850)
Boris Dralyuk

By the Fireplace

The embers fade. A lucid flame
flickers in the half-light,
like a butterfly's azure wing
on a scarlet poppy.

A scattering of motley visions
soothes my tired eyes.
Faces I can't quite distinguish
gaze from the grey ash.

Past happiness and sadness rise –
a friendly, tender pair;
the soul pretends it can get by
without all it held so dear.

(1856)
Boris Dralyuk

*[14]

Evening. I'll go to meet them down the old
familiar road. Light fades. The colour's gone
from all around me – earth, grass, tree and stone –
but overhead the sky has turned to gold.
Its soft warm glow burns brightest where the dark
horizon swells to meet it in a gentle arc.

I'll go no further. Under these oak trees
I'll gladly sit and wait for them till morning,
watching the standing corn sway in the breeze,
and one day's death become another's dawning.
So past and future in my own life meet;
and now the sweetness of the hour, so calm
and free, acts on me like a potent charm,
stilling regret for what's behind, and doubt
of what's in store. My dog lies at my feet,
watching a beetle crawl across the ground.
But what was that? . . . He cocks his head,
alert to catch some distant sound
beyond my ken . . . Yes, he was right:
now, from the west, where still the sky burns bright,
I too can hear the old mare's eager tread.

(1859)
Gordon Pirie

*

The moment I encounter your smile
or the youthful joy in your eye,
I sing – but never to you;
I sing your enchanting beauty.

Word passes from dawn to dawn
that the singer can't help but trill;
he will praise the loved rose for ever
as he stands by her fragrant cradle.

Yet never a word will he hear
from Her to whom the roses belong.
A song can't do without beauty,
but beauty has no need of song.

(1873)
Robert Chandler

Never

And I awoke. Yes, a coffin lid – I
struggle to reach my hands out and I call
for help. Ah yes, I've not forgotten those
agonies before I died – no dream!
I brushed the planks aside as if they were
mere cobwebs. I got up. How bright it seemed,

the wintry light that shone into the vault!
A burial vault – for how could I still doubt?
The glare of snow. There was no door. I set
off home. Would they not be amazed when I
appeared! I knew the park, I knew the way.
But somehow everything was strangely changed.

I run. Great drifts of snow. Lines of dead trees,
stretching their branches high into the air,
devoid of motion. Everything was still –
no sounds, no tracks. The kingdom of the dead
from some old tale. And there – my home! A ruin!
I stood and gazed, disheartened and amazed.

The village slept beneath a shroud of snow;
there was no path across the silent fields.
Yes, there it was – the little church I knew
up on the hill, its fragile ancient tower
pointing forlornly to a cloudless sky –
like some poor pilgrim in a coat of snow.

No winter birds, no insects spot this snow.
I understood: the earth had frozen long
ago and died. For whom, then, did I still
have breath within me? For whom, then, had
the grave returned me? And why this consciousness
in me? What was I called upon to do?

Where can I go, with no one to embrace?
Where can I go, with time now lost in space?
Return then, Death, and hurry to take on
the fateful burden of the one life left.
And you, O frozen corpse of earth, fly on,
taking my own corpse on its last journey.

(1879)
Robert Chandler

Here

Forgotten, cold, my dust will fall asleep
while you are entering your life's sweet May.
One moment then, with magnanimity,
read through these verses that once came to me.

And with a maiden's keen and thoughtful heart
you'll understand my words' wild ecstasy,
and why it was I often left the world
for trembling song, and you will follow me.

Through salutations springing from the grave
the heart's eternal truth will be revealed.
We two shall breathe a life outside of time;
and we shall meet – here – as you read.

(1883)
Robert Chandler

Swallows

Nature's ever indolent spy,
forgetting cares and tasks, I'm fond
of watching darkening swallows fly
above a twilit pond.

I watch an arrow almost touch
the pond's clear glass – until I fear
a hostile element may snatch
this winged lightning from the air.

Once more this upsurge of elation,
once more black water sliding by . . .
But is not this true inspiration?
The very breath of being alive?

Do poets not seek ways forbidden
to beings made from dust and clay?
Do I not dream of what lies hidden
and long to scoop a drop away?

(1884)
Anonymous, revised by Robert Chandler, Boris Dralyuk and Irina Mashinski

*

Not a word will I utter
of what I keep muttering to myself –
not for anything in the world.

Night flowers sleep all summer's day
but leaves wake as sun sets behind a copse –
and my heart starts to blossom.

And into my tired breast wafts a moist
breath of evening. Something flutters, is stirred.
But no, not a word.

(1885)
Robert Chandler

*

You're ringed by fire. Its flashes
delight me too. I am not frightened,
beneath your tender eye-lashes,
of summer lightning.

But I am frightened of high places
where I cannot keep my footing.
How can I hold close what your soul
imparts to me of its beauty?

I fear a look without kindness
may fall on my dulled image –
and I shall be left standing
extinguished and singed.

(1886)
Robert Chandler

September Rose

Her flushed lips parting tenderly
as she breathes in the morning frost,
how strangely this rose smiles
as the September day hurries past.

While blue tits flutter around branches
from which every leaf has now slipped,
how queenlike this rose now appears
with spring's glow on her lips.

How boldly she clings to her hope
that, flying from this cold flower-bed,
she will be the last, intoxicated rose
to cling to the young mistress's breast.

(1890)
Robert Chandler

*

Loving, I am still dumbfounded
by the world and its beauty,
and nothing will make me renounce
the sweetness you grant me.

However hard my breath come,
while I stand here on earth
the sound of new life will be welcome
wherever it stirs.

Submissive to the sun's rays,
roots go down into the grave
to seek from death the strength
to meet spring days.

(1890)
Robert Chandler

Apollon Maikov (1821–97)

Apollon Nikolayevich Maikov translated Goethe, Heine, Mickiewicz and much folk poetry from southern Europe. His 'The Hay Harvest' was once the first poem that Russian children learned by heart. Innokenty Annensky writes with characteristic originality, 'A poet usually chooses their own, particular method of communicating with nature, and often this is sport. Poets of the future may be cyclists or aeronauts. Byron was a swimmer, Goethe a skater, Lermontov a rider, many other of our poets (Turgenev, both Tolstoys, Nekrasov, Fet, Yazykov) were hunters. Maikov was a passionate fisherman and this occupation was in perfect harmony with his contemplative nature, with his love for a fair, sunny day, all of which is so vividly expressed in his poetry.'[15]

The Hay Harvest

The smell of hay is on the field,
   and singing as they go
the women toss the heavy yield
   and spread it row by row.

And yonder where the hay is dry
   each man his forkful throws,
until the wagon loaded high
   is like a house that grows.

The poor old horse who draws the cart
   stands rooted in the heat,
with sagging knees and ears apart,
   asleep upon his feet.

But little Zhuchka speeds away
  in barking brave commotion,
to dip and flounder in the hay
  as in a grassy ocean.

(1856)

Frances Cornford and Esther Polianowsky Salaman

Nikolay Nekrasov (1821–78)

The son of a Polish noblewoman and a Russian officer, Nikolay Alexeyevich Nekrasov grew up on his father's family estate in the province of Yaroslavl, not far from the Volga. His father treated both his wife and his serfs tyrannically. Nekrasov was one of fourteen children; financial problems led his father to take on a job as a police inspector and he often took Nekrasov with him on assignments. Nekrasov thus got to see more of Russian provincial life than most young aristocrats.

In 1838 his father sent Nekrasov to a military academy in St Petersburg. Nekrasov transferred to the university – against the wishes of his father, who cut him off financially. From then, Nekrasov supported himself through journalism and tutoring. At one time he lived in a shelter for the homeless.

In 1842 he began working for *Notes of the Fatherland*, a journal edited by the radical critic Vissarion Belinsky, who encouraged Nekrasov both as a poet and as an editor. In 1846, with the help of friends, Nekrasov managed to purchase *The Contemporary*, the journal founded ten years earlier by Pushkin. During the next two decades Nekrasov published work by almost every major Russian writer and also by foreign writers of the order of Balzac and Flaubert. *The Contemporary* was closed down for political reasons in 1866. Nekrasov then acquired *Notes of the Fatherland*, which he edited more cautiously.

Lyrical poetry was out of favour during this period. Nekrasov, however, was a fighter for social justice and his poetry was popular. He spoke of his Muse as being one 'of vengeance and sadness' and in 'Poet and Citizen' (1855) he wrote:

> You're not obliged to be a poet,
> but you *do* have to be a citizen.

But Nekrasov was not as single-minded as these often-quoted lines suggest. Twenty years later, not long before his death, he returned to the question of the relative claims of politics and art, writing more bleakly:

Struggle hindered me from singing
and song got in the way of struggle.

Nekrasov wrote several long poems about the Russian peasantry. *Who is Happy in Russia?* is about seven liberated serfs who travel around Russia in search of an answer to this question, eventually realizing that no one in Russia is happy; Nekrasov began this ambitious but uneven poem in 1863 and was still working on it at the time of his death. His masterpiece is *Red-Nosed Frost*, a shorter narrative poem about a young widow who, after burying her husband, freezes to death while chopping wood in the forest. The final scene is modelled on a well-known folk-tale encounter between Grandfather Frost and a young girl sent out to die by her stepmother; Nekrasov reverses the tale's happy ending. Here we include most of this scene, as well as part of 'Princess Volkonskaya', an extract from Nekrasov's last completed long poem, *Russian Women*, about two princesses who follow their husbands, participants in the Decembrist Revolt of 1825, into Siberian exile.

Nekrasov was equally at home in very different worlds. At times he lived the life of a déclassé intellectual; at times he enjoyed the lifestyle of a wealthy aristocrat, gambling huge sums and, in 1863, buying a magnificent country estate. In 1866 he appalled his liberal friends by publicly reciting an ode to General Muravyov, a government official notorious for his brutal suppression of the Polish liberation movement in 1863. This occasioned Nekrasov lasting shame, and he has often been charged with hypocrisy. It seems more likely, however, that he was genuinely torn between the different worlds to which he belonged.[16]

Nekrasov died of cancer at the age of fifty-seven. Several thousand people attended his funeral and the main speech was given by Dostoevsky; Nekrasov had been his first publisher.

*

Hay Square, 6 p.m.,
a woman was being whipped.
Young, and a peasant woman.
Not a sound from her lips.

Not a whisper anywhere
but this whip and its whistle.
I said to my Muse,
'Your sister!'

(1848)
Robert Chandler

from Red-Nosed Frost

Not the autumn wind in the forest,
not streams hurtling down to the plains –
what we hear is Frost the Commander,
patrolling his far-flung domains.

Has snow been swept by the blizzards
over every pathway and track?
Is there any bare ground still showing,
any last brown fissure or crack?

Have the oak trees been handsomely dappled,
are the tops of the pines fluffed just right?
Have the ice floes been shackled together
so that every lake is gripped tight?

Frost comes striding over the treetops;
shards of ice crackle under his tread.
Lord Frost moves closer and closer;
beams of sunlight dance in his beard.

What pathway is closed to a wizard?
Ever nearer the widow he draws.
Now Frost is looming above her,
rehearsing his wintry laws.

There he stands in a pine tree,
beating time with his cane,
boasting of his own glory
and repeating his old refrain:

'No need to be bashful, sweet maiden,
see how fine a Commander I am!
Speak truthfully now: have you ever
glimpsed a more handsome young man?

'Blizzards, downpours and whirlwinds –
I can quieten them all in a trice;
I can stroll out over the ocean
and build myself chambers of ice.

'One breath – and the greatest of rivers
lie silenced beneath my yoke,
transformed to the strongest of bridges,
broad roads for the merchant folk.

'I love dropping down into graves
to scatter diamonds over the dead,
to freeze the blood in their veins
and ice the brains in their heads.

'I love frightening a lonely robber
riding home with a purse he's plundered:
in the depth of the forest silence
I make branches resound like thunder.

'Old women go rushing back home,
their heads full of spirits and devils.
But there's more pleasure still to be had
with drunkards returning from revels.

'I don't need chalk to whiten their faces!
I set their noses ablaze without fire!
I freeze beards to reins in a tangle
not even an axe can sever!

'I'm rich, there's no counting my treasure;
my fortune's as great as the world.
Every day I bejewel my kingdom
anew with silver and pearls.

'Dear maiden, I bid you now enter
my empire. Let me make you my queen!
We shall reign in glory all winter,
then let summer slip by in a dream.

'Come, maiden, and let me warm you
in a palace of pale blue ice!'
So Lord Frost sings out above her
as he swings his sparkling mace.

'Are you warm enough there, dear maiden?'
he calls from high in the pine.
'Oh yes,' the young widow answers –
and icy shivers run down her spine.

Now Frost has dropped down lower,
his mace swinging ever so near,
and he whispers softly and tenderly:
'Warm enough?' 'Oh yes, my dear!'

Warm enough – but what does she feel?
Frost's breath has already numbed her
and needles of ice from his beard,
though colder and sharper than steel,
are lulling her into slumber.

'Are you warm enough now?' Frost whispers,
his arms now encircling her waist –
and she hears not Frost but Proklyusha
and all she sees is long past.

On her lips and her eyes and her shoulders
Darya feels the wizard's long kisses –
and she sees not Frost but her husband
and she drinks in his honeyed whispers.

He's talking to her of a wedding,
his words so caressing and sweet
that Darya's eyes are now closing
and her axe lies still by her feet.

And the arc of a smile now parts
the poor lips of the wretched widow.
White flakes now cover her eyelids
and needles of ice her brow . . .

A lump of snow falls on Darya
as a squirrel takes a flying leap,
but Darya does not lift a finger;
she's frozen, enchanted, asleep.

(1864)

Robert Chandler and Boris Dralyuk

A Hymn

Lord, give them freedom who are weak,
and sanctify the people's ways,
grant them the justice which they seek,
and bless their labouring days.

May freedom, but a seed at first,
untrammelled rise to flower and spread.
For knowledge let the people thirst,
and light the path ahead.

Lord, set your chosen followers free,
release them from their ancient bands,
entrust the flag of liberty
at last, to Russian hands.

(1866)

Frances Cornford and Esther
Polianowsky Salaman

from *Princess Volkonskaya*[17]

And Pushkin was there. Oh, I knew him full well [. . .]
When south, to Crimea, all our family went
he came with us, too, like a brother.
And how we enjoyed it! The journey how blest!
When Black Sea and mountains we sighted,
my father, decreeing the horses should rest,
allowed us to walk. We alighted.
Sixteen I was. Tall for my years it was said,
and slender. I gleefully hastened
to run with the curly-haired poet ahead,
and, hatless, my plaits all unfastened,
towards the Black Sea in the sunset I flew . . .
The shores of Crimea lay entrancing,
and breathless the glances around me I threw;
I played with the waves; began dancing;
ran forward to follow the water's recede.
I ran after the waves that forsook me;
then, as they swept in, I ran back at full speed
and laughed as the foam overtook me . . .
And Pushkin looked on, he, too, laughing to see
my boots getting wet, until chiding –

'Be quiet!' There's my governess looking for me,
I whispered, made efforts at hiding
my guilty wet feet . . . And when, later, I found
those exquisite verses, undying,
contained in *Onegin*, my heart gave a bound.
Ah me, how the years have been flying!
'Tis all long ago. I'm an old woman now,
and so there's no need to conceal it:
our poet felt a weakness for me, though, I trow,
for many indeed did he feel it.
But really, I think, he to none gave his heart
excepting his muse. I've a notion
that love, in his mind, did not play a great part
save as image of grief and emotion.

Yursouf was so lovely. Its gardens serene
with valleys far distant were bounded,
the sea at its feet. Adayoug could be seen;
the huts of the Tatars surrounded
the foot of the rocks. On the mountainsides steep
the vines flung their branches so tender,
the poplars a motionless watch seemed to keep,
green columns, majestic and slender.
The house where we lived by a rock was o'er-leant;
the uppermost storey was given
to Pushkin. With fate he was very content,
by mountains and sea he was driven
to rapture. For days quite alone he would stray
no human society seeking.
At night by the sea he would wander away;
to English he set himself, speaking
with Lena, my sister. For Byron was then
his passion, his chief occupation,
and Lena at one time devoted her pen
to making a secret translation
from Byron. To me once her efforts she read
then tore them to pieces, supposing
them worthless. To Pushkin, though, somebody said

that Lena herself was composing.
The fragments that Lena threw out with contempt
he found; our whole circle thus learning
the truth. And he often would praise the attempt
while she with confusion was burning.
In moments of leisure, in sociable mood
he joined us, with welcome unfailing . . .
Just near to the terrace a cypress there stood.
He called it his friend, often hailing
the dawn 'neath its shadow, while musing he lay.
He bade it farewell upon leaving.
A legend sprang up round that cypress, they say,
the folk of that district believing,
that seeking the poet in the watches of night,
a nightingale thence would come winging,
and then, as the moon sailed through Heaven's far height,
both poet and bird would start singing.
All nature stood still the sweet singers to hear,
and ever, as night began falling,
in summer the bird to the cypress drew near
and sang, and complained, as though calling
long after the poet was dead. Still, in vain
the bird came in summer, again and again
and poured out her music enthralling.
At last, when the singer of hope was bereft,
she ceased to return. Sad and lonely
the cypress, deserted and friendless, was left
the sea's distant murmur its only
companion . . . But Pushkin had given it fame
and much of their friendship was spoken,
for years many tourists to visit it came
and broke off a twig as a token.

(1863–78)
Juliet Soskice

5
THE TWENTIETH CENTURY

Innokenty Annensky (1855–1909)

Innokenty Fyodorovich Annensky was born in the Siberian city of Omsk; his father was a public official. He lost both his parents in childhood and was raised in the family of his older brother, a prominent Populist and political activist.

After graduating from St Petersburg University, he taught classical languages and literature. He was Head of a *gymnasium* (an elite secondary school) in St Petersburg from 1886 to 1896 and then Head of the prestigious Nikolayev Boys' Gymnasium in Tsarskoye Selo until his dismissal – for excessive leniency towards his pupils – during the Revolution of 1905. Nikolay Gumilyov, who always revered Annensky, studied at this *gymnasium*. Annensky was no less important to Osip Mandelstam and to Anna Akhmatova.

Annensky first became known for his critical essays and for his translations of the French Symbolists and the complete works of Euripides. He had begun writing poetry in his teens, but it was not until 1904 that he brought out a first collection, *Quiet Songs*. Pathologically self-effacing, he published this under the pseudonym 'Nik. T-o' (*nikto* is the Russian for 'no one').

Annensky's technical brilliance and obvious introversion might lead one to assume he was a champion of art for art's sake, but his range of subject matter is unexpectedly broad. Some of his finest poems deal with political and historical themes. 'Petersburg', for example, looks back both to Pushkin's *The Bronze Horseman* and to Peter the Great himself:

The wizard's gifts were only stone,
the River Neva's yellow brown,
and empty squares like desert wastes
for executions staged at dawn.

Annensky died of a heart attack only a few days before the publication of his second and finer collection, *Cypress Casket*. He had learned from the French Symbolists, but his psychological perceptions are sharper and his ability to elicit emotional power from the slightest and dullest of words is remarkable.

All the Russian modernists – Symbolists, Acmeists, even the Futurists – learned from Annensky. 'I don't mean that everyone imitated him,' Akhmatova wrote. 'But he was moving at one and the same time along so many different paths! In him he bore so much which was new that every innovator turned out to be kin to him.'[1] And Vladimir Kornilov has speculated wryly about whether or not Annensky would be content with his fate – to have exercised such influence yet have had so few readers. We would have liked to do more to expand his readership, but Annensky is exceptionally hard to translate. Our selection is brief.

Flies Like Thoughts

Flies, like black thoughts, have not quit me all day . . .
A. N. Apukhtin (1840–93)

I've grown weary of sleeplessness, dreams.
Locks of hair hang over my eyes:
I would like, with the poison of rhymes,
to drug thoughts I cannot abide.

I would like to unravel these knots . . .
Or is the whole thing a mistake?
In late autumn the flies are such pests –
their cold wings so horribly sticky.

Fly-thoughts crawl about, as in dreams,
they cover the paper in black . . .
Oh, how dead, and how dreadful they seem . . .
Tear them up, burn them up – quick!

(1904)
Boris Dralyuk

In the Train Car

We've done enough, we've said enough –
let's sit in silence, without smiling;
low-lying clouds are shedding snow
and heaven's light is slowly fading.

The brittle willows rage and split
in an unspeakable pitched battle.
'Until tomorrow, then,' I say.
'As for today, let's call it settled.'

Even if boundlessly at fault,
I wish – not dreaming, not entreating –
to stare out at the fields of white
through windows swathed in cotton fleecing.

While you, show off your beauty, shine . . .
assure me that I have your pardon –
shine with that stream of eventide
around which everything has hardened.

(1906)
Boris Dralyuk

Spring Song

Not yet does the current hold sway
but it's drowning the blue ice;
the clouds have not melted away,
yet the snow is drinking in sunlight.

Through a half-open door
my heart hears a whisper . . .
You don't yet love, but no more
can you keep your distance.

(1906)
Robert Chandler

Poppies

The gay day flames. The grass is still.
Like greedy impotence, poppies rise,
like lips that lust and poison fill,
like wings of scarlet butterflies.

The gay day flames . . . The garden now
is empty. Lust and feast are done.
Like heads of hags, the poppies bow
beneath the bright cup of the sun.

(1910)
C. M. Bowra

Winter Sky

Down and away flew the melting snow;
cheeks burned red and glistened.
I had not thought the moon was so small
or the clouds so smokily distant.

Asking for nothing, I'll go away,
for my number is up, for ever.
I had not thought the moon was so fair
or so fearful up in heaven.

Midnight is near. I'm no one, no one's,
worn out by the spectre of life,
marvelling at the moonbeams' smoke
in my treacherous fatherland.

Peter France

Bronze Poet[2]

Clouds that whiten in a dome of blue
and twisted trees sharply delineated,
the dust aglow, each shadow elongated
and phantoms that pass through the heart anew.

Why was the tale so brief? I cannot say.
Was there a second half I didn't know?
In pale skies the clouds dissolve away
and night roams through the blackened trees below.

That man, the bench he sits on in the dusk
are growing heavier and more grotesque . . .
Don't move! For as carnations start to shine

and leafy bushes melt and intertwine,
the poet shakes away his uniform
of tired bronze and springs onto the lawn.

Peter Oram

Fyodor Sologub, pseudonym of Fyodor Kuzmich Teternikov (1863–1927)

Sologub was born in St Petersburg. His father – a tailor and former serf, the illegitimate son of a small landowner – died of tuberculosis in 1867, and his illiterate mother then worked as a domestic servant to an aristocratic family; it was in this household that Sologub and his younger sister grew up. Sologub began publishing in the mid-1880s. He worked as a schoolteacher until he became famous in 1907 with the publication of *A Low-grade Demon* (or *The Little Demon*), one of the greatest novels of the Symbolist period.

Bondage – of all kinds – is a central theme of Sologub's. His best short story, 'In Bondage', is about a boy who believes he has been kidnapped by a wicked fairy pretending to be his mother. Hoping to break the spell with the help of what they call 'winged words' (a phrase from Homer that became the standard Russian for a proverbial expression), his friends fire arrows inscribed with swear-words into his home. Sologub's best short poem, part of which is translated below, treats this same theme directly, without the parody and perversity that characterizes most of his prose.

from *My Boring Lamp*

Lord, if I am a poor and feeble
    word slave,
sentenced to tedious labour
    until the grave,

allow me to transcend myself
    in one eternal prayer,
to compose eight lines,
    whose flame burns clear.

(1898)

Robert Chandler

Zinaida Gippius (1869–1945)

Zinaida Nikolayevna Gippius wrote poems, plays and stories. Along with her husband Dmitry Merezhkovsky she was among the founders of Russian Symbolism; together they ran an important salon. Always flamboyant, she liked to shock both through her behaviour – insulting her guests and wearing male clothes – and poems that she called 'personal prayers', but which others saw as blasphemous. In the early 1900s she and her husband instigated what they called 'The New Church', an attempt to forge links between the intelligentsia and the Church.

Like most of the intelligentsia, the Merezhkovskys welcomed the February 1917 Revolution. But they were hostile to the October Revolution and in late 1919 they left Russia. After settling in Paris, they founded The Green Lamp, a literary and philosophical society attended by most of the more important Russian writers in Paris, including Bunin, Teffi, Khodasevich and Georgy Ivanov. The Merezhkovskys' hatred of Bolshevism, however, eventually led them to a sympathy with the Nazis that alienated most of their colleagues.

Though most of Gippius's poetry now seems too rhetorical, her technical innovations (a greater metrical freedom and the use of assonantal rhyme) were important. Teffi ends her memoir of Gippius by telling how, after her death, she whispered over her coffin the words, 'Friend whom I did not know for long, you did not want to be kind and warm. You wanted to be vicious. Because that is more vivid, isn't it? As for the sweet tenderness that your soul loved in secret, you hid it in embarrassment from the eyes of others.'[3]

*

A shameless thing, for ilka vileness able,
it is deid grey as dust, the dust o' a man.
I perish o' a nearness I canna win awa' frae
its deidly coils aboot my buik are thrawn.

A shaggy poulp, embracin' me and stingin',
and as a serpent cauld agen' my hert,
its scales are poisoned shafts that jag me to the quick –
and waur than them's my scunners' feerfu' smert!

O that its prickles were a knife indeed,
but it is thowless, flabby, dowf, and numb.
Sae sluggishly it drains my benmaist life,
a dozent dragon, dreidful', deef, and dumb.

In mum obscurity it twines its obstinate rings
and hings caressin'ly, its purpose whole;
and this deid thing, whale-white obscenity,
this horror that I writhe in – is my soul!

(1905)

Hugh MacDiarmid

Devillet

I happened upon a devillet
with the body of a child.
Thin and scrawny like a gnat;
his face was sharp, and shy, and old.

win awa' frae get away from *buik* bulk *poulp* octopus
cauld agen' cold against *jag* stab
waur . . . my scunners' feerfu' smert worse . . . fearful pain of my disgust
thowless . . . dowf listless . . . feeble *benmaist* inmost *mum* silent

His body trembled in the rain;
his fur was dark and ruffled.
It was a sorry sight; I feared
this devillet might snuff it.

'Love! Love!' I hear all round me.
But love's beyond me, out of reach.
Pity, though, can sometimes grip me,
and so I caught the little creature:

'Come, come, come into the warm.
Why hang about here on the street?
No, no, don't bristle, don't take fright –
I'll give you sugar lumps to eat.'

'Sugar!' he roared. 'Don't be a fool.
I'll have some soup, a plate of veal.
I'm moving in with you for good.
I'll have a proper meal.'

His voice was rich and resonant –
a masculine, caressing bass.
It was really quite indecent –
so deeply out of place.

His bluster put my back up –
I'd only been trying to help.
So I started to turn my back on
this wretched devil-whelp.

He wrinkled up his little face;
he let out a feeble groan.
I felt another tug of pity –
and dragged the devillet home.

I looked at him in lamp light:
a vile mix, an ancient child.
'I'm sweet, I'm sweet,' I heard him say;
I let him be, grew reconciled.

And soon I felt quite at home,
sharing my home with a devillet.
At noon he frolicked like a goat;
by evening he looked dead.

Now he'd strut about like a man;
now he'd rely on womanly wiles;
and when it rained, he smelt of dog
and licked his fur beside the fire.

For years I'd longed for this or that;
whatever I had, it was never enough.
But now my home almost came to life,
as if growing a coat of fluff.

All was joyless, but all right,
tender and sleepy, in the dark.
Life was dully sweet with a devillet:
child or old man – what did I care?

He was like a decaying mushroom –
ever softer, frailer, sicklier.
Sickly sweet and very tenacious
and stickier, stickier, stickier . . .

Until we were not two, but one.
Now here I am, part of his heart.
And on rainy days I smell of dog
and lick my fur beside the hearth.

(1906)
Robert Chandler

What Have We Done to It?

Our grandads' outlandish dream,
the prison years of our heroes,
our lament and our hope,
the prayer we hardly dared utter –
our scuttled, shattered
Constituent Assembly.[4]

(12 November 1917)

Robert Chandler

Ivan Bunin (1870–1953)

Ivan Alexeyevich Bunin was born in Voronezh into a family of impoverished gentry; among his relatives in previous generations were Vasily Zhukovsky and Anna Bunina (1774–1829), the first Russian woman poet to support herself through her writing. Bunin's first published works were poems and his translation of Longfellow's *The Song of Hiawatha* is considered a classic, but he became better known for his prose; his models were Pushkin, Tolstoy and Chekhov, who became a close friend. In 1920 Bunin left Russia and settled in France, becoming a central figure in the émigré community. In 1933 he was awarded the Nobel Prize for Literature.

In his autobiographical novel *Life of Arseniev*, Bunin said of himself as a young man: 'My sight was so good that I could see all seven stars of the Pleiades; I could hear the whistle of a marmot over half a mile away in the evening fields, and the smell of a lily of the valley or an old book could make me drunk.'

Bunin's admirers included Katherine Mansfield and the Woolfs. D. H. Lawrence and Samuel Koteliansky (an émigré writer from the Ukraine) co-translated his story 'The Gentleman from San Francisco'; before republishing their already outstanding translation, Leonard Woolf improved it still further. During the second half of the twentieth century, however, Bunin was somewhat forgotten in the West – probably because of a general lack of interest in émigré literature. Among his best-known works are *The Village* (1910), a bleak novel about the brutality of village life; *Cursed Days*, the fiercely anti-Bolshevik diary he kept in Moscow and Odessa from 1918 to 1920; and his last and finest collection of short stories, *Dark Avenues* (1946). He is one of the many great twentieth-century Russian prose writers who began their careers as poets; the list includes Fyodor Sologub, Teffi, Andrey Bely, Vladimir Nabokov, Andrey Platonov and Varlam Shalamov.

The Artist (Chekhov)

Grey pebbles crunch: he walks the whole way down
to the garden's end. His eyes just skim
over the ponds. He sits on a bench. Above the house
the treeless peaks seem very close and grim.

Crestfallen and languid, his pet grey crane
shelters in shrubs, hot and distraught,
its leg like a stick. 'Well, bird,' he says,
'we should be in Yaroslavl, the Volga, in the north.'

He imagines the scene as his coffin's borne out
under the sun and the clear blue skies,
turning mourning garb grey, making fire pale
and the house brilliant white. He smiles.

'A fat priest wafts incense, coming down the porch.
Choristers follow. The crane gives a shriek,
clucks with alarm, flies off the fence,
struts round the coffin, and stabs it with its beak.'

His chest is wheezing. Blown from the road,
the dust is hot and very dry. He thinks,
removing his pince-nez, coughing a bit,
'Yes, vaudeville . . . Nothing else makes sense.'

(1908)

Donald Rayfield

Teffi, pseudonym of Nadezhda Lokhvitskaya (1872–1952)

Nadezhda Alexandrovna Lokhvitskaya was born in St Petersburg into a family that treasured literature; she and her three sisters all became writers. Teffi – as she called herself – wrote in many styles and genres. She wrote for the popular satirical journal *Satirikon*. She declaimed her Symbolist poems in salons. She wrote plays and a novel, but her finest works are her short stories and her *Memories* (1928–9), an account of her last journey across Russia, before going by boat from the Crimea to Istanbul in 1919.

Teffi was widely read; her admirers including not only such writers as Bunin, Bulgakov and Zoshchenko, but also both Lenin and the last tsar. After settling in Paris in 1922, Teffi played an active role in the literary life of the Russian émigré community there.

For several decades after her death, Teffi was forgotten. But her stories are now being published ever more widely in Russia, as well as being translated into several languages. Her correspondence with Bunin, a close friend throughout their time in France, has been published in full, though only – as yet – in Russian.

Before a Map of Russia

In a strange house, in a faraway land,
her portrait hangs on the wall;
she herself is dying like a beggar woman,
lying on straw, in pain that can't be told.

But here she looks as she always did look –
she is young, rich, and draped
in the luxurious green cloak
in which she was always portrayed.

I gaze at your countenance as if at an icon . . .
'Blessed be your name, slaughtered *Rus*!'
I quietly touch your cloak with one hand;
and with that same hand make the sign of the cross.

Robert Chandler

Mikhail Kuzmin (1872–1936)

Mikhail Alexeyevich Kuzmin was born into a family of Old Believers in Yaroslavl. The family moved to St Petersburg when he was thirteen. He studied at the St Petersburg Conservatory but did not graduate, perhaps because of his growing interest in poetry, perhaps due to a crisis concerning his homosexuality. In the late 1890s he stayed in Italy, where he was attracted to Catholicism. It seems likely that he then spent some time in the far north of Russia, living in Old Believer settlements and studying their music.

Back in St Petersburg Kuzmin went on composing; he sang his poems in literary salons, accompanying himself on the piano. In 1906 he published *Wings*, the first Russian novel with a homosexual theme; two large editions sold out at once. He also published the verse cycle *Alexandrian Songs* (for which he composed a piano accompaniment). Kuzmin had visited Alexandria ten years earlier; it is unlikely that he and Constantine Cavafy knew of each other, but *Alexandrian Songs* is similar to Cavafy's poetry in both tone and subject matter.

In 1910 Kuzmin published the essay 'On Beautiful Clarity', putting forward ideas later taken up by Gumilyov and the Acmeist poets. Kuzmin and Akhmatova were regulars at The Stray Dog café, a legendary institution where almost every important poet of the time – regardless of political or artistic affiliations – gave readings between 1911 and 1915. Kuzmin wrote a preface for Akhmatova's first book, *Evening*, but perhaps unwilling to admit the extent of his influence on her, she later turned against him; in 'Poem without a Hero' she portrays him as a demonic figure.

Kuzmin published twelve books of poetry. Though still best known for his early poems, he wrote his finest work in the 1920s. He considered his masterpiece to be *The Trout Breaks the Ice* (1929). The book's main poem-cycle is a single, obliquely told narrative of homosexual love, betrayal and reconciliation. The central metaphor is that of a trout caught in a frozen stream: with enough determination, the trout can smash the ice with its tail and so be free. After this book Kuzmin fell silent; in 1936 he died of pneumonia.

As well as poetry, Kuzmin wrote several novels, more than a hundred stories and forty dramatic works – plays, pantomimes and fully scored ballets and operettas. In his struggle to earn a living after the Revolution – and to support both his partner and his partner's mother – he translated a vast amount, including Apuleius's *Golden Ass* and nine Shakespeare plays. His almost complete translation of Shakespeare's sonnets was lost during the Great Terror of 1936–8, when much of his archive was destroyed.

Though Kuzmin is still often seen as a languid aesthete, much of his later work is tragic, complex and profound. His evocations of a cold, hungry, dying Petrograd in the early 1920s are as powerful as Mandelstam's. And in such poems as 'A Message' his subtle shifts of tone serve a true complexity of feeling; his delicate aestheticism has become a courageous loyalty – both to art itself and to distant friends. In 'Good Feelings Overcome Time and Space', a poem no one has yet managed to translate successfully, he writes:

> Though many have departed
> to Paris and Berlin,
> no power on earth can bring them
> closer to my heart.

This remarkable poem is almost a magic spell – a spell with a limp. The first and third lines of each four-line stanza rhyme, but the fourth line does not rhyme with the second. The controlled bathos is especially pronounced in the first stanza. Kuzmin tells us about a wonderful gift he has received; whoever dreams of this gift, he says, 'will not go mad'. For a moment we think that it is not much of a magic gift if this is the most it can do for one. Then we realize how terrible the poet's life must be if he accords such importance simply to staying sane. Kuzmin never defines the gift, but it seems likely that it is his sense of being a part of the Russian poetic tradition.

The two poems we have chosen are in free verse in the original. Kuzmin is one of the few great Russian poets of the last century to have written much free verse – as well as blank verse – though he is no less a master of traditional form.

from *Alexandrian Songs*

I don't know how it happened:
my mother had gone out to the bazaar;
I swept clean the house
and sat at the loom to weave.
I didn't (I swear), I didn't sit at the threshold,
but at the high window.
I wove and sang;
what else? Nothing.
I don't know how it happened:
it was a high window.
He must have rolled up a rock,
or climbed on a tree,
or stood on a bench.
He said:
'I thought it was a robin redbreast,
but this is Penelope.
Why are you at home? Hello!'
'Why are you hopping about in the eaves like a bird
and not writing your sweet scrolls in court?'
'Yesterday we went by boat on the Nile –
my head aches.'
'It obviously does not ache enough
to dissuade you from night revels.'
I don't know how it happened:
it was a high window.

I don't know how it happened:
I thought he couldn't reach it.
'Do you see what I've got in my mouth?'
'What would you have in your mouth
other than strong teeth and a prattling tongue,
and follies in your head.'

'Look, I've got a rose in my mouth.'
'What do you mean, a rose?'
'I'll give it to you, if you wish,
only you must get it yourself.'
I got up on my tiptoes,
I got up on a bench,
I got up on the firm loom base,
I reached for the crimson rose
and he, unfittingly, said:
'With your mouth, your mouth,
only from my mouth to yours,
no, not with your hands, your hands!'
Perhaps my lips touched his, I don't know.
I don't know how it happened,
I thought he couldn't reach.
I don't know how it happened,
I was weaving and singing.
I wasn't (I swear), I wasn't sitting by the threshold,
it was a high window:
who could reach there?
When my mother returned, she said:
'What's this, Zoya,
you've weaved a rose instead of a narcissus?
What's going on in your head?'
I don't know how it happened.

(1906)

Richard McKane

A Message

If, wanderer, you should stay in Berlin,
among a people dear to my heart,
where Hoffmann, Mozart and Chodowiecki
(and Goethe, of course) have also spent time,
give my greetings to the houses and passers-by
and to the old prim lindens
and the flat plains round about.

Everything, no doubt, has changed there;
I wouldn't recognize it if I went,
but I know that out in Charlottenburg,
there on some *strasse* or other,
lives a fair-haired Tamara
with her mother, sister and brother.
Ring the bell, though not too loud,
so Tamara will come down to the door
and pull a sweet little face.
Tell her we're alive and well,
that we remember her often,
that we haven't died, and that
we've even grown stronger, been tempered,
that total sainthood isn't far off,
that we don't eat, drink or wear shoes
and we nourish ourselves with words of the spirit,
that we're poor (but that's hardly news –
when have sparrows ever owned possessions?),
and that we've taken up a fine form of trade:
we sell everything and buy nothing,
look up at the spring sky
and think of our distant friends.
Whether our hearts have grown tired,
whether our hands have grown weak,
let them judge by our new books,
which will one day be published.
Don't bore her, don't be verbose.
But if you go on further
and meet another Tamara[5] –
tremble, wanderer, tremble
and cover your face with your hand
lest you drop dead where you stand,
hearing that unforgettable, winged voice,
seeing the movements of that prophetic Firebird,
watching that fleet sun, that sun with a body.

(1922)

Robert Chandler

Valery Bryusov (1873–1924)

The grandson of a former serf, Valery Yakovlevich Bryusov was born in Moscow. From his schooldays he read widely; as a young man he was determined to make his mark on the literary world. In a diary entry from 1893 he wrote, 'Whether Decadence is false or ridiculous, it is moving forward, developing, and the future will belong to it when it finds a worthy leader. And that leader will be me! Yes, me!'[6]

From 1894 to 1895 Bryusov published three collections of poems entitled *Russian Symbolists: An Anthology*; most of the poems were his own, but he used a number of pseudonyms to make this new 'Decadent' or 'Symbolist' movement seem more impressive. These anthologies also included Bryusov's translations of such poets as Poe, Mallarmé, Verlaine, Oscar Wilde and Émile Verhaeren.

Bryusov was influential not only as the founder, with Konstantin Balmont, of Russian Symbolism but also as an editor. From 1904 he ran the Skorpion publishing house, and from 1904 until 1909 he also edited the influential journal *The Scales*. In 1908 he published a historical novel, *The Fiery Angel*, which Prokofiev later used for an opera libretto. Bryusov's capacity for work was extraordinary. In 1915 he was asked to compile a large anthology of Russian translations of Armenian poetry: he learned the language, read a great deal of background literature and completed most of the translations in less than a year.

In late 1917, when many of his literary colleagues were emigrating, Bryusov declared his support for the Soviet government. In 1920 he joined the Communist Party. There are several accounts of his abusing his position in the Soviet cultural apparatus to attack more gifted colleagues – Khodasevich and Mandelstam among them – of whom he felt envious.

Bryusov is a dull poet. We include the following poem because it has been so well translated by Padraic Breslin, who deserves to be remembered.[7]

*

What if we suffered from the lash
of black defeat and cold and hunger?
Above the world new symbols flash,
the sickle and the workers' hammer.

The soil again our toil will tend,
the hostile sword again we'll shatter;
else why, as gleaming sickles bend,
we raise as one our mighty hammer?

Mount higher, thought, nor fear to drop,
but pierce the cold of stellar spaces.
O cosmic sickle, reap truth's crop!
Break mystery's hold, thou cosmic hammer!

Earth's old! For lies we hold no brief!
As in the fall, ripe fruits we gather.
Bind us, O sickle, in single sheaf!
In single plinth, O forge us, hammer!

But fair outmirrored to the view,
the soul of man is young and happy.
The sickle whet for harvests new,
for coming battles keep the hammer.

(1921)

Padraic Breslin

Maximilian Voloshin (1877–1932)

Born in Kiev, Maximilian Alexandrovich Voloshin spent much of his childhood in the Crimea. He studied at Moscow University but was expelled for subversive political activities – or as he put it, 'agitating in the library'. In the early 1900s, already known as a Symbolist poet and art critic, he moved between Paris, Moscow and St Petersburg. From 1907 he spent much of his time in the Crimea, settling there in 1916. For over a decade his large house in Koktebel, where he both wrote and painted, was a refuge for writers and artists of all political and artistic persuasions. Among his hundreds of guests were Gorky, Gumilyov, Osip and Nadezhda Mandelstam and Marina Tsvetaeva. In 1924 the house became a 'House of Creativity' for Soviet writers, the first of the many such closed-access hotels that became a central part of the Soviet cultural world.

Voloshin published five books of poems. The last, *Poems on the Terror* (1923), was published only in Berlin, but these and other post-1917 poems about Russia's spiritual and political destiny circulated widely in hand-typed copies, loved by both the Reds and the anti-Bolshevik Whites, within and outside Russia's borders. Voloshin's professions of faith in Russia's purification through suffering may now seem facile, but much in these poems is incisive and moving. And Voloshin's success in forging a new, colloquial, sometimes biblical, often violent language – far from the hermetic mysticism of his early poems – is remarkable.

Teffi's *Memories* includes this portrait of Voloshin in Odessa in 1919: 'Wherever I went, I would glimpse his picturesque silhouette: dense, square beard, tight curls crowned with a round beret, a light cloak, knickerbockers and gaiters. Reciting his poems, he was doing the rounds of government institutions and people with the right connections. There was more to this than was at first apparent. The poems served as keys. To help those who were in trouble Voloshin needed to pass through certain doors – and his poems opened these doors. He'd walk into some office and, while people were still wondering whether or not to announce his presence to their superiors, he would begin to recite. His meditations on the False Dmitry[8] and other Russian tragedies were dense and powerful; lines evoking the fateful burden of history alternated with flights of prophecy. An ecstatic crowd of young typists would gather around him, ooh-ing and ah-ing; in blissful horror they would let out little nasal squeals. Next you would hear the clatter of typewriter keys – Voloshin had begun to dictate some of his longer poems. Someone in a position of authority would poke his head around the door, his curiosity piqued, and then lead the poet into his office. The dense, even hum of bardic declamation would then start up again, audible even through the closed door.'

After an account of Voloshin saving a woman poet from execution, Teffi ends: 'In Novorossiisk, in Yekaterinodar, in Rostov-on-Don I would again encounter the light cloak, the gaiters and the round beret crowning the tight curls. On each occasion I heard sonorous verse being declaimed to the accompaniment of little squeals from women with flushed, excited faces. Wherever he went, Voloshin was using the hum – or boom – of his verse to rescue someone whose life was endangered.'

During the Red Terror following the evacuation of the White Army from the Crimea, Voloshin showed still greater courage. His belief in the power of his words – what Marianna Landa refers to as 'his Dostoevskian faith in the divine spark in the soul of the abominable criminal, and his Symbolist belief in the magic of the poetic word'[9] – seems to have been unshakeable; his personal appeals to Red and White officials and commanders, on behalf of individuals, and his verse-prayers addressed to God, on behalf of his country, have much in common. Voloshin believed he could affect the course of events – and sometimes he did. That he escaped arrest and execution is astonishing.

Terror

The working day started at night.
Denunciations, papers, certificates.
Death sentences signed in a hurry.
Yawning, drinking of wine.

Vodka, all day, for the soldiers.
Come evening, by candlelight,
time to read out lists, herd
men and women into a dark yard,

remove shoes, clothes, underwear,
tie the stuff in bundles, pile
it up in carts, take the carts away,
share out rings and watches.

Nightfall, men and women forced
barefoot, naked, over ice-covered stones,
into waste ground outside town,
in wind from the north east.

Rifle-butted to the edge of a gully.
The lantern light wavering.
Machine-gunned for half a minute;
finished off with bayonets.

Into a pit, some not quite dead.
A covering of soil, in a hurry.
And, with a broad-flowing Russian song –
back into town, back home.

At dawn wives; mothers; dogs
made their way to the same gullies;
dug the ground; fought over bones;
kissed the flesh they held dear.

(26 April 1921, Simferopol)

Robert Chandler

In the Bottomless Pit

In memory of Alexander Blok and Nikolay Gumilyov[10]

Day by day more brutal and more savage,
deathly horror holds the night in thrall.
Putrid winds extinguish lives like candles.
No more strength to scream, to help, to call.
Dark the destiny of Russian poets
and inscrutable the roads they trod:
Pushkin stood before a duelling pistol,
Dostoevsky faced the firing squad.
I shall draw my lot and know my fortune,
bitter Russia, fierce infanticide:
I may slip on blood outside the dungeon,
or may perish wretchedly inside,
but your Golgotha I never will abandon,
and your graves shall never be denied.
Whether slain by hunger or by hatred –
I shall choose no other lot instead:
if we die, then let us die together
and arise like Lazarus from the dead.

(November 1921)
Yakov Hornstein

from *Russia*

Great Peter was the first true Bolshevik;
his project: to project his Russia, against
all her customs, all her inclinations,
hundreds of years into some distant vista.
And like us all, he knew no other way
save execution, torture and diktat
to realize truth and justice upon earth.
If not a butcher, you could call the Tsar

a sculptor – his material not marble
but flesh, hacking out a Galatea
and flinging scraps aside. But no man builds
alone. What else was our nobility
but our first Communists? Our nobility
was – all in one – the Party, secret police
and Ivan the Terrible's *Oprichniki*,[11]
a hothouse for the breeding of strange cultures.
[. . .] Bakunin[12] reflects the Russian countenance
in every way – what intellectual boldness,
what sweep of thought, what soaring flights and falls!
Our creativity lies in anarchy.
All Europe took the path of fire – but we
bear in our hearts a culture of explosion.
Fire needs machines and cities, factories,
blast furnaces; an explosion, unless it aims
to pulverize itself, needs the containment
of steel rifling, the matrix of a heavy gun.
This is why Soviet hoops all bind so tight,
why the autocracy's flasks and retorts
were so refractory. Bakunin needed
Nicholas – as Peter's *streltsy* needed Peter,
as Avvakum needed Nikon.[13] This is why
Russia is so immeasurable – in anarchy
and in autocracy alike, and why no history
is darker, madder, more terrible than hers.

(1925)
Robert Chandler

*

The violets of waves, the hyacinths of sea-foam
now blossom on the beach beside the rocks.
The sea salt smells of flowers . . .
On such days
your heart no longer thirsts for any change

or tries to speed the passing moment on,
but eagerly drinks up the golden face
of amber suns that shimmer through the azure.
Autumn brings days like these as one grows old . . .

(1926, Koktebel)
Boris Dralyuk

from *Civil War*

And from the ranks of both armies –
the same voice, the same refrain:
'He who is not with us is against us.
You must take sides. Justice is ours.'

And I stand alone in the midst of them,
amidst the roar of fire and smoke,
and pray with all my strength for those
who fight on this side, and on that side.

(1919)
Robert Chandler

Alexander Blok (1880–1921)

Alexander Alexandrovich Blok was born in St Petersburg. His father was a professor of law in Warsaw, his mother a literary translator and his maternal grandfather the rector of St Petersburg University. His parents separated soon after his birth and he spent much of his childhood at Shakhmatovo, his maternal grandfather's estate near Moscow. There he discovered the religious philosopher Vladimir Solovyov and the poetry of Tyutchev and Fet, both of whom were still surprisingly little known. Shakhmatovo would remain for Blok the image of a lost paradise.

In 1903 Blok married Lyubov Mendeleyeva, the daughter of Dmitry Mendeleyev, the chemist who created the periodic table. It was to Lyubov he dedicated his poem-cycle *Verses about the Beautiful Lady* (1904). For well over a year, however, the marriage remained unconsummated. Eventually, Lyubov seduced him, but this did not help; Blok appears to have felt that sex was humiliating to women. The couple remained together, but their marriage was largely asexual; both had affairs with others.

The idealism of Blok's first book yielded to a recognition of the tension between this idealism and reality – and the Beautiful Lady yielded her place to the more louche figure of the Stranger. 'The Stranger', written when Lyubov was close to leaving Blok for his fellow-poet Andrey Bely, is one of Blok's most famous poems. Here we present it in two translations: English and Scots. As well as some of his best-known love poems, and poems about the Muse, we include two poems in free verse, both imbued with a warmth and a gentle humour not generally associated with Blok.

The greatest of Blok's later poems are meditations on Russia's destiny. 'The Twelve' (1918) is an ambiguous welcome to the October Revolution. In staccato rhythms and colloquial language the poem evokes a winter blizzard in revolutionary Petrograd; twelve Red Guards marching through the streets seem like Christ's Twelve Apostles. Many of Blok's fellow-writers hated this poem for its apparent acceptance of the Revolution.

Most Bolsheviks, on the other hand, disliked the poem for its mysticism.

Blok's biographer Avril Pyman writes, 'Blok had spent two months prior to his composition of "The Twelve" walking the streets, and the snatches of conversation written into the poem, the almost cinematic, angled glimpses of hurrying figures slipping and sliding over or behind drifts or standing rooted in indecision as the storm rages around them work as in a brilliantly cut documentary film. [. . .] Musically, the different rhythms are unified by the wind [. . .] stilled only in the last line.'[14]

Towards the end of his life Blok's chronic depression deepened. For nearly two years between 1916 and 1918 he wrote nothing. After writing 'The Twelve' and one other poem in less than two days – and noting, 'A great roaring sound within and around me. Today, I am a genius' – he sank into a still longer silence. 'All sounds have stopped,' he told Korney Chukovsky. 'Can't you hear that there are no longer any sounds?' During his last three years Blok wrote several prose articles, but only one poem, 'To Pushkin House', an invocation of Pushkin's joy and 'secret freedom'.

Boris Pasternak tells how Mayakovsky once suggested they go together to defend Blok at a public event where he was likely to be criticized: 'By the time we got [there] . . . Blok had been told a pile of monstrous things and they had not been ashamed to tell him that he had outlived his time and was inwardly dead – a fact with which he calmly agreed.'[15]

In spring 1921 Blok did indeed fall ill, with asthma and heart problems. His doctors wanted him to receive medical treatment abroad, but he was not allowed to leave the country, in spite of the pleas of Maxim Gorky. Blok died on 7 August 1921.

Blok was idolized in his day and is still considered one of Russia's greatest poets, but there have always been doubting voices. In his memoir *Petersburg Winters* Georgy Ivanov recounts a conversation between himself and his mentor Nikolay Gumilyov. In reply to Ivanov's claim that, however blasphemous it may be, 'The Twelve' is a work of genius, Gumilyov replies, 'So much the worse if it is! The worse both for poetry and for Blok himself. Don't forget that the Devil is a genius too – so much the worse both for the Devil and for us all.'[16] D. S. Mirsky writes, 'But great though he is, Blok is also most certainly an unhealthy and morbid poet, the greatest and most typical of a generation whose best sons were stricken with despair and incapable of overcoming their pessimism except by losing themselves in a dangerous and ambiguous mysticism or by intoxicating themselves in a passionate whirlwind.'[17] Only four years earlier, Mirsky had said that if he had to choose between 'The Twelve' and all the rest of Russian literature put together, he would hesitate.[18] Few poems can have had such power to polarize opinion – let alone the opinions of a single person.

Akhmatova famously referred to Blok as 'the tragic tenor of the epoch'.[19] And in 'To the Muse' Blok wrote:

> And I knew a destructive pleasure
> in trampling what's sacred and good,
> a delirium exceeding all measure –
> this absinthe that poisons my blood!
> (trans. Stephen Capus)

The Stranger[20]

Over the restaurants on sultry evenings
the stale hot vapours rise,
and a corrupting spirit born of springtime
sounds in the drunken cries.

Over the boredom of suburban villas,
the alleys dusty-dry,
glimmers the golden sign above the baker's,
and tired children cry.

And every night beyond the level crossings,
with bowler hats askew,
saunter the local wits with girls a-giggle,
to criticize the view.

Over the lake is heard the creak of rowlocks,
and female shrieks resound,
while high above, the moon, surprised at nothing,
grins meaningless and round.

And every night my glass reflects my image,
friend of my solitude,
who by the strange wine's aromatic power,
as I am, is subdued.

The sleepy waiters, stuck beside the tables,
watch for an empty glass,
while drunken men, with eyes like rabbits', bellow:
'In vino veritas!'

But every evening at the fated hour –
or is it just my dream? –
a figure moves across the misted window,
a girl in silks that gleam.

Slowly she passes through the drunken rabble,
companionless and fair,
and by the window sits, a mist of perfume
spread round her in the air.

Her silken waist, her hat of sable feathers,
her narrow hand with rings,
seem to exhale a breath of long-forgotten
and legendary things.

Tranced by the wonder of her nearness, striving
to pierce her shadowy veil,
I look on an enchanted shore, a distance
beyond some magic pale.

Unspoken mysteries to me are given,
another's sun is mine;
transfused through every corner of my being,
steals the astringent wine.

Within my brain the drooping ostrich feathers
wave languidly and sweep;
blue on that distant shore the eyes that flower,
immeasurably deep.

Safe in my soul there lies a hoarded treasure,
whose key is only mine –
Oh, you were right indeed, you drunken monsters,
the truth is found in wine.

(1906)

Frances Cornford and Esther Polianowsky Salaman

At darknin' hings abune the howff
a weet and wild and eisenin' air.
Spring's spirit wi' its waesome sough
rules owre the drucken stramash there.

And heich abune the vennel's pokiness,
whaur a' the white-weshed cottons lie,
the Inn's sign blinters in the mochiness,
and lood and shrill the bairnies cry.

The hauflins 'yont the burgh boonds
gang ilka nicht, and a' the same,
their bonnets cocked; their bluid that stounds
is playin' at a fine auld game.

howff tavern *eisenin'* lustful *stramash* uproar *vennel's* alley's
blinters . . . mochiness glimmers . . . dampness
hauflins 'yont young lads beyond *stounds* throbs

And on the lochan there, hauf-herted
wee screams and creakin' oar-locks soon'.
And in the lift, heich, hauf-averted,
the mune looks owre the yirdly roon'.

And ilka evenin', derf and serious
(Jean ettles nocht o' this, puir lass),
in liquor, raw yet still mysterious,
a'e freend's aye mirrored in my glass.

Ahint the sheenin' coonter gruff
thrang barmen ding the tumblers doun;
'In vino veritas' cry rough
and reid-een'd fules that in it droon.

But ilka evenin' fey and fremt
(Is it a dream nae wauk'nin' proves?)
as to a trystin'-place undreamt,
a silken leddy darkly moves.

Slow gangs she by the drunken anes,
and lanely by the winnock sits;
frae'r robes, atour the sunken anes,
a rooky dwamin' perfume flits.

Her gleamin' silks, the taperin'
o' her ringed fingers, and her feathers
move dimly like a dream wi'in,
while endless faith aboot them gethers.

I seek, in this captivity,
to pierce the veils that darklin fa'
– see white clints slidin' to the sea,
and hear the horns o' Elfland blaw.

lochan lake *lift* sky *yirdly roon'* earthly round *derf* taciturn
ettles nocht knows nothing *thrang . . . ding* busy . . . bang
fremt taciturn *winnock* window
frae'r . . . atour from her . . . about *rooky dwamin'* misty, swooning

I ha'e dark secrets' turns and twists,
a sun is gi'en me to haud,
the whisky in my bluid insists,
and spiers my benmaist history, lad.

And owre my brain the flitterin'
o' the dim feathers gang aince mair,
and, faddomless, the dark blue glitterin'
o' twa een in the ocean there.

My soul stores up this wealth unspent,
the key is safe and nane's but mine.
You're richt, auld drunk impenitent,
I ken it tae – the truth's in wine.

Hugh MacDiarmid

*

She came in out of the frost,
her cheeks glowing,
and filled my whole room
with the scent of fresh air
and perfume
and resonant chatter
that did away with my last chance
of getting anywhere with my work.

Straightaway
she dropped a hefty art journal
onto the floor
and at once
there was no room any more
in my large room.

haud hold *spiers my benmaist* asks my inmost

All this
was somewhat annoying,
if not absurd.
Next, she wanted *Macbeth*
read aloud to her.

Barely had I reached
the earth's bubbles[21]
which never fail to entrance me
when I realized that she,
no less entranced,
was staring out of the window.

A large tabby cat
was creeping along the edge of the roof
towards some amorous pigeons.
What angered me most
was that it should be pigeons,
not she and I,
who were necking,
and that the days of Paolo and Francesca
were long gone.

(1908)
Robert Chandler

*[22]

When you stand in my path,
so alive, so beautiful,
yet so tormented;
when you talk only of what is sad,
when your thoughts are of death,
when you love no one
and feel such contempt for your own beauty –
am I likely to harm you?

No . . . I'm no lover of violence,
and I don't cheat and am not proud,
though I do know many things
and have thought too much ever since childhood
and am too preoccupied with myself.
I am, after all, a composer of poems,
someone who calls everything by its name
and spirits away the scent from the living flower.

For all your talk of what is sad,
for all your thoughts of beginnings and endings,
I still take the liberty
of remembering
that you are only fifteen.

Which is why I wish
you to fall in love with an ordinary man
who loves the earth and the sky
more than rhymed
or unrhymed
talk of the earth and the sky.

Truly, I will be glad for you,
since only someone in love
has the right to be called human.

(1908)
Robert Chandler

The Sugar Angel

Through the closed nursery doors, the sugar angel
stares through the chink to see
the children playing at the Christmas party,
the brightly candled tree.

Nana is making up the crackling fire,
a blaze for Christmas Day.
Only the sugar angel – he is German –
wastes, warm and sweet, away.

First comes the softening of his little feathers,
the melting of his feet,
the tiny head falls back, he makes a puddle,
minute and warm and sweet.

And then the puddle dries away. The mistress
looks everywhere in vain,
while old deaf Nana, who remembers nothing,
grumbles and looks again.

You fragile creatures of our dearest daydreams!
Break, melt and vanish away
in the bright-burning blaze of hourly happenings,
the clatter of everyday.

Only a little mischievous girl, recalling
the breath of days departed,
will weep for you in secret for a moment.
A child is tender-hearted.

(1909)

Frances Cornford and Esther Polianowsky Salaman

In a Restaurant

Will I ever forget it, that mythical night:
in the blaze of the setting sun
an abyss divided the sky in two
and the street lamps came on one by one.

I sat in a crowd by the window while somewhere
an orchestra sang about love;
I sent you a rose in a glass of champagne
as gold as the heavens above.

Returning your arrogant look with a mixture
of pride and confusion, I bowed;
with studied disdain you turned to your escort:
'That one, too, is in love with me now.'

All at once the ecstatic strings thundered out
in response . . . But still I could see
from your show of contempt, from the tremor that shook
your hand, that your thoughts were with me.

You jumped up from your place with the speed of a bird
that's been startled; your languid perfume,
the swirl of your dress as you passed, died away
like a vision that's over too soon.

But out of its depths a mirror reflected
your glance as you cried: 'Now's your chance!'
And a gypsy, jangling her beads, sang of love
to the dawn and started to dance.

(1910)
Stephen Capus

from *Dances of Death*

Night, lantern, side street, drugstore,
  a mindless, pallid light.
Live on for twenty years or more –
  it'll be the same; there's no way out.

Try being reborn – start life anew.
All's still as boring and banal.
Lantern, side street, drugstore, a few
shivering ripples on the canal.

(1912)
Robert Chandler

The Kite

Over the empty fields a black kite hovers,
and circle after circle smoothly weaves.
In the poor hut, over her son in the cradle
a mother grieves:
'There, suck my breast: there, grow and take our bread,
and learn to bear your cross and bow your head.'

Time passes. War returns. Rebellion rages.
The farms and villages go up in flame,
and Russia in her ancient tear-stained beauty,
is yet the same,
unchanged through all the ages. How long will
the mother grieve and the kite circle still?

(1916)
Frances Cornford and Esther Polianowsky Salaman

from *The Twelve*

From street to street with sovereign stride . . .
– Who's there? Don't try to hide!
But it's only the wind playing
with the red banner ahead.

Cold, cold, cold drifts of snow.
– Who's there? No hiding now!
But it's only a starving hound
limping along behind.

Get lost, you mangy cur –
or we'll tickle you with our bayonets.
This is the last of you, old world –
soon we'll smash you to bits.

The mongrel wolf is baring his fangs –
it's hard to scare him away.
He's drooping his tail, the bastard waif . . .
– Hey, you there, show your face!

Who is it waving our red banner?
Wherever I look – it's dark as pitch!
Who is it flitting from corner to corner
always out of our reach? [. . .]

Crack-crack-crack! And the only answer
is echoes from house to house.
Only the whirlwind's long laughter
criss-crossing the snows.

Crack-crack-crack!
Crack-crack-crack!

From street to street with sovereign stride,
a hungry cur behind them . . .
While bearing a blood-stained banner,
blizzard-invisible,
bullet-untouchable,
tenderly treading through snow-swirls,
hung with threads of snow-pearls,
crowned with white haloes of roses –
who,
who else
but Jesus Christ?[23]

(1918)

Robert Chandler

Velimir Khlebnikov, pseudonym of Viktor Vladimirovich Khlebnikov (1885–1922)

Alongside Mayakovsky, Khlebnikov is the most important of the Russian Futurists. In much of his work he experiments with language, inventing neologisms and finding significance in the shapes and sounds of individual letters. He treats a wide range of themes: war, revolution and famine; the changing seasons; Slavic mythology; a utopian future where all human knowledge can be disseminated by radio and people live in mobile glass cubicles that can attach themselves to skyscraper-like frameworks. He clung passionately to the belief that a mathematical understanding of the laws of history could allow humanity to predict the future – and so gain the power to shape it. In his long poem 'War in a Mousetrap' he declares that we will one day be able to 'trap' war, as if it is no more than a mouse. And in his unfinished 'The Boards of Fate' he writes, 'Once I was sitting deep in thought, pen in hand. My pen was hanging idly in the air. Suddenly war flew in and, like a merry fly, landed in the inkwell. Dying, it began to crawl across the book and these are the tracks left by its feet as it crawled in a coagulated lump, all covered in ink. Such is the fate of war. War will drown in the writer's inkwell.'[24]

Khlebnikov was born in Astrakhan, on the Volga delta. His mother was close to senior members of the People's Will, a terrorist organization. His father was the official administrator of the Kalmyks, a nomadic Buddhist people who speak a Monogolic language. He passed on to his son not only an interest in Asian cultures but also a love of birds; aged twenty Khlebnikov spent five months on an ornithological expedition in the Urals. Donald Rayfield writes of Khlebnikov's youth: 'The contact with nature combined with familiarity with Tatar, Ukrainian and local dialect to give Khlebnikov an uncanonized lexical store so rich that his own "word-creation" was only a natural step.'[25]

Khlebnikov studied a variety of subjects – biology, mathematics, natural sciences, Sanskrit and Slavic languages and literature – at both Kazan and St Petersburg universities, but he never completed a degree. After an apprenticeship with some of the leading Symbolists, he contributed to the Futurist collection *A Slap in the Face of Public Taste*, its manifesto calling for Pushkin, Dostoevsky and Tolstoy 'to be thrown overboard from the steamship of modernity'. Along with Kazimir Malevich, Natalya Goncharova, David Burlyuk, Pavel Filonov and Mayakovsky, Khlebnikov collaborated on a number of Futurist projects, including the opera *Victory over the Sun* (1913). Nearly all the most important avant-garde artists of the time illustrated one or another of his books.

Central though he was to the avant-garde, Khlebnikov was in many ways an unlikely Futurist. While his comrades enjoyed shocking the public, painting their faces and dressing as clowns, he himself was a poor public performer. A lover of myth and folklore, he wrote about mermaids and shamans, often in archaic language. He wrote movingly about the place of animals in our lives: 'Man has taken the surface of the terrestrial globe away from the wise community of beasts and plants and become lonely; he has no one with whom to play tag and blind-man's buff; in an empty room with the darkness of non-existence all around, there is no play and no comrades. Whom is he to have fun with? All around is an empty "nothing". Driven out of their carcasses, the souls of beasts have thrown themselves into him and inhabited his steppes with their law. They have built beastly cities inside his heart.'[26]

Khlebnikov often uses seemingly childish, made-up words (always, however, formed in a logical manner, and from Slavic roots) to refer to his most deeply held beliefs. In 1904 – long before the first use of the term 'noosphere' – he coined the term *myslezem* ('thought-earth') to refer to the earth's 'brain-tissue', its intellectual and spiritual space. Another important concept for him (though it was Alexey Kruchonykh, a less-gifted Futurist, who coined the word) is that of *zaum* ('beyond mind'). The translator Paul Schmidt brilliantly rendered this as 'beyonsense'. Khlebnikov used it of the languages 'of the birds' and 'of the stars' in which he wrote parts of his late 'super-tale' *Zangezi*.

Khlebnikov welcomed the revolution of February 1917 and – at least initially – the October Revolution. Back in Astrakhan he worked for the local military-political newspaper *Red Soldier* – while also helping his father to organize a nature reserve in the Volga delta. He spent the last four years of his life wandering. He left Moscow for Kharkov in early 1919, but the city was captured by the Whites and Khlebnikov only narrowly avoided conscription into the White Army by feigning madness. In 1920 he took part in the 'First Congress of Eastern Peoples' in Baku on the Caspian Sea. He wrote to his sister Vera that in evening classes for the workers, 'I announced to the Marxists that I represented Marx squared, and to those who preferred Muhammad I announced that I was the continuation of the teachings of Muhammad, who was henceforth silenced since the Number had now replaced the Word.'[27]

From Baku Khlebnikov travelled in April 1921 to Iran as a 'lector' in the 'Persian Red Army', sent to northern Iran to support a short-lived Persian Soviet Republic. There he wore Persian robes and was known as 'the Russian Dervish' and 'the priest of flowers'. Back in Russia by August, he witnessed the terrible Volga famine. He was attacked and robbed and lost most of his manuscripts. He died in June 1922, after years of malnutrition and several bouts of typhus and malaria.

Khlebnikov has much in common with Guillaume Apollinaire. Both lived short lives. Both had a gift for drawing and both were provincials, acclaimed as geniuses on moving to their country's capital. Both were close to the greatest visual artists of their time: Apollinaire to Picasso; Khlebnikov to Filonov and Vladimir Tatlin, who staged and directed *Zangezi*, himself playing the lead role.

Both poets are known for their more experimental work, but both also wrote poems that embody deep and unexpected perceptions in more traditional forms; both were uncommonly open to experience of all kinds, willing to follow a thought or feeling wherever it may lead. Much of their work is boldly simple, informed by a deep compassion. Many other examples of avant-garde rhetoric now seem dated, but Khlebnikov's 'Appeal by the Chairmen of the Terrestrial Globe', inspired as it is by a justified horror at the nature of modern warfare, retains its power. And no other writer has left us so profound a poetic response to the Volga famine of 1921.

Khlebnikov was admired even by poets with little sympathy for Futurism. Kuzmin called him 'a genius and a man of great vision'. Gumilyov admired his first publications and Osip Mandelstam later wrote, 'Every line of his is the beginning of a new long poem. [. . .] What Khlebnikov wrote was not even verses, not even long poems, but a vast all-Russian prayer book or icon case.'[28]

Laugh Chant[29]

after Khlebnikov

Laugh away, laughing boys!
Laugh along, laughmen!
So they laugh their large laughter, they laugh aloud laughishly.
Laugh and be laughed at!
O the laughs of the overlaughed, the laughfest
of laughingstocks!
Laugh out uplaughingly the laugh of laughed laughterers!
Laughily laughterize laughteroids, laughtereens,
laughpots and laughlings . . .
Laugh away, laughing boys!
Laugh along, laughmen!

(1908)

Christopher Reid

Menagerie

to Vyacheslav Ivanov[30]

Zoo! Zoo!
Where the iron of the cages is like a father, reminding brothers that they are brothers, and stopping their bloody skirmish.
Where Germans come to drink beer.
And pretty ladies sell their bodies.
Where eagles sit like centuries, defined by a present day that still hasn't reached its evening.
Where the camel, whose high hump is denied a rider, knows the mystery of Buddhism and has concealed the smirk of China.
Where a deer is nothing but terror, flowering like a wide stone.
Where the people's costumes are terribly fancy.
Where people go about frowning and trying to be clever.
And Germans blossom with health.
Where the black gaze of the swan, who exactly resembles winter but whose yellow-black beak is a little grove in autumn, is slightly guarded and mistrustful even for the swan itself.
Where the dark-blue pretty peacock, pretteacock, drops a tail that is like Siberia seen from the rock of Pavda,[31] when over the gold leaves and the green forest is thrown a blue net of clouds, and all this takes on various shades from the soil's unevenness.
Where you feel the desire to pull out the Australian lyre-birds' tail-feathers and pluck them like guitar strings and sing of Russian exploits.
Where we clench our fists as if holding a sword and whisper an oath: to keep the Russian species separate, at the price of life, at the price of death, at any price.
Where the monkeys get angry in different ways and show off their various extremities and are always annoyed at the

presence of people, apart from the sad ones and the mild ones.

Where the elephants, twisting like mountains twist in an earthquake, beg children for food, adding their ancient meaning to the more general truth: 'I wanna eat! Gimme something to eat!' – and then they slump to the ground as if to beg for mercy.

Where the agile bears climb up and look down, and wait for their keeper's command.

Where the pipistrelles hang overturned, like the heart of a modern Russian.

Where the falcon's breast reminds us of the feathery clouds before a storm.

Where the low-slung pheasant drags a golden sunset after itself, and all the coals of its fire.

Where in the tiger's face, framed by a white beard and with the eyes of an elderly Muslim, we honour the Prophet's first follower and read the essence of Islam.

Where we start to think that faiths are the retreating waves whose advance is the various species.

And that there are so many beasts on the earth because they see God in different ways.

Where the beasts, tired of roaring, stand up and look at the sky.

Where the torments of sinners are vividly recalled in the seal, howling as it drags itself round its cage.

Where the ridiculous fish-wing penguins care for each other with the tenderness of Gogol's Old World landowners.

Zoo, Zoo, where the gaze of a beast means more than books learned by heart.

Zoo.

Where the eagle complains about something, complaining like a tired child.

Where the husky kicks up the Siberian dust, completing the ancient ritual of enmity under the gaze of a cat that is licking itself clean.

Where the goats beg by sticking their cloven hooves through the wires, and wave them, their eyes taking on a self-satisfied or happy expression once they've got what they wanted.

Where a too-tall giraffe stands and stares.
Where the noon cannon makes the eagles stare up at the sky
in expectation of a storm.
Where the eagles fall from their tall perches like idols during
an earthquake from the roofs of temples and houses.
Where one eagle, tousled as a little girl, looks up at the sky
and then down at its foot.
Where we see a wooden totem in the face of the motionless
stag.
Where an eagle sits with its back to the people and looks at
the wall, holding its wings strangely wide. Does it think
that it is hovering high over the mountains? Or is it
praying? Or is it too hot?
Where an elk kisses the smooth-horned buffalo through a fence.
Where the deer lick the cold iron.
Where a black seal slides along the floor leaning on its long
flippers, with the movements of a man tied up in a sack,
like a cast-iron monument caught by a fit of the giggles.
Where the lion, shaggy-haired 'Vyacheslav Ivanov', rushes
around and beats its paw angrily against the iron
whenever the keeper calls it 'comrade'.
Where all the lions dream with their faces against their paws.
Where the deer unwearyingly knock against the wire with
their horns and beat it with their heads.
Where all the ducks of one particular species in their dry cage
cry out in unison after a brief shower of rain, as if
offering a prayer – does it have feet and a beak? – a
prayer of thanks to their deity.
Where the guineafowl are sometimes loud gentlewomen with
naked stripped necks and an ashy-silver body made to
measure by the same tailor who caters to the night sky.
Where I refuse to recognize a fellow northerner in the honey
bear and instead discover the Mongol hidden within him,
and want to take revenge on him for Port Arthur.[32]
Where the wolves show compliance and devotion in their
twisted attentive eyes.
Where, as I enter their stuffy house where it is difficult to stay
for long, I am showered with a unanimous cry of

'prrrrick!' and the husks of seeds by the idle parrots, who chatter fluently.

Where the fat and shining walrus waves its black slippery fan-shaped foot like a tired coquette and then falls into the water, and when it drags itself up onto the ramp once more, its powerful greasy body is topped by the moustachioed spiny head and smooth brow of Nietzsche.

Where the jaws of the white, tall, black-eyed llama and that of the smooth, short buffalo, and those of all other ruminants move evenly to the right and to the left, just like the life of the country.

Where the rhinoceros holds in his red-white eyes the unquenchable fury of a deposed tsar and alone of all the beasts does not hide his contempt for mankind, like contempt for a slave rebellion. He conceals Ivan the Terrible within himself.

Where the gulls with their long beaks and their cold ice-blue eyes that seem to exist inside round spectacles look like international businessmen, something we find confirmed in the innate skill with which they steal on the wing the food that is meant for the seals.

Where, remembering that Russians used to call their great chieftains 'falcon', and remembering also that the eye of the Cossack, sunk deep beneath a brooding brow, and of this bird – the race of royal birds – are identical, we begin to know who it was who taught the Russians the art of war. O hawks, piercing the breasts of herons! And the heron's sharp beak pointed to the sky! And the pin where that rare person – endowed with honesty, truthfulness and a sense of duty – mounts his insects!

Where the red duck who stands on his webbed feet reminds you of the skulls of Russians who have fallen for their motherland, in whose bones his ancestors built their nests.

Where, in the golden forelock of one breed of bird, dwells the flame of that strength that is only characterized by a vow of celibacy.

Where Russia pronounces the name 'Cossack' like an eagle's screech.

Where the elephants have forgotten their trumpet calls and make a sound that seems to mourn their condition. Could it be that, seeing us so insignificant, they have started to consider it a sign of good taste to make such insignificant sounds themselves? I do not know. O grey wrinkled mountains! Covered with lichen and with grass growing in your ravines!
Where in the beasts some kinds of beautiful possibilities are dying, like – written in a Book of Hours – the *Lay of Igor's Campaign*[33] during the fire of Moscow.

(1908–11)
James Womack

*[34]

People, years and nations
run away forever
like a flowing river.
In nature's supple mirror
we're the fish,
dark's ghosts are gods,
and the constellations
knot night's net.

(1915)
Robert Chandler

from *An Appeal by the Chairmen of the Terrestrial Globe*[35]

We alone, who have rolled *your* three years of war
into the single scroll of a terrible trumpet –
we alone sing and shout, sing and shout,
drunk on the charm of the truth
that the Government of the Terrestrial Globe
already exists.
We are it. [. . .]

In the meantime, mothers,
carry away your children
if ever a state shows up anywhere.
And you, young men, run away
and hide in caves
if you see a state anywhere.
Young women, and anyone who can't bear the
smell of the dead,
fall into a faint at the word 'frontiers':
they smell of corpses.
Every executioner's block, after all,
was once a fine pine tree,
a curly-haired pine.
An executioner's block is black,
an executioner's block is a blot
only because
it's where people have their heads chopped off.
It's no different with you, state.
'State' is a very fine word from a dream.
In it are five sounds
(or eleven in my original Russian)
and much that is fresh and useful.
You grew in a forest of words,
same as an ash tray, a match or a fag end,
an equal among equals.
But why does a state feed on people?
Why does a Fatherland become a people-eater,
and a Motherland become his wife?
Hey! Listen!
In the name of all humanity
we offer to negotiate
with the states of the past:
if you, O states, are as splendid
as you like to make out you are,
as you make your servants make out you are,
then why this food of the gods?
Why do we people get crunched up in your jaws
by your incisors and molars?

Listen, states that stretch over space,
for three years now
you have given the impression
that humankind is no more than a pastry,
a sweet rusk that melts in your mouth.
But what if this rusk were to jump up like a razor
and say 'Màmochka!'
What if we were sprinkled over it
like poison?
From now on we order that the words 'By the Grace of God'
be changed to
'By the Grace of Fiji.'[36]
Is it seemly for the Lord Terrestrial Globe
to encourage collective people-eating
within his domain?
And is it not the height of servility
on the part of people, people who are being eaten,
to defend their supreme Eater?
Listen! Even an ant
squirts formic acid on the tongue of a bear. [. . .]
Standing on the deck of the word 'star-suprastate',
and needing no stick or crutch in this perilous hour,
we ask, 'What is higher?
We – by virtue of our right of insurrection,
incontestable in our supremacy,
protected by the patents of true invention,
we who have proclaimed ourselves Chairmen of the
    Terrestrial Globe –
or you, governments
of the separate countries of the past,
those everyday remnants beside the slaughter-houses
of the two-legged oxen
with the moisture of whose corpses you have been smeared?'
As for us – leaders of a humankind
that we have constructed according to the laws of rays
and with the help of the equations of fate –

we reject the lords
who call themselves rulers,
states, and other publishing houses
and trading companies of 'War and Co.'
and who claim to have placed the mills of a delightful
prosperity
beneath what is now a three-year waterfall
of your beer and our blood, now flowing
in a defencelessly red wave. [. . .]
Like switchmen
where the tracks of Past and Future meet,
we look with the same composure
on the replacement of your states
by a scientifically constructed humanity
as we do on the replacement of bast sandals
by the hyaline glow of a train.
Comrade workers, don't complain about us:
we, as worker-architects,
follow a special path, to a shared goal.
We are a special kind of weapon.
And so, the gauntlet of five words has been
thrown down:
Government of the Terrestrial Globe.
Cut through by a red lightning,
the pale blue banner of non-possession,
the banner of windy dawns, morning suns,
now flutters high over the earth.
There it is, my friends!
The Government of the Terrestrial Globe!

(1917)

Robert Chandler

from *Night in a Trench*

We need flowers to lay on coffins,
but coffins tell us we are flowers
and last no longer than a flower.

(1920)
Robert Chandler

from *The One Book*

I saw the black Vedas,
the Koran and the Gospels,
and, in their silken boards,
the books of Mongolian Buddhists,
build a bonfire –
as Kalmyk women
do at dawn –
from the dust of the steppes,
from sweet-smelling sheep dung.
And I saw these books lie down on it
of their own accord –
white widows disappearing
in a cloud of smoke –
in order to hasten the coming
of the One Book
whose pages are great seas
trembling like the wings of a deep-blue butterfly
and where the silk thread of a bookmark
marking how far a reader's eyes have journeyed
is a blue torrent of huge rivers:
the Volga, where they sing of Razin[37] at night,
the yellow Nile, where they pray to the sun,
the Yangtze-Kiang, where people are a dense swill,

and you, Mississippi, where the Yankees
wear the starry sky as if it were trousers,
where they wrap their legs in the starry sky,
and the Ganges, where dark people are trees of mind,
and the Danube, where white people in white
stand over the water in white shirts,
and the Zambezi, where people are blacker than a boot,
and the stormy Ob, where a god is thrashed
and turned to face the corner
before people eat something rich,
and the Thames, where there is grey boredom.
The human race is the book's reader
and the cover bears its creator's name –
my name in pale-blue letters. [. . .]
The whale leaps in these pages
and the eagle, skirting the page's corners,
alights on the waves, on the seas'
breasts, to rest on the osprey's bed.

(1920–21)
Robert Chandler

Love Flight[38]

Will you turn
your twisted plait
to a bowstring for me?
Hold
me to the burnished bow
of your brow –
and I,
with finer feathers,
will outfly
the swiftest storm!

(1921)
Robert Chandler

Night in Persia

The seashore.
Sky. Stars. I feel calm. I'm lying down.
My pillow's neither stone nor down
but a sailor's cast-off holey boot.
It was on Samorodov's foot
in the Red days, when he led a mutiny at sea[39]
and brought the White ships to Krasnovodsk,
into Red water.[40]
It's getting dark. It's dark now.
'Give us a hand, comrade!'
calls an Iranian, black like cast iron.
He's got a pile of brushwood to lift.
I pull on his strap
and help him shoulder his load.
'Saoul!' (That's their word for 'Thank you!')
He vanished in the darkness.
In the darkness I whispered,
the name 'Mahdi!'[41]
'Mahdi?'
A beetle, flying straight off the black
and noisy sea,
made straight for me,
circled twice over my head,
folded his wings
and settled in my hair.
He was gently silent and then
suddenly squeaked,
articulating a familiar word
in a language we both understood.
Firmly and courteously,
he had his say.
Enough. We had understood each other!
The night's dark pact
had been signed by the squeak of a beetle.
Hoisting his wings like sails,

the beetle flew off.
The sea erased both his squeak
and the kiss on the sand.
This happened!
It's true
to the last full stop!

(1921)
Robert Chandler

Hunger[42]

Why are elk and hares leaping through the forest,
making themselves scarce?
People have eaten the bark of poplars,
the green shoots of firs . . .
Women and children wander the forest,
gathering birch leaves
for soup, for broth, for borsch,
the tips of fir trees and silver moss –
food of the forest.
Children, forest scouts,
wander through thickets.

They roast white worms in a bonfire,
wild cabbage and fat caterpillars,
or big spiders – they're sweeter than nuts.
They catch moles, grey lizards,
shoot arrows at hissing reptiles
and bake goose-foot pastries.
Hunger drives them after butterflies –
they've collected a whole sack of them.
Today Màma
will be making butterfly borsch.
Enraptured, as if in a dream,
not believing the truth,
the children watch

with big eyes made holy by hunger
as a hare leaps tenderly through the trees.
It might be a vision from the world of light –
but the vision is agile and soon gone –
nothing left but the black tip of an ear.
An arrow sped after it,
but too late – the ample dinner had fled.
The children stand as if under a spell . . .
'Look – a butterfly! Quick! After it!
Over there now! Pale blue!'
The woods are dark, a wolf from far away
comes to the spot
where a year before
he had eaten a lamb.
He circled round and round like a top, sniffed
    everywhere,
but nothing remained –
the ants had worked hard – save one dry hoof.
Embittered, the wolf tightened his lumpy ribs
and made off beyond the trees.
There with his heavy paw he'll crush
crimson-browed grouse and grey capercaillie
that have gone to sleep beneath the snow –
and he too will get sprinkled with snow.
A vixen, a fiery ball of fluff,
clambered onto a tree stump,
and contemplated her future:
should she become a dog?
Should she become a servant to humans?
Many traps had been laid –
she could take her pick.
No, it wouldn't be safe;
they'd eat a red fox
quick as they eat dogs!
And the fox began to wash herself with her
    downy paws,
spinning her fiery tail into the air
like a sail.

A squirrel grumbled:
'Where are my nuts and acorns?
The people have eaten them!'
Quietly, transparently, evening came.
With a quiet murmur, a pine kissed a poplar.
Tomorrow they may
be chopped down
and broken up for breakfast.

(1921)
Robert Chandler

from *Hunger*[43]

Fire-eye,
without its lashes
of downpours and rain,
has been burning our earth, our fields
and whole nations of stalks of grain.
Rippling like dry straw,
fields smoked and ears of grain yellowed,
faded and withered into a dry death.
Scattered, the grain fed mice.
Is the sky ill? Is the sky a sick person?
It has no moist eyelashes,
no mighty downpours, none
of the weather that makes for fine harvests.
Burning the grass, the fields and our gardens,
the eye of the heat remained cruelly yellow,
always golden, with no brows of clouds.
People sat down submissively to wait
for a miracle – but there are no such things – or death.
This was a pale-blue doom.
This was drought. Among beloved years –
a stepson.
Everything – grain and rain –

had betrayed the farmer's labour.
Had not the ploughman's hands,
sweating as always, scattered
good grains that very spring?
Had not the farmer's eyes
looked in hope at the sky
all summer long,
in expectation of rain?
The naked eye of the heat,
this eye of golden fire,
was burning with golden rays
the cornfields of the Volga.

Through the ravine in the forest,
raising clouds of dust,
the crowd hurried to the green hills and the three pines.
All in a rush and agitated,
holding sticks in their hands,
long beards like wedges,
they hurried along.
All of them, children and adults, were running.
This was hunger.
It was to find the holy clay,
that can be eaten like bread,
that you don't die from,
that people were in such a rush.
Clay – you alone remained
when everything let us down!
Clay! Earth!
Hunger was herding humanity.
Men, women and children,
filling the ravine,
were hurrying to find the holy clay
that is as good as bread.
Clay – the mute saviour
beneath the roots of hundred-year-old pines.

And that was when the mind of scientists,
aspiring towards other worlds,
was trying to construct, from lands
subordinate to thought, a dream of life.

(1921)
Robert Chandler

*

The air is split into black branches,
like old glass.
Pray to Our Lady of Autumn!
The windows of autumn's chapel,
smashed by a hurtling bullet,
are wrinkling.
A tree was burning,
a bright spill in the golden air.
It bends; it bows down.
Autumn's flint and steel angrily
struck the sparks of golden days.
A forest at prayer. All at once
golden smells fell to the ground.
Trees stretch out – rakes
gathering armfuls of the sun's hay.
Autumn's tree resonantly evokes
a sketch of Russia's railroads.
The golden autumn wind
has scattered me everywhere.

(1921)
Robert Chandler

*[44]

Moscow, who are you?
Enchantress or enchanted?
Forger of freedom
or fettered lady?
What thought furrows your brow
as you plot your worldwide plot?
Are you a shining window
into another age?
O Moscow, are you femme fatale
or fetter-fated,
fated or fêted?
Does scholarship decree
your crucifixion
beneath the razorblades of clever scholars
frozen over an old book
as pupils stand around their desk?
O daughter of other centuries,
powder keg,
explosion of your fetters.

(1921)
Robert Chandler

*

A police station's a fine place:
it's where the State and I have trysts.
It's where the State reminds me
that it still exists.

(1922)
Robert Chandler

from *Zangezi*

They are the bright blue stilland,
the sky full of bright blue eye-fall
never-never fleeing things
whispering on irrelevant wings.
Ledglings in flight, seeking their selfland,
flocking through darkness to vanishment.
A swelling of heavenly neverings,
a swirling of wing-welling overings.
They have flown, fading and groaning,
forgetting their getting, their names,
unwillingly lulled in their own unwantings.
Cryers and callers, all whirled into wasteland,
earth's own backward, the everlasting everlost of heaven,
into the goneness of here and the notness of now,
hovering haveless through star-frost and sea-spray
towards elsewhere. Wayfarers on the evening air,
thistening like thought-secrets, heaven's harriers,
these nestlings of nowhere, a lattering flutter
of wings in flight to some elsewhere,
of ledglings in flight, seeking their selfland!
Hover-home, breeder of streaming light,
of strange unattainable flutter and fluxion!
Wing-wavers white as drifting down,
weary wizards of downward drift,
wavering dowers of dawn.
River of blue skystead
weary wings of the dreamstead,
broad harmonies of the downstead.
Barefooted in star clusters,
there you died.
Heaven hovers in their hair,
heaven hovers in their voices!
Streaking the eastern streams of everland,
they fly away into their neverland.

With the nevering eyes of earthlings
like notnesses of earth-law,
fleet flight to the blue of heaven,
flight fleet into blue, hovering.
Shrouded in all-knowing sorrow,
they fly to the source of pre-knowledge,
winglings of no-where, mouths of now-here!
Winglings of not-here, mouths of no-there!
Heaven hovers in their faces:
they are the dwellers in the blue places.
High heaven's harriers, a flood of flame,
the heavenly fire-river over us all.
The untamed eyes all vanishing vision,
their untamed eyes saying: not here.

(1921–2)
Paul Schmidt

*

I, a butterfly that has flown
into the room of human life,
must leave the handwriting of my dust
like a prisoner's signature
over the stern windows,
across fate's strict panes.
The wallpaper of human life
is grey and sad.
And there is the windows'
transparent 'No'.
I have worn away my deep-blue morning glow,
my patterns of dots,
my wing's light-blue storm, first freshness.
The powder's gone, the wings have faded
and turned transparent and hard.
Jaded, I beat

against the window of mankind.
From the other side knock eternal numbers,
summoning me to the motherland,
asking one single number
to return to all numbers.

(1921)
Robert Chandler

The Solitary Player[45]

And while over Tsarskoye Selo
poured Akhmatova's songs and tears,
I, unwinding the thread of the enchantress,
dragged myself like a sleepy corpse through a desert
where impossibility lay dying.
  A tired player,
    I strode on regardless.
And meanwhile the curly brow
of the underground bull in the dark caves
was chomping bloodily, eating people
in the smoke of immodest threats.
And wrapped in the will of the moon,
like an evening wanderer in a sleepy cloak,
I leaped in sleep over abysses
and walked from cliff to cliff.
Blind I walked, while
the wind of freedom moved me
and beat me with slanting rain.
And I removed the bull's head from the mighty meat and bones
and placed it against the wall.

Like a warrior of truth, I shook it above the world:
Look – here it is!
          Here is the curly brow for which crowds once blazed!
And with horror
I understand that I was invisible to all:
that it was necessary to sow eyes,
that a sower of eyes must appear.[46]

(1921–2)
Robert Chandler

*

Once more, once more,
I am
your star.
Woe to the sailor who takes
a wrong bearing
between his boat and a star.
He will smash against rock
or sandbar.
Woe to you all, who take
a wrong bearing
between your heart and me.
You will smash against rock
and be rock-mocked
as you
once
mocked me.

(1922)
Robert Chandler

Sofia Parnok (1885–1933)

Sofia Yakovlevna Parnok was born into a Jewish family in the southern city of Taganrog on the Sea of Azov. Her father was a pharmacist; her mother, a doctor, died when Sofia was six. As a young woman, she studied music at the Conservatory of Geneva, and law in St Petersburg, before deciding to devote herself to poetry. In 1909, after divorcing her husband, she settled in Moscow. She then converted to Orthodox Christianity; Parnok appears always to have seen herself as Russian rather than Jewish, and Orthodoxy remained important to her throughout her life.

In 1914 she met Marina Tsvetaeva and they fell passionately in love. Tsvetaeva wrote about their affair in her poem-cycle 'The Girl-Friend'; Parnok in her first book, *Poems* (1916). No Russian poet before Parnok had written so directly about female – let alone lesbian – sexuality.

In the 1920s Parnok published four collections of poetry, all with small print runs. The last two were brought out by The Knot, a publishing co-operative she co-founded in 1926. She also continued to publish influential criticism; in 1923 she had picked out the four now conventionally seen as the greatest Russian poets of the last century: Akhmatova, Pasternak, Mandelstam and Tsvetaeva. After the closure of The Knot in 1928, she was unable to publish her own work. In 1929 she wrote the libretto for a successful opera, but she was now supporting herself mainly through her translations from French; these include poems by Baudelaire and several novels.

Intelligent, independent, lesbian and Orthodox Christian, Parnok was deeply isolated. Among the few poets close to her were Korney Chukovsky, Khodasevich (who emigrated) and Voloshin (who, like her, lived in the Crimea). In 1927 Parnok spoke of herself as an 'invisible woman' in Russian poetry. She called her last book *In an Undertone* (1928) and her last unpublished cycle 'A Useless Good'. These last poems, mostly addressed to the physicist Nina Vedeneyeva (her 'grey-haired

Eve') in whose arms she died, are her finest – as sexually bold as they were politically dangerous. One poem ends with an irreverent reference to Stalin's first five-year economic plan, 'Leave hurried love to hasty youths – / I'm planning on a five-year kiss'. In 1933 Parnok died of a heart attack.

A Childhood Memory

for Khodasevich

A childhood memory: those pears,
wrinkled, little, tight,
and hidden inside –
tart flesh that puckered the mouth:
exactly so my delight
in the bitter shards of your verse.

(1927)
Catriona Kelly

*

They've cut a hole in the deep
dense blue of the ice:
a breathing space for big fish and little,
water for bringers of buckets,
a way out for a weary traveller
if she and life turn out after all
to be travelling different roads
and she has nowhere to go.

(1931)
Robert Chandler

*

I pardon all your sins –
but two I can't abide:
you read poems in silence
and kiss aloud.

So sin, blossom, be merry –
but take my advice:
a kiss, my darling, is not for the ear,
and music is not for the eyes.

(1931)
Robert Chandler

Nikolay Gumilyov (1886–1921)

Nikolay Stepanovich Gumilyov was born near St Petersburg at the naval base of Kronstadt, where his father served as a physician. He studied in Tsarskoye Selo at the *gymnasium* (high school) where Annensky was head teacher; Gumilyov later referred admiringly to Annensky as 'the last swan of Tsarskoye Selo'.[47]

Gumilyov published his first book of poems, *The Way of Conquistadors*, in 1905, and his second, *Romantic Flowers*, in 1908. From 1907 he travelled a great deal, first to France and Italy and then to Africa; fascinated by Africa, he went there almost yearly. In late 1910 Gumilyov was one of the founders of the Guild of Poets, which developed into the movement that became known as Acmeism; the other main figures were Osip Mandelstam, Sergey Gorodetsky and Anna Akhmatova – whom Gumilyov had married earlier that year. Acmeism was, in essence, a reaction to the confused mysticism of the Symbolists. In Gorodetsky's words, 'For the Acmeists the rose has once again become beautiful in itself, through its petals, scent and colour, and not through its imagined similarities to mystical love or whatever else.'[48]

Like Ezra Pound and the Imagists, the Acmeists valued craft and attention to specific detail. And whereas the Symbolists had aspired to bring poetry to the condition of music, the Acmeists wanted poetry to be more like architecture. This ideal was realized, above all, in Osip Mandelstam's first book, *Stone*.

Gumilyov's interests continued to develop along a path similar to Ezra Pound's; in 1918, three years after Pound published his versions of Chinese poems in *Cathay*, Gumilyov published *Porcelain Pavilion*, poems adapted from Chinese via French. Pound and the Acmeists also shared a love of Dante. Mikhail Lozinsky, the finest Russian translator of the *Divine Comedy*, was an Acmeist, and Dante came to mean more and more to both Mandelstam and Akhmatova. Asked two decades later to define Acmeism, Mandelstam replied, 'A yearning for world culture.'

In 1914 Gumilyov chose to enlist. He fought bravely and was awarded two Crosses of St George. In Paris at the time of the Revolution, he returned to Russia in 1918. To someone who advised him to stay in Paris, he is said to have replied, 'I have hunted lions and I don't believe the Bolsheviks are much more dangerous.' For the next three years Gumilyov lived in or near Petrograd (as St Petersburg had been called since 1914) writing and publishing many of his finest poems, teaching younger poets and taking part – as both translator and editor – in the ambitious translation projects initiated by Maxim Gorky. Among the poets he translated are Villon, Blake, Wordsworth, Coleridge ('The Rime of the Ancient Mariner'), Heine, Leopardi, Gautier, Baudelaire and Rimbaud. In collaboration with Vladimir Shileyko, the Assyriologist who became Akhmatova's second husband, he translated *The Epic of Gilgamesh*. Gumilyov was also a perceptive critic, able to appreciate talents very different from his own; among the poets he praised at the start of their careers are both the Futurist Khlebnikov and the more classically inclined Khodasevich.

In August 1921 Gumilyov, always openly hostile to the Bolsheviks, was arrested. Falsely accused of taking part in a monarchist conspiracy, he was executed towards the end of the month. Gorky interceded on his behalf, but to no avail.

from *Stars' Terror*

All this happened when the night was golden,
golden was the night but also moonless.
He was running, running across country,
stumbling down, and standing up, and panting,
turning madly like a wounded rabbit,
and a flow of ceaseless tears was streaming
down his nose and cheeks so sere and wrinkled,
down his goaty beard, wet and dishevelled.

He was followed by his breathless children
and by his grandchildren, also breathless,
and, forgotten in their tent behind them,
his great-grandchild filled the air with yelling.

'Father, stop!' his children cried in anguish,
his grandchildren wrung their hands in prayer,
'No misfortune's happened. Belladonna
has not poisoned any sheep or oxen,
nor has rain put out the sacred fire,
neither lions nor the cruel Zend folk
have disturbed the peace of field and village.'

Just ahead of him a ditch was gaping,
but the old one could not see in darkness;
and he fell, his bones and sinews cracking.
Even then he tried to move by crawling,
but his children seized him by his clothing,
his grandchildren helped them, weak and trembling.
Then he stopped and spoke to them as follows:

'Woe and horror! Fright, abyss and downfall
wait for him who dwells between the rivers!
For the mighty black one looks upon him
from the sky, intense and many-eyed,
and espies the secret of his secrets.
Yesternight I went to sleep as usual,
wrapped in skins, my face, as usual, downwards,
dreaming of a cow, well-fed and healthy,
full of milk appeared her swollen udder.
Thinking I would suck the creamy liquid,
I crawled under her, just like an adder,
but she kicked me suddenly and wildly,
turned me on my back, and I awakened;
I was wrapped no more, my face looked upward.
I was lucky when that poisonous beetle
burned one of my eyes with stinking fluid.

For had both my eyes been looking skyward
I should be by now as dead as mutton.
Woe and horror! Fright, abyss and downfall
wait for him who dwells between the rivers!'

Looking down and silent stood his children,
his grandchildren tried to hide their faces.
Patiently they waited for the answer
from his eldest son, grey-haired and bearded.
And the firstborn spoke to them as follows:

'Long has been my life and always peaceful,
and I hear my heartbeats prophesying
that the future also bears no evil.
I shall now with both my eyes discover
what it is that roams the sky above us.'

So he spoke, and did as he had promised:
on his back he lay, not on his belly.
All the tribe around him stood and waited,
long they stood and waited, still and breathless.
Then the old one asked him, all a-tremble:
'Son, what see you?' But there came no answer
from his eldest son, grey-haired and bearded.
When the brothers bent over their brother,
they could see he was no longer breathing,
that his face was queer and darkly tarnished,
and that death had maimed his manly features.
Fearful moaning started from the women,
seconded by yells of crying children;
and the old one swore, blaspheming hoarsely,
pulling at his beard with crooked fingers.
Now eight brothers sprang up, strong and wiry:
'Let us shoot,' they said, 'our arrows skywards;
let us kill for good that wandering mischief,
let us put an end to all this trouble!'
But the dead man's widow shouted wildly:
''Tis my vengeance, it is not your vengeance!

I myself will see his evil features,
with my teeth I'll tear his dirty goitre,
scratch the eyes out of his ghastly forehead!'

Then she threw herself before the others
on the ground, and raved, and murmured magic,
tearing at her breasts, her fingers biting.
Then, at last, she looked around her, grinning,
cooing like some silly bird and cackling: [. . .]
And when she with her continued yelling,
yelling like a dog who's lost his senses
sped to the abyss that had no bottom,
no one followed her or tried to stop her.

They returned with heavy hearts and dismal,
sat around their tents, afraid and nervous.
Time drew nearer midnight. The hyena
barked but once and stopped, and all was silent.
And the people said: 'The one above us,
God or beast, must badly want an offering.
We must sacrifice to him a virgin
free of sin and young in mind and body,
such a one on whom no man has ever
thrown a glance of passion or desire.
Garr is dead, Garaya lost her senses,
but their daughter here counts but eight summers,
she may do as well, it's worth to try her.'

So the women fetched the little Garra
and they dragged the child before the people.
And the old one raised his axe of granite,
thinking it was best to break her temples,
for it was his grandchild that he pitied.
But the others did not let him, saying:
'What a sacrifice with broken temples!'

So they lay the girl, her face turned upward,
on the stone on which the sacred fire
had been burning till it died neglected.

Looking down they stood around her waiting.
'Soon she'll die,' they thought, 'and we'll be going
home to snatch a little sleep till sunrise.'
But she lay and did not think of dying,
she looked up and right towards her brothers.
Then once more into the sky, and wanted
to get off the cold and stony surface.
But the old one did not let her, saying:
'What is it you see?' – and she retorted:

'Nothing do I see; the sky is empty:
black and curved and empty; it is full of
tiny lights that flicker, as in summer
do the flowers in the bogs and marshes.'
Pensive grew the old one then and ordered:
'Look again!' And so the child continued
to regard the sky, intense and thoughtful.
'No,' she said, 'those lights, they are not flowers,
they are simply fingers, bright and golden,
they are pointing to the fields and pastures,
to the sea and mountains of the Zend-folk;
and they show us everything that happened,
that is happening and that will happen.'

All the tribe around her stood in wonder:
for apart from children, even menfolk
never spoke such words until the present.
Garra's cheeks were flaming with excitement,
eyes were sparkling, and her lips had parted;
upward rose her arms, as if she wanted
here and now to fly away and skyward.
She began to sing, and sang so sweetly,
like the wind among the ferns in forests,
in the wooded valleys of the Tigris.

Mella counted almost eighteen summers
but no man had ever touched her body.
She lay down beside the little Garra,

looked into the sky and started singing.
And with Mella – Akha, and with Akha
her betrothed, Urrh, and then all people
followed, lying down and singing, singing,
just as larks do on a sunny morning
or as frogs do on a rainy evening.
But the old one stood aside in anger,
sealing up his ears with fists and fingers;
bitter tears were chasing one another,
running from his only eye like water.

He was thinking of his fall, his battered
hands and knees, his cuts and wounds and bruises,
and of Garr and his demented widow.
And he wept for olden times, when people
looked at simple things and were contented:
at the pastures where their sheep were grazing,
at the river where their sails were passing,
at the meadows with their playing children,
never looking at the starry blackness,
strange, and inaccessible and foreign.

(1911)
Yakov Hornstein

*

You shall recall me yet, and more than once –
recall my world, uncommon and exciting:
a clumsy world, fashioned of flame and songs,
but, unlike others, wholly undesigning.

It could have been yours, too, but no. It had
proven too little, or perhaps too vast.
My verse, it seems, must have been very bad,
my pleading with the Lord for you, unjust.

But every time, drained of your strength, you'll yield
and utter: 'I don't dare recall those nights.
A different world has fascinated me
with all its simple, less refined delights.'

(1917)
Boris Dralyuk

Ezbekiya

How very strange – it is ten years today
since I inhaled the scents of Ezbekiya,
the splendid park in Cairo which that night
was full of voices and of festive moonlight.

I came there broken, tortured by a woman,
and neither salty breezes from the sea,
nor the exotic tumult of bazaars
could cure my wounded soul or give me solace.
Ten years ago I prayed to God for death
and was prepared to hasten its approach.

But then that garden seemed a holy grove,
a sacred forest of the new-born world:
tall graceful palm-trees lightly raised their branches
as virgins do when visited by gods;
there, on the hills, like wise prophetic druids,
majestic, lofty platans proudly crowded,
and underneath, a rushing waterfall
loomed through the darkness like a unicorn.
Night-butterflies were everywhere and flew
amid the many flowers that grew so tall,
or 'mid the stars – the stars came down so low,
looking like ripening berries on a bush.

And I recall exclaiming: 'More than grief,
deeper than death is life. This is, O God,
my voluntary vow: whatever pain,
distress, humiliation be my lot,
I will not plan an easy death, before
again I walk on such a moonlit night
under the graceful palms of Ezbekiya.'

How very strange – it is ten years today,
and I must think again of palms and platans,
and of that rushing whitish waterfall,
looming in darkness like a unicorn.
And suddenly a multitude of voices,
the droning of the wind, the silent night,
the sound of distant speech, they all unite
in one mysterious whisper: Ezbekiya.

Yes, just ten years, but, gloomy wanderer,
I must again go forth, must see once more
the clouds and seas and unfamiliar faces,
all that has no more charm for me, and enter
that splendid garden, to repeat my vow,
or else, to say that it has been fulfilled,
and that I now am free . . .

(1918)

Yakov Hornstein

The Lost Tram

I was walking down an unfamiliar street,
and suddenly I heard the caws of crows,
and distant thunder, and a ringing lute:
a tram flew by before my eyes.

Just how I ran onto its running board
remains a mystery.
The tail it trailed, even in daylight,
was firebird-fiery.

It raced on like a dark and winged whirlwind,
adrift in time's abyss . . .
Stop, tram-driver,
Stop this tram at once.

Too late. We've turned the corner,
glided through a palm-oasis,
and rocked our way across three bridges –
the Neva, the Nile, the Seine.

Slipping past the window, an ancient beggar
threw us a searching stare –
the beggar who died in Beirut, of course,
only last year.

Where am I? Languid, anxious,
my heart beats in response:
'Look – it's the station! They're selling tickets
to India of the Soul – depart at once!'

A sign . . . It announces in blood-swollen letters:
'Greengrocer.' I know that instead
of cabbage heads, swedes and rutabagas
they sell the heads of the dead.

The executioner, with a face like an udder,
red-shirted, stout as an ox,
has chopped off my head. Along with the others,
it lies at the bottom of a slippery box.

On a side street, a house of three windows,
a fence made of boards, greying grass . . .
Stop, tram-driver,
Stop this tram at once!

Mashenka, you lived and sang here.
Here's where you wove me a carpet.
Where are they now – your voice, your body?
Dearest, are you truly among the dead?

Oh how you moaned in your chamber,
while I, in a powdered wig, your groom,
went to present myself to the Empress –
never to glimpse you again.

I've grasped it at last: our freedom
is only a light pulsating from far –
people and shadows stand at the entrance
to the zoo of the wandering stars.

A sweet and familiar wind, of a sudden,
and over the bridge, flying my way –
a horseman's hand in a glove of iron,
and two great hooves, raised to the sky.

Steadfast stronghold of Orthodoxy,
St Isaac's spire is etched on high.
Prayers must be sung for Mashenka's health
and a memorial service for me.

And still, my heart is forever sullen.
It's hard to breathe, and it hurts to live . . .
Mashenka, I could never have known
of such a love, of such a grief.

(1920)
Boris Dralyuk

The Sixth Sense

Good is the wine that is in love with us,
and good is bread, our generous friend;
and good the woman who brings us torment
yet yields her sweetness to us in the end.

But what are we to do with sunset fires?
With joys that can't be eaten, drunk or kissed?
And what are we to do with deathless verse?
We stand and watch – as mysteries slip past.

Just as some boy too young to know of love
will leave his play to gaze, his heart on fire,
at maidens swimming in a lake, and gaze
and gaze, tormented by obscure desire;

or as within the gloom of ancient jungle
some earthbound beast once slithered from its lair
with wing buds on its back, still tightly closed,
and let out cries of impotent despair;

so year on year – how long, Lord, must we wait? –
beneath the surgeon's knife of art and nature,
our flesh is wasted and our spirit howls
as one more sense moves slowly to creation.

(1920)

Robert Chandler

Vladislav Khodasevich (1886–1939)

Vladislav Felitsianovich Khodasevich was born in Moscow, but his family were culturally Polish-Lithuanian; his mother (of Jewish ancestry, but brought up Catholic) introduced him to Adam Mickiewicz and Polish poetry when he was a child, before he had read any Russian poetry. Evidently feeling unable to take his place in Russian culture for granted, he wrote of his Russian wet nurse that she gave him 'the excruciating right to love and to curse the resounding power of Russia'.[49] Khodasevich published his first book in 1907, but it was only with 'The Grain's Path', a poem he published in late 1917, that he won recognition. This became the title poem of the first of the three great collections of his maturity.

In 1918 he published an anthology of Hebrew verse in Russian translation, and he went on to translate from Polish, French and other languages, working sometimes from the original, sometimes from a crib. In December 1920 he moved to Petrograd, where he lived, along with many other writers, in the State-subsidized House of Arts, a former palace. There he wrote many of the poems that form the second of his mature collections, *The Heavy Lyre* (1922). His article 'The House of Arts' evokes this period in the life of the city that had been Russia's capital for two hundred years until March 1918: 'Moscow, without the bustle of trade and administration, would probably have seemed pitiful. Petersburg became majestic. Along with the brass signs and plaques, it shed all superfluous gaudiness. [. . .] Even the most ordinary buildings took on the sternness and clear outlines that, until then, had belonged only to palaces. In this magnificent but strange city, scholarly, literary, artistic and theatrical life all came to the surface and took on an unusual distinctness. The Bolsheviks were trying to take control of this life but had not yet succeeded – and this life was living out its last days of freedom in a state of true creative elation. Hunger and cold did nothing to diminish this elation; they may even have intensified it.'[50]

In June 1922 Khodasevich left Russia with Nina Berberova, now best known for her memoir *The Italics are Mine*. They lived in Berlin, in Maxim Gorky's villa in Sorrento, again in Berlin and then in Paris. Khodasevich published *European Night*, his last collection, in 1927. From the mid-1920s he had been writing less and less poetry – probably because of poverty, poor health and depression. He did, however, write literary criticism – his only source of income. As well as articles about Pushkin and contemporary literature, he wrote a fine biography of Derzhavin. Shortly before his death, he published *Necropolis*, a memoir of his last eighteen months in Petrograd. He also did much to help a younger colleague, Vladimir Nabokov; one of the heroes of Nabokov's *The Gift* is modelled on Khodasevich.

Khodasevich's own loyalty was not to any literary or political grouping but to Pushkin. Soon after leaving Russia, he wrote that he was carrying his Motherland around with him in the form of eight small volumes – i.e., Pushkin's complete works. More than twenty years later, in 1944, Boris Slutsky, then a Red Army commissar, came across a fine library of émigré literature on an estate in Bosnia. He already knew Khodasevich's early poetry and he seized the opportunity to read his later work. This influenced not only his own poetry, but also, through him, the work of many other Soviet poets of the post-Stalin era.[51] With Slutsky's help, Khodasevich began his long and slow return journey to Russia.

The Grain's Path

The sower walks down the even furrows;
his fathers all followed the path he follows.

The young seed glitters gold in his hand,
but it must fall into the black ground.

There, amid the tunnels of the blind worm,
it will die on its due day – and grow again.

So now my soul treads the path of the grain –
down into darkness – and spring's return.

And you, my people, and you, my native land,
you will die and live, when the dark months end,

for we have been granted only this one truth:
whatever lives must follow the grain's path.

(1917)
Robert Chandler

The Monkey[52]

A day of heat. The woods burning. Time
hanging heavy. From a neighbouring plot
a cock was crowing. I went through the gate.
There, on the bench, his back against the fence,
a wandering Serb, dark-skinned and lean, sat dozing.
A heavy silver crucifix hung down
among the rolling drops of sweat that coursed
his half-bared chest. Above him, on the fence,
a monkey squatted, wearing a red skirt,
and ravenously made a meal
of dusty lilac leaves. A leather collar
straining backwards on a chain
compressed its neck. Hearing me, the Serb
awoke, and mopped the pouring sweat, and asked for water.
But as soon as he had put it to his lips
to see if it was cold, he set the saucer
down upon the bench, at which the monkey
its fingers dabbling in the water, seized
the dish with both its hands,
and, crouching down upon all fours, its elbows
leaning on the bench, began to drink.
Its chin was nearly resting on the boards,
its back went arching high up in the air

above its balding crown. In such a way
must Darius once have stooped and crouched to drink
from some small roadside pool the day he fled
before the might of Alexander's phalanx.
When all the water had been drunk, the monkey
flipped the dish down from the bench, stood up,
and – shall I ever now forget this moment? –
the creature offered me its hand to shake,
its black and calloused hand, still freshly cool
    with moisture . . .
I have shaken hands with famous beauties,
with poets, with national leaders – but not one
whose hand possessed lineaments
of such nobility! Not one whose hand
touched mine with such a sense of brotherhood!
God knows, no human creature ever looked
into my eyes so wisely or so deep,
truly, to the bottom of my soul.
The sweetest legends of profound antiquity
that miserable creature woke in me,
and in that moment life for me was full,
and, as it seemed, a choir of stars and waves,
of winds and spheres, came bursting in my ears
like organ music, thundering as it did
of old, in other immemorial days.
The Serb went off, pattering his tambourine.
The monkey, riding on his left-hand shoulder,
sat swaying to the rhythm of his walk –
a maharajah on an elephant.
Up in the opalescent smoke, the sun
hung huge and crimson, shorn
of all its rays. The heavy heat, still thunderless,
pressed down upon the fields of scrawny wheat.

That was the day on which the war broke out.

(1918–19)

Michael Frayn

To a Guest

Bring visions when you ring my bell
or all the loveliness of hell,
or God, if you belong to that band.
But little acts of meaning well –
just leave them outside on the hat stand.

On this small pea in endless space
be shining angel or be demon.
But not mere man, though, for to be one
is to pass by and leave no trace.

(1921)
Michael Frayn

Ballad of the Heavy Lyre

I sit where the light is above me,
my circular room is my sphere;
I gaze at a plasterwork heaven
where the sun is an old chandelier.

And likewise illumined around me,
the chairs and the table and bed.
Should I sit with my hands in my pockets,
or where might I put them instead?

Silently, frost on the window
grows palm-trees and icy white flowers;
my watch ticks away in my waistcoat,
metallically counting the hours.

O my life is so worthless, a quagmire
where I'm stuck with no way to get free!
And who can I tell of my pity
for the things that I own, and for me?

And hugging my knees where I'm sitting,
I'm rocking, quite gently at first,
when out of the trance that I've entered
a chorus of verses has burst.

It's nothing but passionate nonsense!
Whatever it means, it's absurd,
but sound is more honest than meaning,
and strongest of all is a word.

And a music, the music of music
is twined in the song of my life,
and piercing me, piercing and piercing,
is the blade of the slenderest knife.

I find myself rising above me,
from where I exist but am dead;
my feet are in underground fire,
and a galaxy streams at my head.

I watch with my eyes ever wider –
how a serpent might see through the gloom –
I see my wild song is entrancing
the comfortless things in my room,

and the things begin dancing a measure,
with gracefully circling charms;
and somebody's heavy lyre comes
from out of the wind to my arms.

And there is no plasterwork heaven,
no chandelier sun any more;
but the blackness of slippery boulders
and Orpheus, his feet on the shore.

(1921)

Peter Daniels

*

Twilight was turning to darkness outside.
Under the eaves a window banged wide.

A curtain was lifted, a light briefly shone,
a swift shadow fell down the wall and was gone.

Happy the man who falls head first to death:
at least for a moment his viewpoint is fresh.

(1922)
Michael Frayn

Shape Ships to Seek

Shape ships to seek some shining shore,
or, if you choose, chirp chants in churches.
But seize your chance – shout one shy cheer,
and shoot up starwards, sharp and sheer . . .
I shift the chairs – a cheerless chore . . .
What tosh you chunter in these searches
for shoes and spectacles, to be sure!

(1922)
Michael Frayn

In Front of the Mirror

Nel mezzo del cammin di nostra vita[53]

'I, I, I' What a strange word he's saying!
That man there – can he really be 'I'?
Such a creature my mother watched playing –
ashen skin, and the hair slightly greying,
as all-wise as a snake, and as sly?

The boy dancing at country-house dances
in Ostankino's summer-night heat –
was that I, who at each of my answers
can read loathing and fear in the glances
of the half-fledged young poets I meet?

Can that boy who poured out all his feeling
in debates that went on half the night
be myself – the same self that grew steeled in
sadder talk where I learned to conceal,
to say nothing, or keep my words light?

But all this is the traveller's hazard
on the journey by which life is spanned:
you look up, for no cause you could guess at,
and you're lost in a featureless desert,
your own tracks even vanished in sand.

No black tigress in Paris defied me –
I can't claim a Bohemian past –
and I've no ghostly Virgil to guide me. –
Merely loneliness standing beside me
in the frame of the truth-telling glass.

(1924)
Michael Frayn

Plainsong

Choke all week in the fumes and air stinking
of fear, for the bare means of life;
spend the Saturday dozing and drinking,
with your arm round an unlovely wife.

Then on Sunday by train for an outing,
with a rug to spread out on the grass,
just to doze off again, never doubting,
that for pleasure this stands unsurpassed.

And then wake up and put on your jacket,
drag the rug and wife back to the flat,
and not once curse the rug and attack it
with your fists. The world, too. Look, like *that!*

With the same kind of modest expression
do the bubbles in soda ascend,
in a meek and well-ordered procession,
up and up, one by one, to their end.

(1926)

Michael Frayn

The Dactyls

1.

He had six fingers, my father. Across the stretch of canvas,
  Bruni tutored the soft trail of his brush.
Where the Academy sphinxes have stared each other out,
    he would
  dash in a summer jacket across the frozen Neva.
He returned to Lithuania, the cheerfully penniless painter
  of murals in many churches, Polish and Russian.

2.

He had six fingers, my father. That kind of birth is lucky.
  Where the pear trees are standing on the green boundary,
the Viliya bringing its azure waters into the Neman,
  he met his joy in the poorest of poor families.
As a child I found in a drawer Màma's veil and bridal slippers.
  Màma! To me you are prayers; love; faithfulness; death.

3.

He had six fingers, my father. We would play at 'Master Magpie'
  of an evening on the divan that we loved. That's when
I would painstakingly fold his fatherly fingers over,
  one by one – that's five. And the sixth one is me.

Half a dozen children. And truly, by hard work he brought
five up to adulthood, but he didn't last into mine.

4.

He had six fingers, my father. That tiny superfluous pinky
he could hide neatly inside the fist of his left,
and so inside his soul for ever, unmentioned under a bushel,
he would hide his past, his grief for his sacred craft.
He went into business out of need, not a hint or a word
of a memory, a murmur. He liked just to say nothing.

5.

He had six fingers, my father. How many streaks of
paint did he
tightly conceal in his dry and handsome palm?
The artist considers the world – judges it, and with a bold
will, the will of his demon, creates a new one.
But he had closed his eyes, his painting gear put away,
not to create or to judge . . . the hard, sweet vocation!

6.

He had six fingers, my father. His son? He has inherited
neither the humble heart, the brood of children,
nor the six fingers. Like placing a bet on a dubious card
he stakes his soul, his fate, on a word, on a sound.
Now on a January night, drunken with six-fingered metre and
six-fingered verses, the son remembers his father.

(1927–8)

Peter Daniels

Whyever Not?

Whyever not the four-foot iamb,
cherished from before the flood?
And what to sing, if not to sing
the iamb's gift, so rich and good?

The angels brought it down from heights
above the stars, where Muses dwell,
more glorious than all Russia's flags,
and stronger than a kremlin wall.

Consumed by years, the names of who
had fallen at Khotín, and why:
and yet the Ode upon Khotín[54]
for us was life's initial cry.

That day a Russian muse arose
upon the snowy hills, and stood
to sing her first prodigious note
to all her distant sisterhood.

Since then in strict diversity,
as in the famous 'Waterfall',[55]
across the same quartet of steps
the Russian verses foam and boil.

The more they spring from off the cliff,
the more the whirlpool twists away
more secret in its harmonies,
and higher leaps the sparkling spray –

that spray where, like a radiant dream
suspended joyfully in its height,
there plays chromatically with sense
the rainbow of ideal delight.

. . . . . .

Its nature is mysterious,
where spondee sleeps and paeon sings,
one law is held within it – freedom.
Freedom is the law it brings . . .

(1938)
Peter Daniels

Janus

In me things end, and start again.
I am, although my work is slight,
a link in an unbroken chain –
one joy, at least, is mine by right.

And come the day my country's great
again, you'll see my statue stand
beside a place where four roads meet
with wind, and time, and spreading sand.

(1 January 1928)
Robert Chandler

The Monument

I am an end and a beginning.
So little spun from all my spinning!
I've been a firm link nonetheless;
with that good fortune I've been blessed.

New Russia enters on her greatness;
they'll carve my head two-faced, like Janus,
at crossroads, looking down both ways,
where wind and sand, and many days . . .

Michael Frayn

Anna Akhmatova, pseudonym of Anna Gorenko (1889–1966)

Anna Andreyevna Gorenko's father was a maritime engineer. She was born near Odessa, but her family moved to Tsarskoye Selo, near St Petersburg, before she was one year old. She began publishing poetry in her late teens; since her father considered this unrespectable, she adopted her grandmother's Tatar surname – Akhmatova. In her last years she wrote this of her name:

> Dense, impenetrable, Tatar,
> drawn from God knows when,
> it clings to every disaster,
> itself a doom without end.

In 1910 she married Nikolay Gumilyov, whom she had first met seven years earlier and who had encouraged her in her writing. She was a key member of Gumilyov's Guild of Poets and of the Acmeist movement into which it developed. Though Akhmatova always remained loyal both to Acmeism in general and to Gumilyov's memory, their marriage seems to have been unhappy from the beginning. Another important early relationship was with the Italian artist Amadeo Modigliani, then young and unknown, with whom Akhmatova spent time in Paris in 1910 and 1911. Modigliani made at least sixteen drawings of her, though few have survived.[56]

In 1918 Akhmatova and Gumilyov divorced. Akhmatova married the Assyriologist Vladimir Shileyko but separated from him after two years. During the 1920s and early 1930s she lived with the art critic Nikolay Punin; both Punin and Lev Gumilyov, Akhmatova's son by her first husband, were to serve several terms in the Gulag.

Between 1912 and 1921 Akhmatova published five books, to much acclaim; most of the poems are love lyrics, delicate and concise. In 1921, however, Gumilyov was shot for alleged participation in a monarchist conspiracy and it became difficult, eventually impossible, for Akhmatova to publish her own work. She wrote little between 1922 and 1940 and during most of her life she supported herself through translation; the poet Anatoly Naiman remembers her translating every day until lunchtime. Although she translated a few poems by Victor Hugo, Leopardi and other European poets, she worked mostly with languages she did not know, using cribs; she appears to have valued her translations of Serb epics and Korean classical poetry, though most of this work was no more than a necessary routine.[57] She also wrote perceptive, scholarly articles about Pushkin.

Many of Akhmatova's friends emigrated after the Revolution, but Akhmatova made a conscious choice to share the destiny of her country. From the mid-1920s she embraced the role of witness to the tragedies of her age. She recalled later that by 1935 every time she went to see off a friend being sent into exile, she would find herself greeting countless other friends on the way to the railway station; there were always writers, scholars and artists leaving on the same train.[58] As well as political epigrams, Akhmatova wrote two important long poems. The first, 'Requiem', is a response to the Great Terror of 1936–8. 'Poem without a Hero' (composed from 1940 to 1965) is longer and more cryptic; in it Akhmatova revisits her Bohemian past with mingled guilt, horror and pity. Neither poem was published in Russia until the late 1980s.

During the Second World War Akhmatova – along with Shostakovich and other Leningrad artists – was evacuated to Tashkent. In late 1945 and early 1946 the philosopher Isaiah Berlin, then attached to the British Embassy, visited her in her apartment. He impressed her deeply, and he appears several times in her later poetry as a mysterious 'guest from the future'. Soon after this visit, Akhmatova and the satirist Mikhail Zoshchenko were expelled from the Union of Soviet Writers. This was simply a part of the general post-war crackdown, but Akhmatova firmly believed it was a punishment for her meetings with Berlin.

Akhmatova's son Lev Gumilyov was rearrested in late 1949. Hoping to bring about his release, she wrote a poem in praise of Stalin. Her son, however, remained in the camps until 1956.

During her last years Akhmatova was a mentor to Joseph Brodsky and other younger poets. She was allowed to travel to Sicily to receive the Taormina Prize, then to England to receive an honorary doctorate from Oxford University. Her last public appearance was at the Bolshoy Theatre in October 1965, during a celebration of the 700th anniversary of the birth of Dante. There she read her poem about Dante's exile and quoted other poems about Dante by Gumilyov and Mandelstam, neither of whom had yet been republished in the Soviet Union. In her notes for this talk she wrote, 'When ill-wishers mockingly ask what Gumilyov, Mandelstam and Akhmatova have in common, I want to reply "Love for Dante".'[59]

In November 1965 Akhmatova suffered a heart attack, and she died in March 1966. Her life during her last decades was recorded in detail by Lydia Chukovskaya in her *Akhmatova Journals*.

Osip Mandelstam said that Akhmatova 'brought into the Russian lyric all the huge complexity and psychological richness of the nineteenth-century Russian novel'.[60] Boris Pasternak wrote, 'All her descriptions, whether of a remote spot in a forest or of the noisy street life of the metropolis, are sustained by an uncommon flair for details.'[61] Akhmatova herself noted in 1961, 'I listened to the Dragonfly Waltz from Shostakovich's Ballet Suite. It is a miracle. It seems that it is being danced by grace itself. Is it possible to do with the word what he does with sound?'

Akhmatova's poems are always graceful and the finest attain the intensity of prayers or spells. Almost all are in rhyme, though we have not always reproduced this. The second epilogue to 'Requiem' proved particularly difficult. All our attempts at reproducing its rhyming couplets seemed to compromise the dignified tone and almost architectural structure of the original.

*

The pillow's just as hot
when I turn it over.
And now a second candle
is guttering, and crows
are cawing louder than ever.
Not a wink . . . And it's too late
even to think of sleep.
White, blindingly white –
a blind on a white window.
Good morning!

(1909)

Robert Chandler

Song of a Last Encounter

I walked without dragging my feet
but felt heavy at heart and frightened;
and I pulled onto my left hand
the glove that belonged to the right one.

There seemed to be countless steps,
though I knew there were only three,
and an autumn voice from the maples
whispered, 'Die with me!

I have been undone by a fate
that is cheerless, flighty and cruel.'
I replied, 'So have I, my dearest –
let me die one death with you . . .'

The song of a last encounter:
I glanced up at a dark wall:
from the bedroom indifferent candles
glowed yellow . . . And that was all.

(1911, Tsarskoye Selo)
Robert Chandler

*

Careful, puss, there's an owl
embroidered on the chair.
Grey puss, don't growl –
or Grandpapa will hear.
The candle's gone out;
there are mice on the stair.
I'm afraid of that owl.
Nanny, who put it there?

(1911)
Robert Chandler

*

We're all boozers and floozies here,
altogether a joyless crowd!
On the walls, the flowers and birds
yearn for clouds.

You sit puffing your black pipe;
smoke is rising, strange and dim.
This tight skirt makes me look
slimmer than slim.

The windows boarded up for good –
what's out there? Lightning? Snow?
Like those of a cautious cat
your eyes glow.

What is my heart longing for?
Am I waiting for Death's knell?
And the woman dancing now
is bound for Hell.

(1913)
Margo Shohl Rosen

*

We had thought we were beggars,
with nothing at all,
but as loss followed loss
and each day
became a day of memorial,
we began to make songs
about the Lord's generosity
and our bygone wealth.

(1915, St Petersburg, Trinity Bridge)
Robert Chandler

Prayer

Grant me years of sickness and fever;
make me sleepless for months at a time.
Take away my child and my lover
and the mysterious gift of rhyme.

As the air grows ever more sultry,
this is the prayer I recite:
and may the storm cloud over my country
be shot through with rays of light.

(11 May 1915, Day of the Holy Spirit, St Petersburg)

Robert Chandler

from *Epic Motifs*[62]

I would gaze anxiously, as if into a mirror,
at the grey canvas, and with every week
my likeness to my new depiction grew
more strange and bitter . . .

(1914–16)

Boris Dralyuk and Margo Shohl Rosen

The Muse

I feel my life hang by a hair
as I wait at night for the Muse;
youth, freedom, fame melt into air
as my guest appears with her flute.

She enters, tosses back her shawl;
her half-closed eyes let nothing pass.
'So it was *you* who sang of Hell
to Dante?' 'Yes,' she says, 'it was.'

(1924)

Robert Chandler

In Memory of Sergey Yesenin

There are such easy ways
to leave this life,
to burn to an end
without pain or thought,
but a Russian poet
has no such luck.
A bullet is more likely
to show his winged soul
the way to Heaven;
or else the shaggy paw
of voiceless terror will squeeze
the life out of his heart
as if it were a sponge.

(1925)
Robert Chandler

Epigram

Here the loveliest of young women fight
for the honour of marrying the hangmen;
here the righteous are tortured at night
and the resolute worn down by hunger.

(1928)
Robert Chandler

Voronezh

for Osip Mandelstam

All the town's gripped in an icy fist.
Trees and walls and snow are set in glass.
I pick my timid way across the crystal.
Unsteadily the painted sledges pass.
Flocks of crows above St Peter's, wheeling.
The dome amongst the poplars, green and pale in
subdued and dusty winter sunlight, and
echoes of ancient battles that come stealing
out across the proud, victorious land.
All of a sudden, overhead, the poplars
rattle, like glasses ringing in a toast,
as if a thousand guests were raising tumblers
to celebrate the marriage of their host.

But in the exiled poet's hideaway
the muse and terror fight their endless fight
throughout the night.
So dark a night will never see the day.

(1936)

Peter Oram

Imitation of the Armenian

I shall come to you in a dream,
a black ewe that can barely stand;
I'll stagger up to you and I'll bleat,
'Shah of Shahs, have you dined well?

You are protected by Allah's will,
the world is a bead in your hand . . .
And did my son's flesh taste sweet?
Did your children enjoy their lamb?

(1937?)
Robert Chandler

Answer

I'm certainly not a Sibyl;
my life is clear as a stream.
I just don't feel like singing
to the rattle of prison keys.

(1930s)
Robert Chandler

Mayakovsky in the Year 1913

Although I didn't know your days of glory
I was present at your tempestuous dawn
and today I'll take a small step back in history
to remember, as I'm entitled to, times gone.
With every line, your words increased in power!
Unheard-of voices gathering in swarms!
Those were no idle hands that threw up such towering
and menacing new forms!
Everything you touched suddenly seemed
somehow altered, different from before,
and whatever you destroyed, remained
that way, and in every syllable the roar
of judgement. Often dissatisfied, alone,
driven on by an impatient fate,
you knew how fast the time was nearing when
you'd leap, excited, joyful, to the fight.
We could hear, as we listened to you read,

the reverberating thunder of the waters
and the downpour squinted angrily as you slid
into your wild confrontations with the city.
Your name, in those days unfamiliar, flashed
like streaks of lightning through the stuffy hall.
It's with us still today, remembered, cherished
throughout the land, a thundering battle call.

(1940)

Peter Oram

from *Requiem*

Instead of a Preface

During the terrible years of the Yezhov Terror I spent seventeen months waiting in the queues outside the Leningrad prisons. Once someone happened to 'recognize' me. Then a woman with pale blue lips who was standing behind me, and who had never before even heard of me, awoke from the blank numbness common to all of us and said in my ear (everyone there spoke in a whisper):

'Can you describe this?'

And I answered:

'Yes.'

Then something resembling a smile slid over what had once been her face.

(1 April 1957)

Second Epilogue

Once more the hour of remembrance:
I can see you all, hear you all, sense you all:

one they could barely help to the window,[63]
one who no longer treads this earth,

one who once tossed her beautiful head
and said, 'It's like coming back home.'

I'd wanted to call each one by name,
but the list's gone and there's nowhere to ask;

I've woven a broad shroud for them
out of thin words I heard from their lips.

I remember them always, everywhere;
even new sorrows won't make me forget;

and if they gag my worn-out mouth
through which a hundred million people

scream, then may I be remembered too,
each anniversary of my death.

And if ever in this country of mine
they should decide to put up a statue

to me, then I will accept this honour
on one condition: that it be placed

neither where I was born, by the sea –
my last tie with the sea has been torn –

nor by the tree stump I love in that charmed park,
the haunt of a spirit I can't console,

but here, where I stood for three hundred hours
and they never drew back the bolts:

because I fear that, in the bliss of death,
I may forget the rumble of Black Marias,

forget how they slammed that vile door
and a woman howled like a wounded beast.

And may its unmoving bronze eyelids
stream with tears of melting snow;

may a prison dove call in the distance,
and ships sail quietly by on the Neva.

(1940, Fountain House)
Robert Chandler

Music

for D. D. Sh.

Something miraculous burns brightly;
its facets form before my eyes.
And it alone can speak to me
when no one will stand by my side.

When my last friends had turned and gone
from where I lay, it remained close –
burst into blossom, into song,
like a first storm, like speaking flowers.

(1958)
Boris Dralyuk

from *Three Poems*[64]

The poet was right: once again –
lantern, side-street, drugstore,
silence, the Neva and its granite . . .
A monument to our century's

first years, there he stands, as when,
waving goodbye to Pushkin House,
he drank a mortal weariness –
as if such peace
were more than he deserved.

(1960)
Robert Chandler

Boris Pasternak (1890–1960)

Boris Leonidovich Pasternak was born in Moscow into an assimilated Jewish family. His father was a painter, his mother a concert pianist; their friends included Tolstoy, Rachmaninov, Scriabin and Rilke. Pasternak's first ambition was to be a composer. Next he studied philosophy at Moscow University, spending one semester in Germany at the University of Marburg. In 1912 he returned to Moscow via Italy, now certain that his vocation was poetry.

In 1917 Pasternak wrote the poems that make up his collection *My Sister Life*. With its clusters of metaphor, unusual rhymes and headlong rhythms, this has been described as 'a blinding illumination or flash-photo of the poet's simultaneous experience of love, poetic creation and revolution'.[65] Angela Livingstone has noted some of the responses of other poets: 'Tsvetaeva wrote: "Downpour: the whole sky onto my head, plumb-down . . . A downpour of light." And: "Pasternak is all wide-open – eyes, nostrils, ears, lips, arms." And further: "The whole book is the affirmation 'I am!' And yet how little is said directly about himself. Unmindful of himself." A year later, Mandelstam wrote: "To read poems by Pasternak is to get one's throat clear, to fortify one's breathing, to renovate one's lungs." '[66]

Unlike many of his friends and family, Pasternak chose not to emigrate after the October Revolution. Though soon shocked by the regime's violence, he always saw Russia as his only possible home. He continued to live in or just outside Moscow almost all his life.

It is natural to wonder how Pasternak survived the Stalin era. This may have been in part because he somehow, perhaps guided by some unconscious instinct of self-preservation, established what one could call a 'personal' relationship with Stalin. This began after the suicide of Stalin's wife in 1932. Thirty-three other writers published a collective letter in the *Literary Gazette*; Pasternak somehow managed to append a separate, almost intimate, message of his own.

In April 1934 Pasternak was one of a dozen people to whom Mandelstam recited his 'Stalin Epigram'. 'I didn't hear this, you didn't recite it to me,' Pasternak said to him. 'I'm afraid the walls have ears and perhaps even these benches on the boulevard here may be able to listen and tell tales. So let's make out that I heard nothing.'[67] But when Mandelstam was arrested, Pasternak begged Nikolay Bukharin, the editor of the newspaper *Izvestiya*, to intercede for him. Soon afterwards Stalin telephoned Pasternak in person, asking him whether Mandelstam was a 'master'. Pasternak's reply was evidently long and incoherent. Stalin put down the receiver, saying, 'I see, you just aren't able to stick up for a comrade.'[68] Ashamed, Pasternak tried unsuccessfully to phone Stalin back. Pasternak retold this story many times over the years; both Akhmatova and Nadezhda Mandelstam considered that he had acquitted himself at least relatively well.

Like almost all Soviet writers, Pasternak joined in some of the denunciations of prominent politicians during the show trials of the mid-1930s. He refused, however, to sign an open letter calling for the execution of Marshal Tukhachevsky and other senior generals accused of treason. Ignoring his refusal, the authorities included Pasternak's signature in the published text of the letter. Pasternak then wrote to Stalin, saying that, having been brought up as a Tolstoyan, he could not act as a judge of life and death. Pasternak also wrote to Stalin about Mayakovsky, and about the Georgian poetry he was translating. The unusual tone of his letters, their odd fusion of reverence and intimacy, may have made an impression on a tyrant concerned about his place in history. Whether Stalin truly said 'We won't touch this cloud-dweller!' is uncertain, but we know that he kept at least one of Pasternak's letters in his personal archive.

Throughout much of his life Pasternak supported himself mainly through translation; between 1932 and 1940, probably because of depression, he wrote no original work. Poets he translated include Shakespeare (both parts of *Henry IV* and all the tragedies), Goethe (*Faust*), Schiller, Verlaine and Rilke and several Georgian poets. All his translations are free. His mistress Olga Ivinskaya wrote, 'Whenever [he] was provided with literal versions of things which echoed his own thoughts or feelings [. . .] he worked feverishly, turning them into masterpieces. I remember his translating Paul Verlaine in a burst of enthusiasm like this – *L'Art poétique* was after all an expression of his own beliefs about poetry.'[69]

In the West Pasternak is best known as the author of *Doctor Zhivago*. Rejected by Soviet publishers, this was smuggled to Milan and published there in 1957. In 1958 Pasternak was awarded the Nobel Prize, but, under pressure from the Soviet authorities, he wrote to the Nobel Committee to 'renounce this undeserved distinction'. All this, of course, generated publicity, and the English translation of *Zhivago* headed *The New York Times* bestseller list for six months.

In 1960 Pasternak died of lung cancer in the writers' village of Peredelkino, on the outskirts of Moscow. The authorities did not publicize the date and time of his funeral, but handwritten notices were posted throughout the Metro and thousands of mourners travelled to Peredelkino. His funeral turned into a spontaneous public demonstration. One member of the public recited Pasternak's poem 'Hamlet', in which Pasternak conflates the figures of Hamlet, Christ and his own self; this poem had yet to be published. Someone else said, 'Sleep peacefully, dear Boris Leonidovich! We do not know all your works, but we swear to you at this hour: the day will come when we shall know them all.'[70] During the next few decades, Pasternak's grave became, in effect, a shrine for Soviet dissidents.

Pasternak's early, obviously complex poems and his later, apparently simpler poems present equal difficulties to translators. According to Livingstone, 'Especially hard to translate are two qualities: the impression of movement [. . .] and a certain elusiveness. Marina Tsvetaeva wrote in 1932 that "with Pasternak we can never find our way through to the theme; it's as if we keep catching at a sort of tail disappearing beyond the left edge of the brain, like trying to recall a dream". Far from being a form of vagueness, this goes along with a precision of detail and an intensity of focus that, to quote Tsvetaeva again, are "like looking through exceedingly powerful lenses, not adapted to your eye".'[71] Irina Mashinski writes, 'He is my teacher of energy and joy, which are much more difficult to convey in a poem than sadness or fear.'

February

February. Get ink and weep!
Burst into sobs – to write and write
of February, while thundering slush
burns like black spring.

For half a rouble hire a cab,
ride through chimes and the wheels' cry
to where the drenching rain is black,
louder than tears or ink –

where like thousands of charred pears
rooks will come tearing out of trees
straight into puddles, an avalanche,
dry grief to the ground of eyes.

Beneath it – blackening spots of thaw,
and all the wind is holed by shouts,
and poems – the randomer the truer –
take form, as sobs burst out.

(1913)
Angela Livingstone

Spring

What hundreds of buds – gluey, blurry –
stuck on twigs like cigarette-butts!
April is kindled. The park sends out
a mood of maturity, woods shout back.

And the forest's neck is tightly noosed
by feathered throats – a buffalo netted,
groaning the way a cathedral organ,
steel gladiator, groans in sonatas.

Poetry! Be a Greek sponge with suckers –
I'll put you down on the damp green
plank of a garden bench beneath
all this sticky foliage – grow

lush frills and enormous fringes,
drink clouds in, absorb ravines.
And, poetry, at night I'll squeeze you out
to the health of thirsting paper.

(1917)
Angela Livingstone

Weeping Garden

Dreadful! It drips and it listens –
whether it's all alone in the world
crushing a twig like lace at the window,
or is someone watching?

Palpable, though, is the pressure
of porous earth's taut swellings,
and far off, audible as in August,
midnight ripens in fields.

No, no sound, no witness.
Convinced there's no one there,
back it goes to its game of rolling
down roofs and across gutters.

I'll lift it up to my lips and listen –
whether I'm all alone in the world,
ready to burst out in sobs if I need to,
or is someone watching?

Silence. Not a leaf moving.
No dot of light, just weird
gulps and splashings about in slippers,
the lulls full of sighs and tears.

(1917)
Angela Livingstone

Storm, Instantaneous Forever

Then summer took leave of the platform
and waiting room. Raising his cap,
the storm at night for souvenir
took snap after dazzling snap.

The lilac darkened. And the storm
came bounding in from the meadows
with a sheaf of lightning flashes
to light the office windows.

And when malicious delight ran
down corrugated iron in torrents,
and like charcoal on a drawing
the downpour crashed against the fence,

the avalanche of consciousness began
to glimmer: light, it seemed, would soon
flood even those corners of reason
where now it is bright as noon.

(1919)
Jon Stallworthy and Peter France

from *In Memory of Marina Tsvetaeva*

It's as hard to imagine
you don't exist
as to imagine you a miser-millionaire
among starving sisters.

What can I do for you? Say.
There's a quiet reproach
in the way
you've gone your way.

Losses are riddles. In vain
I try to find
an answer.
Death has no outline.

Half-words, tongue-slips, delusion –
and only
faith in resurrection
by way of direction.

Winter makes a splendid memorial:
a glimpse of twilight,
add currants, pour on wine
– and there's your remembrance meal!

An apple tree in a drift, the town
wrapped in snow,
seemed all year long
to be your grave, your headstone.

Facing God, you reach out
towards him, from earth,
just as before
your days had reached their final count.

(1943)
Robert Chandler

Hamlet[72]

The hum dies down; alone on stage,
my back against the wall, I try
to sense within a distant echo
the twists and turns of destiny.

A thousand glinting opera glasses
focus the dark into my eyes.
O Father, should it be possible –
allow this cup to pass me by.

I like your stubborn, bold design,
and I've agreed to play this part.
But other forces are at play now –
this once, please count me out . . .

The acts cannot be rearranged
and there's no turning from the road.
Alone, a sea of cant all round me:
Life is not a walk across a field.

(1946, included in *Doctor Zhivago*)
Robert Chandler

Christmas Star[73]

The winter was deep.
Wind whistled and howled.
In the cave in the hills it was bitterly cold
but the child lay asleep,

for the breath of an ox kept the coldness at bay.
Farm animals' breathing
was rising and wreathing:
a warm haze hung over the crib where he lay.

The shepherds arose though they'd not woken quite,
shook the chaff off their coats
from the barley and oats,
stared out from their cliff through the depths of the night.

Far away, snowy fields, with a chapel nearby
old graves and their railings,
a snowbound farm trailer
and over the graveyard the star-studded night.

Close by, to one side, unfamiliar to them
and shy, like the light
in a hut in the night,
the star lit the way towards Bethlehem.

Like a great stack of hay, set apart from the sky
and from God and, as though
it reflected the glow
of a farm set on fire, it was blazing away.

This haystack, hung burning bright, towering high
in the midst of creation.
With great consternation
creation observed this new star in its sky.

And observing its halo of reddening flame
which so urgently shone
and which beckoned them on
the three wise astronomers hurriedly came.

They were followed by camels with gifts laden high,
then donkeys came tripping in harness downhill
in order of ever-diminishing size.
And the whole of the future seemed somehow revealed
in a vision that whispered through faraway skies.

All the centuries' thoughts, all the worlds and the dreams,
all future museums and art galleries,
all fairyland pranks and all conjurors' schemes,
and all the bright garlands and Christmas trees,
all of childhood's hopes, all the flickering flames,
the tinsel's magnificent colourfulness . . .
. . . and ever more bitter the wind on the plains . . .
. . . all the apples and baubles of golden glass . . .

Though a part of the pond was obscured by the trees
the shepherds could see the remainder between
the uppermost branches and rook colonies,
and the camels and donkeys could clearly be seen
as they passed by the pond-edge. 'Let's travel together
and seek out this wonder and offer our praise,'
they said, tightening their furs to keep out the cold weather.

But at least all this tramping through snow helped them keep
themselves warm, and the prints that their bare feet
were marking,
like slivers of mica, which gleamed in the deep
starlit snowfields so brightly they set the dogs barking,
led up to the cave where the child lay asleep.

The night was a frosty cold fable where some
silent figure unnoticed emerged now and then
from the snowdrifts and joined with the men.
The dogs stuck by the shepherd-boy, nuzzling him,
and yapped nervously, fearing the worst was to come.

And among all the crowds in that very same land
on those same roads walked many an angel who, though,
being bodiless, was quite invisible, so
it was only his footprints he left behind.

The crowds were assembling around a great stone
as the first light revealed the trunks of the cedars.
'Now tell me your name,' Mary asked each in turn.
'A bunch of poor shepherds and learned astrologers,
come here to offer the two of you praises.'
'You won't all fit in! Wait a while by the door . . .'

In the ashy-grey hours of earliest morning
the shepherds and herdsmen were stamping about.
Among farmers and horsemen discussions broke out
as they gathered in crowds round the watering spout,
while the asses kept kicking and camels kept groaning.

Day broke, and brushed out like hot cinders the last
of the stars from the sky. Of the whole motley crowd
that hoped to go past
the threshold the magi alone were allowed.

He was sleeping, all radiant, and shone like a moonbeam
inside a dark recess, in his oaken hay-box.
Instead of a fur or a sheepskin to warm him,
was muzzle of donkey and nostril of ox.

For a while they stood whispering there in the shadows,
but found little to say, until one of them felt
a hand nudging him forward. He looked up and saw
in the doorway, not far
from him, gazing at Mary, like some special guest,
the Nativity star.

(1947, included in *Doctor Zhivago*)

Peter Oram

Osip Mandelstam (1891–1938)

Osip Emilievich Mandelstam was born in Warsaw to a Polish Jewish family; his father was a leather merchant, his mother a piano teacher. Soon after Osip's birth the family moved to St Petersburg. After attending the prestigious Tenishev School, Mandelstam studied for a year in Paris at the Sorbonne, and then for a year in Germany at the University of Heidelberg. In 1911, wanting to enter St Petersburg University – which had a quota on Jews – he converted to Christianity; like many others who converted during these years, he chose Methodism rather than Orthodoxy.

Under the leadership of Nikolay Gumilyov, Mandelstam and several other young poets formed a movement known first as the Poets' Guild and then as the Acmeists. Mandelstam wrote a manifesto, 'The Morning of Acmeism' (written in 1913, but published only in 1919). Like Ezra Pound and the Imagists, the Acmeists valued clarity, concision and craftsmanship.

In 1913 Mandelstam published his first collection, *Stone*. This includes several poems about architecture, which would remain one of his central themes. A poem about the cathedral of Notre-Dame de Paris ends with the declaration:

> Fortress Notre-Dame, the more attentively
> I studied your stupendous ribcage,
> the more I kept repeating: in time I too
> will craft beauty from sullen weight.

In its acknowledgement of earthly gravity and its homage to the anonymous masons of the past, the poem is typically Acmeist.

Mandelstam was also a great love poet. Several women – each an important figure in her own right – were crucial to his life and work. An affair with Marina Tsvetaeva inspired many of his poems about Moscow. His friendship with Anna Akhmatova helped him withstand the persecution he suffered during the 1930s. He had intense affairs with the singer Olga Vaksel and the poet Maria Petrovykh. Most important of all was Nadezhda Khazina, whom he married in 1922.

Osip and Nadezhda Mandelstam moved to Moscow soon after this. Mandelstam's second book, *Tristia*, published later in 1922, contains his most eloquent poetry; the tone is similar to that of Yeats's 'Sailing to Byzantium' or some of Pound's first *Cantos*. Several poems were inspired by the Crimea, where Mandelstam had stayed as a guest of Maximilian Voloshin. Once a Greek colony, the Crimea was for Mandelstam a link to the classical world he loved; above all, it granted him a sense of kinship with Ovid, who had also lived by the Black Sea. It was while exiled to what is now Romania that Ovid had composed his own *Tristia*.

The final section of Mandelstam's 1928 volume *Poems* (the last collection he was able to publish in his life) is titled 'Poems 1921–25'. These twenty poems differ from any of his previous work. Many are unrhymed, and they are composed in lines and stanzas of varying length. This formal disintegration reflects a sense of crisis that Mandelstam expresses most clearly in 'The Age':

Buds will swell just as in the past,
sprouts of green will spurt and rage,
but your backbone has been smashed,
my grand and pitiful age.

And so, with a meaningless smile,
you glance back, cruel and weak,
like a beast once quick and agile,
at the prints of your own feet.

For several years from 1925 Mandelstam abandoned poetry – or, as he saw it, was abandoned by poetry. Alienated from himself and the world around him, he supported himself by translating. He also wrote memoirs, literary criticism and experimental prose.

What helped Mandelstam to recover was a journey to Armenia from May to November 1930. The self-doubt of 'Poems

1921–25' yields to an almost joyful acceptance of tragedy. Armenia's importance to Mandelstam is not surprising: it is a country of stone, and one of the arts in which Armenians have long excelled is architecture. And to Mandelstam Armenia represented the Hellenistic and Christian world where he felt his roots lay; there are ruins of Hellenistic temples not far from Yerevan and it was on Mount Ararat – which dominates the city's skyline – that Noah's Ark is believed to have come to rest. Mandelstam drew strength from a world that felt more solid, and more honest, than the Russia where he had become an outcast.

In the autumn of 1933 Mandelstam composed an epigram about Stalin, then read it aloud at several small gatherings in Moscow. It ends:

> Horseshoe-heavy, he hurls his decrees low and high:
> in the groin, in the forehead, the eyebrow, the eye.
> Executions are what he likes best.
> Broad is the highlander's chest.
>
> (trans. Alexandra Berlina)

Six months later Mandelstam was arrested. Instead of being shot, he was exiled to the northern Urals; the probable reason for this relative leniency is that Stalin, concerned about his own place in the history of Russian literature, took a personal interest in Mandelstam's case. After Mandelstam attempted suicide, his sentence was commuted to banishment from Russia's largest cities. Mandelstam and his wife settled in Voronezh. There, sensing he did not have long to live, Mandelstam wrote the poems that make up the three *Voronezh Notebooks*. Dense with wordplay yet intensely lyrical, these are hard to translate. A leitmotif of the second notebook is the syllable 'os'. This means either 'axis' or 'of wasps' – and it is the first syllable of both Mandelstam's and Stalin's first names ('Osip' and 'Iosif' are, to a Russian ear, just different spellings of a single name). In the hope of saving his own life, Mandelstam was then composing an Ode to Stalin;[74] he evidently imagined an axis connecting himself – the great poet – and Stalin – the great leader.

In May 1938 Mandelstam was arrested a second time and sentenced to five years in the Gulag. He died in a transit camp near Vladivostok on 27 December 1938. His widow Nadezhda preserved most of his unpublished work and also wrote two memoirs, published in English as *Hope Against Hope* and *Hope Abandoned*.

*

Cautious, toneless sound
of fruit from a tree
to the constant
melody of forest silence . . .

(1908)

John Riley

*

From the dimly lit hall
you slipped out in a light shawl.

The servants slept on,
we disturbed no one . . .

(1908)

James Greene

*

To read only children's tales
and look through a child's eye;
to rise from grief and wave
big things goodbye.

Life has tired me to death;
life has no more to offer.
But I love my poor earth
since I know no other.

I swung in a faraway garden
on a plain plank swing;
I remember tall dark firs
in a feverish blur.

(1908)
Robert Chandler

*

Newly reaped ears of early wheat
lie in level rows;
fingertips tremble, pressed against
fingers fragile as themselves.

(1909)
James Greene

Silentium[75]

She has yet to be born:
she is music and word,
and she eternally bonds
all life in this world.

The sea breathes gently;
the day glitters wildly.
A bowl of dazed azure
sways pale foam-lilac.

May I too reach back
to that ancient silence,
like a note of crystal
pure from its source.

Stay, Aphrodite, as foam.
Return, word, to music.
Heart, be shy of heart,
fused with life's root.

(1910)
Robert Chandler and Boris Dralyuk

*

No, not the moon – the bright face of a clock
glimmers to me. How is it my fault
that I perceive the feeble stars as milky?
And I hate Batyushkov's unbounded arrogance:
What time is it? someone simply asked –
and he replied to them: *eternity!*[76]

(1912)
Boris Dralyuk

The Admiralty[77]

A dusty poplar in the northern capital,
a transparent clock face lost in the leaves;
and, shining through this green – a brother
to both sky and water – a frigate, an acropolis.

Aerial craft, touch-me-not mast, straight edge
repeating to Peter's heirs this golden rule:
beauty is no demi-god's caprice
but a plain carpenter's rule, his raptor's eye.

Four elements rule over us benignly;
free man is able to create a fifth.
Doesn't this ark, this chastely crafted ark
deny the sovereignty of space?

Angry and whimsical, the jellyfish cling on;
anchors lie rusting like discarded ploughs –
we cast away the chains of Euclid's space
and the world's seas open before us.

(1913)
Robert Chandler

Dombey and Son

The shrillness of the English language
and Oliver's dejected look
have merged: I see the youngster languish
among a pile of office books.

Charles Dickens – ask him; he will tell you
what was in London long ago:
the City, Dombey, assets' value,
the River Thames's rusty flow.

'Mid rain and tears and counted money,
Paul Dombey's curly-headed son
cannot believe that clerks are funny
and laughs at neither joke nor pun.

The office chairs are sorry splinters;
each broken farthing put to use,
and numbers swarm in springs and winters,
like bees perniciously let loose.

Attorneys study every letter;
in smoke and stench they hone their stings,
and, from a noose, the luckless debtor –
a piece of bast – in silence swings.

His foes enjoy their lawful robbing,
lost are for him all earthly boons,
and lo! His only daughter, sobbing,
embraces checkered pantaloons.

(1913)
Anatoly Liberman[78]

Concerning the chorus in Euripides

The shuffling elders: a shambles
of sheep, an abject throng!
I uncoil like a snake,

my heart an ancient ache
of dark Judaic wrong.
But it will not be long

before I shake off sadness,
like a boy, in the evening,
shaking sand from his sandals.

(1914)
James Greene

*

On the black square of the Kremlin
the air is drunk with mutiny.
A shaky 'peace' is rocked by rebels,
the poplars puff seditiously.

The wax faces of the cathedrals
and the dense forest of the bells
tell us – inside the stony rafters
a tongueless brigand is concealed.

But inside the sealed-up cathedrals
the air we breathe is cool and dark,
as though a Russian wine is coursing
through Greece's earthenware jars.

Assumption's paradise of arches
soars up in an astonished curve;
and now the green Annunciation
awakens, cooing like a dove.

The Archangel and Resurrection
let in the light like glowing palms –
everything is secretly burning,
the jugs are full of hidden flames.

(1916)

Thomas de Waal

Solominka[79]

1.

When you lie there, Salome, in your vast
room, when you can't sleep, when you lie and wait
for the tall ceiling to descend, to brush
your delicate eyelids with its grave weight; [. . .]

when you can't sleep, things seem to gain in weight
or else are lost – the silence is so full;
white pillows glimmer palely in the glass;
the bed is mirrored in a circling pool;

and pale blue ice is streaming through the air.
Salome, broken straw, you sipped at death,
drank all of death, and only grew more sweet.
December now streams out her solemn breath.

Twelve moons are singing of the hour of death,
the room is gone, the Neva takes its place,
Ligeia, winter herself, flows through my blood,
and I have learned to hear you, words of grace.

2.

Lenore, Solominka, Ligeia, Seraphita.
The heavy Neva fills the spacious room.
Salome, my beloved straw, Solominka,
poisoned by pity, slowly sips her doom.

And pale blue blood runs streaming from the stone.
From all I see only a river will remain.
Twelve moons are singing of the hour of death.
And Salome will never dance this dance again.

(1916)
Robert Chandler

*

The thread of golden honey flowed from the bottle
so heavy and slow that our hostess had time to declare:
Here in melancholy Tauris, where fate has brought us,
we are not bored at all – and glanced back over her shoulder.

On all sides the rites of Bacchus, as if the world
held only watchmen and dogs, not a soul to be seen –
the days roll peacefully by like heavy barrels:
away in the hut are voices, you can't hear or reply.

We drank tea, then went out to the huge brown garden,
dark blinds were down like lashes over the eyes,
we walked past the white columns to look at the vineyard
where the somnolent hills are coated in airy glass.

I said: The vines are alive like ancient battles,
where curly horsemen are fighting in curving order,
in stony Tauris the science of Hellas lives on –
and the noble rusty array of golden acres.

And in the white room quiet stands like a spinning wheel,
smells of vinegar, paint and wine that is fresh from the cellar.
Remember, in that Greek house, the much-loved wife –
not Helen – the other wife – how long she embroidered?

Golden fleece, oh where are you now, golden fleece?
All the journey long the heavy sea waves were loud,
and leaving his ship, his sails worn out by the seas,
full of space and time, Odysseus came home.

(1917)

Peter France

*

Heaviness, tenderness – sisters – your marks are the same.
The wasps and the honeybees suck at the heavy rose.
Man dies, heat drains from the once warm sand,
and on a black bier they carry off yesterday's sun.

Oh, you tender nets and you heavy honeycombs,
easier to lift a stone than to speak your name!
Only one care is left to me in the world:
a care that is golden, to shed the burden of time.

I drink the mutinous air like some dark water.
Time is turned up by the plough, and the rose was earth.
Slowly they eddy, the heavy, the tender roses,
roses of heaviness, tenderness, twofold wreath.

(1920)
Peter France

*

Take from my palms some sun to bring you joy
and take a little honey – so the bees
of cold Persephone commanded us.

No loosing of the boat that is not moored,
no hearing of the shadow shod in fur,
no overcoming fear in life's dense wood.

And kisses are all that's left us now,
kisses as hairy as the little bees
who perish if they fly out of the hive.

They rustle in transparent depths of night,
their home dense forests on Taigetos' slopes,
their food is honeysuckle,[80] mint and time.

So for your joy receive my savage gift,
a dry and homely necklace of dead bees
who have transmuted honey into sun.

(1920)
Peter France

*[81]

I was washing at night out in the yard,
the heavens glowing with rough stars,
a star-beam like salt upon an axe,
the water butt cold and brim full.

A padlock makes the gate secure,
and conscience gives sternness to the earth –
hard to find a standard anywhere
purer than the truth of new-made cloth.

A star melts in the water butt like salt,
cold water in the butt is blacker still,
death is more pure, disaster saltier
and earth more truthful and more terrible.

(1921, Tbilisi)
Peter France

The Horseshoe Finder (A Pindaric Fragment)

We look at a forest and say:
Here's a forest for ships, for masts,
rose-shadowed pines,
right to their very tops free of shaggy burdens,
they ought to creak in a windstorm,
like solitary Italian pines,
in the furious forestless air.
Beneath the wind's salt heel the plumbline holds,
set in the dancing deck,
and a seafarer,
in his insatiable thirst for space,
dragging the brittle instrument of the geometer across
sodden ruts,
collates against the pull of earthly breast
the ragged surface of seas.

But drinking the scent
of resinous tears, which show through the ship's planking,
admiring the timber,
riveted, well-jointed into bulkheads,
not by that quiet carpenter of Bethlehem, but another –
the father of voyages, the seafarer's friend –
we say:
They too once stood on land,
ungainly, like a donkey's spine,
their tops overlooking their roots,
upon the ridge of some renowned mountain,
and clattered beneath fresh cloudbursts,
suggesting vainly that the heavens exchange their noble burden
for a pinch of salt.

Where shall we start?
Everything cracks and reels.
The air shivers with similes.
One word's no better than another,
the earth drones with metaphors,
and lightweight carts
harnessed garishly to flocks of birds dense with strain
burst to pieces,
competing with the snorting favourites of the hippodrome.

Thrice blessed, he who guides a name into song;
the song adorned with nomination
lives longer among the others –
she's marked among her friends by a fillet on her brow,
which saves her from fainting, from powerful stupefying smells,
whether it be the closeness of a man,
or the smell of fur from a powerful beast,
or merely the scent of savory, crushed between palms.

The air grows dark, like water, and all things living swim
through it like fish,
fins thrusting aside the sphere,

compact, resilient, barely warm, –
a crystal, in which wheels spin and horses shy,
damp humus of Neaira, furrowed anew each night,
by pitchforks, tridents, hoes, and ploughs.
The air is mixed as solidly as the earth:
one can't get out of it, to enter it is difficult.

A rustle runs along the trees like some green ball.
Children play at knucklebones with vertebrae of dead animals.
The fragile chronology of our era is drawing to its close.
Thanks for everything that was:
I made mistakes myself, fell astray, botched my reckoning.
The era rang, like a golden sphere,
hollow, molded, sustained by no one,
at every touch responding 'Yes' or 'No'.
It answered like a child:
'I'll give you an apple' or 'I won't give you an apple',
its face a perfect copy of the voice that speaks these words.

The sound's still ringing, though the source of sound has
vanished.
A horse slumps in the dust and snorts in a lather,
but the sharp turn of its neck
still keeps the memory of racing forward with its out-flung
hooves –
when there weren't only four of them,
but numerous as stones upon the road,
rekindled in four shifts,
as numerous as the ground-beats of the blazing horse.

So,
the finder of a horseshoe
blows off the dust
and burnishes it with wool, until it shines.
Then
he hangs it over the threshold,
to take a rest,
so it no longer needs to strike out sparks from flint.

Human lips,
for which there's nothing more to say,
retain the form of their last-spoken word,
and weight continues tangible in the hand
although the jug,
spilled half
while carried home.

What I'm saying now, I do not say,
but has been dug from the earth, like grains of petrified wheat.
Some
portray a lion on their coins,
others –
a head.
Assorted copper, gold and bronze lozenges
lie with equal honour in the earth.
The age, which tried to gnaw them through, imprinted teeth
on them.
Time lacerates me, like a coin,
and I'm no longer ample for myself.

(1923, Moscow)
Steven J. Willett

Armenia

Here labour is understood
as an awesome, six-winged bull;[82]
and, swollen with venous blood,
pre-winter roses bloom.

1.

You rock the rose of Hafez
and dandle your wild-beast children;
your lungs are the octahedral shoulders
of bull-like peasant churches.[83]

Coloured in raucous ochre,
you lie far beyond the Mountain;[84]
here we have only a picture,
a water transfer peeled from a saucer.

2.

Oh, I can't see a thing and my poor ear's gone deaf,
and there are no colours left but red lead and this raucous ochre.

And somehow I found myself dreaming of an Armenian
morning,
I felt like seeing how a tomtit gets by in Yerevan,

how a baker plays at blind man's buff with the bread,
stooping to scoop the moist warm hides from the oven . . .

Oh, Yerevan, Yerevan! Were you sketched by a bird?
Or did a lion colour you in, like a child with a box of crayons?

Oh, Yerevan, Yerevan! More a roast nut than a city,
how I love the Babels and Babylons of your big-mouthed streets.

I've fingered and mauled my life, like a mullah his Koran,
I have frozen my time, never spilt hot blood.

Oh, Yerevan, Yerevan! There's nothing more that I need –
I don't want your frozen grapes!

3.

You longed for a dash of colour –
so a lion who could draw
made a long paw
and snatched five or six crayons from a box.[85]

Country of blazing dyes
and dead earthenware plains,
amid your stones and clays
you endured sultans and red-bearded sardars.[86]

Far from anchors and tridents,
where a continent withers to rest,
you put up with those ever-so-potent
potentates who loved executions.

Simple as a child's drawing,
not stirring my blood,
your women pass by, bestowing
gifts of their graceful lionhood.

How I love your ominous tongue,
your young coffins,
where each letter's a blacksmith's tong
and each word a cramp-iron.

4.

Covering your mouth like a moist rose,
octahedral honeycombs in your hands,[87]
all the dawn of days you stood
on a world's edge, swallowing your tears.

You turned away in shame and sorrow
from the bearded cities of the East –
and now you lie amid clays and dyes
as they take your death mask.

5.

Wrap your hand in a kerchief
and plunge it, through the celluloid thorns,
into the heart of the wreath-bearing briar.
Snap.
Who needs scissors?
But mind it doesn't just fall apart –
scraps of pink, confetti, a petal of Solomon,
a wildling without oil or scent,
no use even for sherbert.

6.

Realm of clamouring stones –
Armenia, Armenia!
summoning the raucous mountains to arms –
Armenia, Armenia!

Soaring forever towards the silver trumpets of Asia[88] –
Armenia, Armenia!
Lavishly flinging down the Persian coins of the sun –
Armenia, Armenia!

7.

No, not ruins but what remains of a round and mighty forest,
anchor-stumps of felled oaks from a Christianity of beasts
    and fables,
capitals bearing rolls of stone cloth, like loot from a heathen
    marketplace,
grapes each the size of a pigeon's egg, scrolls of eddying
    rams' horns,
and ruffled eagles with the wings of owls, still undefiled by
    Byzantium.[89]

8.

The rose is cold in the snow:
which lies three fathoms deep on Sevan . . .
The mountain fisherman has made off with his azure sledge
and the whiskered snouts of stout trout
police the lime-covered lake bed.

While in Yerevan and Echmiadzin
the vast mountain has drunk all the air.
I need to entice it with an ocarina,
tame it with a pipe
till the snow melts in my mouth.

Snow, snow, snow on rice paper,
the mountain swims towards my lips.
I'm cold. I'm glad . . .[90]

9.

Clip clop against purple granite,
a peasant's horse stumbles
as it mounts the bald plinth
of the realm's sovereign stone,
while some breathless Kurds run behind
with bundles of cheese wrapped in cloth –
peacemakers between God and the Devil
and backers of both.[91]

10.

What luxury in an indigent village –
The thread-like music of the water!
What is it? Someone spinning? Fate? An omen?
Don't come too close. There's trouble on the way.
And the maze of the moist tune
conceals something dark, stifling, whirring –
as if a water nymph were paying a visit
to a subterranean watchsmith.

11.

Clay and azure . . . azure, clay . . .
What more do you want? Just squint,
like a myopic shah over a turquoise ring,
over a book of ringing clays, a bookish earth,
a festering text, a precious clay,
that hurts us like music,
like the word.

12.

I shall never see you again,
myopic Armenian sky;
never again screw up my eyes
at Mount Ararat's nomad tent;
and in the library of earthenware authors

I shall never again open
the hollow volume of a splendid land
that primed the first people.

(1930, Tbilisi)
Robert Chandler

*

Help me, O Lord, through this night.
I fear for life, your slave.
To live in Peter's city is to sleep in a grave.

(1931)
Robert Chandler

*

After midnight, clean out of your hands,
the heart seizes a sliver of silence.
It lives on the quiet, it's longing to play;
like it or not, there's nothing quite like it.

Like it or not, it can never be grasped;
so why shiver, like a child off the street,
if after midnight the heart holds a feast,
silently savouring a silvery mouse?

(1931)
Robert Chandler

*

Gotta keep living, though I've died twice,
and water's driving the city crazy:
how beautiful, what high cheekbones, how happy,

how sweet the fat earth to the plough,
how the steppe extends in an April upheaval,
and the sky, the sky – pure Michelangelo . . .

(1935)
Andrew Davis

*

Drawing the youthful Goethe to their breast,
those Roman nights took on the weight of gold . . .
I've much to answer for, yet still am graced;
an outlawed life has depths yet to be told.

(1935)
Robert Chandler

*

Goldfinch, friend, I'll cock my head –
let's check the world out, just me and you:
this winter's day pricks like chaff;
does it sting your eyes too?

Boat-tailed, feathers yellow-black,
sopped in colour beneath your beak,
do you get, you goldfinch you,
just how you flaunt it?

What's he thinking, little airhead? –
white and yellow, black and red!
Both eyes check both ways – both! –
will check no more – he's bolted!

(1936)
Andrew Davis

*

Deep in the mountain the idol rests
in sweet repose, infinite and blest,
the fat of necklaces dripping from his neck
protects his dreams of flood tide and of slack.

As a boy, he buddied with a peacock,
they gave him rainbow of India to eat
and milk in a pink clay dish,
and didn't stint the cochineal.

Bone put to bed, locked in a knot,
shoulders, arms and knees made flesh,
he smiles with his own dead-silent lips,
thinks with his bone, feels with his brow,
and struggles to recall his human countenance . . .

(1936)
Andrew Davis

*

You're not alone. You haven't died,
while you still, beggar-woman at your side,
take pleasure in the grandeur of the plain,
the gloom, the cold, the whirlwinds of snow.

In sumptuous penury, in mighty poverty
live comforted and at rest –
your days and nights are blest,
your sweet-voiced labour without sin.

Unhappy he, a shadow of himself,
whom a bark astounds and the wind mows down,
and to be pitied he, more dead than alive,
who begs handouts from a ghost.

(1937)
Andrew Davis

*

Where can I hide in this January?
Wide-open city with a mad death-grip . . .
Can I be drunk from sealed doors? –
I want to bellow from locks and knots . . .

And the socks of barking back roads,
and the hovels on twisted streets –
and deadbeats hurry into corners
and hurriedly dart back out again . . .

And into the pit, into the warty dark
I slide, into waterworks of ice,
and I stumble, I eat dead air,
and fevered crows exploding everywhere –

But I cry after them, shouting at
some wickerwork of frozen wood:
A reader! A councillor! A doctor!
A conversation on the spiny stair!

(1937)
Andrew Davis

*

Breaks in round bays, and shingle, and blue,
and a slow sail continued by a cloud –
I hardly knew you; I've been torn from you:
longer than organ fugues – the sea's bitter grasses,
fake tresses – and their long lie stinks,
my head swims with iron tenderness,
the rust gnaws bit by bit the sloping bank . . .
On what new sands does my head sink?
You, guttural Urals, broad-shouldered Volga lands,
or this dead-flat plain – here are all my rights,
and, full-lunged, gotta go on breathing them.

(1937)
Andrew Davis

*

Armed with wasp-vision, with the vision of wasps
that suck, suck, suck the earth's axis,
I'm filled by the whole deep vein of my life
and hold it here in my heart
and in vain.

And I don't draw, don't sing,
don't draw a black-voiced bow over strings:
I only drink, drink, drink in life and I love
to envy wasp-
waisted wasps their mighty cunning.

O if I too
could be impelled past sleep, past death,
stung by the summer's cheer and chir,
by this new air
to hear earth's axis, axis, axis.

(1937)
Robert Chandler

*

I'll say this in a whisper, in draft,
because it's early yet:
we have to pay
with experience and sweat
to learn the sky's free play.

And under purgatory's temporal sky
we easily forget:
the dome of heaven
is a home
to praise forever, wherever.

(1937)
Robert Chandler

Anna Prismanova (1892–1960)

The daughter of a doctor, Anna Semyonovna Prismanova was born in Latvia. The family moved to Moscow in 1918 and Prismanova left Russia in the early 1920s. By 1924 she had moved to Paris. Writing for her was a full-time yet private activity; she played little part in the cultural life of the Russian émigré world. Her imagery is bold and she breaks grammatical rules. Her work remains undervalued.

Catriona Kelly sees her as one of a very few Russian women poets 'who explicitly acknowledged her affiliation to women's writing in a historical sense'.[92] To illustrate how Prismanova challenged traditional ideas of femininity, she translates the last stanza of 'Granite':

> One might suppose that I shall not forget you,
> but that won't be because I loved you so,
> rather because you chanced to be the fire
> which I myself employed to hew my soul.

The nearest English-language parallel to Prismanova may be her contemporary, the American poet Louise Bogan; both poets develop vivid metaphysical conceits with concision, crafting adamantine lyrics that carry an intense emotional charge.

The Jolt

The jolt must come from far away:
the start of bread is in the grain.
A stream, although still underground,
aspires to reflect the sky.

A future Sunday's distant light
reaches us early in the week.
The jolt must come from far away
to trigger earthquakes in the heart.

A shoulder alien to me
controls the movement of my hand.
In order to acquire such strength,
the jolt must come from far away.

(late 1930s or early 1940s)

Boris Dralyuk

Blood and Bone

1.

My nature has two cornerstones,
and mother, singing hushabye,
rocked not a single child, but twins:
bone of sobriety and blood of fire.

This blood, this bone – of equal zeal
and locked in battle from the start –
have sealed my fate with a sad seal,
forever splitting me apart.

2.

Music, is it you I hear
above me in the early hours?
You place a cross upon my roof
and build a temple from my house.

All-mighty music, you unite
this blood, this bone within yourself.
I can't be sure you'll help my life,
but you are sure to help my death.

(1946)

Boris Dralyuk

Marina Tsvetaeva (1892–1941)

Marina Ivanovna Tsvetaeva was born in Moscow. Her mother was a gifted pianist, her father a classicist and the founder of what is now the Pushkin Museum of Fine Arts. Like Pasternak, Tsvetaeva was steeped from childhood in art and music.

In 1902 Tsvetaeva's mother contracted tuberculosis. In hope of a cure, the family spent most of the next four years abroad. For a while they lived near Genoa. Frequent moves reinforced Tsvetaeva's knowledge of Italian, French and German. Around this time she gave up the strict musical studies imposed on her by her mother, who died in 1906, and turned to poetry.

Along with many other writers and artists, Tsvetaeva stayed during subsequent years in the Crimea, at the home in Koktebel of the legendarily hospitable Maximilian Voloshin. There she met the poet Sergey Efron, whom she married in 1912. After the October Revolution, Tsvetaeva remained in Moscow, even though Efron was fighting in the White Army. Tsvetaeva left her younger daughter Irina, aged three, in a state orphanage, hoping they would feed her better than she could herself, but Irina died of starvation. In May 1922 Tsvetaeva and her surviving daughter left Moscow for Berlin, where they were reunited with Efron. In August that year they moved to Prague, then in 1925 to Paris.

Tsvetaeva remained devoted to Efron, despite her many affairs. The most significant of these were with Osip Mandelstam; with Sofia Parnok; and, in Prague, with Konstantin Rodzevich, who inspired her two great cycles of love poems, *Poem of the Mountain* and *Poem of the End*.

During her fourteen years in Paris, Tsvetaeva grew increasingly isolated. She offended most of the émigré community by praising Mayakovsky; mistakenly branding her as pro-Soviet, the editors of the important journal *The Latest News* stopped publishing her work. Tsvetaeva had been a regular contributor and was supporting her family – her husband, their daughter Ariadna and her young son Georgy – through her literary earnings.[93] Tsvetaeva's isolation became complete when, in 1937, it emerged that Efron had been working as a Soviet agent; not only had he recruited for the NKVD[94] (the Soviet security service), but he had also been complicit in several murders. Though fiercely anti-Soviet herself, she had no choice but to follow her husband back to the Soviet Union; how much she knew about his work for the NKVD is uncertain.

Despite the extreme Romanticism of many of her views, Tsvetaeva was always clear-headed about political matters. In May 1917, while many writers were being seduced by what they heard as the music of the Revolution, she had written:

> You stepped from a stately cathedral
> onto the blare of the plazas . . .
> – Freedom! – The Beautiful Lady
> of Russian grand dukes and marquises.
>
> A fateful choir's rehearsing –
> the liturgy still lies before us!
> – Freedom! – A street-walking floozy
> on the foolhardy breast of a soldier!
> (trans. Boris Dralyuk)

And 'God Be With You!' a short poem from June 1934, ends: 'Follow after Hitler, Stalin / uncover from the sprawling corpses / a star, or the hooks of a swastika.'[95]

Tsvetaeva uses every linguistic register. She coins words and draws freely on vulgarisms and archaisms. Her work has more rhythmic energy even than Mayakovsky's. Her constant interrogation of words – of their sounds, meaning and origin – can make a reader feel that he or she is being taken into the very heart of the Russian language. Among her finest works are the collections *Craft* (1923) and *After Russia* (1928), and *The Ratcatcher* (1925), a lyrical-satirical version of the Pied Piper legend in which the Bolshevik rats come to resemble the German burghers they have ousted. Her translations include not only Russian versions of Goethe and Rilke, but also French versions of poems by Pushkin. She wrote diaries, literary criticism and verse dramas. Throughout much of 1926 she kept up an intense correspondence with Rilke and Pasternak; these exchanges have been published in full. In a poem addressed to Pasternak a year earlier, she had written:

> Distances divide, exclude us.
> They've dis-welded and dis-glued us.
> Despatched, disposed of, dis-inclusion –
> they never knew that this meant fusion
> of elbow grease and inspiration.
> (trans. Peter Oram)

In her last years Tsvetaeva, like Khodasevich – and like Pushkin and Lermontov – turned increasingly to prose, most of it as emotionally and intellectually charged as her poetry. Her essay 'Pushkin and Pugachov' is a masterpiece. She also wrote a long article about the artist Natalya Goncharova.

Tsvetaeva returned to the Soviet Union in 1939. Unable to publish her own work, she translated two ballads about Robin Hood, poems by Lorca, Baudelaire's 'Le Voyage' and some two thousand lines of the Georgian poet Vazha-Pshavela.

Both Efron and Ariadna were arrested in 1939. Efron was shot; Ariadna sent to the Gulag. Tsvetaeva was evacuated from Moscow, but she then hanged herself in the town of Yelabuga; she may have been under pressure to act as an informer for the NKVD. No one attended her funeral.

To Osip Mandelstam

Nothing's been taken away!
We're apart – I'm delighted by this!
Across the hundreds of miles
that divide us, I send you my kiss.

Our gifts, I know, are unequal.
For the first time my voice is still.
What, my young Derzhavin, do
you make of my doggerel?

For your terrible flight I baptize you –
young eagle, it's time to take wing!
You endured the sun without blinking,
but my gaze – that's a different thing!

None ever watched your departure
more tenderly than this
or more finally. Across hundreds
of summers, I send you my kiss.

(1916)
Peter Oram

*

Black as the pupil of an eye, sucking at light
like the pupil of an eye, I love you, far-sighted night.

Give me the voice to sing of you, godmother of every hymn,
you in whose hand lie the bridles of the four winds.

Calling on you, extolling you, I am no more than
a shell where the sea-swell goes on roaring.

Night! I have looked long enough into human eyes.
Now, emblaze me, make ash of me, black-sun-night!

(1916)
Robert Chandler

from *Death is a No*

Death is:
an unfinished house,
an unbrought-up son,

an unbound-up sheaf,
an unbreathed-out sigh,
an uncried-out cry.

(1920)
Boris Dralyuk

Roland's Horn[96]

Like a jester complaining of the cruel weight
of his hump – let me tell about my orphaned state.

Behind the devil there's his horde, behind the thief there's
his band,
behind everyone there's someone to understand

and support him – the assurance of a living wall
of thousands just like him should he stumble and fall;

the soldier has his comrades, the emperor has his throne,
but the jester has nothing but his hump to call his own.

And so: tired of holding to the knowledge that I'm quite
alone and that my destiny is always to fight

beneath the jeers of the fool and the philistine's derision,
abandoned – by the world – with the world – in collision,

I blow with all my strength on my horn and send
its cry into the distance in search of a friend.

And this fire in my breast assures me I'm not all
alone, but that some Charlemagne will answer my call!

(1921)
Stephen Capus

To Mayakovsky

Beyond the chimneys and steeples,
baptized by smoke and flame,
stamping-footed archangel,
down the decades I call your name!

Rock-steady or change-at-a-whim!
Coachman and stallion in one!
He snorts and spits into his palm –
chariot of glory, hold on!

Singer of city-square wonders,
I salute that arrogant tone
that rejected the brilliant diamond
for the sake of the ponderous stone.

I salute you, cobblestone-thunderer!
– see, he yawns, gives a wave, then he swings
himself back into harness, back under
the shafts, his archangelic wings.

(1921)
Peter Oram

An Attempt at Jealousy

How is your life with the other one,
    simpler, isn't it? One   stroke of the oar
then a long coastline, and soon
    even the memory of me

will be a floating island
    (in the sky, not on the waters):
spirits, spirits, you will be
    sisters, and never lovers.

How is your life with an ordinary
woman? without godhead?
Now that your sovereign has
been deposed (and you have stepped down).

How is your life? Are you fussing?
flinching? How do you get up?
The tax of deathless vulgarity
can you cope with it, poor man?

'Scenes and hysterics I've had
enough! I'll rent my own house.'
How is your life with the other one
now, you that I chose for my own?

More to your taste, more delicious
is it, your food? Don't moan if you sicken.
How is your life with an *image*
you, who walked on Sinai?

How is your life with a stranger
from this world? Can you (be frank)
love her? Or do you feel shame
like Zeus' reins on your forehead?

How is your life? Are you
healthy? How do you sing?
How do you deal with the pain
of an undying conscience, poor man?

How is your life with a piece of market
stuff, at a steep price?
After Carrara marble,
how is your life with the dust of

plaster now? (God was hewn from
  stone, but he is smashed to bits.)
How do you live with one of a
  thousand women   after Lilith?

Sated with newness, are you?
  Now you are grown cold to magic,
how is your life with an
  earthly woman, without a sixth

sense? Tell me: are you happy?
  Not? In a shallow pit how is
your life, my love? Is it as
  hard as mine with another man?

(1924)

Elaine Feinstein

from *The Ratcatcher*

'Stop!
This isn't a rustic hop!
Do you pipe your tunes at our Council?
Less fast! Andante! I do recall
something was said of Jew and devil,
but of "music-makers" – nothing at all!

Oh, after the service it's "Come inside,
friend, with your piping and fiddling" –
of course musicians are welcome at weddings:
just not at the side of the bride!

Marry a piper? A semiquaver!
Mere sound! A reed with incisions!
It's unheard-of! Who would ever
get married to a musician?

What? A piper? A bag of nerves!
My daughter? Sooner a blacksmith!
What would she do with his fifths and thirds
in the matrimonial blankets?

Marry a piper? A naked bean!
In England perhaps – but listen:
in Hamlin it's never been heard or seen
that our daughters marry musicians.'

'What is music? Twitter of birds!'
'Pastime! A children's plaything!'
'What is music? Noise in your ears.'
'Jollying up for a wedding.'

'Inconsequential scrape of strings.'
'Shouts of "Bravo!" Anguish.'
'Music? It isn't even the goose,
it's merely the goose's garnish.'

'Mustn't forget that when I was young
I too was one of the lads!'
'Just a piece of wood and some feline gut,
combined with a certain knack.'

'Scatters your wits! A narcotic fume!'
'No, when we hire a singer,
it's so they'll sing us a soothing tune
to help digest our dinner.'

'With women around, and a tankard of beer,
it's pleasant to have a song . . .
A tune or two before turning in . . .
though it mustn't last too long.'

(1925)

Angela Livingstone

from *Phaedra*

(An old servant is telling Hippolytus how Antiope [Hippolytus' mother, brought up as an Amazon] once fought beside Theseus [Hippolytus' father], against her own people.)

Taking aim, not just with eye and
elbow but with every pulsing
vein, aiming her whole, aimed,
body, equal of men – no: equal
of gods (her never-used-up quiver
fuller than a horn of plenty),
radiant under the foe's arrows,
there she stood – afraid of nothing.
Bowstring taunting tauter bowstrings,
fleshless bosom turned aside and
merging with the chest-tight bow so
close the arrows seemed to fly
not from the string but from the heart! Those
arrows passionate for destruction,
so thick and fast, in endless sequence,
that they could have been (but was it
war or thread she span?) a single
arrow flying from the string.
Was that a lion fighting beside her?
No, for in that cruel battle
even a god would have seemed timid.
Facing arrows, spurning pleasures,
thus she fought beside your father.

(1927)

Angela Livingstone

from *To Mayakovsky*

[. . .] Shot a bullet into his soul,
as if it were his own enemy.
The wrestler who wrestled God
has destroyed another temple. [. . .]
He destroyed many temples,
but none more precious than this.
Give peace, O Lord, to the soul
of this your deceased enemy.

(1930)
Robert Chandler

Homesickness

Homesickness! that long
exposed weariness!
It's all the same to me now
where I am   altogether lonely

or what stones I wander over
home with a shopping bag to
a house that is no more mine
than a hospital or a barracks.

It's all the same to me, captive
lion   what faces I move through
bristling, or what human crowd will
cast me out   as it must

into myself, into my separate internal
world, a Kamchatka bear without ice.
Where I fail to fit in (and I'm not trying) or
where I'm humiliated   it's all the same.

And I won't be seduced by the thought of
my native language, its milky call.
How can it matter in what tongue I
am misunderstood by whoever I meet

(or by what readers, swallowing
newsprint, squeezing for gossip)?
They all belong to the twentieth
century, and I am before time,

stunned, like a log left
behind from an avenue of trees.
People are all the same to me, everything
is the same, and it may be the most

indifferent of all are these
signs and tokens which once were
native but the dates have been
rubbed out: the soul was born somewhere.

For my country has taken so little care
of me that even the sharpest spy could
go over my whole spirit and would
detect no native stain there.

Houses are alien, churches are empty,
everything is the same:
but if by the side of the path one
particular bush rises
the rowanberry . . .

(1934)
Elaine Feinstein

Vladimir Mayakovsky (1893–1930)

Vladimir Vladimirovich Mayakovsky was born in Georgia, where his father was a forest ranger. After his father's sudden death in 1906 the family moved to Moscow. Aged fifteen, Mayakovsky joined the Bolsheviks; imprisoned three times, he began writing poetry in 1909, during a period of solitary confinement. In 1911 he entered the Moscow Art School, where he met David Burlyuk and other leading Futurists; he first published his poetry a year later, in the Futurist collection *A Slap in the Face of Public Taste*.

Mayakovsky's Futurist poems depend mainly on image and sound, but his work soon began to include more narrative, as well as impassioned discourse about both art and revolution. *A Cloud in Trousers* (1915) is his first long poem; for all the colloquial language, inventive rhymes and mockery of Romantic cliché, it remains deeply Romantic; the speaker – clearly Mayakovsky himself – is in despair, unable to imagine life without his beloved. *The Backbone Flute* (1916) and *Man* (1918) are no less Romantic.

In the summer of 1915 Mayakovsky fell in love with Lilya Brik, the wife of his publisher Osip Brik. The three remained close for the rest of Mayakovsky's life, but this triangular relationship brought Mayakovsky great pain. He later fell in love with other women, but they too were either already married or living abroad.

In Petrograd in 1917 Mayakovsky recited his political poetry to audiences of workers and revolutionary sailors. Back in Moscow he worked for the Russian State Telegraph Agency, creating more than 600 cartoon-like drawings with witty rhymed captions. He also wrote advertising slogans for state stores. Mayakovsky has been accused of prostituting his talent, and he himself, in his unfinished long poem *At the Top of My Voice* (1930), admits to having 'stepped on the throat' of his own song. These commissions may, nevertheless, have been valuable, as technical exercises and as an antidote to his early Romanticism.

During the 1920s, as well as editing *LEF* (the journal of the

Left Front of Arts) and other avant-garde journals, Mayakovsky travelled not only throughout the Soviet Union but also to western Europe and the United States. He published a prose memoir, *My Discovery of America*, and he wrote poems on such subjects as Brooklyn Bridge, his criticisms of capitalism mixed with expressions of wonder at the American capacity for innovation. In 1929 and 1930 he wrote two plays, *The Bedbug* and *The Bathhouse*; here his satire is directed against Soviet philistinism and bureaucracy.

On the evening of 14 April 1930 Mayakovsky shot himself. For at least the next fifty years discussion of his death was politicized. The view put forward by those sympathetic to the Soviet Union was that he killed himself because of a failed love affair – because, as he wrote in his last poem, 'love's boat smashed against the daily grind';[97] the anti-Soviet view was that he killed himself because of his disillusion with the Soviet Union. With time, however, Mayakovsky's suicide has come to seem almost inevitable; suicide is a central theme throughout all periods of his work.

This anthology includes a number of poems written in response to the suicides of Yesenin, Mayakovsky and Tsvetaeva. Mayakovsky's poem on Yesenin is one of the finest of these; few poets have written of suicide with such breadth of understanding. Mayakovsky is remonstrating not only with Yesenin but also with himself, trying to argue *himself* out of committing suicide. In a later article, 'How to Make Verses', he almost admits this, saying he found the poem hard to write because he was, at the time, leading an unsettled life all too similar to Yesenin's.

In 1935 Stalin declared Mayakovsky the greatest poet of the Soviet epoch. Mayakovsky survived this canonization (Pasternak called it his 'second death'), remaining an inspiration to many poets, including the Turkish Nâzim Hikmet, the Chilean Nobel laureate Pablo Neruda, and Louis Aragon, the French Surrealist (and later, Communist) poet who married Lilya Brik's sister. And in the 1960s and 1970s Mayakovsky was important to such younger poets as Voznesensky and Yevtushenko.

Yevtushenko writes: 'As a boy, Mayakovsky would climb into a huge clay wine vat and read poetry aloud, trying to swell the power of his voice with the vat's resonance. Mayakovsky was not only Mayakovsky but also the powerful echo of his own voice: oratorical intonation was [. . .] his very character.'[98] This is a memorable vignette, but it would be wrong to think of Mayakovsky as no more than a wild loudmouth; his best poems are thoughtful and compassionate, and his 'general animal sadness' is as important as his revolutionary fervour.

'A Good Attitude to Horses', included in both Scots and English, is one of only a dozen poems Mayakovsky wrote during the two years immediately after the October Revolution. Mayakovsky loved animals and often identified with them. This plea for people to show greater kindness – towards animals and towards one another – is central to his work.[99]

What About You?

I splintered the landscape of midday
by splashing colours from a tumbler.
I charted on a tray of aspic
the slanting cheekbones of Atlantis.
Upon the scales of an iron turbot,
I found ladies' lips, aloof.
And you, could you have played a nocturne
using a drainpipe for a flute?

(1913)

Maria Enzensberger

from *The Backbone Flute*

To all of you –
those I liked or like –
cherished as icons in the cave of my soul,
solemnly, I raise as a goblet of wine
the skull filled with my poetry.

I contemplate –
so often –
ending my days
with the full stop of a bullet.
This evening,
for all of you –
just in case –
I am giving a farewell concert.

Memory,
pack the brain's auditorium
with inexhaustible swarms of beloveds.
Spatter laughter from eye to eye,
sate the night with former weddings' glory.
Fill every soul with a jocular mood
so that this night is forgotten by no one.
Today, I shall play the flute –
my backbone.

(1916)

Maria Enzensberger

from *A Cloud in Trousers*

Maria!
The streets are running wild.
The crowd scratches my cheek with its fingers.

Open up!
It hurts!
Look, I've been stuck in the eye
with a hatpin!

She opened up.
Dearest!
Don't be scared
of this other

woman who hugs tight to my neck, smelling of animal sweat
and wet with grief –
it is my fate to drag
a million huge clean capital-L Lovers
and a billion dirty little lovelets with me through life.

Don't be scared
that once again
in a foul-weather excess
I will snuggle up to a thousand pretty faces –
'Mayakovsky's exes!' –
they're just ghosts –
a dynasty of deposed princesses.

Maria, come closer!
I won't make you tremble naked before me,
just give me the matchless charm of your lips:
my heart has never grown up as far as May,
but a full life holds at least a hundred Aprils.

Maria!
A poet is happiest when he's writing,
but I'm a man,
I'm made of flesh and blood –
I'm asking for your body,
asking like a Christian:
'Give me this day my daily bread.'

Maria, give it to me!
Maria, I'm scared of forgetting your name,
like a poet fears
losing the perfect words,
born at midnight in his bed.
I will care for your body and love it, like a wounded soldier,
an unnecessary man,
a nobody,
cares for his remaining leg.

Maria –
you don't want to?
You don't want to!
Ha!

Well, dark and downcast,
I'll take up my heart once again
and carry it off
crying
like a dog carries
his paw
back to the kennel,
after it's been run over by a train.

My heart's blood will make the road happy,
the red flowers show bright among the dust
on my coat. Like the sun round the earth, a thousand times
Salome
will dance round the head of the Baptist.

And when my tally of years
finally plays itself out
a million drops of blood will cover
the road to my father's house.

I'll climb up to heaven –
I'll be dirty (I slept in the gutter).
I'll stand next to him, bend down
and speak into his ear:

'Listen up, mister god!
Don't you get bored up here in the sky,
spending all day looking down?
Here's a plan – let's chop down that tree
(the one in your garden . . .) and make it into a merry-go-round!

'If you're omnipresent, you can get into all
the cellars and bring some quality wine back up –
then maybe, just maybe, Peter the Apostle
can be persuaded to lighten up.
And let's get some Eves back among the heavenly host:
I'll show you –
this evening I'll gather the most
beautiful girls from the boulevards for you.

'You want to?
                    You don't want to?
                                        Do you shake your head,
goldilocks? Are you frowning? Do you think that all this . . .
all this wingèd
nonsense here has a clue about what love is?

'I'm also an angel, I was one back down there –
I looked out through these eyes like a little
lamb. But I'm wasting my sweetness on the desert air:
it's like setting up a china shop and whistling for a bull!
You're omnipotent, and you thought up hands
and you gave everybody a head,
                                        or something –
how come you couldn't work out a plan
so we could kiss, kiss, kiss without suffering?

'I thought you were all-powerful, the real god-almighty,
but you're just a dimwit, a crusty little godkin.
See, I bend down,
                         and from the top of my
boot, pull out my shiv, my bare bodkin.
You scoundrel, you with your wings!
It's only in heaven you have any presence!
You must be scared – your feathers are bristling!
I'll slice you from here to Alaska, you and your incense!

'Goodbye!'
They can't stop me.
I may be right or wrong, but I can't settle down.
Look – they've got blood all over the sky
and they've beheaded the stars again.

Hey you!
Sky!
Take off your hat! Can't you see
I'm coming?

Needs to wash out its ears.

The universe is asleep,
and one huge ear –
covered in stars like fleas –
flops over its paws.

(1914–15)
James Womack

A Good Attitude to Horses

Hooves beat,
seem to sing:
'grib – grab – grob – grub'.

Drunk on wind,
shod with ice,
the street skidded.
A horse crashed
down on its crupper.
And straight away
gaper on gaper –
trouser-flarers along the Kuznetsky –
ganged up, guffaws
rang out, raucous:

'Horse gone down!'
'Down with a horse!'
All Kuznetsky Street was laughing.
I alone
didn't mix my voice in the howl at the horse.
I went up and saw
the horse's eyes . . .

The street tipped over,
flowed on as usual . . .

I went up and saw
how drop after drop
rolled down the muzzle,
hid in the hair . . .

And a sort of general
animal sadness
poured from me, splashing,
and ran down, rustling.
'Horse, don't cry.
Horse, please listen –
Why should you think you're worse than they are?
Little one, look:
all of us are to some extent horses,
each of us is a horse in his own way.'
Perhaps it was old
and didn't need nannying
or perhaps it thought my idea was stupid –
anyway,
the horse got up on its feet with a jerk,
gave a neigh . . .
and off it went,
waving its tail,
a red-haired youngster.
Reached home cheerfully,
stood in its stall,

feeling as though it was still a colt,
and life was worth living
and work worth doing.

(1918)

Angela Livingstone

A Richt Respeck for Cuddies

Horse-cluifs clantert
giein their patter
crippity
crappity
croupity
crunt.

Bleezed in the blaffert,
wi ice-shoggly bauchles,
the street birled and stachert.
The cuddy cam clunk,
cloitit doon doup-scud
and wheech
but the muckle-mou'd moochers werna lang
in makin theirsels thrang,
gawpus eftir gawpus, aa gaw-hawing
alang the Kuznetsky in their bell-bottom breeks.
'Aw, see the cuddy's doon!'
'Aw, it's doon, see the cuddy!'
And aa Kuznetsky gaffit.

cuddies horses *cluifs clantert* hooves clumped along
crunt quick heavy blow *Bleezed . . . blaffert* hit . . . gusts
wi ice-shoggly bauchles with ice-shaky old shoes
birled and stachert spun and staggered
cloitit doon doup-scud thumped down onto his buttocks
muckle-mou'd moochers many-mouthed watchers
aa . . . gaffit all . . . laughed

Aa but me.
I didna jyne the collieshangie.
I cam and kest
a gliff intil
the cuddy's ee . . .
The street's owrehammelt
in its ain breenges . . .

I cam and I saw
the muckle draps that scrammelt
doon the cratur's niz-bit
to coorie in its haffits . . .

And oh but the haill
clanjamfry o craturly
cares cam spillin and splairgein
fae my hert wi a reeshle!
'Ned, Ned, dinna greet!
Listen to me, Ned –
Ye think thae buggers are the saut of the erd?
My chiel,
neds are we all, to be honest wi ye;
nae man's unnedlike, in his ain wey.'
Aweel, it micht be
the beast was an auld yin
and had nae need o a fyke like me,
or was my thochts a wheen corse for a cuddy?

Onywey
Ned
gied a loup whaur he liggit

collieshangie uproar *kest* cast *gliff intil* glance into *ee* eye
owrehammelt capsized *breenges* rushing
coorie . . . haffits nestle . . . mane *clanjamfry o* mob of
reeshle rustle *dinna greet* don't cry *saut of the erd* salt of the earth
o a fyke of a fusspot
gied a loup whaur he liggit gave a leap where he was lying

stoitert to his feet,
gied a nicher
and the flish
o his tail doon the street.
My chestnut chiel!
Back home to his stable
lauchin like a pownie
staunin by the stable-waa
feelin in his banes able
to dree the darg and the dowie
for the life that's worth it aa.

Edwin Morgan

To Yesenin

You've left us,
    as they say,
        and gone off cruising
through emptiness,
    to other worlds
        beyond the stars.
There's no more credit for you,
    no more boozing,
        no more bars.
No, Yesenin,
    I'm
        not trying to take the piss
this lump in my throat's
    not laughter,

nicher whinny
dree the darg and the dowie endure the day's work and the sadness

but bitter moans.
I see you, hand slashed open,
round the twist,
swing back and forth,
a sack
of your own bones.
Stop!
Pack it in!
Have you gone mad or what?
Letting
your cheeks
go white like that,
like death!
For turning things
around
you'd always got
the knack,
and better
than anyone else on earth.
Why?
What was gained?
Astonishment confuses.
The critics mumbled:
'His failure's due, we think
to this . . .
or that . . .
but the main trouble is,
he loses
the thread, because of too much
of the drink . . .'
They say
if you'd swapped
decadence
for Class
you'd have been changed,
and avoided heavy scenes.
You think
the working-class

gets off on kvass?
In drinking matters
they're not
exactly green.
They say
if there'd been
someone to keep you under
control,
your talent
might have started soaring.
But
you'd have written,
day after day,
hundreds
of lines
as long as Doronin's[100]
and just as boring.
I know
if I'd produced
that kind of crap
I'd also
be bent on self-eradication.
But I'd far rather
vodka wipe me off the map
than bored frustration.
The reason
for so much blood
pointlessly spilled
neither noose
nor pocket-knife explains.
If
the Angleterre's[101] inkwells
only had been filled
there mightn't
have been a need
for slashing veins.

Imitators cheered:
Encore! Encore!
Whole platoons
were poised for
self-destruction.
We've suicides
enough –
why raise the score?
Better
to raise
the rate of ink production.
The tongue's
now locked
behind the teeth
for good.
Such mystery-making's
serious,
and absurd.
The nation,
and the wordsmiths' brotherhood
have lost
the apprentice-drunkard
of the word.
And people come
with their supply of trashy verse,
unchanged
from previous deaths,
regurgitated,
defile your grave
with doggerel
or worse –
Is that
how poets' lives
are celebrated?
Your monument
still hasn't been erected.
Where is it –
the ringing bronze,

the granite hunk?
The railing's there, though:
and on it
they've inflicted
a load
of verbose and nostalgic junk.
I hear your name
in little hankies snivelled.
Sobinov quotes you,
drools your verse to death.
Beneath the withered birch
you hear him drivel:
'Not a wor-r-r-d,
my f-r-r-iend,
no-o-o, not a b-r-r-reath . . .'
Oh,
I really can't find an expletive which is
strong enough for these
Lohengriniches![102]
I ought to drum up
a thundering great scandal.
I can't see
poetry
mutilated – tell
them where to go, yes
whistle out
these vandals,
tell them to bugger off and go to hell!
Let's
rid ourselves
of talentless infections,
blast coat-tails
till
they billow like black sails,
see Kogan[103]
scattered out in all directions –
and who cares
who

his spiked moustache impales!
There's still
a lot of crap
around these days
and much to do
just to keep up with things.
Human life
must learn
to change its ways.
Once it's changed,
then its praises can be sung.
It's true, these times
are hard ones for the pen
but tell me,
you
wimps and cripples of today:
where
is there a single one
of all great men
who chose
the trodden path,
the easier way?
The word's
the captain of all man's powers.
March on!
Let time
break through
with bullets
from behind!
Leave nothing
to the old days
past and gone
except for
the hair that's ruffled by the wind.
We're ill-equipped
to build
a happy world.
So

tear joy
        from the days
                as they arrive!
In this life
        to die's
                not difficult.
It's hard as hell
        to be alive.[104]

(1926)
Peter Oram

Anent the Deeference o Tastes

A cuddy,
goavin at a camel,
        lauchit:
'Whit
kinna cuddy's yon,
        aa bim-bam-bauchlt?'
The camel shrieked:
        'Ye caa yirsel a cuddy?
Ye're naethin
but a scrunty
        shilpit camel!'
– Ach ,
lat auld Frosty-Pow abune unscrammle
the twa puir craturs;
he
kens the brose fae the gundy.

(1928)
Edwin Morgan

cuddy horse *goavin* staring *aa bim-bam-bauchlt* all misshapen
shilpit puny *Frosty-Pow abune* Grey-Head above
kens the brose fae the gundy knows the porridge from the toffee

Georgy Ivanov (1894–1958)

Along with his fellow émigré, Marina Tsvetaeva, Georgy Vladimirovich Ivanov is one of the very greatest Russian poets of the last century.

As a young man he had been close to the Acmeists. For several years after settling in Paris with his wife (the poet and memoirist Irina Odoevtseva) Ivanov wrote little, but in the late 1920s he began the poems for which he is remembered – poems of brilliant despair that at once anticipate Existentialism and look back to the French Symbolists, and to their Russian translator, Innokenty Annensky. Ivanov went on writing more and more subtly, his perfect mastery of traditional form offsetting an ever more startling emotional directness. He composed much of his finest work during his last few months, when he knew he was dying.

Ivanov was a controversial figure. He enraged Akhmatova, Nadezhda Mandelstam and others by publishing a memoir, *Petersburg Winters*, that mixes fact, rumour and personal fantasy and was taken more literally than Ivanov intended. He was accused of Nazi sympathies, although he had been writing thoughtfully, from as early as 1933, of the dangers of Nazism and the temptation it held for Russian émigrés. He was even accused of complicity in a murder in St Petersburg – a false rumour that pursued him nearly all his life as an émigré.

This hostility towards Ivanov can best be understood as symptomatic of a general malaise. The Russian émigrés were as cut off from French culture as from the Soviet Union. Most French writers – both before and after the Second World War – were pro-Soviet and they and the émigrés looked on one another with suspicion. In their isolation the Russians were all too prone to feuding, and Ivanov fought his corner fiercely, although a recent biographer calls him a 'lamb in wolf's clothing'.[105]

Until the last years of the Second World War the Ivanovs were wealthy; Odoevtseva's father, a rich lawyer in Riga, supported them during their first decade in Paris and left Odoevtseva a large inheritance when he died in 1933.[106] Much of the hostility directed at the Ivanovs was probably inspired by envy. But by the end of the war they were penniless. Their gold had been stolen; their fine villa in Biarritz had been destroyed during an Allied bombing raid and – with Latvia now a part of the Soviet Union – there was no more income from their property in Riga. In 1955 the Ivanovs had to leave Paris. From then until Ivanov's death they lived not far from Nice – in a home for old people with no citizenship.

Poems 1943–58 – the last book Ivanov himself prepared – came out soon after his death. Odoevtseva then compiled the cycle 'Posthumous Diary', writing down some poems from memory. G. S. Smith writes of Ivanov's last poems: 'An ageing, careworn man, almost always alone and speaking to himself (except in a few love poems, among the most delicate ever written in Russian), quietly probes the balmy-rosy atmospheric permutations of an alien Mediterranean coastline into which remembered snowstorms threaten to intrude. Among provocatively offhand gestures about the pointlessness of it all, potentially redemptive values drift in with the snow, evoked and guided by the formal mastery of their verbal articulation.'[107]

In summer 1918 Maxim Gorky initiated an ambitious publishing venture: 'World Literature'. Its aim was to make the great works of world literature accessible to the masses and also to provide a source of income for Petrograd's starving writers and scholars. Many important writers – Blok, Mandelstam, Gumilyov, Khodasevich, Zamyatin, Chukovsky – were involved. Among the poets Ivanov translated were Gautier and Baudelaire and (with the help of a crib) Wordsworth, Coleridge and Byron. His rhythmically inventive translation of Coleridge's 'Christabel', edited by Gumilyov, always remained important to him; Ivanov revised it over the decades and was trying to republish it as late as 1953.

In 1956 Ivanov referred to Kuzmin as 'the teacher of my youth';[108] earlier, in *Petersburg Winters*, he wrote that Kuzmin had taught his generation to celebrate the everyday – calmly, intimately, without the hysteria of the Symbolists. In several late poems he remembers Gumilyov and Mandelstam; he seems never to have broken off his inner dialogue with both. Ivanov's post-war work, always in traditional forms, is startlingly fresh in its colloquial diction; some poems are as simple and musically perfect as the best of Verlaine; others as bold in their thoughts and imagery as the later work of Paul Celan. In *Poems 1943–58* Ivanov alludes several times to 'I go outside to find the way', Lermontov's eloquent expression of a sense of isolation from other human beings and of unity with the cosmos; having to learn this poem by heart, at the age of fifteen, was the beginning of Ivanov's love of poetry.[109] In his very last poems Ivanov, like so many Russian poets before him, turns to Pushkin: 'Posthumous Diary' opens with one of the most moving poems ever addressed to him.

*

It's good that Russia has no Tsar,
it's good that Russia's just a dream,
it's good that God has disappeared,

that nothing's real, except the stars
in icy skies, the yellow gleam
of dawn, the unrelenting years.

It's good that people don't exist,
that nothingness is all there is,
that life's as dark and cold as this;

until we couldn't be more dead,
nor ever were so dark before,
and no one now can bring us aid,
nor even needs to any more.

(1930)
Stephen Capus

*

The stars glow blue. The trees are swaying.
A routine evening. Routine winter, too.
All is forgiven. Nothing's forgiven.
Music and gloom.

We are all heroes, we are all traitors;
all words are worthless, each and every one.
My dear contemporaries –
having fun?

(1934)
Maria Bloshteyn

*

Everything's changed, nothing has changed
in the strange chill, strange chill of dawn.
I've dreamed many dreams over the years
and now I awake – with the years all gone.

Here we go, here I stand in an autumn field
(changed, unchanged, I don't understand) –
as if I've been given my freedom
and my last hope has been torn from my hand.

(1944–5)
Robert Chandler

*

Thirty years now Russia's lived in fetters,
in Magadan,[110] in Kolymà –
but the Russia that will live for ever
is the one now dying in Kolymà.

(1947)
Robert Chandler

*

Nothing, nothing will be returned;
love, forgiveness – unearned, unlearned;
though we can never learn to forget.

Sweet is the sleep of an alien land.
We sense spring, hear the sea's even sound
in this world of eternal torment.

(1949)
Robert Chandler

*

Where can I look, where can I go,
to find that almost Alpine snow,
all sacrificed so life can grow,
all turned by May to splash and flow,
to breath of dandelion and rose,
to mighty wave or shining billow –
into that foolish question posed
by François Villon long ago?

(1951)
Robert Chandler

*

Led by what is shining,
the sleepwalker looks into a blank,
black is the death beneath him
and there's no knowing
where the moon's thin ledge
will slide him.

The innocent are executed
in a universal night –
look the other way.
Look into cold nothing
and let its moonshine take you
beyond all understanding.

(1948)
Robert Chandler

*

Some things succeed, and some things fail;
everything's nonsense that passes away . . .

But even so this reddish-brown grass
which grows by a gate in the fence will last.

. . . If Russian speech has the power to go
back to the land where the Neva flows –
from Paris I send these muddled words,
though even to me they sound absurd.

(1950)
Stephen Capus

*

One mirror must mirror another;
each mirror mismirrors the other.

Not that evil cannot be defeated,
only that we cannot escape defeat;

I believe in the ash left behind by the fire;
not in the music that burned my life.

(1950)
Robert Chandler

*

No more Europe, no more America.
The end of Tsarskoye, of Moscow, too.
A fit of nuclear hysteria –
life atomized into a radiant blue.

Transparent, all-forgiving haze will stretch
over the seas. And he who could have done
something yet chose not to, will be left
in the expanse of pre-eternity, alone.

(1953)
Robert Chandler

*

I love a despairing peace:
chrysanthemum blossoms in fall,
lights adrift in a river of mist,
a sunset that has turned pale,

nameless graves, all the clichés
of a Symbolist 'wordless romance' –
what Annensky loved with such greed
and Gumilyov couldn't stand.[111]

(1954)
Robert Chandler

*

I still find charm in little accidental
trifles, empty little things –
say, in a novel without end or title,
or in this rose, now wilting in my hands.

I like its moiré petals, dappled
with trembling silver drops of rain –
and how I found it on the sidewalk,
and how I'll toss it in a garbage can.

(1956)
Boris Dralyuk

To Alexander Pushkin

I dearly, dearly long to be with you,
to sit and chat with you, drink tea with you.

You'd do the talking – I would be all ears;
your voice grows ever dearer with the years.

You, too, knew grief and fury and disdain;
you, too, died slowly, slowly and in pain.

(1958)
Robert Chandler

* 112

No more brushing of teeth
or shaving of cheeks.
'There are things you must say
before you die.'

Eternity's door stands open wide.
And 'It's time, my friend, it's time!'
Time for mind and heart to be clear
and give life a heart-warming cheer.

Time for the wise words of the old
whose soul is at peace with the world . . .
Before I die
I have nothing to say.

(1958)
Robert Chandler

*

After plodding year after year
through towns in an alien land,
we have ground enough to despair –
and despair is where we must end.

For despair is our final refuge –
as if, in midwinter, we had come
from Vespers in a nearby church,
through Russian snow, to our home.

(1958)
Robert Chandler

*

The smokey blotches of the neighbours' windows,
and windswept roses bending, drawing breath –
if I could think that life is but a dream,
that we cannot help waking after death.

To wait in heaven – heaven is so blue –
to wait in that cool bliss without a care.
And then, never to part with you.
With you for ever. Do you see? For ever . . .

(1958)
Boris Dralyuk

*

Spring exultation, nightingales, the moon
on southern seas – they make my poor head spin
with boredom. More than that. I disappear.
The real me lives elsewhere. Far to the north.

Berlin, poor Russian Paris, filthy Nice –
a dream from which I soon will find release.

Petersburg. Winter. Gumilyov and I
walk by an ice-bound Neva, bright with snow.
The river Lethe. Side by side, we walk
and talk as poets did, so long ago.

(1958)
Robert Chandler

*

Say a few more words to me,
don't fall asleep before the dawn.
I need to feel you close to me.
My journey's almost done.

May the last poem I have made
take on new life through your sweet lisp,
your quiet wrestle with sounds
you cannot get your tongue round.[113]

(1958)
Robert Chandler

Sergey Yesenin (1895–1925)

Born into a peasant family in the province of Ryazan, Sergey Alexandrovich Yesenin began writing poetry at the age of nine. He moved to Moscow in 1912, working as a proofreader and then studying for eighteen months at Moscow University. In 1915 he moved to Petrograd, where he became known in literary circles – largely thanks to the support of Alexander Blok – as a leading figure in a new group of 'peasant poets'. His first book, *Ritual for the Dead* (*Radunitsa*) won him wider popularity. In late 1918 he founded his own publishing house and, together with Anatoly Mariengof, a literary movement known as Imaginism. With its emphasis on startling imagery, this is best seen as a precursor of Surrealism; it has nothing in common with the more classically inclined Imagist movement founded in London by Ezra Pound.

In late 1921 Yesenin met the American dancer Isadora Duncan. Knowing almost nothing of each other's languages, they married in May 1922. Yesenin accompanied his wife on a tour of Europe and the United States, but the marriage (Yesenin's second) lasted less than a year; Yesenin's first and third marriages were equally short-lived. An affair in 1924 with the poet Nadezhda Volpin produced one son, Alexander Yesenin-Volpin, who became a poet and a leading Soviet dissident.

During 1924 and 1925 Yesenin wrote many of his finest poems. But his alcoholism grew severe and in November 1925 he was hospitalized after a nervous breakdown. On 27 December, two days after his release, he cut his wrists and wrote a farewell poem in his own blood; the following morning he hanged himself in the icon corner of his room in the Hotel Angleterre in Leningrad, where he had stayed in 1921 with Isadora Duncan. His farewell poem is remarkable for its grace.

A Romantic, Yesenin had welcomed the Revolution but had soon been disillusioned. His long poem 'Pugachov' (1921), about the eighteenth-century peasant rebel, was a coded expression of sympathy for the huge peasant uprising against the Bolsheviks that year in the province of Tambov. He wrote poems in praise of Lenin after his tour of Europe and the United States, but his central themes – peasant Russia and low-life Moscow – were seen as anti-Soviet and he was harassed by the secret police. Both before and after his death (about which conspiracy theories still abound) Party officials made out that his work was corrupting Soviet youth. These attacks on Yesenin were an important stage in the process of the 'sovietizing' of Russian literature and it was in their context that Mayakovsky wrote his own poem on Yesenin's death (page 324). Though not uncritical of Yesenin, Mayakovsky reserves his fiercest criticisms for his attackers.

Yesenin is often considered sentimental, but his best poems are strikingly honest. His regret for the passing of 'village Russia' coexists with a clear acknowledgement that he himself could never return to that world. His 1924 collection *Moscow of the Taverns* evokes the lives of thieves, prostitutes and down-and-outs with affection but without false glamour. And he is honest about himself. 'The Black Man', written a month before his death, begins:

> My friend, my friend,
> I'm ill, I'm very ill.
> I don't know where this illness has come from:
> whether it's the wind
> whistling over a deserted field
> or whether it's alcohol
> stripping my brain
> like a grove of trees in September.

Yesenin also writes well about animals. One poem describes a bitch dragging herself back home after watching her puppies being drowned; for a moment she sees the moon over her owners' hut as one of these puppies, still alive. Another poem describes a colt in the steppe, racing after a train as if unaware that a railway engine is now worth as much 'as many tons of horseflesh and skin'. Shalamov – whom no one could call sentimental – has written, 'A large part of nature – animals – has been left outside the remit of lyric poetry. Only children's poets and composers of fables ever write about animals. It is Yesenin who shows us with what powerful kindness, with what spiritual warmth, it is possible to write about animals.'[114]

Shalamov also tells us that Yesenin was much loved by the Russian criminal underworld. A general contempt for women coexisted in this world with a cult of the mother, and 'literally every criminal' knew Yesenin's 'Letter to my Mother' by heart. They also often had his lines tattooed on their bodies. Among the most popular were the last words of the poem beginning 'Poor poet': 'I bet on the Queen of Spades, / but I played the Ace of Diamonds.' The Ace of Diamonds, sewn on the back of prisoners' uniforms in tsarist times, was a general symbol for criminality.

Recalling her childhood in the 1970s, Irina Mashinski writes: 'Every day, on my way to and from school, I would cross Yesenin Boulevard, where there was a funny-looking statue of a musing poet with a book in his hand. Local drunks – of whom there were many – would gather there at night, not necessarily to recite poems. But they loved Yesenin and considered him one of them.'

*

Mist climbs from the lake.
Fields bare after harvest.
Beyond blue hills
the sun rolls to its rest.

Splintered, deep in ruts,
the weary road thinks
it cannot be long now
till grey-haired winter.

In the misty, resonant grove
I watched yesterday
as a bay moon, like a foal,
harnessed herself to our sleigh.

(1917)
Robert Chandler

The Backstreets of Moscow

The farmhouse is lonely without me,
and my old dog is gone from the door;
God sent me to die in the backstreets
and I can't go home any more.

I'm in love with this overdone city,
though it's dirty and falling apart;
it reminds me of stories at bedtime,
and the street sounds hurt my heart.

I go out for a fix after midnight,
and the fix that I'm after is fame,
so I head for a bar in the backstreets
where everyone knows my name.

It's noisy and dirty and drunken
but nobody there drinks alone –
the bartenders buy me my vodka
and the hookers cry at my poems.

My heart beats faster and faster,
and I say to the drunk by the door –
'I'm like you, my life's a disaster,
and I can't go home any more.'

Oh, the farmhouse is lonely without me,
and my old dog is gone from the door;
God sent me to die in the backstreets
and I can't go home any more.

(1922)
Paul Schmidt

Cigarette Pedlars

Avenues so wretched,
snowbanks, bitter frost.
Desperate little urchins
with trays of cigarettes.
Wandering dirty avenues,
enjoying evil games –
all of them are pickpockets,
all are jolly thieves.
That bunch takes Nikitskaya,
this – Tverskaya Square.
They stand, sombrely whistling,
the livelong day out there.
They dash to all the barrooms
and, with some time to spare,
they pore over Pinkerton
out loud over a beer.
Let the beer be bitter –
beer or not, they're soused.
All rave about New York,
all dream of San Frantsisk . . .
Then again, so wretchedly,
they walk out in the frost –
desperate little urchins
with trays of cigarettes.

(1923)
Boris Dralyuk

Letter to My Mother

Greetings, old woman! How are you?
Are you well? As for me – I'm all right;
and I hope our old house is still bathed in
that ineffable evening light.

But I hear that you fret for my safety,
though you try to conceal your distress;
that you're often seen wandering the highway
in your old-fashioned country dress.

And they say that you see a recurring
dream as the dusk starts to fall –
of some hooligan thrusting a dagger
through my heart in a barroom brawl.

Cheer up, old woman! Don't worry:
it's all a preposterous lie;
for, although I'm a scandalous drunkard,
still, I'll see you before I die.

I'm the same loving son as always,
and my only ambition's to come
back alive from this chaos and madness
to visit once more my old home.

I'll return in the spring when the blossom
has covered our garden in white;
but promise you'll no longer wake me,
as before, with the first morning light!

Don't fret over what never happened,
don't revive the old dreams – let them go;
from my earliest days disappointment
is all I've been fated to know.

And don't teach me to pray – it's not worth it!
The old days will never come back;
you alone are my one consolation,
you alone are the light which I lack.

So forget your imaginary worries
and learn how to curb your distress;
and stop wandering about on the highway
in your old-fashioned country dress.

(1924)
Stephen Capus

To Kachalov's Dog

Give me your paw, Jim, for good luck.
I've never seen such paws – not ever.
Let's sit beneath the moon and bark
at all this boring, noiseless weather.
Give me your paw, Jim, for good luck.
But please, old boy – don't lick, don't lick.
Just try and get this simple thing.
Friend, you don't know what life is like,
and don't know what it takes to live.
Your master's kind and widely known;
you've had so many guests before –
and, smiling, every one has longed
to pet you, touch your velvet fur.
In your dog's way, you're bloody handsome,
with such a kind and trusting face.
And, needing nobody's permission,
just like a drunk, you kiss and kiss.
Dear Jim, among your guests you've had
some of all sorts, some out of sorts.
But *she* – most silent and most sad –
has she happened to call round, old sport?
If she does come, I give you a command.
Since I'll be gone, please stare into her eyes
and tenderly, for me, please lick her hand –
for all my faults – and faults that weren't my fault.

(1925)
Boris Dralyuk

*

Poor poet, was that really you,
addressing the moon in rhyme?
My eyes were dulled so long ago
by love, by cards and wine.

The moon climbs through the window frame.
White light, so white it blinds you . . .
I bet on the Queen of Spades,
but I played the Ace of Diamonds.

(1925)
Boris Dralyuk

*

Oh, to hell with this storm, damn this snow and hail –
pounding on the rooftop, driving in white nails!
But me – I'm not frightened, and I know my fate:
my wastrel heart has nailed me to you – nailed us tight!

(1925)
Boris Dralyuk

*

Farewell, dear friend, farewell –
you're present in my heart.
We'll meet again, the stars foretell,
though now we have to part.

Goodbye for now, goodbye, dear friend –
no handshake, words or grief.
To die is nothing new – but then,
what new is there in life?

(1925)

Robert Chandler and Anthony Rudolf

Nikolay Oleinikov (1898–1937)

Born in a village in the Donets Basin, an industrial area in the east of what is now Ukraine, Nikolay Makarovich Oleinikov broke with his prosperous Cossack family and served in the Red Army during the civil war. Mainly self-educated, he was a man of great energy and varied gifts – a Cossack warrior, a womanizer, a mathematician, a writer, a practical joker. Robin Milner-Gulland tells how Oleinikov arrived in Leningrad in 1925, 'equipped with a document from his village council testifying that "citizen Oleinikov is authentically beautiful: issued to gain admission to the Academy of Arts" (he had persuaded the council chairman that only beautiful people were admitted)'.

Oleinikov published little of what he wrote for adults, making his living as a children's writer and the editor of two children's journals, *Yozh* (Hedgehog), which he founded, and *Chizh* (Finch). He was close to the group of avant-garde writers, at one time known as the OBERIU ('Association of Real Art'), that included Kharms, Vvedensky and Zabolotsky. And like them, he owed a great deal to the generosity, courage and good judgement of Samuil Marshak, the translator and children's poet who was chief editor of Detgiz, the children's section of the State Publishing House.[115] Alice Nakhimovsky refers to the offices of Detgiz – known familiarly as the 'Marshak Academy' – as 'the single official place in Leningrad where Vvedensky and Kharms found themselves surrounded by the like-minded'. She continues: 'One young writer [. . .] remembers wandering around the [building] in search of what he imagined as dignified figures, only to find them marching around on all fours "pretending to be camels".'[116]

The importance of Soviet children's literature – both in its own right and as a refuge for disaffected writers – can hardly be overestimated. Sarah Suzuki, from the Museum of Modern Art in New York, writes, 'Producers of art and literature were already attuned to children's own creativity: they had borrowed the principles of invented and nonsense languages for transrational poetic experiments, had hung kids' drawings alongside their own in avant-garde exhibitions and salons, and had experimented with purposefully naive compositional strategies. They now turned to work made to inspire and challenge young readers.'[117]

A Party member since 1920, Oleinikov understood the nature of the Soviet regime. In 1933 he feigned illness to avoid being seconded to a grain-requisitioning detachment in his native steppe. His poetry grew increasingly subversive, mocking state propaganda and the strictures of Socialist Realism. Like hundreds of thousands of others, he was executed in 1937 at the height of the Great Terror.

Oleinikov appears to have been a disconcerting figure. Yevgeny Shvarts, the poet, playwright and editor who first invited Oleinikov to move to Leningrad, described him as 'my friend and vicious enemy and abuser'.[118] Zabolotsky, who wrote two poems about him, saw him as someone 'with the special privilege of "speaking truths" that no one else dared pronounce or wanted to hear'.[119] Kharms wrote poems both to and about Oleinikov, and he is the model for Sakerdon Mikhailovich in Kharms's story 'The Old Woman'.

Oleinikov had a particular gift for composing parodic declarations of love. 'An Epistle to a Theatrical Actress' begins:

> Miss, I saw you yesterday
> first in clothing, then without.
> The sensation was, no doubt,
> greater than I can convey.[120]

His finest work, however, goes beyond parody. Rather than mocking something specific, Oleinikov often seems to be targeting *all* aspects of human endeavour. In 'The Beetle' he continues a fable begun by Captain Lebyadkin, the mad poet from Dostoevsky's *The Demons*. Anatoly Liberman's translation incorporates anachronisms that Oleinikov would, I believe, have enjoyed.

The Beetle

In a beaker sits a beetle,
sits and sucks his tawny leg.
He's been caught. He has been sentenced,
and for ruth he does not beg.

He casts glances at the sofa,
in his sorrow half-alive;
there he sees the vivisectors,
honing axes, whetting knives.

An efficient young assistant
boils the scalpel on the heater,
at the same time gently whistling
something from the early Beatles.

He can whistle, brainless monkey,
licensed butcher from the dregs!
And the beetle in the beaker
sits and sucks his tawny legs.

He observes the surgeons closely,
and his eyes begin to roll . . .
He would not have been so frightened
had he known there is a soul.

But we've learned from modern scholars
that the soul is not at issue:
fat and kidneys, blood and choler
are the soul's immortal tissue.

All that makes us hustle-bustle
are some ligaments and muscles.

This is science. Facts are stubborn
but are easy to apply.
And he wrings his arms (the beetle),
he is ready, he will die.

Now the resident approaches,
the MD who cuts and rips;
on the beetle he discovers
what he needs between the ribs.

And he throws and sticks the patient,
as he might have stuck a boar,
then he bares his teeth and, beastlike,
fills the workroom with his roar.

Whereupon the vivisectors
grab the beetle's carcass, and
some explore his chest with pincers,
some dismember him by hand.

And they kicked him, flicked him, pricked him,
and they tore to death their victim.
Lacerated by that thug,
dies of injuries the bug.

He is cold. His eyes don't tremble . . .
Then the brigands stopped their pranks
and retreated, somewhat sobered,
stepping back in serried ranks.

Torture, anguish – all is over.
There is nothing more to lose.
The remaining subsoil waters
from his body slowly ooze.

In a chink, inside the closet,
waits his son and hums a song –
'Daddy, Daddy, where're you, Daddy?'
Pauvre garçon!

He will never see his father,
who could not have travelled farther.

There he stands, his vivisector,
bending over with the lads –
ugly, shaggy, grinning bravely,
with his pincers and his adze.

You elitist, sexist mugger,
scoundrel, scholarly and smug!
Read my lips: this little bugger
is a martyr, not a bug.

Soon the window will be opened
by the coarse, unfeeling guard,
and he'll find himself, our darling,
on the driveway in the yard.

Near the porch, amid the garbage,
he will rot (his body hacked,
with his legs all pointing upward)
and await the final act.

Neither rain nor sun will quicken
him who thus unburied lies.
And a chicken – yes, a chicken –
will peck out his beady eyes.

(1934)

Anatoly Liberman

Nikolay Zabolotsky (1903–58)

Nikolay Alexeyevich Zabolotsky's father was an agronomist of peasant stock; his mother was an assistant schoolteacher, descended from a line of priests. Nikolay spent much of his childhood in the remote province of Vyatka. After briefly studying medicine and philology in Moscow, he moved to Petrograd in the early 1920s to study at the pedagogical institute. In 1928 he and two younger writers, Kharms and Vvedensky, founded the OBERIU[121] ('Association of Real Art'), the last avant-garde grouping in the Soviet Union. Their dream was to create not only plays, prose and poetry but also music, painting and film. Kharms and Zabolotsky both studied with the painter Pavel Filonov. Shostakovich knew both Kharms and Oleinikov; in 1930 the Maly Theatre nearly commissioned him to write an opera with a libretto based on a poem by Oleinikov.[122]

Many of the poems in Zabolotsky's first collection, *Columns* (1929), are grotesque vignettes of city life. In 1933 he published 'The Triumph of Agriculture', a part-humorous, part-moving poem about a utopian future. Eugene Ostashevsky, one of Zabolotsky's translators, writes, 'The poem's human agitator, a soldier like those who came back from the front in 1917, promises animals that the arrival of the tractor will free them from exploitation; in the future, they will live and work in scientific institutes, where "horses, friends of chemistry" eat "polymeric soup" and "a cow in formulas and ribbons" bakes "pie out of elements". The text ends with the communal destruction of old farm tools, portrayed as instruments of oppression.'[123]

Zabolotsky may truly have been trying to explore a better future, but the poem was seen as satirical. A large collection of his work, already in proof, was cancelled. Zabolotsky then made his living from translations and children's literature. Amongst much else, he wrote versions of Rabelais and parts of *Gulliver's Travels*.

In 1937 Zabolotsky managed to publish a booklet of seventeen poems, many of them about nature or on philosophical themes. The presence of poems about Stalin and Kirov allowed critics to speak of Zabolotsky 'freeing himself from earlier mistakes' but did not prevent him from being arrested a year later, charged with writing anti-Soviet propaganda. Despite a brutal interrogation, he refused to sign 'confessions' that would have incriminated others. He was sent to Siberia; astonishingly, he composed 'Forest Lake' during a sixty-day journey in a crowded cattle truck. Of all his poems this may be the most visionary. The natural world overcomes its innate violence and the lake becomes a pure and bottomless chalice, shining like the eye of a sick and despairing man who has glimpsed the evening star:

> And crowds of animals and feral beasts
> all peered through the fir-trees, with antlered faces
> reaching towards their baptismal chalice,
> and bowing to drink the life-waters of truth.
> (trans. Anna Razumnaya)

Zabolotsky was released in August 1944. While still in Kazakhstan, he resumed work on his translation of the medieval epic poem *The Lay of Igor's Campaign*, begun before his arrest. In January 1946 he was allowed to return to Moscow; reinstated in the Union of Soviet Writers, he published his translation of the *Lay*. This was the first of many translations he undertook during his last years; he translated nearly a thousand pages from Georgian alone. He continued translating after Stalin's death, even though he no longer felt he was risking his life by working on his own poetry.

In late 1956 Zabolotsky's wife Yekaterina Vasilievna left him for Vasily Grossman. Zabolotsky began to live with a much younger woman, Natalia Roskina, only to separate from her in February 1957. In September 1958 he and his wife began living together again, but he died of a heart attack on 14 October.

Critics often split Zabolotsky's career into two halves – an avant-garde youth and a classical period after his years in the camps – but this is mistaken. There is a classical detachment even in his early work, and there are echoes in his last poems not only of Tyutchev but also of Khlebnikov, Pasternak and Mandelstam. His concern with the problem of man's place in the natural world remained constant and he stayed true to his faith – a faith not shared by his OBERIU colleagues – in both science and poetry as sources of absolute truth. In a late note he wrote, 'The poet works with all his being simultaneously: with reason, heart, soul and muscles. He works with all his organism, and the more harmoniously integrated this work, the higher its quality. For thought to triumph he embodies it in images. For language to work he draws from it all its musical might. Thought – Image – Music: that is the ideal trinity towards which the poet strives.'[124]

The Face of a Horse

Animals do not sleep. In the dark of night
they stand, a wall of stone, above the world.

The cow's sloping head
rustles the straw with its smooth horns,
the rocky brows a wedge between age-old cheekbones,
the mute eyes revolving sluggishly.

The horse's face is handsomer, more knowing.
He hears the murmur of leaves and stones,
and, attentive to the wild beast's cry,
hears, too, the nightingale's gurgle in the copse.

And knowing all, to whom may he recount
his wondrous visions?
Cimmerian darkness!
Over the skyline, constellations rise.
The horse stands, like a knight on guard,
the wind plays in his hair,
his eyes burn, like two huge worlds,
his mane spreads, like the imperial purple.

And should a man but see
the horse's magic face,
he would tear out his own pathetic tongue
and give it to the horse. In truth,
this magic beast is worthy of it.

Then we would hear words.
Words, big like apples,
thick, like honey or curds,
words that penetrate like fire
and, once within the soul, as in some hut,
illuminate its wretched trappings,
words that will not die,
and which, in song, we celebrate . . .

But now the stable is empty,
the trees, too, have dispersed,
pinch-faced morning has swathed the hills,
opened the fields up for work.
And the horse, in its cage of shafts,
dragging a covered cart,
looks with submissive eyes
at the enigmatic, stationary world.

(1926)

Daniel Weissbort

The Wedding

A long ray gushes through the window,
the mighty house stands in the dark,
the fire spreads about, enkindled,
and flashing in its shirt of stone.
The kitchen sheds delightful heat.
Like golden draft horses, today
there ripen, not at all in vain,
baked loafs, and *babas*,[125] and *pirogs*.[126]

There a coquettish *kulebyaka*[127]
shines as the meaty heart of being.
Above, turned blue from being rinsed,
a chick casts curses on his childhood.
He's shut his childish little eyes,
furrowed his multicoloured forehead,
and laid his sleepy little corpse
into a delftware table-casket.
Above him no priest brayed a Mass,
waving a cross up in the air;
for him no cuckoo cared to sing
her guileful, crafty little song:
chained in the clap of cabbages,
he lay there, in tomatoes dressed;
a dainty leg of celery
descended on him, like a cross.
And so he slumbered, in life's prime,
a paltry midget among men.

The clock resounds. Night has arrived.
The feast is fervent, effervescent.
The wine decanter cannot keep
its fiery head from toppling over.
A giant flock of meaty women
sit in a circle, feathers shining,
and balding wreaths of ermine, greased
by sweating, century-old maids,
crown their enormous, heaving breasts.
They eat the densest of the sweets;
they wheeze in their voracious passion;
and, spreading free their bellies, press
close to their plates and to the flowers.
Their balding husbands sit erect,
straight as the whistle of a bullet,
their necks unable to escape
from fatty trenches of loose meat.
And breaking through the manifold

monotony of crystalware,
like some dream of a happy world,
a wedding speech's winged moral.

O bird of god, have you no shame?
And what does he add to your honour –
this groom, now tacked on to a bride,
who's traded in the clap of hooves?
The forms of his conforming face
still bear a wedding-crown's faint trace;
the golden ring upon his finger
glints brightly with a daring air.
Meanwhile, the priest, perennial guest,
his beard splayed out, like some great visor,
sits like a tower over the party,
with a guitar upon his shoulder.

Strike up, guitar! Widen the circle!
Ton-heavy goblets roar aloud.
Startled awake, the priest now bellows
and lashes at the golden strings.
To the guitar's primordial thunder,
lifting their glasses to the sky,
the rabid couples hurtle blind
into the mirrors' bare abysses.
And in their tracks, across the yards,
witless from incessant wailing,
the giant house, shaking its rump,
spins into the expanse of being.
And there – the awful dream of silence,
the greying hordes of factories,
and far above the masses' stations –
the law of labour and creation.

(1928)

Boris Dralyuk

*

Everything in the soul, it seemed, had been lost again
and I lay in the grass, weary with sad reproach,
and a flower's splendid body was rising above me
and beneath it a small grasshopper was keeping watch.

And then I opened my book in its heavy binding
and saw a drawing of a plant on the first page.
And either the flower's truth or a lie locked within it
reached out into nature from this printed page.

And the flower looked at its reflection in surprise,
as if trying to understand an alien word.
A strange movement of thought was trembling in its leaves,
a tension of will that cannot be told.

And the grasshopper raised his trumpet and nature awoke
and the sad creature struck up a *Gloria* to the mind.
And the flower's likeness in my old book began to wake
and so my heart moved too, towards it, to respond.

(1936)
Robert Chandler

Goodbye to Friends

In your long jackets, broad-brimmed hats,
with notebooks of your poems,
you disintegrated long ago in dust
like fallen lilac blossom.

Yours is a country free of ready forms,
where all is mingled, fractured, dislocated,
where there's no sky – only a grave mound –
and the moon's orbit never changes.

A synod of soundless insects sings
in a language foreign to our ear,
and a beetle-man holds out a tiny lantern
to greet acquaintances as they appear.

Are you at peace, my comrades?
Free of all memories? At ease?
Your brothers now are ants and roots,
dust pillars, grass-blades, sighs.

Your sisters now are pinks, sprays of lilac,
chickens, little chips of wood;
and your language has no power
to recall a brother left behind.

Your brother has no home yet in the land
where, shadow-light, you lighted long ago
in your long jackets, broad-brimmed hats
with notebooks of your poems.

(1952)
Robert Chandler

*[128]

Somewhere not far from Magadan,
in the grip of miseries and danger,
slowly, through the breaths of icy fog,
they trudged on behind a sledge.

From the soldiers, from their iron throats,
from the predatory crooks and thieves –
only the infirmary could save one,
or being sent for flour into town.

So they trudged along, in battered coats –
two ill-fated Russian men –
two old peasants yearning for their huts,
the far-off huts where they'd been born.

Burnt out by life, they'd no heart left,
far away from all their folk;
and the weariness that hunched their bodies
now consumed their very souls.

Up above them all the forms of nature,
all of life proceeded on its course.
But the stars, those harbingers of freedom,
were no longer looking down at men.

The mystery of the universe might still
have been unfolding in the northern skies,
but these two – they were no longer
pierced by those penetrating fires.

Round about them whirled a blizzard,
spreading on the stumps a snowy cloak.
And on this snow the freezing men now sat,
without a word, without a look.

The horses stopped. Labour was now over –
over now, the life that they'd been dealt . . .
A sweet somnolence embraced them,
took them, sobbing, to a distant land.

Now the guards would never overtake them,
never would the escort catch them up –
only Magadan's bright constellations
will catch fire high up above.

(1956)

Boris Dralyuk

from *Last Love*

1. *Thistles*

They set a bouquet of thistles
on the table – before me now
rises a jostling, a blazing,
a crimson round-dance of lights.
These stars, with their sharpened points,
these sprays of the northern dawn
clatter and wail with their bells;
their torches glow from within.
This, too, is creation's image –
an organism, woven from light rays,
the flare of unfinished scrimmage,
a flash of swords upraised.
It's a tower of rage and glory,
spear standing by spear,
where bundles of flowers, heads bloodied,
are plunged into my heart.
I dreamt of a prison turret,
and of bars, black as the night,
and behind them, a fairytale bird –
the bird that can't be helped.
And I, too, it appears, live badly,
for I can't help her break free.
And a wall of thistles is planted
between my joy and me.
A wedge-like thorn pierces my breast,
And I am dazzled one last time
by the sad and beautiful gaze
of her inextinguishable eyes.

4. *Last Love*

The car rumbled and came to a stop.
Two emerged into the space of evening,
and the driver, exhausted by work,
slumped down wearily onto the wheel.

Constellations of lights, far away,
trembled gently through the windshield.
The aged passenger lingered a while
with his lady beside the flowerbed.

And the driver, through sleepy eyelids,
suddenly noticed two faces,
turned to each other for eternity,
completely forgetting themselves.

Two hazy and delicate lights
shone from them, and all around
the passing summer's beauty
embraced them with hundreds of arms.

Here there were fire-like cannas,
like glasses of bloody wine,
and the grey plumes of aquilegias,
and daisies in golden crowns.

Awaiting autumnal minutes,
and grief's unavoidable taste,
the lovers were surrounded
by a fleeting ocean of bliss.

And leaning close to each other,
like homeless children of the night,
they strolled silently through the flowers
in the electric glow of the light.

While the car stood in the darkness,
and the engine rumbled to a start,
and the driver gave a weary smirk,
rolling down the window at his side.

He knew that the summer was ending,
that soon there'd be rain and snow,
that their little song had been sung –
but they, they didn't know.

(1957)

Boris Dralyuk

Alexander Vvedensky (1904–41)

Born in St Petersburg, Alexander Ivanovich Vvedensky studied in the early 1920s with Mikhail Matyushin and other artists from former Futurist circles. In 1928, along with Kharms and other poets and artists, he founded the avant-garde OBERIU group; together they staged readings, plays and what would later have been called 'happenings'. Like Kharms, Vvedensky made his living from writing and translating children's books. In late 1931 he and Kharms were arrested, accused of belonging to a group of anti-Soviet children's writers. After a year of 'internal exile' (they were forbidden to live in any of the main cities), they were allowed to return to Leningrad. In 1936 Vvedensky moved to Kharkov, in the Ukraine.

In 1941, after the German invasion, Vvedensky was arrested again. He was accused of plotting to stay in Kharkov under Nazi occupation; in reality, he and his family had attempted to leave but been unable to push their way onto a crowded evacuation train. On 19 December Vvedensky died of typhus on board a prison train.

Only about a quarter of Vvedensky's work survives. That any survives at all is thanks to Yakov Druskin, a close friend of Vvedensky and Kharms. During the worst months of the Siege of Leningrad, after Kharms too had been rearrested, Druskin (himself almost starving) went to Kharms's room, which had been sealed by the NKVD, and removed a suitcase of Kharms's papers, among which were also poems by Vvedensky. For around fifteen years Druskin alone preserved the work of both poets. Between 1978 and 1984 his disciple Mikhail Meilakh managed to get Russian-language editions of their work published in the West – though this led to Meilakh himself being imprisoned for 'anti-Soviet literary activity'.

There are parallels between Vvedensky's suggestion that one should 'respect the poverty of language' and the minimalism of Samuel Beckett. Like Beckett, Vvedensky often writes as if from a world where art is no longer possible. In 'Where. When', however, Vvedensky treats his main themes – time, death and

God – with an emotional directness seldom to be found in his earlier work. The poem is reminiscent of prayers spoken by an extreme Russian sect, the Skoptsy. Before undergoing an initiation rite that entailed castration, men used to say a prayer that began, 'Goodbye sky, goodbye earth, goodbye sun, goodbye moon, goodbye stars, goodbye lakes, rivers and hills, goodbye all elements of heaven and earth.'[129] Remarkably, the judge at Vvedensky's first trial had called his poetry 'a literary liturgy'.

In her closing statement at the Pussy Riot trial in late 2012 – eighty years after Vvedensky's first arrest and trial – the artist Nadezhda Tolokonnikova said: 'The highbrow and refined pursuits of the OBERIU poets, their search for thought on the edge of meaning, were realized at the cost of their lives, carried away by the meaningless and entirely inexplicable Great Terror. [. . .] The OBERIU poets inadvertently proved that their basic sense of meaninglessness and alogism was correct: they had felt the nerve of their epoch. Thus art rose to the level of history. [. . .] The dissidents and the poets of OBERIU are thought to be dead, but they are alive. They are punished, but they do not die.'[130]

Conversation about the Absence of Poetry[131]

Twelve people were sitting in a room. Twenty people were sitting in a room . . . people were sitting in a room. There was a concert in the hall. A singer was singing.

> Poets can there be a doubt
> that all your songs have been sung out
> and bards lie sleeping in the earth
> like misers in their final berth?

The singer paused. A couch appeared. The singer continued:

> A tree stands silent in the ground
> night without honour flows
> the sun like science makes no sound
> and bakes the boring groves.

The singer paused. The couch disappeared. The singer continued:

Clouds drift richly in the air
wisely stallions gallop on
but poems are no longer there
all is silent, all is wan.

The singer paused. The couch appeared. The singer continued:

Most likely all the poets died
musicians and singers by their side.
And somewhere all these bodies sleep
like tranquil misers in the deep.

The singer paused. The couch disappeared. The singer continued:

O look at nature's visage bold

At this point everybody went to the windows and started looking at the miserable view.

The silent forest trees.

Everybody looked at the trees of the forest, which were not making a single sound.

Today our public has grown cold
to sounds of birds like these.

All over the place the public was standing and spitting when it heard the birds sing. The singer paused. The couch appeared. The singer continued:

Autumn. Leaves with crimson kissed.
The cemetery of bards grows still.
Silence. A nocturnal mist
has settled on the hill.

The singer paused. The couch disappeared. The singer continued:

> The sleeping poets rose and said
> right you are, we're all quite dead
> our funeral's been sung and thus
> the yellow grass now covers us.

The singer paused. The couch appeared. The singer continued:

> Music in the earth keeps time
> worms with verses sing along.
> Rivers memorize their rhyme
> beasts drink the sound of song.

The singer paused. The couch disappeared. What did he prove by that?

(1938)

Alice Stone Nakhimovsky

Where. When

1. *Where*

Where he stood leaning against a statue. With a face overflowing with thoughts. He stood. He was turning into a statue himself. He had no blood. Behold what he said:

> Goodbye dark trees,
> goodbye black forests,
> revolution of heavenly stars
> and voices of carefree birds.

He must have got it into his head to travel somewhere sometime.

> Goodbye steppe cliffs,
> I've observed you for hours.
> Goodbye living butterflies,

I've hungered along with you.
Goodbye rocks, goodbye storm clouds,
I've loved and tormented you.

With yearning and belated repentance he began to examine the ends of grass blades.

Goodbye splendid ends.
Goodbye flower. Goodbye water.
Mail couriers rush past.
Fate and disaster rush past.
I walked a prisoner in the steppe,
I embraced a path in the forest,
I scared away a crowd of oaks,
saw a grave house made from oak,
and found it hard to lead my song around.

He imagines and remembers how once or never he would appear by the river.

I used to come to you, river.
Goodbye river. My hand is shaking.
You were all shining, all flowing
and I stood before you,
dressed in a glass caftan,
and listened to your river surf.
How sweet it was for me to enter
you and once again come out.
How sweet it was for me to enter
me and once again come out,
where oaks noised like finches,
where oaks were crazily able,
oak noise scarcely audible.

But now he ponders how it would be were he also to see the sea. Goodbye sea. Goodbye sand.

How high you are, O mountain land.
May waves beat. May spray spray.
I sit on a stone, a pipe in my hand,
while the sea plashes step by step.
And all is far at sea.
And all is far from the sea.
Cares rush by like a tedious joke.
Goodbye sea. Goodbye Paradise.
O mountain land how high you are.

He also remembered about the last thing in nature. He remembered about the wilderness.

Goodbye to you too
wild places and lions.

And so, having said goodbye to everything, he neatly laid down his weapon and, taking a temple out of his pocket, shot himself in the head. And here began the second part – the parting of all with one.

The trees waved their arms as if they were wings. They pondered all they could and replied:

You used to visit us. Behold,
he died. So shall you all.
He mistook us for minutes.
He was worn, crumpled, bent,
wandering out of mind
like an icy winter.

But what does he now tell the trees? Nothing. He is going numb.

The cliffs or rocks did not move. Through silence, through passing over in silence and through absence of sound, they intimated to us and to you and to him.

Sleep. Goodbye. Your course is done.
Your worldly courier is come.
Now is come your final hour.
Lord have mercy on us.
Lord have mercy on us.
Lord have mercy on us.

But what does he now answer back to the rocks? Nothing. He is turning to ice.

The fish and the oaks presented him with a bunch of grapes and a small amount of last joy.

The oaks said: We grow.
We swim, spoke the fish.
The oaks asked the time.
Have mercy on us too,
spoke the fish.

But what will he say to the fish and the oaks? Nothing – he will not know how to say thank you.

River powerfully rushing over the earth. River powerfully flowing. River powerfully bearing its waves. River as tsar. Saying goodbye in such a way. Like this. While he lay there right on its bank like a notebook.

Goodbye notebook.
Dying is difficult and not nice.
Goodbye world. Goodbye paradise.
Human land how far away you are.

What will he do to the river? Nothing – he is turning to stone.

And the sea, grown weak from its own long storms, contemplated death with sorrow. Did the sea have a faint look of an eagle? No, it did not.

Will he glance at the sea? No, he cannot.

But hark! Of a sudden, somewhere, the sound of trumpets. Savages – or not-savages. He glanced at human beings.

2. *When*

When he half-opened his own swollen eyes, he half-opened his own eyes. He recalled by heart everything as it is. I forgot to say goodbye to the rest, that is, he forgot to say goodbye to the rest. Here he recalled, he remembered the whole instant of his own death. Those sixes and sevens all the time. All that fussing about. All that rhyme. Which had been a loyal friend to him, as Pushkin had said before him. Oh Pushkin, Pushkin, that very Pushkin who had lived before him. Here the shadow of universal disgust lay on everything. Here the shadow of the universal lay on everything. Here the shadow lay on everything. He did not understand anything but he held himself back. And the savages, or maybe not-savages, appeared and with a lament like the rustle of oaks, like the humming of bees, like the plash of waves, like the silence of stones and the look of a desert, holding plates over their heads, came down without hurry from the heights onto the sparse earth. Oh Pushkin, Pushkin.

(1941)

Robert Chandler

Daniil Kharms, pseudonym of Daniil Yuvachov (1905–42)

Daniil Ivanovich Yuvachov was born in St Petersburg. He adopted the pseudonym 'Kharms' (partly, at least, in homage to Sherlock Holmes) while still at school. Of its several possible transliterations, he himself preferred 'Charms', punning on the English 'harm' and 'charm'. An admirer of Edward Lear and Lewis Carroll, he cultivated the manner of a pipe-smoking English eccentric even during the 1930s.

His father, a member of the terrorist organization the People's Will, was arrested as a young man; after four years in solitary confinement and eight years of penal servitude, he returned to St Petersburg in 1895 and became a devout member of the Orthodox Church. His son seems to have inherited both his courage and his spiritual concerns. Kharms was interested in mystic literature, including the Kabbalah, and his favourite books included Hoffmann's stories and Knut Hamsun's *Mysteries*. Among his friends were Vladimir Propp, author of an influential analysis of the structure of the magic tale, and Maria Yudina, a pianist who made no secret of her devotion to Orthodoxy. Kharms drew and painted throughout his life and was close to several important artists, some of whose work is only now being rediscovered.[132]

In his early twenties Kharms studied at a technical college but never graduated; later he enrolled on a film course, which he also failed to complete. In 1928 he helped found the avant-garde OBERIU. In early 1930 this was disbanded, and in December 1931 Kharms and his friend Vvedensky were arrested. Though sentenced to 'internal exile' for three years, they were allowed to return to Leningrad in early 1933.

Kharms earned his living by writing for children, publishing twelve books of stories during the last twelve years of his life. But after publishing the poem beginning 'A man once walked' in a children's magazine in 1937, Kharms was unable to publish anything for a year; the poem was evidently read as an allegory of the purges. Rearrested in 1941, after the German invasion, Kharms died in a Leningrad prison hospital. Only in 1988 was his work for adults first published in book form in the Soviet Union.

Kharms wrote poems, stories and plays. We include examples of his prose as well as his poetry, which is more personal. The difference between his poetry and his prose has been well described by Nakhimovsky: 'The world of Kharms's personal works [i.e., his poetry] is an ordinary one, illuminated from time to time by a desire for faith or the flash of a grotesque imagination. In Kharms's fiction, the grotesque takes leave of the narrator's thoughts and becomes reality itself.'[133]

Prayer before Sleep 28 March 1931 at Seven O'Clock in the Evening

'Lord, in broad daylight
apathy overcame me.
Allow me to lie down and fall asleep Lord,
and while I sleep fill me Lord
with your strength.
There is much I want to know,
but neither books nor people
will tell me this.
May You alone Lord enlighten me
by means of my verses.
Wake me strong for the battle with meanings,
swift in the arrangement of words
and zealous to praise the name of God
for ever and ever.'

Robert Chandler

The Constancy of Merriment and Dirt

Cool water gurgles in the river
and the mountains' shadow lies on the fields
and light fades in the sky. And birds
are already flying in dreams.
And the yardman with the black moustache
stands all night by the gate
and under his dirty hat he scratches
the back of his head with dirty hands.
And through the window come merry shouts,
the stamping of feet and the ring of bottles.

A day goes by, then a week,
and then the years go by
and people vanish
in neat ranks into their graves.
While the yardman with the black moustache
stands for years by the gate
and under his dirty hat he scratches
the back of his head with dirty hands.
And through the window come merry shouts,
the stamping of feet and the ring of bottles.

The moon and the sun have paled,
constellations have changed shape,
motion has become sticky
and time has become like sand.
While the yardman with the black moustache
stands again by the gate
and under his dirty hat he scratches
the back of his head with dirty hands.
And through the window come merry shouts,
the stamping of feet and the ring of bottles.

(1933)

Robert Chandler

A Fairy Tale

There once was a man by the name of Semyonov.
And Semyonov went out for a walk and lost his handkerchief.
And Semyonov started looking for a handkerchief and lost
his hat.
And looking for a hat, he lost his jacket.
He began to look for a jacket and lost his boots.
– Yes – said Semyonov – this *is* a loss – I shall go home.
Semyonov began walking home – and he got lost.
– No – said Semyonov – I'd rather sit. And he sat down.
And he sat on a stone, and fell asleep.

(1933)
Katie Farris and Ilya Kaminsky

Blue Notebook, No. 10

There once lived a red-headed man who had no eyes or ears. He also had no hair, so he was only in a manner of speaking called red-haired.

He couldn't speak, since he had no mouth. He had no nose either.

He didn't even have arms or legs. And he had no stomach, and he had no back, and he had no spine, and he had no innards at all. He had nothing at all! So there's no knowing who we are talking about.

We'd better not talk about him any more.

(1937)
Robert Chandler

Old Women Falling Out

Excessive curiosity made one old woman fall out of a window, plummet to the ground and break into pieces.

Another old woman poked her head out of a window to look at the one who had broken into pieces, but excessive curiosity made her too fall out of the window, plummet to the ground and break into pieces.

Then a third old woman fell out of a window, then a fourth, then a fifth.

When a sixth old woman fell out, I felt I'd had enough of watching them and I went off to the Maltsev Market where I heard that a blind man had been given a knitted shawl.

(1937)
Robert Chandler

*

Here's the rain crashing down,
time has stopped.
The clocks go on helplessly knocking.
Grow, grass, you don't need time.
Speak, Holy Spirit, you don't need words.

(1937)
Robert Chandler

*

This is how hunger begins:
first you wake in good cheer,
then weakness begins,
and then boredom,
and then comes the loss

of the power of swift reason
and then comes calm –
and then the horror.

(1937)
Robert Chandler

*

A man once walked out of his house
with a walking stick and a sack,
and on he went,
and on he went:
he never did turn back.

He walked as far as he could see:
he saw what lay ahead.
He never drank,
he never slept,
nor slept nor drank nor ate.

Then once upon a morning
he entered a dark wood
and on that day,
and on that day
he disappeared for good.

If anywhere by any chance
you meet him in his travels,
then hurry please,
then hurry please,
then hurry please and tell us.

(1937)
Matvei Yankelevich and Eugene Ostashevsky

Varlam Shalamov (1907–82)

Born in Vologda, Varlam Tikhonovich Shalamov saw himself as a writer from childhood. His father was a priest who had served twelve years in Alaska as a missionary; his mother, a schoolteacher, passed on to him her love of poetry. In 1926 Shalamov began studying law at Moscow University, but in 1928 he was expelled – probably for having taken part in a demonstration against Stalin on the tenth anniversary of the October Revolution. In 1929 he was sentenced to three years in a labour camp in the Urals; he had been involved in an attempt to print and distribute a suppressed letter Lenin wrote before his death, recommending that Stalin be removed from his post as General Secretary of the Party.

In 1932 Shalamov returned to Moscow, where he worked as a journalist and published several short stories. Rearrested in 1937, he was sentenced to five years in Kolyma, the vast labour-camp empire in the far north-east of the Soviet Union. In 1943 he was given an additional ten years for 'anti-Soviet propaganda'. In 1945 he spent several months in a camp hospital; not for the first time he was close to death. Later that year he survived several months in a punishment camp. In spring 1946 he was again close to death, but a doctor saved him, risking his life by enrolling Shalamov on a medical training course for which he was ineligible. After completing this course, Shalamov worked as a medical assistant at a hospital and in a lumber camp. From 1949 he was able to write poems, which he later collected in his *Kolyma Notebooks*.

In 1951 Shalamov was released, though he remained in Kolyma, still working as a camp medical assistant. In 1952 he sent some of his poems to Pasternak, who praised them; the two writers met in Moscow in November 1953 and remained on friendly terms for some years, with Pasternak doing what he could to help Shalamov publish his work. From late 1953 Shalamov lived in the Kalinin province, but in 1956 he was allowed to return to Moscow; by then he had begun work on the *Kolyma Tales*, his thousand-page cycle of stories set in the Gulag.

Alexander Solzhenitsyn writes that, on first reading Shalamov's poems in samizdat (hand-typed copies) in 1956, 'I trembled, as if from meeting a brother.'[134] He invited Shalamov to collaborate with him on *The Gulag Archipelago*, but Shalamov refused, at least in part because he disagreed with Solzhenitsyn's belief in the ennobling effect of suffering.

During much of the 1960s Shalamov was part of a circle that met at the home of Nadezhda Mandelstam, but in 1968 he broke off relations with her. *Kolyma Tales* was smuggled out to the West in the late 1960s, but it attracted little attention. In 1972 Shalamov alienated many of his friends and admirers by publishing a letter protesting against the publication of his stories in the West. He was disillusioned with dissident circles; Western publishers did indeed appear to have treated his work casually;[135] and he knew that his letter would enable him to join the Union of Soviet Writers and publish a fourth selection of poems.

Shalamov spent his last years in poverty and isolation and was moved to an old people's home in 1979. Blind, deaf and suffering from Huntington's disease,[136] he went on composing fine poems until his last months. He was no longer able to write, but visitors took dictation. He died on 17 January 1982, after being transferred, in bitter cold and without proper clothing, to a psychiatric hospital.

Kolyma Tales is recognized by Russian readers as a masterpiece of Russian prose and the greatest of all works of literature about the Gulag. Leona Toker has written movingly of the form of Shalamov's epic story-cycle being 'grounded in an ethical intention so genuine that its artistic merit seems to be the natural consequence of its truth'.[137] Shalamov's poetry, however, is still little read. This may be because we tend to pigeonhole writers; it is hard to imagine that the author of the bleak and sober *Kolyma Tales* could also have written poems of such ecstatic joy.

In 1966 Shalamov wrote that late Pushkin and early Pasternak are 'the best of Russian poetry'.[138] He also loved Baratynsky and Tyutchev. Fet and Blok became ever more important to him in his last years. Some of his historical poems bear the imprint of Mandelstam, and one of the earliest of the *Kolyma Tales*, 'Cherry Brandy', is an imagined account of Mandelstam's death in a labour camp. Remarkably, Shalamov managed to read this aloud, in May 1965, during the first public event in Moscow in honour of Mandelstam. During this same event Shalamov also paid a moving tribute to the Acmeist movement as a whole: 'The principles of Acmeism proved so vital and healthy that the list of participants is like a roll call of martyrs. If the Symbolists had been subjected to such trials, there would have been a general retreat into monasteries, into mysticism. There were healthy seeds in the theory of Acmeism that helped these poets to live through their lives and go on writing. Neither Akhmatova nor Mandelstam renounced the principles of their poetic youth; they did not change their aesthetic views.'[139]

The longest poem in this selection, 'Avvakum in Pustozyorsk', is written in the voice of the Archpriest Avvakum (1620–82), the archetypal Russian dissident and the most famous of the so-called Old Believers.[140] His refusal to accept the changes to the Orthodox ritual introduced by Patriarch Nikon led to his being exiled to Siberia. Then he was taken to the north of European Russia, to the military outpost of Pustozyorsk; after being imprisoned for fourteen years in a sunken, log-framed hut, he was burnt at the stake. His account of his life, written with verve and in colloquial language, is the first work of modern Russian prose; it circulated widely in manuscripts before the first printed edition in 1861. Shalamov's admiration for Avvakum seems unqualified, but in 'Boyarynya Morozova', a poem about a famous Old Believer from the high nobility, his characteristic admiration for strength of will is tempered with what may be a note of criticism:

> Not love, but rabid fury, has led
> God's servant to the truth. Her pride
> is justified – first high-born lady
> to seek a convict's fate.

Gripping her Old Believers' cross
tight as a whip between her hands,
she thunders out her final curses;
the sleigh slips out of sight.

So this is how God's saints are born . . .
Her hate more ardent than her love,
she runs dry fingers through her dry,
already frost-chilled hair.

Shalamov can be seen as a modern schismatic: as a young man he belonged to a Trotskyist group and several of the most positive figures in *The Kolyma Tales* are Social Revolutionaries (i.e., members of the party that was the Bolsheviks' main rival). He may, in these stanzas, be pondering a faultline in his own psyche; during his last years Shalamov quarrelled irreconcilably with almost everyone close to him. It is equally possible that the apparent criticism of Morozova is not intended; Shalamov may have considered the intensity of her (and his own) hatred entirely justified. Nevertheless, it is hard to believe that he was not, at some level, aware that those who hate evil more intensely than they love good are in a dangerous position.

Somewhat like Paul Celan and Primo Levi, Shalamov seems in the end to have been defeated by the destructive forces he withstood so bravely and for so long. His own life story may be the most tragic of all the Kolyma tales.

*

Flying in at my window,
a moon like a snow jay
scrapes claws on walls,
flutters over my pillow.

Scared of confinement
in page or dwelling,
my homeless darling –
in midnight finery.

Robert Chandler

*

Snow keeps falling night and day –
some god, now turned more strict,
is sweeping out from his domain
scraps of his old manuscripts.

Sheaves of ballads, songs and odes,
all that now seems bland or weak –
he sweeps it down from his high clouds,
caught up now by newer work.

(1950)[141]
Robert Chandler

Roncesvalles

I was captivated straight away,
tired of the lies all around me,
by that proud, tragic tale
of a warrior's death in the mountains.

And it may have been Roland's horn[142]
that called me, like Charlemagne,
to a silent pass where the boldest
of many bold fighters lay slain.

I saw a sword lying shattered
after long combat with stone –
a witness to forgotten battles
recorded by stone alone.

And those bitter splinters of steel
have dazzled me many a time.
That tale of helpless defeat
can't help but overwhelm.

I have held that horn to my lips
and tried more than once to blow,
but I cannot call up the power
of that ballad from long ago.

There may be some skill I'm lacking –
or else I'm not bold enough
to blow in my shy anguish
on Roland's rust-eaten horn.

Robert Chandler

Baratynsky[143]

Three Robinson Crusoes
in an abandoned shack,
we found a real find –
a single, battered book.

We three were friends
and we quickly agreed
to share out this treasure
as Solomon decreed.

The foreword for cigarette paper:
one friend was delighted
with a gift so unlikely
he feared he was dreaming.

The second made playing cards
from the notes at the back.
May his play bring him pleasure,
every page bring him luck.

As for my own cut –
those precious jottings,
the dreams of a poet
now long forgotten –

it was all that I wanted.
How wisely we'd judged.
What a joy to set foot in
a forgotten hut.

(1949)
Robert Chandler

*

Memory has veiled
much evil;
her long lies leave nothing
to believe.

There may be no cities
or green gardens;
only fields of ice
and salty oceans.

The world may be pure snow,
a starry road;
just northern forest
in the mind of God.

Robert Chandler

*

By candlelight,
    in midday dark, I'll warm
your words beside the stove;
    frost's bitten them.

Frost's wordless spell
    had made your letter dumb.
The letters melt, drip tears;
    calling me home.

Robert Chandler

I Believe

Off once more to the post:
will I find your letter?
My mind races all night
and daytime's no better.

I believe, I believe in omens,
in dreams and spiders.
I have confidence in skis,
in slim boats on rivers.

I have faith in diesel engines,
in their roars and growls,
in the wings of carrier pigeons
in tall ships with white sails.

I place my trust in steamers
and in the strength of trains;
I have even dreamed of
the right weather for planes.

I believe in reindeer sledges,
in the worth of a compass
and a frost-stiffened map
when there is no path;

in teams of huskies,
in daredevil coachmen,
in tortoise indolence
and the snail's composure.

I believe in the powers
of that wish-granting pike,[144]
in my thinning blood . . .
I believe in my own endurance;
and in your love.

(1952)
Robert Chandler

Purple Honey

From a frost-chilled
  line of poetry
my anguish will drop
  like a ripe berry.

Rosehip juice will dye
  fine crystals of snow –
and a stranger will smile
  on his lonely way.

Blending dirty sweat
  with the purity of a tear,
he will carefully collect
  the tinted crystals.

He sucks tart sweetness,
this purple honey,
and his dried mouth
twists in happiness.

(1954)
Robert Chandler

Tools

Our tools are primitive
and simple:
a rouble's worth of paper,
a hurrying pencil,

we need no more
to build a castle –
high in the air –
above the world's bustle.

Dante needed nothing else
to build gates
into that Hell hole
founded on ice.

(1954)
Robert Chandler

*

And so I keep going;
death remains close;
I carry my life
in a blue envelope.

The letter's been ready
ever since autumn:
just one little word –
it couldn't be shorter.

But I still don't know
where I should send it;
if I had the address,
my life might have ended.

Robert Chandler

*

They say we plough shallow,
always tripping and slipping,
but it's hard to plough boldly
on the soil we've been given.

We plough in a graveyard
just tickling the topsoil,
afraid our blade may turn up
bones of dead people.

(1955?)
Robert Chandler

*

All that is human slips away;
everything was mere husk.
All that is left, indivisible,
is birdsong and dusk.

A sharp scent of warm mint,
the river's far-off noise;
all equal, and equally light –
all my losses and joys.

Slowly, with its warm towel
the wind dries my face;
moths immolate themselves
in the campfire's flames.

(1955)
Robert Chandler

Avvakum in Pustozyorsk

The walls of my church
are the ribs round my heart;
it seems life and I
are soon bound to part.

My cross now rises,
traced with two fingers.[145]
In Pustozyorsk it blazes;
its blaze will linger.

I'm glorified everywhere,
vilified, branded;
I have already become
the stuff of legend:

I was, people say,
full of anger and spite;
I suffered, I died
for the ancient rite.

But this popular verdict
   is ugly nonsense;
I hear and reject
   the implied censure.

A rite is nothing –
   neither wrong nor right;
a rite is a trifle
   in God's sight.

But they attacked our faith
   in the ways of the past,
in all we'd loved as children,
   and taken to heart.

In their holy garments,
   in their grand hats,
with a cold crucifix
   in their cold hands,

in thrall to a terror
   clutching their souls,
they drag us to jails
   and herd us to scaffolds.

We don't mind about doctrine,
   about books and their age;
we don't debate virtues
   of fetters and chains.

Our dispute is of freedom,
   and the right to breathe –
about our Lord's free will
   to bind as he please.

The healers of souls
   chastised our bodies;
while they schemed and plotted,
   we ran to the forests.

Despite their decrees,
   we hurled our words
out of the lion's mouth
   and into the world.

We called for vengeance
   against their sins;
along with the Lord,
   we sang poems and hymns.

The words of the Lord
   were claps of thunder.
The Church endures;
   it will never go under.

And I, unyielding,
   reading the Psalter,
was brought to the gates
   of the Andronikov Monastery.

I was young;[146]
   I endured every pain:
hunger, beatings,
   interrogations.

A winged angel
   shut the eyes of the guard,
brought me cabbage soup
   and a hunk of bread.

I crossed the threshold –
   and I walked free.
Embracing my exile,
   I walked to the East.

I held services
   by the Amur River,
where I barely survived
   the winds and blizzards.

They branded my cheeks
  with brands of frost;
by a mountain stream
  they tore out my nostrils.

But the path to the Lord
  goes from jail to jail;
the path to the Lord
  never changes.

And all too few,
  since Jesus's days,
have proved able to bear
  God's all-seeing gaze.

Nastasia, Nastasia,
  do not despair;[147]
true joy often wears
  a garment of tears.

Whatever temptations
  may beat in your heart,
whatever torments
  may rip you apart,

walk on in peace
  through a thousand troubles
and fear not the snake
  that bites at your ankles –

though not from Eden
  has this snake crawled;
it is an envoy of evil
  from Satan's world.

Here, birdsong
  is unknown;
here one learns patience
  and the wisdom of stone.

I have seen no colour
 except lingonberry
in fourteen years
 spent as a prisoner.

But this is not madness,
 nor a waking dream;
it is my soul's fortress,
 its will and freedom.

And now they are leading me
 far away and in fetters;
my yoke is easy,
 my burden grows lighter.

My track is swept clean
 dusted with silver;
I'm climbing to heaven
 on wings of fire.

Through cold and hunger,
 through grief and fear,
towards God, like a dove,
 I rise from the pyre.

O far-away Russia –
 I give you my vow
to return from the sky,
 forgiving no foe.

May I be reviled,
 and burned at the stake;
may my ashes be cast
 on the mountain wind.

There is no fate sweeter,
   no better end,
than to knock, as ash,
   at the human heart.[148]

(1955)
Robert Chandler

*

Our court nightingale,
   beak open wide,
can let out the loudest
   trills in the world.

The creature is stunned
   by what pours from his throat –
but it was he who spurred
   Derzhavin to write

that praise and flattery
   are by no means the same:
a slave can flatter
   but he can't do praise.

Robert Chandler

*

Alive not by bread alone,
   I dip a crust of sky,
in the morning chill,
   in the stream flowing by.

Robert Chandler

*

I felt in soul and body,
for the first time in years,
the silence after a blizzard,
the even light of the stars.

Should the magi wish to see
their kindness to the end,
they'd bring me sheets of paper.
A candle. Matches. And a pen.

(1954)
Robert Chandler

*

I went out into the clear air
and raised my eyes to the heavens
to understand our stars
and their January brilliance.

I found the key to the riddle;
I grasped the hieroglyphs' secret;
I carried into our own tongue
the work of the star-poet.

I recorded all this on a stump,
on frozen bark,
since I had no paper with me
in that January dark.

(1955)
Robert Chandler

*

I thought they would make us the heroes
of cantatas, posters, books of all kinds;
that hats would be flung in the air
and streets go out of their minds.

We had returned.
We were unbowed.
We had stayed true.

But the city had thoughts of its own;
it just muttered a word or two.

(1961)
Robert Chandler

*

Not to set fire to myself
or be burned like Avvakum,
I do what I can
to chase away thought.

I now orbit the earth
in low-level flight,
life's burdens and vanities
far out of sight.

(1981)
Robert Chandler

Arseny Tarkovsky (1907–89)

Arseny Alexandrovich Tarkovsky was born in what is now Ukraine. His father was of Polish origin; his mother Russian with some Polish blood. From 1925 to 1929 he studied in Moscow, on a course run by the All-Russian Union of Poets; there he met the poets Georgy Shengeli and Maria Petrovykh. In 1933, Shengeli invited several young poets – Tarkovsky and Petrovykh among them – to work as translators for the State Publishing House; all were finding it hard to publish their work and Shengeli's invitation proved a lifeline. For the next thirty years Tarkovsky supported himself by translating, with the help of cribs, from Armenian, Georgian and the languages of Central Asia. The poets who meant most to him[149] were the Arab Abul 'Ala al-Ma'arri; the Turkmen Magtymguly Pyragy and Mämmetweli Kemine; and the Georgian Vazha-Pshavela. In 1973 Tarkovsky wrote: 'The poetry of the East has deeply penetrated my life – it is my central theme.'[150]

Tarkovsky's first collection of his own work, *Before the Snow*, was published only in 1962; in a review Anna Akhmatova called it 'an unexpected and precious present to the contemporary reader'.[151] During the 1960s Tarkovsky ran a regular seminar for young poets; as someone who had known most of the great poets of the preceding generation and who had gone on writing 'for the drawer' throughout Stalin's rule, he was an important teacher. Larissa Miller, a poet who attended his seminar, refers to him as 'a keeper of the flame'; a few years later, it was he who first showed her poems by Khodasevich and Georgy Ivanov.[152]

Tarkovsky often addresses spiritual and aesthetic questions and has been called the last poet of the Silver Age; yet in 'How It Was' he locates his first inspiration in the joy of being given a flatbread made from rotten potato. According to his daughter Marina this poem is autobiographical. 'Field Hospital' is no less so. In 1943 Tarkovsky, who had repeatedly petitioned to be sent to the front, was seriously wounded; he underwent several gradual amputations to one leg.

Tarkovsky's poem about Paul Klee – one of several poems about painters – is all the more remarkable for being written as early as 1957, when information about modern art was still scarce in the Soviet Union. Boris Dralyuk writes, 'Tarkovsky reconciles the childlike side of Klee with his more apocalyptic vision: even after he sees death, his art remains childlike. Tarkovsky's Klee intimates the darkness he has glimpsed, but he does not infect us with it. The poem is appropriately childlike in tone; Tarkovsky is protecting us.'

Tarkovsky's daughter includes the civic-minded Nekrasov – along with Pushkin, Tyutchev and Lermontov – as one of the poets Tarkovsky saw as teachers. In 1972 Tarkovsky played an important role in helping Shalamov to join the Union of Soviet Writers.[153] Along with Joseph Brodsky, Tarkovsky was present at Akhmatova's funeral, and he spoke the last words over her grave. His poems, quoted at length, form an integral part of the films made by his son Andrey.

On the Bank

He was sitting by the river, among reeds
that peasants had been scything for their thatch.
And it was quiet there, and in his soul
it was quieter and stiller still.
He kicked off his boots and put
his feet into the water, and the water
began talking to him, not knowing
he didn't know its language.
He had thought that water is deaf-mute,
that the home of sleepy fish is without words,
that blue dragonflies hover over water
and catch mosquitoes or horseflies,
that you wash if you want to wash, and drink
if you want to drink, and that's all there is

to water. But in all truth
the water's language was a wonder,
a story of some kind about some thing,
some unchanging thing that seemed
like starlight, like the swift flash of mica,
like a divination of disaster.
And in it was something from childhood,
from not being used to counting life in years,
from what is nameless
and comes at night before you dream,
from the terrible, vegetable
sense of self
of your first season.

That's how the water was that day,
and its speech was without rhyme or reason.

(1954)
Robert Chandler

Paul Klee

Over the meadows, beyond the mountains,
    there once lived a painter called Klee,
and he sat on his own on a path
    with various bright-coloured crayons.

He drew rectangles and he drew hooks,
    an imp in a light-blue shirt,
Africa, stars, a child on a platform,
    wild beasts where Sky meets Earth.

He never intended his sketches
    to be like passport photos,
with people, horses, cities and lakes
    standing up straight like robots.

He wanted these lines and these spots
to converse with one another
as clearly as cicadas in summer,
but then one morning a feather

materialized as he sketched.
A wing, the crown of a head –
the Angel of Death. It was time
for Klee to part from his friends

and his Muse. He did. He died.
Can anything be more cruel?
Though had Paul Klee been any less wise,
his angel might have touched us all

and we too, along with the artist,
might have left the world behind
while that angel shook up our bones,
but – what help would that have been?

Me, I'd much rather walk through a gallery
than lie in some sad cemetery.
I like to loiter with friends by paintings –
yellow-blue wildlings, follies most serious.

(1957)
Robert Chandler

First Trysts

Every moment of our trysts
we celebrated as an epiphany,
alone in all the world. Bolder you were
and lighter than a bird's wing. Heady
as vertigo, you hurtled down, touching
only alternate stairs, then led me
through damp lilac into your domain
beyond the looking glass.

When night came, a grace was given
me, the altar gates were opened
and there, in the darkness, was shining,
and slowly bending down, a nakedness –
and waking, 'Be blessed!', I would say,
knowing my blessing was impertinent;
you were asleep, lilac was stretching
from the table to touch your eyelids
with the universe's deepening blue,
and, touched by such blue, your eyelids
were peaceful and your hand was warm.

Rivers ran pulsing in the crystal, mountains
were smoking, seas were glimmering,
and you were holding in your palm
the crystal sphere and sleeping on a throne
and – Just God! – you were mine.
You awoke, and you transformed
the human dictionary of every day
and speech was filled, was overflowing
with resonant power, and the word *thou*
revealed its new meaning: *King*.

Nothing in the world but suffered change,
even simple things – a washbasin, a jug,
when water stood between us, layered,
steadfast, as if on guard.

We were led we knew not whither.
Like mirages, cities built by miracle
made way for us. Mint laid itself
beneath our feet, and birds were going
our way, and fish swimming upstream
and the sky unfolded before our eyes . . .

While fate followed in our steps,
a madman with a razor in his hand.

(1962)
Robert Chandler

Field Hospital

They turned the table to the light. I lay
upside down, like meat slapped onto a scale;
my soul swayed, dangling on a string,
I saw myself from the side:
balanced without makeweights,
against a fat mass from the market.
This
was in the middle of a snow shield,
chipped along its western edge,
surrounded by icy swamps,
by trees on broken legs,
and railroad halts with their skulls
cracked open, looking black
beneath their snowy caps, some double,
and some triple.

Time stopped that day,
clocks didn't run – the souls of trains
no longer flew along the mounds,
lightless, on grizzled fins of steam.
No gatherings of crows,
no blizzards, no thaws inside that limbo
where I lay naked in disgrace,
in my own blood, outside the pull
of future's gravity.

But then it shifted, circling on its axis –
the shield of blinding snow.
A wedge of seven airplanes

turned low above me. And the gauze,
like tree bark, stiffened on my body,
while someone else's blood now ran
into my veins out of a flask, and I
breathed like a fish tossed on the sand,
gulping the hard, earthy, mica-like,
cold, and blessed air.

My lips were chapped, and then,
they fed me with a spoon, and then,
I couldn't recall my name,
while King David's lexicon
awoke upon my tongue.

Then
snow melted away, and early spring
stood on her toes and wrapped
the trees with her green kerchief.

(1964)

Boris Dralyuk and Irina Mashinski

How It Was

Nowhere anything for eating,
all of Russia fading, freezing,
selling gramophones and blankets,
hats and chairs and anything
in exchange for wheat and millet
in the year nineteen-nineteen.

Elder brother killed already,
and my dad already blind,
all our furniture long bartered,
home was like an empty tomb,
yet we lived, we still had water,
bread we baked from angry nettles.

Màma was all hunched and aged,
all grey-haired though only forty,
nothing but a beggar's rags
clinging to her skinny body.
When she slept, I kept on checking:
was she breathing, was she not?

Guests were few and far between
in the year nineteen-nineteen.
Sick at heart, our poor old neighbours,
just like little birds in cages,
tiny birds on withered perches,
lived like we did, lived in hell.

Then one of these poor old neighbours
brought a gift – rotten potato.
'Think what riches,' she began,
'once belonged even to beggars!
See how Russia's being chastised
for Rasputin and his doings!'

Evening came. 'Eat!' said Màma,
holding out a splendid flatbread.
And the Muse dressed all in rose,
came to me all of a sudden,
hoping she could make me sleepless,
hoping I'd be hers for ever.

So I wrote my primal poem,
sang how Màma on a Sunday
baked a flatbread from potato.
So I had my first encounter
with poetic inspiration
in the year nineteen nineteen.

(1977)

Robert Chandler

Maria Petrovykh (1908–79)

Maria Sergeyevna Petrovykh was born near Yaroslavl, where her father worked as an engineer. She moved to Moscow in 1925. As a student on a course newly instigated by the All-Russian Union of Poets, she met the poets Georgy Shengeli and Arseny Tarkovsky.

Petrovykh married soon after moving to Moscow, but the marriage did not last. She married again in 1936 and gave birth to a daughter the following year, but her husband was arrested and sent to a labour camp. He died in 1942. Two of her uncles, both priests, also died during the Great Terror: her maternal uncle died in prison; her paternal uncle was shot.

Petrovykh was known to most readers only as a translator, for the main part from Armenian and Polish. She barely published her own work, but it includes some remarkable love lyrics. Akhmatova, Pasternak and Tarkovsky all admired her work and Osip Mandelstam was for a while in love with her. Tarkovsky wrote the preface to *A Distant Tree* (1968), the only collection published during her life. From 1959 to 1964, along with David Samoilov, Petrovykh ran a seminar for young translators.

from *Spell*

I won't give you up to death.
I will stand before her.
With my heart
I will shield
your heart.
If you see me
pale,

it is not from pain;
it is from joy
that you are invulnerable.[154]

(1933)
Robert Chandler

*

Love me. I am pitch black,
sinful, blind, confused.
But if not you, who else
is going to love me? Face
to face, and fate to fate.
See how stars shine bright
in the dark sky. Love me
simply, simply, as day
loves night and night loves day.
You have no choice. I am
pure night, and you – pure light.[155]

(1942)
Robert Chandler

*

March saw winter gain in strength –
bitter cold and unrelenting storms.
In reckless fury, blinding spite,
the wind blew only from the north.

No hint of spring. Gripped by inertia,
the heart slips all too close to places
of no return: no self, no words,
mere apathy and voicelessness.

Who can bring back our sight, our hearing?
Who can retrace the way to hearth
and home now that all trace of home
is gone, wiped from the earth?[156]

(1955)
Robert Chandler and Irina Mashinski

The Line of the Horizon

It's just how it is, it's the way of the ages;
years pass away, and friends pass away
and you suddenly realize the world is changing
and the fire of your heart is fading away.

Once the horizon was sharp as a knife,
a clear frontier between different states,
but now low mist hangs over the earth –
and this gentle cloud is the mercy of fate.

Age, I suppose, with its losses and fears,
age that silently saps our strength,
has blurred with the mist of unspilt tears
that clear divide between life and death.

So many you loved are no longer with you,
yet you chat to them as you always did.
You forget they're no longer among the living;
that clear frontier is now shrouded in mist.

The same sort of woodland, same sort of field –
you probably won't even notice the day
you chance to wander across the border,
chatting to someone long passed away.

(1957)
Robert Chandler

*

I'm nothing to you, I mean zero.
I know, there's nothing more to say.
And yet I love you still more dearly,
ecstatically and without mercy,
and like a drunk, I stumble, reel,
and loiter in a lightless alley,
insisting that I love you still –
no mercy, and ecstatically.

(1959)
Boris Dralyuk

*

Words lying empty, without breathing –
that don't know why they exist at all.
Words with no goal, words with no meaning,
that shelter no one from the cold
and haven't fed a single soul.
Words of impotence – of the weak!
Words that don't dare, too shy to speak.
They give no heat, they shed no light,
but, with an orphan's grief, go mute,
not knowing they are mutilated.

(1970s)
Boris Dralyuk

Olga Berggolts (1910–75)

Olga Fyodorovna Berggolts was born in St Petersburg; her half-Latvian father was a surgeon. Between 1925 and 1935 she published poems, stories, journalism and children's literature. She then suffered a number of tragedies: the deaths of both her daughters and the arrest and execution of her ex-husband, the poet Boris Kornilov (1907–38). In December 1938 she too was imprisoned. She was released after seven months, but only after suffering a miscarriage from being beaten during interrogations.

Officially exonerated in 1939, she was allowed to join the Communist Party in 1940. She remained in Leningrad throughout the Nazi blockade, although she could (like Akhmatova, Shostakovich and many others) have been evacuated to Central Asia. Her second husband died in 1942. She spoke almost daily on Leningrad radio, reading both news items and her own poems. These broadcasts were important to those trapped in the city, and she became known as the 'Voice of the Blockade'. According to Yakov Druskin, a Leningrad poet and translator, it was her straightforwardness, above all, that won people's hearts: 'It was as if the woman from next door had happened to get into the Smolny [the Party headquarters], hear the latest news and was now sharing it not with the entire city but with the other people in her own apartment.'[157] The best of her poems from this time are equally straightforward. In one she tells how she was walking home one evening, clutching her minuscule bread ration: a woman begs her to swap the bread for a dress, saying she needs to bury her dead child and that the carpenter will only agree to make her a coffin in exchange for bread. Berggolts refuses but invites the woman back home; there she shares the bread with her, saying, 'Now – eat a piece. Forgive me! And don't think I begrudge bread to the living!' In another poem she writes of the tin swallow she wore on her lapel, a sign that she was waiting for a letter: 'we understood that only a plane, / only a bird, could reach Leningrad / from the Motherland we loved.' And her well-known 'February Diary', written after the death of her second husband, begins:

It was a day like any other.
A woman-friend of mine called round.
Without a tear she told me she'd
just buried her one friend.
We sat in silence till the morning.
What words were there to say to her?
I'm a Leningrad widow too.

Berggolts remains best known for her wartime poetry and prose – and, above all, for the poem she was asked to write for the Memorial Wall of the Piskaryovskoye Cemetery in Leningrad, where most of the 500,000 civilian victims of the Blockade are buried. The poem's last words, 'No one is forgotten, nothing is forgotten', have been repeated countless times in memorial speeches and inscriptions throughout the Soviet Union – and in post-Soviet Russia. Much of Berggolts's work, however, was published only long after she wrote it. A few of her prison poems were, surprisingly, included in her collection *The Knot* (1965). Other poems and diary extracts were first published only in 1990; more extracts were published in 2010.

Many of Berggolts's poems are hackneyed, but the best show a piercing self-awareness. She was one of the few writers to stay in contact with Akhmatova after the official attacks on her in August 1946, but she evidently criticized herself for not being still more courageous. Heavily alcoholic in her last years, she died in 1975 of cirrhosis of the liver. Though her death was little reported, thousands attended her funeral. Like the funerals of Pasternak and Akhmatova – though on a smaller scale – this was a show of true feeling, a spontaneous demonstration the authorities were unable to stifle.

from *Ordeal*

[. . .] And once again
you will have the strength
to see and recognize
how all you have ever loved
will begin to torment you.
And at once, like a werewolf,
a friend will appear
before you and slander you,
and another will push you away.
And the temptations will start:
'Renounce! Disavow! Forswear!'
And your soul will writhe
in the grip of anguish and fear.
And you will have the strength,
once again, to repeat one thing:
'I forswear nothing – nothing –
of all I have lived my life by.'
And once again, remembering
these days, you will have the strength
to cry out to all you have loved:
'Come back! Come back to me!'

(January 1939, Cell 33)
Robert Chandler

*

You took me –
I was sullen, without affection,
with only black thoughts
and convict ravings
and a widow's unhealed anguish
and a past love that wasn't past.

You took me as a wife –
not for joy's sake,
not of your own accord
but out of love.

(1942)
Robert Chandler

*

We pronounced
the simplest, poorest words
as if they had never been said.
We were saying
sun, *light*, *grass*
as people pronounce
life, *love*, *strength*.

Remember how we cleared
that eternal, accursed glacier
from the city streets – and an old man
stamped his foot against the pavement,
shouting, 'Asphalt, friends, asphalt!'

As if he were a sailor long ago,
calling out, 'Land, land!'

(1945)
Robert Chandler

*

Oh don't look back
at that ice,
at that dark;
there, waiting greedily
for you is a look
that will demand an answer.

I looked back today. And suddenly,
I saw him – alive and with living eyes,
looking at me out of the ice,
my one and only, for all time.

I hadn't known it was like that;
I'd thought I lived and breathed another.
But Oh, my joy, my dream, my death,
I only live beneath your gaze.

I have been faithful to *him* alone;
in that alone I have done right:
to all the living, I'm *his* wife;
to you and me – your widow.

(1947)
Robert Chandler

*

I spent all day at the meeting,
  either lying or voting.
I'm surprised I didn't go grey
  or die of shame.
I wandered about the streets,
  where I could be myself again.

I had a smoke with a yardman –
  then a drink in a cheap kiosk
along with two amputees,
  who had fought at Krasny Bor.
Their complaints were something else –
  their conversation was real.
One memory led to another,
  as we stirred the ash in our hearts:
penal battalions sent on reconnaissance
  straight across minefields.
One man would return bemedalled;
  others would lie down for ever,
their trumped-up sins now redeemed
  with daredevil blood.
And I said in a drunken rage,
  barely able to string thoughts together,
'Oh how I hate our righteous ones,
  Oh how I love our sinners!'

(1948–9)

Robert Chandler

Semyon Lipkin (1911–2003)

Born in Odessa, Semyon Israilievich Lipkin moved to Moscow in 1929. Unable from 1934 to publish his own work, he turned to translating, mainly from Persian and the Turkic languages of Central Asia. His first collection of his own poetry appeared only in 1967. He also wrote a novel about Stalin's deportation of the Chechens, and a memoir of Vasily Grossman. It was Lipkin who initiated the process that led to the text of Grossman's *Life and Fate* being smuggled out to the West.

By the Sea

The waves crashed under the flicker of the lighthouse
and I, in my ignorance, heard a monotone.
Years later the sea speaks to me and I begin to understand
there are birds and laundresses, sprites and sorcerers,
laments and curses, moans and profanity, white horses
and half breeds who rear up unexpectedly.
There are waves who are salesgirls with buxom hips
who sell foam from the counter, they tremble fluent or airy.
Nature can't be indifferent, she always mimics us
like a loan, a translation; we're the blueprint, she's the copy.
Once upon a time the pebble was different
and so the wave was different.

(1965)
Yvonne Green

*

He who gave the wind its weight,
and gave measure to the water,
pointed lightning on its path,
and showed rain what rules to follow –
he once told me with quiet joy:
'No one's ever going to kill you:
How can dust be broken down?
Who has power to ruin beggars?'

(1981)

Robert Chandler

Lev Ozerov, pseudonym of Lev Adolfovich Goldberg (1914–96)

Born in Kiev, Lev Ozerov studied in Moscow, then worked as a front-line journalist after the German invasion. After the liberation of Kiev in 1943 Ilya Ehrenburg commissioned him to write an article for *The Black Book* (a planned documentary account of the Shoah on Soviet soil)[158] about the massacre at Babi Yar, a ravine just outside the city. In the course of six months the Nazis shot a hundred thousand people, nearly all of them Jews. Ozerov also wrote a long poem about Babi Yar, published in early 1946.[159] Here, though, we include a later, terser poem that fuses images of the Shoah, the war and the Gulag.

From 1943 Ozerov taught in the Translation Faculty at the Gorky Literary Institute, translating poetry from Yiddish, Hebrew and Ukrainian (languages he knew well), Lithuanian (which he could read) and other languages of the Soviet Union with the help of a crib. He also wrote many books of literary criticism and did much to enable the publication of writers who had suffered or perished under Stalin. He was the first editor to publish Zabolotsky (his translation of *The Lay of Igor's Campaign*) on his return from the Gulag in 1946.

Ozerov has yet to win due recognition. His finest book, *Portraits without Frames*, published after his death, comprises fifty accounts, told in a variety of tones and with deceptive simplicity, of meetings with important figures, many – though not all – from the literary world. One poem tells how Yevgenia Taratuta, an editor of children's literature, kept her sanity during brutal interrogations by reciting Pushkin and Mayakovsky to herself. A second describes Ozerov's first meeting with Zabolotsky on his return from the Gulag. The poem ends with Zabolotsky's daughter telling Ozerov, decades afterwards, how later that day her father had said to her: 'I had thought I was forgotten, but people still seem to remember me.' Ozerov writes with compassion not only about such great and courageous writers as Shalamov but also about such writers as Fadeyev, a Soviet literary boss who shot himself when Stalin's crimes, and his own complicity, began to be exposed under Khrushchev.

Among the subjects of other 'portraits' are Babel, Platonov, Shostakovich, Tatlin, Kovpak (a Ukrainian partisan leader) and the ballet dancer Galina Ulanova. One poem tells of Slutsky's generosity in making his room available to couples who had nowhere to sleep together; one evening he returns home to find a note: 'Boris, / you are a great humanist, / and the heavenly powers / will reward you. The sins of others, / sins that are not yours, / will bring you blessings.'

* [160]

An oar is lying now on the sand.
It tells me more of space and motion
than all the vast and violent ocean
that brought it to dry land.

(1940 or earlier)
Robert Chandler

*

The dead are speaking. Without full stops.
Or commas. And almost without words.
From camps. From isolation cells.
From buildings as they blaze.
The dead are speaking. A letter. A will.
Diaries. Exercise books from school.
On rough pages of uneven brick –
the cursive of a hurrying hand.

With slivers of tin on a bed-board,
with shards of glass on a wall
or a thin stream of blood on a barrack floor,
life signed off as best it could.

(1962)
Robert Chandler

*

The world's too big; it can't be scanned in verse.
We two. And silence. And the universe.
Two can be company enough. And silence –
a silence we can share is more than silence.

(1990s)
Robert Chandler

Pasternak

Khrushchev's sevenfold retinue
were falling over themselves,
doing all they could
to disgrace the man.
But their idea of disgrace
brought him glory.

He refused to leave Russia.
So they demanded
he leave Moscow
during Macmillan's visit
in 1959.
It's not that Pasternak took fright
or lost his head,
tormented as he was.
I saw him

in those troubled days.
No. Like a forest or a garden
before a storm,
he was prepared to take the hit
not out of meekness,
but out of faith
in life,
which he had, after all, called his sister.
Saying farewell, he looked at me
in such a way, and smiled so brightly,
that I flinched.
It scared me.
Pasternak left for Tbilisi.
With his wife.
Ten days of February,
six of March.

In Georgia, he warmed up
among his old, faithful friends –
in Tabidze's home,
now a museum.
The worries, grief and bitterness
of the preceding days and weeks –
the racket, scandals, quarrels –
wore off. At the sight of Tbilisi
and its surroundings,
they fell away,
like turbid mountain torrents.
Tbilisi brought him back to younger days.
Through distant smoke, through dove-grey haze
he saw the light of heaven,
the colour blue,
which he had always loved.
Would he have the chance
to spend time here
at least once again?
On the eve of his departure,

he set off early
to say farewell to Svetitskhoveli.
He removed his cap and entered the cathedral.
He felt the breath of the eleventh century.
Can anyone not love this place,
the grandeur of this space,
stretching eastward,
inspiring thoughts of eternity,
of the eternal life of the soul?
This place doesn't make you feel small –
it brings you peace.
Pasternak needed this,
like air,
in a world where he was suffocating.

These four free-standing pillars,
holding the dome up like the sky!
These reliefs, these carvings!
Stone, coolness, calm.
He stepped out, his soul uplifted.
He looked at the cathedral, then the sky –
the sky, then the cathedral.
Saying farewell
proved difficult.
But he was glad that he'd spent time here.
When he turned his attention to the earth,
he noticed people
looking closely at him.
Let them look – that's their business.
But one of them, loud-voiced and young,
approached and asked,
'You're Pasternak, aren't you?'
'No, no, I'm not Pasternak,'
he answered, horrified,
and took off in a hurry –
yes, almost at a run,
like Pushkin's Eugene

from the Bronze Horseman.
'You Pasternak?'
someone was shouting after him.
'No, no, you're wrong,'
he answered, without looking back.

(1990s)
Boris Dralyuk

Shmuel Halkin[161]

He was in Maleyevka[162]
when they came for him.
They led the sick man to the car.
He managed to hand his stick to Prishvin,
who was standing in the snow with his dog,
looking bewildered:
'Where are you going, Samuil Zalmanovich?'
'Goodbye!' said Halkin.
He thought this was the end for him,
but it wasn't . . .
In the labour camp, deep in a mine,
he said to the poet Sergey Spassky,[163]
'Would you like me to stay alive?
Then read me every day
one stanza,
even just one line
that I don't know.
It doesn't need to be your own –
other people's will do.'

There was no paper,
but Halkin was writing.
Poems piled up.
A terrible burden.
More dangerous, perhaps, than gunpowder.

He wrote them down
on the paper of memory
and day by day
his memory grew heavier.
Poems with sharp elbows
were elbowing one another
out of the way.
And when he'd filled
his last scrap of memory,
he met a prisoner
who knew Yiddish.
A great rarity.
A real find.
This prisoner
was a sheaf of paper,
paper for new lines.
When Halkin returned home,
worn out by the camps,
he wrote down his poems
and his memory emptied
and new poems
came flooding in.

He returned home
handsome and heavy-hearted,
eyes filled with a sorrow
that lay beyond the limits of sanity,
yet he had not forgotten
youth and a thirst for life.
When he read,
he would begin quietly,
as if to the beat of his heart.
He would catch fire quickly.
He would flare up wildly.
He would stand up on tiptoe
and then stand on the table
and then stand on the windowsill.

Growing weak again, he would
call out, 'Maria! Ma – !'
And his wife would come running.
Along with their son and daughter,
they would take him down
from the windowsill
and put him to bed, half-dead.
He was still living.
He was still writing.

And then he died.
On the day of his funeral
a bearded man in a wadded jacket
came up to me in the cemetery
and asked, 'Are you a relative?
Or do you know
any relatives of the deceased
or, maybe, any close friends?'
'I'm not a relative.
I'm a friend. A translator.
What can I do for you?'
'I've brought with me
a number of poems
dictated to me by Halkin.
I learned them by heart.
I'm his manuscript.'
This man's jacket
was the uniform of a *zek*.[164]
I introduced this man
to Halkin's wife and children.
We sat at the table for a long time
and talked about Halkin.
And he dictated many lines –
the cycle *Mayn Oytser*,
'My Treasure' –
his posthumous collection of poems.
This *zek* read us an unwritten book
and Halkin came to life in his own poems,

line by line and stanza by stanza,
in poems honed by grief
to a diamond glitter
and sharpness.

(1990)
Robert Chandler

Shalamov

Forward and to one side,
like a knight on a chessboard,
with a knapsack on his back,
Varlam Shalamov plods on,
battered by Kolymà.
Lonely, almost sullen,
he has the air of a sad
Russian peasant or scholar or writer
whom life has stung hard,
whom life has pressed down on
but not yet utterly crushed.
Deep in his soul
there is still strength,
still the will
to fight fate.
His wrinkled face is a hieroglyph
of all he has lived through
and keeps quiet about.
It's a cold day.
We go into a café.
Not much to eat,
but it's warm.
'Varlam Tikhonovich,
read me some new poems.'
He turns one ear towards me.
Without a word he takes off
his rough, wind-battered knapsack.

Inside it a wooden spoon
hobnobs with crusts of bread,
notebooks
and documents –
death, after all,
can creep up on you
any moment.
He reads slowly,
separating each word:
each word
ready to drop into the abyss.
Getting the words
out is easier
with pauses for breath.
'Thank you,' I say.
'No, it's for *me*
to thank *you*. Who
nowadays asks anyone
to read poems?' he says
hoarsely, with feeling.
'I've got an awful lot
of them.
How do I choose?'
He reads at random
jumping about, whatever
he happens on.
Reading aloud,
he warms up.
'All right. Enough of that.'
Someone brings coffee,
sausages, bread.
Steam rises from the cup.
Steam rises from the plate:
the renowned fragrance
of a Moscow
people's café.
Shalamov tries not to eat
too quickly,

not to show
that he's very hungry.
I don't ask about Kolymà
and he doesn't mention it:
as if it hadn't happened.
As he eats the bread,
he holds one hand
just below his chin.
Crumbs fall
into his palm.
Shalamov eats them greedily,
with particular relish.
His long experience
of malnutrition
is apparent.
This mouth accustomed to hunger
opens slowly, mistrustfully,
almost unwillingly, as if in shame.
Shalamov eats in silence,
with tried and tested
deliberateness,
sensibly, with pauses,
and to me he seems
not to be thinking
about food.
What is Shalamov
thinking about?
How can I ever know?
He puts his manuscript
back in his knapsack.
Out we both go
into the winter outside.
'It's a cold day,' I say.
'What do you mean?' he says.
'It's warm.'

Robert Chandler

Konstantin Simonov (1915–79)

Konstantin Mikhailovich Simonov was born in Petrograd, the son of a tsarist officer and a princess from Russia's oldest royal dynasty. His father left Russia in 1917 and died in Poland in 1921.

From 1931 to 1935 Simonov worked in a factory, and in 1936 he published his first poems. During the Second World War he was a correspondent for *Red Star*, the army newspaper; he also wrote plays, a novel about Stalingrad and two books of poems. 'Wait for Me', addressed to the actress he later married, was the best known poem of the time. In the words of one of his editors, 'Soldiers cut it out of the paper, copied it out as they sat in the trenches, learned it by heart and sent it back in letters to wives and girlfriends; it was found in the breast pockets of the killed and wounded.'[165] His novel *The Living and the Dead* (1959) was the first relatively honest description of the catastrophic retreats of 1941 to be published in the Soviet Union.

An important bureaucrat and a competent writer who at least sometimes tried to be honest, Simonov was Secretary of the Union of Soviet Writers from 1946 until 1959, and from 1967 until 1979. Here we include two poems that show how, as a young man, he was endowed with a true lyric gift.

Tears Cost Her Nothing Anyway

Just let her cry and have her say;
tears cost her nothing anyway.
Lermontov, 'Testament'

Born beautiful, I hear them say,
you'll have good fortune all the way.

Poor child, misfortune, suffering, praying,
your death itself will be in vain,
you'll not defeat the foolish saying,
the cunning comfort of the plain.
They'll say you snatch by beauty's art
all that is yours by warmth of heart.

Be tender, faithful, what you will,
but still the same old tale is told,
the beautiful are heartless still,
the fortunate are always cold.
They'll hear what love is poured on you
– that only shows what looks can do!

Perhaps you'll marry out of guile,
still, still to beauty love's denied,
they'll credit you with all that's vile,
the lust and greed that they must hide.
With pride your husband you adore?
– Because you need him, nothing more!

Your husband dies: his faults are spared,
but still on you their verdict's damning.
Forget him – then you never cared,
or don't forget – and then you're shamming.
And let her cry, you'll hear them say,
tears cost her nothing anyway!

Yet quiet pain wins no belief
nor hidden tears. They do not care
that when a child, unchildish grief
befell you in the market-square.
You suffered wounds too deep to heal?
The beautiful can scarcely feel!

I was not angry when of late
  you scorned me too with unbelief,
the beautiful and fortunate
  can only trust in loss and grief.
Oh, if you'd known all this ahead
your beauty would have withered dead.

You'll reach perhaps felicity,
  or pine from gnawing pain within,
or live, uncomforted by me,
  but the unholy saw will win: –
Born beautiful, I hear them cry,
you're fortunate until you die!

(1941)
Frances Cornford

Wait for Me

to Valentina Serova

Wait for me, and I'll come back!
Wait with all you've got!
Wait, when dreary yellow rains
tell you, you should not.
Wait when snow is falling fast,
wait when summer's hot,
wait when yesterdays are past,
others are forgot.
Wait, when from that far-off place,
letters don't arrive.
Wait, when those with whom you wait
doubt if I'm alive.

Wait for me, and I'll come back!
Wait in patience yet
when they tell you off by heart
that you should forget.

Even when my dearest ones
say that I am lost,
even when my friends give up,
sit and count the cost,
drink a glass of bitter wine
to the fallen friend –
Wait! And do not drink with them!
wait until the end!

Wait for me and I'll come back,
dodging every fate!
'What a bit of luck!' they'll say,
those that would not wait.
They will never understand
how amidst the strife,
by your waiting for me, dear,
you had saved my life.
Only you and I will know
how you got me through.
Simply – you knew how to wait –
no one else but you.

(1941)
Mike Munford

Alexander Galich, pseudonym of Ginzburg Alexander Arkadievich (1918–77)

As a young man, Alexander Galich was a successful playwright and screenwriter. A trusted member of the Soviet elite, he was allowed to travel to Paris to work on Franco-Soviet film collaborations. In the late 1950s, however, he began writing songs and singing them to his own guitar accompaniment, creating the new genre of 'bard song'. Most of his songs – like those of his fellow singer-songwriter Vladimir Vysotsky – treated taboo themes: from the Gulag and the Shoah to the contempt often shown by Soviet wartime commanders for the lives of their own soldiers. Disseminated through bootleg recordings, Galich's songs quickly became popular.

Galich's ever-sharper criticisms of the regime, along with publication of his songs in the West, led to his expulsion from the Union of Soviet Writers in 1971, and then from the Cinematographers' Union. In 1972 – like a surprising number of Soviet Jews in the 1960s and 1970s – he was baptized into the Orthodox Church; information about Judaism was scarce, and some Jews saw baptism as the only available way to reconnect with a spiritual tradition.[166] Though brought up with little knowledge of Judaism, Galich had always been eager to assert his Jewish identity. In his memoir *Dress Rehearsal* he tells how, in the summer of 1952, at a time of growing State-sponsored anti-Semitism, he tried to attend a meeting of the Yiddish section of the Moscow branch of the Union of Soviet Writers. The chairman, the poet Perets Markish, told Galich (who did not know Yiddish) that he was an outsider and that he should leave. Bewildered and humiliated, Galich obeyed. Two weeks later this whole section of the Union was arrested; Galich realized that Markish had probably saved his life.[167]

Anti-Semitism is one of Galich's main themes. One song includes the lines:

Ivanov writes on our form that he's Russian –
the real thing, but don't make any bets.
See, he's born in that Jew-town of Bobruisk,
and his grandmother's last name was Kats.
So you'll have to make a note of that grandma
(keep Ivanov himself in the dark),
but put his form into a separate file,
and mark it off with a separate mark.[168]

In 1974 Galich was expelled from the Soviet Union. He lived in Norway, then Munich, then Paris. On 15 December 1977, his wife found him electrocuted; he had fallen onto a Grundig antenna he was plugging into a socket. A French court concluded that his death was an accident, but there is ground for doubt. His concerts, his new poems and his work for Radio Liberty had infuriated the Soviet authorities; his relatives had been receiving anonymous threats and his wife died soon afterwards, also in strange circumstances.

'I remember 15 December 1977, the day of his death, very well,' Irina Mashinski writes. 'I was in my second year at university. A close friend called to tell me the news and invite me to his parents' apartment where there would be a gathering that night in memory of Galich. My friend's physicist parents were close to dissident circles and they had known Galich personally. There was a huge pile of bulky winter coats by the door and the room was crowded, but we were all very quiet. This was the first time I realized how many people Galich was important to, how many people there were in the world who thought and felt the same way as I did.'

As well as Galich's first song, 'Lenochka', which he composed on the Red Arrow (the night train between Moscow and Leningrad) and which he has described as 'the beginning of his life's path', we include a song about the Soviet leaders and a song about survivors of the Gulag. Galich played an important role in creating the alternative, anti-establishment myth of Soviet culture; many of his songs are homages to poets who suffered, or were executed, during the Stalin regime. The best known of these is dedicated to Boris Pasternak; Galich castigates himself and his fellow intellectuals for priding themselves on the fact that Pasternak died in his own bed, not through suicide like Tsvetaeva or in the Gulag like Mandelstam. Two lines from this song quickly became almost proverbial in dissident circles:

> We shall remember by name
> all those who raised a hand.

Galich has in mind the Union of Soviet Writers meeting on 31 October 1958 that voted for Pasternak to be expelled. Among the other writers to whom Galich dedicated songs are Akhmatova, Mandelstam and Kharms.

Lenochka

One April night our Lenochka
was standing at her post,
that chestnut-haired young beauty
was standing at her post.
So stunning and sublime she was –
one look and you were toast!
At city's exit Lenochka
was standing at her post!

And that's the story for you,
she was standing at her post.

If you become a cop, you see,
you have to swear all day,
don't matter if you're shy or not,
you have to swear all day.
Her girlfriends sniffed the lilacs,
went into town to play,
but she patrolled the highways
so she had to swear all day!

> And that's the story for you,
> she had to swear all day!

So Lenochka was standing there,
a sergeant on patrol,
a girl out of Ostankino
a sergeant on patrol.
To each her very own, you see,
while others had a ball,
our Lenochka was standing there,
a sergeant on patrol.

> And that's the story for you,
> a sergeant on patrol!

When suddenly she noticed
a cavalcade of lights!
From Moscow's central airport
a cavalcade of lights!
The sirens were all blaring,
security's airtight!
Some foreigners were coming:
a cavalcade of lights!

> And that's the story for you,
> a cavalcade of lights!

So Lenochka just waved them through,
her hand, it didn't shake!
Her knees went kind of wobbly,
but her hand, it didn't shake!
These weren't local taxis, see,
but cars of foreign make!
And Lenochka just waved them through,
her hand, it didn't shake!

> Oompah-oompah-oompah,
> her hand, it didn't shake.

But suddenly the lead car
slowed down along its route,
though everything was fine, you see,
it slowed down on its route.
The KGB surrounded it
like something was afoot,
but right beside our Lenochka
it slowed down on its route.

And that's the story for you,
it slowed down on its route!

In that car sat a gorgeous
young Ethiopian stud.
He stared at our Lenochka
that Ethiopian stud,
and rising from his leather seat
(he would not miss, by God!)
he tossed her a chrysanthemum,
that Ethiopian stud!

Oompah-oompah-oompah,
that Ethiopian stud!

A messenger arrived at dawn from
CC CPSU,[169]
he zoomed in on a fancy bike from
CC CPSU.
He hurried right to Lenochka,
he was giving her the cue:
'They're calling L. Potapova to
CC CPSU!'

Right there on the Old Plaza
was that Ethiopian guy,
he was getting all the honours,
that Ethiopian guy.
He thanked them very regally

and that is not a lie,
'cause it turned out he's a royal,
that Ethiopian guy!

His retinue drank vodka,
but he stared at the door,
he held on to his souvenirs
and he stared at the door.
They hailed the regal ally,
but he grunted like a boar,
just then the music sounded
and they opened up the door . . .

All sheathed in tulle and velvet,
she walked into the hall.
Left everybody speechless
when she walked into the hall.
So that the royal stud himself,
Ahmed Ali and all,
cried out, 'I must be dreaming!'
when she walked into the hall.

Oompah-oompah-oompah,
when she walked into the hall!

And afterwards our Lenochka
around the world was known,
a girl out of Ostankino
around the world was known.
When Prince Ali did his daddy in,
and got the royal throne,
the Sheik's wife L. Potapova
around the world was known!

(1961)

Maria Bloshteyn

Behind Seven Fences

We rode out into the country,
far away from dirt and grime,
there we saw the fenced-in houses,
where our leaders spend their time!

There the grass is greener
and the air is clear!
There they've got mint candies,
truffles and éclairs!

Behind seven fences,
under seven seals,
there they crunch mint candies,
after fancy meals!

They've got flora, they've got fauna,
they've got caviar and drinks,
but if you as much as peek in,
you'll be picked up by their finks.

Guards patrol the fences
in civilian duds,
while Stalin's loyal comrades
chew their shish kebabs.

Behind seven fences,
locked by seven locks,
Stalin's favourite comrades
chew their shish kebabs!

And when it's fun they're after,
as Stalin's high command,
they get to screen the movies
that they themselves have banned.

And they all breathe heavily,
as they stare up at the screen:
'cause they like the raunchy blonde
that looks just like Marilyn.

Behind seven fences,
under seven seals,
they sure like the raunchy blonde
that looks just like Marilyn!

We walked about awhile
round the fences in the rain,
then we sighed at one another
and took the homebound train.

And as we rode the train back
we heard a radio talk
on democratic freedoms
enjoyed by Soviet folk.

But behind seven fences,
locked by seven locks,
they were too busy feasting
to hear that radio talk!

(1961)

Maria Bloshteyn

Clouds

See the clouds float by, clouds float by,
they float slowly by like on film,
while I eat chicken here, Georgian-style,
I downed my brandy, all five hundred ml.

See the clouds float to Abakan,
they don't rush, they float on and on,
they're warm, I bet, way up there,
while I'm frozen for eons to come.

Horseshoe-like I froze into the road,
into ice that I hacked with my axe,
not for nothing I spent twenty years
breaking my back in those camps.

To this day I see the snows mound,
to this day I hear the guards yell,
so now fetch me more of that brandy,
and a pineapple or something as well.

See the clouds float by, clouds float by,
to Kolymà, that old cherished land.
They don't need any kind of an amnesty,
or a lawyer to give them a hand!

As for me, no complaints, life is good,
twenty years, like small change, are all spent,
I drink brandy here like some lord,
even false teeth I've got, a full set!

Clouds float east toward the dawn,
they don't have a care in the world!
But my pension comes on the fourth
and again on the twenty-third.

And on those days, just like me,
half the country sits drunk in these dives
and like our memory to those lands
clouds float by, clouds float by.

(1962)

Maria Bloshteyn

Boris Slutsky (1919–86)

Boris Abramovich Slutsky spent his childhood and youth in Kharkov, in what is now Ukraine; his parents were Jewish, his father a manual worker. From 1937 he studied at the Moscow Institute of Law; from 1938 he was also studying at the Gorky Literary Institute. During the war he served as a political instructor, joining the Communist Party in 1943. He was awarded several decorations and was wounded, suffering severe concussion. Two trepanations in the late 1940s left him with unrelenting headaches and severe insomnia.

After being demobilized in 1946 Slutsky lived on a small disability pension, and on what he earned from radio work and as an editor and translator; the anti-Jewish campaigns of the time made it impossible for him to find full-time employment. He wrote poems criticizing Stalin as early as 1953 and was an important figure in the literary revival after Stalin's death. After publishing his first collection of poems in 1957 he managed to bring out another every two or three years. Altogether he wrote more than two thousand poems; a few of the most controversial circulated in samizdat, but more than half of his work became known only long after his death.

Slutsky grew up in a household where both Russian and Yiddish were spoken, and in 1963 he edited the anthology *Poets of Israel*. Like many Soviet poets, he translated from a variety of languages with the help of cribs. Of the many poets he translated, those who meant most to him were probably Nâzim Hikmet, the Turkish Communist then living in exile in the Soviet Union, and Bertolt Brecht. He once explained to Lev Ozerov that Brecht was a pleasure to translate because he was cleverer than he was himself; Brecht was someone he could learn from.[170]

Slutsky referred to his own poetry as 'plain as porridge',[171] but this is misleading. If he tends to avoid the high style, it is because – as G. S. Smith writes – 'he always prefers to make workaday language work harder rather than venturing into stylistic and conceptual borderlands'.[172] And in the words of Joseph Brodsky: 'Slutsky almost single-handedly changed the diction of post-war Russian poetry. His verse is a conglomeration of bureaucratese, military lingo, colloquialisms and sloganeering . . . His tone is tough, tragic and nonchalant – the way a survivor normally talks, if he cares to, about what, or into what, he has survived.'[173]

Some aspects of Slutsky are perplexing. Avowedly a sceptical atheist, he once told the poet Vladimir Kornilov that he had heard voices all his life – which had led his father to call him an 'idiot'; Kornilov adds that Dostoevsky's *The Idiot* was Slutsky's favourite novel. Sometimes it is hard to tell whether Slutsky's cool rationality indicates an inability to feel or an overwhelming intensity of feeling. It is hard to reconcile his awareness of tragedy, and of the enormity of both Nazi and Soviet anti-Semitism, with his moments of extreme banality.[174] And it is hard to reconcile his criticisms of Stalinism with his apparent loyalty to the regime. Kornilov writes: 'In the 1950s he told me he wanted to write for intelligent secretaries of provincial Party Committees. He was slow to realize that they had a different cast of mind and had no need for the kind of poems he wrote.'[175] Kornilov then quotes a poem Slutsky wrote in 1952, while Stalin was still alive. It ends:

Back to the wall, life hanging on a thread,
I still believe in the construction plan.
I build on what I still believe is rock
and yet it slips away from me like sand.

Liberals were shocked by a speech Slutsky gave at a Union of Soviet Writers meeting after the award of the Nobel Prize to Boris Pasternak. There were probably several reasons why Slutsky joined in the attacks on Pasternak: a confused sense of Party loyalty; fear of expulsion from the Union of Soviet Writers, to which he had only recently been admitted; and a sincere belief that it was unpatriotic of Pasternak to publish *Doctor*

Zhivago abroad. Slutsky's poem about an unspecified act of cowardice – an act that has left in his blood a sediment 'like the most bitter, biting salt' – is probably about this incident.[176]

While Slutsky's criticism of Pasternak is still held against him, his many acts of courage and generosity are too seldom remembered.[177] It was Slutsky who published the first review – a passionately enthusiastic one – of Varlam Shalamov's first collection of poems; and it was Slutsky's support that enabled Semyon Lipkin to publish his first collection in 1967. Slutsky had an equally keen sense of his duty to his predecessors; it was thanks to Slutsky that Khlebnikov (who had died in a remote village) was reburied in 1960 in Moscow's most prestigious cemetery, the Novodevichy. Slutsky was, in many ways, an important mediator; in the words of a younger poet, Genrikh Sapgir, he 'was somehow the link between us [clandestine writers] . . . and the "official" world'.[178]

Slutsky wrote about the war, about the Shoah, about various aspects of his Jewish heritage, about Stalin, about returnees from the camps, about other writers, about almost every aspect of everyday life. Some of his themes were acceptable to the authorities; others were not. What nearly all his poems have in common is a focus on the specific and a wariness of dogma. Slutsky is a careful, modest explorer of human experience, closer to Chekhov or Vasily Grossman than to Tolstoy or Solzhenitsyn. Slutsky did, in fact, know Grossman. During the late 1950s, when both were living in the same building, Slutsky regularly read his new poems aloud to Grossman or left him copies of poems he had recently typed out.[179]

Like Grossman, Slutsky is often bleak, but this allows him to give voice to important truths. A poem about German prisoners-of-war ends:

> Sooner or later, every post-war period
> becomes a pre-war period.
> The outcome of the Sixth World War
> will depend on how we have treated
> the prisoners-of-war from the Fifth.

Slutsky said of his war poems: 'The life that I lived for four years [. . .] was brutal and tragic and it seemed one needed to write tragedies about it, but since I was unable to write true tragedies, I wrote ballads – shortened, crumpled and concise tragedies.'[180]

Slutsky remained an atheist, but he did not forget his cultural roots. Not only Yiddish but also the Hebrew he had learned as a child remained important to him, if only as deeply felt absences. Thus, in 'Relearning Solitude' (1977), he writes:

Just as I once learned one ancient tongue
enough to read its texts,
and I forgot the alphabet –
I've forgotten solitude.
This all must be recalled, recovered, and relearned.
I remember how once I met
a compiler of words
in the ancient tongue that I had learned
and lost.
Turned out, I knew two words: 'heavens' and 'apple'.
I might have recalled the rest –
All beneath the heavens and beside the apples –
But the need wasn't there.
(trans. Marat Grinberg and Judith Pulman)

Slutsky is having to 'relearn solitude' in 1977 because of the recent death of his wife Tanya. For three months after this – before falling into the depressed silence of his last nine years, during which he wrote nothing – Slutsky wrote some of the finest poems of love and mourning in the Russian language; these have yet to receive due recognition.

*

This sulking man with a self-inflicted wound
stares up at me, transfixed and terrified,
not trying to hide the question in his eyes,
to which no answer can be found.

'Investigating officer'. Can this be me?
Investigate – what's that? Officiate?
I could just let him off to walk away
or order him put up against a tree.

Am I the fiercest foe or the first friend
of him, this criminal, this outcast?
Should I report the matter closed
or portion him an ounce of lead?

Some words are coming from his lips,
his fixed stare pleads
for me to take his part;
and it's enough to pierce my heart
and take away my wits.

Now, though, some words are coming off my tongue,
but I can't seem to find the proper mien.
This fearsome right is wrong for me –
investigating right and wrong.

(1950s)[181]
G. S. Smith

The Hospital

With 'Messers' still raking across our hearts,
and riflemen,
so close,
still letting loose –
our charging cheer still urging us ahead,
that Russian yell, 'Hurrah-rara-rara!'
– a line
of twenty syllables,
no less . . .

A village church,
refitted as a club.
Beneath production diagrams
we lay.
The crannies reeking still of putrid God –
we need a country priest here, no mistake!
Anathema is strong though faith be cautious.
A lousy priest to cense away this smell!
Such frescoes gleaming in the corners!
The heavens hail!
Halved
with the howls
of hell.

Down on the floor, its clay long trodden smooth,
there lies a devil,
with a stomach wound.
Frescoes above, chill corner of the room –
a knocked-out Wehrmacht corporal, on the ground.

Close by,
on a low bed, still but a youth –
a Soviet colonel, soon to breathe his last.
With medals gleaming on his battledress.
He. Breaks the rule. Of silence.
And cries out!
(In a whisper – dead men do.)

Demanding as an officer and Russian,
as human being, at this extreme hour,
this greenish,
red-haired,
rotten non-com Prussian
not die here, right beside these lads of ours!

He keeps on stroking down his decorations,
and smoothing down
his service tunic's breast,
and weeping,
weeping,
weeping in frustration,
that nobody will honour his request.

Two paces off, in his unheated corner,
flat on the floor, that knocked-out corporal.
An orderly picks up this helpless man,
and carries him away, far as he can,
that he might not
with his dark final breath
besmirch a Soviet officer's shining death.
Silence comes down again.
Some old sweats
training up
a new recruit:
'That's how it is,
that's what it's like,
this war!
It's clear, my lad,
you don't much like it,
huh?
So go ahead,
fight it
the way *you* want!'

(1957)
G. S. Smith

About the Jews[182]

Jews don't plant any crops, –
Jews do deals in their shops;
Jews prematurely go bald,
Jews grab more than they're owed.

Your Jew's a conniving bastard;
he's not much good in the army:
Ivan in a trench doing battle,
Avram doing trade at the market.

I've heard it since I was a child
and soon I'll be past any use,
but I can't find a place to hide
from the cries of 'The Jews! The Jews!'

Not a single deal have I pulled,
never stolen and always paid,
but I bear this accursed blood
within me like the plague.

From the war I came back safe
so as to be told to my face:
'No Jews got killed, you know! None!
They all came back, every one!'

(1950s)
G. S. Smith

God

Once we all used to abide
together with God, side by side.
He didn't dwell in the sky,
we'd see him from time to time

alive, on the mausoleum.
He was much more clever and evil
than that other God, the old one,
known to the world as Jehovah,
whom he overthrew with a crash
and reduced to a heap of ash,
then subsequently restored
and recruited to serve the cause.
For once we all used to abide
together with God, side by side.

One day as I wandered around in
the Arbat, I met God on parade
with five limousines and surrounded
by guards wearing mousy grey
overcoats, hunched in dread.
It was early and late – overhead
the grey light of morning was showing
as he gazed with his cruel, all-knowing
eyes through the hearts of men,
unmasking deviants and traitors.

For we lived in an era when
God himself was our neighbour.

(early 1950s)
Stephen Capus

The Master

My master – he disliked me from the start.
He never knew me, never saw or heard me,
but all the same he feared me like the plague
and hated me with all his dreary heart.
When I bowed my head before him,
it seemed to him I hid a smile.
When he made me cry, he thought

my tears were crocodile.
And all my life I worked my heart out for him,
each night I lay down late, and got up early.
I loved him and was wounded for his sake.
But nothing I could do would ever take.
I took his portrait everywhere I went,
I hung it up in every hut and tent,
I looked and looked, and kept on looking,
and slowly, as the years went past,
his hatred hurt me less and less.
And nowadays it hardly seems to matter:
the age-old truth is men like me
are always hated by their master.

(1954?)

Margo Shohl Rosen

*

June would be clammy, January crisp;
and concrete solid, sand unstable.
For there was order. Real order.

People got up and went to work.
And then they watched *The Happy Fellas*
at cinemas. For there was order.

In pedigrees and in parades,
political police, and apparatus,
even in parodies – there was order.

People made fun, and were afraid,
only of those they were supposed to,
for there was order, real order.

An order of the bent and bashed.
In hours, in minutes, and in seconds,
in years as well, there was real order.

It would have gone on without end,
but then a certain person fell,
and all this order went to hell.

(early 1960s)
G. S. Smith

All Rules are Incorrect

All rules are incorrect,
all laws remain perverse,
until they're firmly set
in well-wrought lines of verse.

An age or era will
be merely a stretch of time
without a meaning until
it's glorified in rhyme.

Until the poet's 'Yes!',
entrusted by his pen
to print, awards success
to this or that – till then

the jury will be out,
the verdict still in doubt.

(early 1960s)
Stephen Capus

*

With that old woman[183] I was cold-polite.
I knew her minuses, esteemed her merits,
especially that calm dignity she had,
that frosty, even icy kind of passion.

As a republican bred in the bone,
I couldn't accept the regal attitude,
the bearing, halo, coronation progress,
the world of masters – therefore, that of slaves.

Her hutch was inches deep in flattery,
like ashes after a long-burning blaze.
The way she shook my hand – *significant*.
I got the picture: flattery's the way.

That universe I'd laboured to transform
to chaos – painfully, tormentedly –
was here back in its primal state, for shaping
into a pedestal. That's all there was.

Perhaps, though, I was making a mistake,
and, at a time when human dignity
was being trampled,
                        she'd assumed this mission
herself, and chosen, of all rights,
the most important ones, those *she* desired –
no matter how the menials might quake,
no matter how the common folk might whistle,
no matter how authority might rage.

I could not take this path, but path it was.
When there were almost no paths left to tread,
the price for this was heavier than most.
And I esteemed that cold and mournful passion.

(early 1970s)

G. S. Smith

Strange Things

Such a strange sort of freedom:
do everything you want,
say, and write and publish
everything you want.
But to want the thing you want,
this was impossible.
You had to crave
what you had to have.

Daily life was also strange:
your living quarters cost you almost nothing.
The world's finest women
were cheaply to be bought.
Middling petty bosses
all had private cars
with private drivers.
A servant girl,
though called 'domestic worker',
continued resolutely serving.

Only cutlets had high value
without a side dish
and especially with a side dish.
Victory was easier to procure
than victuals.
The victor over Hitler's hordes
didn't even get a rouble for a bottle,
though he liberated half the world.

Most surprising was the law.
The criminal code
had to be handled carefully.
You only had to squeeze it
and blood would spurt out.
You met death in its pages
more often than in ballads.

Such a strange sort of freedom!
Across the border we broke the prisons open
and blew them up. From the rubble
we built prisons of our own.

(late 1960s)
Margo Shohl Rosen

*

Brought up in greedy simplicity
and the iron needs that go with it,
I spend on what's useful and edible;
Tanya prefers to buy flowers.

A flower lasts only for hours.
A day, two days – then fades.
Tanya hears me in silence –
and keeps to her old ways.

Her shadow flicks by on the wall,
a light flares on the table –
and something lights up in me.
A flower, a flower, is visiting,
calling me
to some small sublimity.

(c. 1970)
Robert Chandler

*

I was at fault all round,
but Tanya said tenderly,
near the last full stop
on her road of torment:
'Forgive me.'

Breaking the awful bond
between poor body and sick bed,
she raised herself up on her elbows –
to ask my forgiveness.

I was blinder than blind.
A tear was burning, burning,
since I was at fault all round
and I was alive
while she was dying.

(1977)
Robert Chandler

*

What did they do
with the relatives of Christ?
What did they do with them?
No written source
will tell you a damned thing –
nothing but crossings out, emptiness.
What the hell did they do with them?

What did they do
with those simple people,
simple craftsmen, men who worked on the land?
Were all marched off to some nearby wilderness,
lined up and machine-gunned?

Whatever happened then, two centuries later
there were no demands for compensation
or calls for revenge.
Total posthumous rehabilitation of Jesus
led to no rehabilitation of kin.

And now flowers are growing from the relatives
of Christ.
Below them lie depths, above them rise heights,
yet world history has found no place
for those relatives of Christ.

(1977)

Robert Chandler

*

I had a bird in my hand
but my bird has flown.
I held a bird in my hand
but am now all alone.

My small bird has left me
full of anger and rage;
my blue bird has left me
alone in a cage.

(1977)

Robert Chandler

*

Always busy, plagued by anxiety,
guilt-ridden, duty to be done –
husbands should be the first to die;
never the ones who're left alone.

Wives should grow old slowly. Aim
for the four-score-and-twenty mark, even;
not every day, but from time to time
remembering their men.

You should not have left the way
you did. That was wrong.
With a kind smile on your face
you should have lived on,
you should have lived long.

Until their hair turns white –
for wives, that's the way to wait,

getting on with things around the home,
breaking the odd heart if they can,
and even (well, where's the harm?)
toasting the memory of their old man.

(1977)
G. S. Smith

David Samoilov, pseudonym of David Samuilovich Kaufman (1920–90)

The son of a doctor, David Samoilov studied from 1938 to 1941 at the Moscow Institute of Philosophy, Literature and History; during these years he became friends with Boris Slutsky. The poets he most admired were Khlebnikov, Pasternak, Mayakovsky and Mandelstam, all of whose first collection, *Stone*, he knew by heart.

An infantry officer during the Second World War, Samoilov was wounded and hospitalized. After returning to active service, he ended the war in Berlin. During the next ten years he wrote little and published still less, working mainly as a translator. His first collection of his own poems appeared in 1958. From then, he published poems regularly, while continuing to work both as a translator and as a children's writer.

Much of Samoilov's work has a cool, gently ironic air. Boris Dralyuk writes of 'The Forties': 'The poem develops with a remarkably natural movement – like a life slowly reconstructed as one flips through a photo album.'

The Forties

The forties, fateful,
warring, frontline,
with funeral notices,
clattering trains.
The hum of the rails.
All is cold, high and barren.
Their houses have burned –
they're heading east.
That's me at the station
in my scruffy wool cap.
The star's not standard issue –

it's cut from a can.
Yes, here I am in the world,
skinny, happy, carefree.
I've got tobacco in my pouch –
I have a stash of rolling papers.
I joke with the girls,
and limp a little overmuch.
I break my rationed bread in half,
and I know everything on earth.
Imagine! What coincidence –
war, horror, dreams and youth!
And all of it sank deep inside me . . .
and only later did it wake.
The forties, fateful,
lead and gun smoke . . .
War wanders through the land.
and we are all so young!

(1961)
Boris Dralyuk

The Ballad of a German Censor

In Germany once lived a censor
of lowly rank and title.
He blotted, struck and cancelled
and knew no other calling.

He sniffed out harmful diction
and smeared it with Indian ink.
He guarded minds from infection
and his bosses valued his work.

On a winter day in forty-three
he was dispatched 'nach Osten'.
And he stared from the train car's window
at fields, graveyards, snowstorms.

It was cold without a fur coat.
He saw hamlets without homes or people.
Only charred chimneys were left,
creeping by, like lizards or camels.

And it seemed to him that Russia
was all steppe, Mongoloid, bare.
And he thought he was feeling 'nostalgia',
but it was really just the chill and fear.

He arrived at his field post office:
such-and-such region and number.
Table, chair, iron cot and mattress,
three walls – in the fourth, a window.

Russia's short on *Gemütlichkeit!*
He had to climb over snowdrifts.
And the work? No shortage of that:
cutting, deleting, smearing.

Before him lay piles of letters,
lines and lines – some straight, some wavy.
Generals wrote to their comrades,
soldiers wrote to their families.

There were letters, messages, queries
from the living, from those who'd been killed.
There were words he judged 'non-Aryan',
but it was really just fear and the chill.

He would read nearly all day round,
forgetting to eat or shave.
And inside his tired mind
something strange began to take place.

Words he'd blotted and excised
would come and torment him at night,
and, like some eerie circus,
would parade there before his eyes . . .

Lines, killed by black ink,
turned tyrannical, like a tirade:
'In the East, the East, the East,
we will not, will not be spared . . .'

The text was composed of black mosaics;
each word clung fast to the next.
Not the greatest master of prose
could have come up with such a text.

Long thoughts, like wagon trains,
shook the joints and ridges
of his tired and weakened brain;
battered its fragile bridges.

He turned unfriendly to all his friends
and grew brusque, unsociable, sad.
He was brilliant for a few days
and then broke down and went mad.

He awoke, from the fear and chill . . .
with a wild, choking feeling.
The dark was impenetrable –
the window blacked out with ink.

He realized that bravado leads nowhere,
that existence is fragile,
and the black truth invaded his soul
and wiped away the white lie.

The poor censor was born a pedant.
He reached for a small notebook
and truthfully – that is, with talent –
set everything down, in order.

The next morning he took up, with zeal,
his . . . No – a different task:
he underlined all that was real
and crossed out everything else.

Poor censor, he'd lost his mind!
Little man, like a grain of millet!
He informed on himself in a day
and was taken away that minute . . .

There once lived a censor in Germany.
His rank and title were low.
He died and was promptly buried,
and his grave fell under the plough.

(1961)

Boris Dralyuk

Rasul Gamzatov (1923–2003)

Rasul Gamzatovich Gamzatov's father was a traditional bard, well known among his people, the Avar. Gamzatov himself became the best-known modern poet writing in Avar – one of the many languages of Dagestan, in the north-eastern Caucasus.

Gamzatov wrote 'Cranes' in 1968, after seeing the paper cranes in the museum of the Peace Memorial Park at Hiroshima; and, on the same day, receiving news of his mother's death. The poem was translated into Russian by Naum Grebnev (a gifted translator) and later revised by Mark Bernes, a popular singer. Bernes recorded the song in 1969 and it became a staple of the Soviet repertory – a truly Soviet, rather than Dagestani or Russian, song.

Irina Mashinski, who translated 'Cranes', writes: 'Maybe it is the multilayered authorship of this text that has made it, in Soviet perception, almost anonymous, like an ancient Egyptian poem. Having lost the author's biography, the poem loses its individual poetics, too – or at least so it seems to a Russian reader. It does not represent an ethnographical peculiarity or a national tradition. All that remains is breadth, simplicity and height. "Cranes" is a unique case of an epic elegy.' The song's great popularity has led to white cranes becoming generally associated with dead soldiers; many war memorials in the former Soviet Union bear either an image of flying cranes or lines from this song. Boris Dralyuk writes from Los Angeles: 'There is a large, Soviet-style memorial to Russian veterans of the Second World War in my neighbourhood park – a meeting place for the city's large population of Russian émigrés. The memorial is a jutting hunk of granite, inscribed with four lines from Gamzatov, a flock of cranes soaring above them.'

Much official support was given to having the poetry of the Soviet Union's national minorities translated into Russian. It was supposed that this would help forge a truly Soviet culture, transcending national divisions. This hope proved illusory, but the project did at least enable many Russian writers – often unable to publish their own work – to earn a living.

At the same time, this emphasis on translation often led to absurdities. Because of the dominance of Russian, and because so many of the best Russian poets were working as translators, a translation often assumed far greater importance than the original. In a talk for Radio Liberty the émigré Russian novelist Sergei Dovlatov once recalled a visit to the Kalmyk city of Elista. A local poet presented him with what he called 'a literal version' of a short poem of his: 'I love my steppes. I love the sun. I love my collective farm's sheep. But most of all I love the Communist Party.' When Dovlatov asked to hear the original, so as to get a sense of the poem's sound, the poet admitted that there *was* no original, only this 'literal version'.[184]

Cranes

Sometimes I think that soldiers, who have never
come back to us from the blood-covered plains,
escaped the ground and didn't cross the River,
but turned instead into white screeching cranes.

And since that time the flock is flying, narrow
or wide, or long – and maybe that is why
so often and with such a sudden sorrow
we stop abruptly, staring at the sky.

On flies the wedge trespassing every border –
a sad formation, ranks of do-re-mi,
and there's a gap in their open order:
it is the space they have reserved for me.

The day will come: beneath an evening cloud
I'll fly, crane on my right, crane on my left,
and in a voice like theirs, shrill and loud,
call out, call out to those on earth I've left.

(1968)
Irina Mashinski

Alexander Mejirov (1923–2009)

Alexander Petrovich Mejirov was born in Moscow to Jewish parents. He took part in the defence of Leningrad from 1941 to 1943, but was seriously wounded. His first collection of poetry (1947) was criticized for its 'excessively personal' representation of wartime experiences. Mejirov was a mentor to some of the poets who began to publish in the late 1950s, during the period known as the Thaw. He emigrated to the United States in 1992.

*

I began to grow old
        when I turned forty-four,
and at the eating place on the corner,
        I was already taken
for a lonely retiree,
        forgotten
        by every soul
        on earth,
forsaken by his children
and ignored by the rest of his kin.

Well, this is the law of life, isn't it?
        Yet I confess
        that at first,
Whenever I entered the place
        and looked around
        for a vacant table,
this circumstance depressed me.

But later
    I found in it
    the emergency exit in the building called life.

Yes, I submerged
    into the muffled hubbub of voices
of that place
    in almost a cellar,
    where my ailing spirit
    was strangely healed,
as I carried a pea soup
    on a quavering piece of plastic,
a spoon, a fork and a knife,
    still dripping,
    and a hunk of bread on a plate –
also wet.

I came to love
    those
    crudely panelled
    walls,
that line to the counter,
    the trays
    and the meagre menu card.
'Blessed are,'
    I muttered,
    'Blessed are,
    Blessed are,
    Blessed are . . .'
That blessed squalor
    I shall never betray.

I came to love
    the defeat at the game of life,
and the faded traces
    of decorations
    on old uniforms,

and I could now enter
    the world of shadows just like another shadow,
without farewell salvos,
    solemn faces,
    or fuss.

(1973)

Lev Navrozov

Bulat Okudzhava (1924–97)

Although born in Moscow to a Georgian father and an Armenian mother, Bulat Shalvovich Okudzhava spoke and wrote only in Russian. His father, a high-ranking Party member, was executed in 1937; his mother spent eighteen years in the Gulag.

After fighting in the Red Army during the war, Okudzhava studied at Tbilisi State University. He then worked as a teacher of Russian Language and Literature. In 1956 he returned to Moscow, and in 1961 he became poetry editor of the important *Literaturnaya Gazeta*. It was during these years that he began to compose songs.

Okudzhava had no formal training in music, but he had a natural gift for melody and his melodies blend perfectly with his lyrics. Amateur recordings of him singing these songs, to his own simple guitar accompaniment, spread across the Soviet Union. No official recordings were released until the late 1970s, but his songs were featured in several films and lines from their lyrics entered the language. Okudzhava was seldom directly political, but – after the grandiosity of most Stalin-era music and literature – his gentleness and modesty lent his songs a freshness almost equivalent to a political stance; he made it seem acceptable for people living in a supposedly Communist state to have personal feelings. For a while, at least, he was able to restore meaning to concepts – 'honour', 'comradeship', even 'the Motherland' – long devalued by official propaganda. Among his main themes are Moscow life, friendship and love, and the brutality of war. One well-known song is about Mozart:

Mozart is playing his faithful old fiddle:
Mozart is playing, the fiddle just sings.
Mozart plays on though he's caught in the middle,
never selecting the countries, the kings.

(trans. Eric Hill)

Better known still is a song about the night's last trolleybus, a blue trolleybus that rescues the lost and lonely and grants them a sense of wordless communion:

> The last trolleybus glides along the city.
> Moscow grows dim and, like a river, fades.
> And the pain that thrashed at my temple
> slowly abates.
> (trans. Maria Bloshteyn and Boris Dralyuk)

Gentle and welcoming, Okudzhava's songs *are* this blue trolleybus; his songs brought intimacy into a world that had been ruled by intimidation.

During the Khrushchev 'Thaw' Okudzhava often performed to large crowds in football stadiums, sometimes along with such poets as Akhmadulina, Voznesensky and Yevtushenko. Though never a political activist, he consistently supported liberal reform. Shostakovich admired his melodies, but Okudzhava saw himself primarily as a poet and seems not to have taken his songs seriously. During the 1980s he also published historical novels and autobiographical stories.

Even in the original, his lyrics seem insubstantial without their music. We include only one example – often assumed to be about Stalin, though its import is broader.

Black Cat

There's a courtyard in our building,
that's where you'll find the back door,
and behind it lives a Black Cat –
ensconced here like some lord.

There's a smirk behind his whiskers,
darkness shields him like a wall,
and this Black Cat remains quiet
while all others caterwaul.

He keeps smirking in his whiskers,
hasn't caught a mouse of late,
catches us on our loose lips,
on a bit of tempting bait.

He does not request or order –
when his yellow eye burns bright,
every one of us forks over,
thanking him with all our might.

He won't meow and he won't purr –
he just gorges, drinks and gloats.
And he paws at dirty floorboards
like he's clawing at our throats.

This is why the place we live in
is so dark and dreary still,
we should really hang a light bulb –
but can't seem to foot the bill.

(1957–9)

Maria Bloshteyn

Yevgeny Vinokurov (1925–93)

After serving in the artillery during the Second World War, Yevgeny Mikhailovich Vinokurov studied at the Gorky Literary Institute, publishing his first poems in 1948. As co-editor of the poetry section of the journal *October*, he published both Slutsky and Zabolotsky.

Daniel Weissbort writes: 'His poems often strike me as akin to pencil sketches . . . [There is] a discretion, a discipline, a restraint, that relates more to line and form than to colour. And yet, as with all master draughtsmen, he manages to convey *everything*.'[185]

Missing the Troop Train

There's something desperate about trains . . .
I stood alone on the icy platform,
lost in the Bashkir steppes.
What can be more fantastic, more desolate
than the light of an electric lamp
rocking in a small station at night?
Trains swept past from time to time.
Their roar engulfed me,
I was submerged in coal dust,
and each time, I grabbed hold of my cap –
it looked as though I was greeting someone.
The bare, stunted tree by the side of the platform
reached out after them . . .
I waited for one train at least
to stop, for God's sake!
In the distance was the dark forest mass.
I lifted my head –
over me, a vast
host of stars:

regiments,
divisions,
        armies of stars,
all bound for somewhere.
An hour earlier, I'd got out of the train
to fetch some boiling water . . .
I could be court-martialled for this.
I stood there,
the snow melted round my boots,
and the water in the aluminium kettle I was holding
had already iced over.
Above the forest mass I saw
a little star,
fallen a long way behind the others.
I looked at it
and it looked at me.

(1965)
Daniel Weissbort

Inna Lisnianskaya (1928–2014)

Born in Baku, Inna Lisnianskaya published her first collection in 1957. Three years later she moved to Moscow. In 1979 she and her husband Semyon Lipkin resigned from the Union of Soviet Writers in protest at the expulsion from the Union of two other writers, Viktor Yerofeyev and Yevgeny Popov. For the next seven years her work was published only abroad. From 1986 she was able to publish regularly, winning several important prizes.

We have chosen three of her later poems. The first two were written not long before the death of her husband; the last shortly afterwards.

Jealousy

I look out the window at the retreating back.
Your jealousy is both touching and comical.
Can't you see I am old and scary, a witch,
and apart from you no one needs me at all!

Well, what's so touching and funny in that?
Jealous, you're keen to send all of them packing
away from our home, with its roof's mossy coat,
and our life which consists entirely of sacking.

But they do not desist, out of kindness of sorts –
from scraping away the moss, checking a rafter,
and they bring flowers as well, to thank me
for your still being alive and so well looked after.

And they steal away with something else, a notion
of how to survive as the years advance
and still be loved, and, with time running out,
to listen to eulogies, fresher than the news.

And my attachment, the truth of my love, no less,
they envy. So keep your jealousy buttoned up!
In this world, with its surfeit of painful loss,
let me open the door with a smile on my lips.

(2001)
Daniel Weissbort

Our Meeting

The woodpecker chips at the bark – easy route to the worm?
I take my time waking you, though I rose at dawn.
Your war is over – to each his own frost.
You skated on the Volga, iced Ladoga kissed,
but my frost was the morgue: from orphan to orderly,
so as not to starve, I pulled funeral trolleys.
There's a sacred meaning in this meeting of fate and fate –
it was to unfreeze life that you and I met.

(2001)
Daniel Weissbort

*

Naked thoughts live unembellished.
That saying's a lie, you can't
twice and so forth, whatever it is.
A thousandth time I enter the same river.

And I see the same grey stones on the bottom,
the same carp with its gristly fins,
the same sun in the blue patch of sky
washes the yellow spot for ages.

In the same river the willow weeps,
the same waters ripple tunefully,
no day passes but into the same river
I enter, the very same life.

(2003)
Daniel Weissbort

Vladimir Kornilov (1928–2002)

Vladimir Nikolayevich Kornilov's father was a construction engineer. From 1945 until 1950 Kornilov studied at the Gorky Literary Institute, from which he was three times expelled for truancy and 'ideologically false verse'.

Kornilov published his first book of poems in 1964. A year later he signed letters of protest against the arrest of Andrey Sinyavsky and Yury Daniel, who had published abroad. In 1977, after himself publishing work abroad, Kornilov was excluded from the Union of Soviet Writers. As he says in his poem in homage to Andrey Platonov, he then worked briefly as a street-cleaner.[186] He is, however, mistaken about Platonov, who never, in reality, worked as a street- or yard-cleaner. The origin of this legend – a part of 'intelligentsia folklore' for many years – is that Platonov sometimes *chose* to sweep the yard of the Literary Institute (LitInstitute) building where he lived.

Kornilov composed around forty poems about Russian writers. He writes about the courage with which Gumilyov, 'the Kipling of Tsarskoye Selo', faced his executioners in 1921. He writes admiringly of Akhmatova, one of his sponsors when he was admitted in 1965 to the Union of Soviet Writers. He also reflects on the paradox of Lermontov's fate; what led him to fight his last duel was a peculiar blend of courage, pain and spite – but its tragic outcome somehow made Lermontov appear an embodiment of love: 'And boys writing poems at night, / hope for a similar fate.'[187]

Forty Years Later

A foundling of the worthless muses
and other brutes,
I languish all the livelong day
at the LitInstitute.

And dream up rhymes and other good-
for-nothing schemes . . .
Outside the window, a janitor sweeps
the pavement clean.

Slouching, gaunt, and hollow-cheeked,
he's gloomy, ill.
But to hell with him and all his woes –
I'm full of myself.

. . . And all the while he was the one
whose words the Genius
of Humanity had banished from
the magazines.

Thus the writing of that time
grew strangely inept,
while at the LitInstitute the yard
was nicely swept.

. . . My whole life I looked into myself –
at others, rarely.
But all the same, his fate did touch
something in me.

Now I've become a poet – good,
bad, who knows? –
declining like the century,
sentenced to sweep snow.

Who envies either of our lives?
His life was destroyed
by *M. tuberculosis*, and mine –
by my wretched thyroid.

. . . I bear being outcast unbowed,
I kowtow to none,
but before *you* I'll bow down,
Andrey Platonov.

And forty years later I pray:
in your distant heaven,
forgive the folly of my youth,
forgive everything –

my hubris, hard-heartedness, but mostly
forgive the boredom
with which I gazed through that window
on your torment.

(1985)
Katherine E. Young

Freedom

I'm not ready for freedom yet.
Am I the one to blame?
You see, there was no likelihood
of freedom in my time.

My great-great-grandad, my great-grandad,
my own grandad never
dared to dream of
'Freedom now!'
None of them saw it: ever.

What's this thing that they call freedom?
Does it bring satisfaction?
Or is it helping others first
and putting oneself last?

An overwhelming happiness,
pride and envy expelled,
throwing open one's own soul,
not prying in anyone else's.

Here are oceans composed of sweat,
Himalayas of toil!
Freedom's a lot harder than
unfreedom to enjoy.

For years I, too, awaited freedom,
waited till I trembled,
waited till I ached – yet I'm
unready, now it's come.

(1986)
Katherine E. Young

Andrey Voznesensky (1933–2010)

Andrey Andreyevich Voznesensky was the son of a professor of engineering. As a teenager, he sent some of his poems to Boris Pasternak, who responded warmly. The two became friends.

Voznesensky published his first poems in 1958; with their strong rhythms and unusual metaphors they captured the mood of the coming decade. A brilliant public performer, he won international fame, travelling worldwide and meeting such luminaries as Picasso, Jean-Paul Sartre and Marilyn Monroe. His English translators included many of the best-known poets of the day, from W. H. Auden to Allen Ginsberg.

Since the 1970s Voznesensky's reputation has declined; he may not have been as poetically or politically daring as his admirers once thought. During his last two decades, on the other hand, he was impressively ready to court unpopularity by speaking out about such controversial subjects as Russian anti-Semitism.

To Bella Akhmadulina

There were loads of us. Well – about four.
The car was careering pell-mell.
And with us the orange-haired driver,
sleeves rolled up, stylish as hell.

Oh Belka, most reckless of roadhogs!
What an outlandish, angelic sight!
I adore your porcelain profile
like a lamp that's brilliantly white.

In Hades they fire up the griddle
and send a patrol to the gates
when your speedo's gone way past the middle
and you recklessly roll cigarettes.

I love it when, racing still faster,
in a voice clear as crystal you say:
'Oh dear, it's such a disaster.
They've taken my licence away . . .

. . . You see, they booked me for breaking the speed limit
while in a state of emotional excitement, but
I was just driving normally . . .'

Oh Belka, don't stress out your liver.
Our dear sergeant cannot do wrong –
the speed of his gearbox, however,
just can't match the speed of your song.

It's a poet's first duty, in spite
of the traffic restrictions, to fly,
bringing sound at the speed of light
like the angels that sing in the sky.

And though after travelling light years
we may in a flash disappear,
though we may not collect any prizes –
it was we who first got into gear.

So Bel, press the celestial lever,
though our bones find nowhere to rest.
Long live the song-gear, for ever!
Of all gears the deadliest!

What's engraved in the future to meet us?
There are few of us. Well – about four.
But we race on –
and since you're a goddess,
the majority's ours for sure.

(1963)

Peter Oram

Yevgeny Yevtushenko (b. 1932)

Yevgeny Alexandrovich Yevtushenko was born in Siberia, to a family of German, Russian, Tatar and Ukrainian origin. His father was a geologist, his mother a singer; both his grandfathers had been arrested during Stalin's purges. In 1961 he published 'Babi Yar', about the Nazi massacre of Kiev Jews. This poem – set to music by Shostakovich in his Thirteenth Symphony – was all the more controversial for addressing not only the massacre itself, but also Soviet anti-Semitism. The authorities had refused to allow a memorial for the Jewish victims; Babi Yar had come to epitomize not only the Shoah itself, but also official attempts to suppress its memory.

Yevtushenko's greatest popularity was during the late 1950s and 1960s. Brodsky and others accused him of hypocrisy, of being outspoken enough to win attention but taking care never to endanger his privileged position. This seems harsh: though no dissident, he certainly did more good than harm. Yevtushenko has also worked in film, as an actor and as a writer/director. In 1993 he published a large anthology, *Twentieth-Century Russian Poetry*. He is now working on a multi-volume anthology, in Russian, of poetry from the eleventh to the twentieth century.

Loss

Russia has lost Russia in Russia.
Russia searches for itself
        like a cut finger in snow,
        a needle in a haystack,
like an old blind woman madly stretching her hand in fog,
searching with hopeless incantation for her lost milk cow.

We buried our icons.
        We didn't believe in our own great books.
        We fight only with alien grievances.

Is it true that we didn't survive under our own yoke,
becoming for ourselves worse than foreign enemies?
Is it true that we are doomed to live only in the silk
nightgown of dreams, eaten by moths? –
        Or in numbered prison robes?

Is it true that epilepsy is our national character?
Or convulsions of pride?
        Or convulsions of self-humiliation?
Ancient rebellions against new copper kopeks,
against such foreign fruits as potatoes are
now only a harmless dream.

Today's rebellion swamps the entire Kremlin
        like a mortal tide –
Is it true that we Russians have only one unhappy choice?
The ghost of Tsar Ivan the Terrible?
        Or the Ghost of Tsar Chaos?
So many imposters. Such 'imposterity'.

Everyone is a leader, but no one leads.
We are confused as to which banners and
slogans to carry.
And such a fog in our heads
        that everyone is wrong
        and everyone is guilty in everything.

We already have walked enough in such fog,
in blood up to our knees.
Lord, you've already punished us enough.
Forgive us, pity us.

Is it true that we no longer exist?
Or are we not yet born?
We are birthing now,
but it's so painful to be born again.

(1991)

James Ragan and Yevgeny Yevtushenko

Sergey Chudakov (1937–early 1990s?)

The son of a labour-camp director, Sergey Ivanovich Chudakov spent much of his childhood in Kolyma. Expelled from Moscow State University, he supported himself by writing articles under pseudonyms; he was also a pornographer, pimp and book thief. Sometimes called 'the Russian Villon', he is thought to have died or been murdered in the early 1990s.

*

They played Pushkin on a grand piano.
They killed Pushkin in a duel one day.
He had asked them for a plate of cloudberries
and, lying near a bookshelf, passed away.

In icy water, full of frozen clods,
they buried Pushkin, hallowed be his name.
And we too tend to meet too many bullets;
we hang ourselves, and open up our veins.

All too often we are hit by cars,
get tossed down stairwells in a drunken state.
We live – and all our petty intrigues
wound little Pushkin in some way.

Little, cast in iron, celebrated –
in a park deserted thanks to frost –
he stands (his understudy and replacement),
bitterly regretful at the loss

of youth, and of the title *Kammerjunker*,
of songs, of glory, of the girls in Kishinyov,
of Goncharova in her white lace petticoat,
and of death that cannot be shrugged off.

Boris Dralyuk

Bella Akhmadulina (1937–2010)

Izabella ('Bella') Akhatovna Akhmadulina was the only child of a Tatar father and a Russian-Italian mother. As a schoolgirl she attended a poetry circle run by Vinokurov. She went on to study at the Gorky Literary Institute, from which she was temporarily expelled in 1959 for her defence of Pasternak during the controversy over *Doctor Zhivago*. Later she defended both Solzhenitsyn and the nuclear physicist Andrey Sakharov. Her own poetry is apolitical, but she was clear and consistent in her support of other writers.

Although her poetry was well known, she managed to join the Union of Soviet Writers only with difficulty; she was first accepted not as a poet but as a translator. Like many other Soviet poets, she translated from a variety of languages with the help of cribs. She had several close friends among Georgian poets.

During the 1960s she read regularly in stadiums, often with Voznesensky and Yevtushenko, her first husband. Her poetic voice, however, is quieter than theirs. Her work includes love poems, poems about the creative process, and many poems about Akhmatova, Mandelstam, Tsvetaeva and other poets.

This extract from 'I Swear', a rhetorically structured, tightly rhymed poem of fifty-two lines, illustrates the degree to which Tsvetaeva's suicide, like Sylvia Plath's, has taken on the status of myth. Akhmadulina addresses Tsvetaeva directly, speaking of Yelabuga, the small town where she hanged herself, as if it were some murderous monster, a Russian witch or Baba Yaga:

> I swear by your sad rest in Paradise
> where you're bereft of torment and of craft;
> I swear by your yelabuga that I shall kill
> your cruel yelabuga – so that our grand-
> children can sleep in peace. Old women will
> still frighten them at night, not knowing that

yelabuga is gone, that I've despatched her:
Hush, hush, sleep tight – or blind yelabuga
will come for you.

Here, though, we include a more joyful poem, also addressed to Tsvetaeva.

Music Lessons

I love the fact that you, like me, like so
many of us, Marina –
(I can't speak –
my throat is frozen!) you, like light! like snow! –
(I try to say it, but I almost choke,

as if I'd swallowed ice!) – that you, you too
had piano lessons. A parody of learning!
The gods above both laugh and weep – as though
a candle could be taught the art of burning!

You and the piano, two equal darknesses,
just didn't get on: two perfect, separate rings,
miserable in the mutual deaf-muteness
of mutually exclusive foreign tongues.

Two sombre and suspicious specialists –
a hostile and impossible encounter.
You and the piano – two potent silences,
throats still too weak for speaking or resounding.

Yet your degree of orphanhood was greater
and settled the matter. Piano? – a mere prisoner
of silence, until some collaborator
presses the C sharp with her little finger.

You stood alone – no need of such liaison,
and music's struggle was, for you, to find
a way, without disturbing pain's foundations,
to open up a bleeding wound of sound.

Doh for a-*do*-lescence! Doh, Marina,
for declamation, destiny, all those
new dawning days! Alike, we bow heads in the
child-piano-player's archetypal pose –

like you! like you! – to seize the piano stool,
useless Gedike's carousel, and instead
to send the snatched-off beret into a whirl
so that it whistles round and round your head!

That's all, for good luck's sake, I meant to do:
to let for once the lovely words come leaping
out – *Marina, I'm like you, like you!* . . .
I meant to shout with joy, but see – I'm weeping.

(1963)
Peter Oram

Vladimir Vysotsky (1938–80)

Vladimir Semyonovich Vysotsky was born in Moscow. The youngest of the three well-known singer-songwriters of the 1960s and 1970s, he became *the* spokesman for his era. With his characteristic humour, he describes his first years in 'Ballad about Childhood':

Conception time I recall only vaguely,
my memory is somewhat askew,
but it was both nocturnal and sinful,
and I got out when my time was through.
I was born neither anguished nor angry –
I was out in nine months not nine years.
Still, I served my first term in the womb,
(nothing much to write home about there). [. . .]

Back there we lived life modestly – one was the same as all:
a corridor, thirty-eight rooms, and just one washroom stall.
Not walls, but thin partitions, so you really couldn't choose
but listen as your neighbours were knocking back the booze.
There it was always freezing, no matter what we wore,
and I got plenty lessons in what money's worth and more.

Warning sirens did not scare our neighbour,
bit by bit, Mum got used to them too,
as for me, well, at three, I just didn't care
about air raids and what they could do.
Not all from above hails from the Lord:
fire bombs must be snuffed without fail,
so to help with the war, I donated
my play sand and my rusty little pail. [. . .]

(trans. Maria Bloshteyn)

In 1956 Vysotsky joined the Moscow Art Theatre Studio-Institute. His literature teacher there was Andrey Sinyavsky, a gifted writer who became a prominent dissident. In 1961 Vysotsky wrote 'Tattoo', the first of his many songs about the criminal underworld. In June 1963, while acting in a film, Vysotsky recorded a cassette of his songs; copies soon spread across the entire Soviet Union. In 1964 the director Yury Lyubimov invited Vysotsky to join his new theatre, the Taganka. There Vysotsky took part in productions based on poems by Mayakovsky and Voznesensky and, famously, played Hamlet in a production that began with him reciting Pasternak's poem 'Hamlet'. He also continued to act and sing in films.

Throughout the 1960s and 1970s Vysotsky went on composing his songs – many of them almost miniature plays – accompanying himself on a guitar and singing in a voice as hoarse as Bob Dylan's. His lyrics were so convincing that former mountaineers, prisoners, war veterans, etc., were often unshakeable in their belief that Vysotsky was one of them, that he, too, had been through whatever they had been through.

Vysotsky evidently had a rare gift, even as a child, for absorbing slang and jargon. Against the background of the blandness of so much of Soviet culture, the impact of his realism was overwhelming. He was popular among all classes – writers, students, down-and-outs and ordinary workers. The Party bosses he mocked would invite him to their grand dachas. Even Leonid Brezhnev loved his songs.

In the late 1970s, to counteract his hangovers, he began using morphine, heroin and amphetamines. This is probably why he died in 1980. After a vast, unauthorized gathering at the Taganka, Vysotsky was buried at the Vagankovskoye Cemetery. Tens of thousands of people lined the streets as his coffin passed by.

His well-known 'Wolf Hunt' alludes to a poem by Yesenin in which the poet identifies with a hunted wolf. Yesenin's wolf is killed – but Vysotsky's, though apparently doomed, manages to escape. First, he asks:

> So, pack leader, explain if you can,
> why we're hurtling toward the gunshot
> and not trying to break through the ban?

He appears to resign himself to convention, to the inevitable:

Wolves cannot and must not do otherwise.
So it looks like my time here is done.
And the one for whom I am intended
has just smiled and raised up his gun.

But then he breaks free:

In defiance, I am running riot
across the flags with life itself the prize!
And I joyfully hear how, behind me,
the crowds cry out in surprise.
(trans. Maria Bloshteyn)

Another important poem, and one that Vysotsky often chose to recite rather than sing, is 'Monument'. As well as alluding to poems by Derzhavin and Pushkin (see pp. 13, 101), he evokes the fate of Mayakovsky, who was canonized by Stalin. The poem begins with a description of a bronze and granite monument:

When I went and died without warning,
canny loved ones of mine cast a death mask –
they could hardly have done this faster!
And I don't know who made them do it,
but my jutting Asiatic cheekbones
got chiselled off the plaster.
I had never imagined or dreamed it –
never dreamed that I was in danger
of turning out deader than dead.
But the mask had been sweetly polished
and a sepulchral dullness wafted
from my toothlessly smiling head.

But when this is unveiled, to the accompaniment of saccharine versions of his songs, Vysotsky comes back to life; he refuses to be canonized. With a wild shriek, he crashes down:

And my fall both bent me and broke me,
but as the dust settles,
my angular cheek bones jut out
from the metal.
I couldn't stay mum like I ought to –
wouldn't can it!
That's not me: I openly
left the granite.
(trans. Maria Bloshteyn and Boris Dralyuk)

Dense with wordplay and references to aspects of Soviet life for which English lacks words, these songs are hard to translate. We include only excerpts. Here is the last half of 'Wayward Steeds'.

from *Wayward Steeds*

A bit slower, my steeds, a bit slower!
If the whip thinks it's boss – it's wrong!
But it looks like my steeds are wayward,
I didn't live enough and can't finish my song.

I will let my steeds drink,
I will let myself sing,
for a little while longer, I'll stand at the brink!

We're on time – no one's late for appointments with God.
Why then are angels singing with such fury?
Or is it the sleigh bell, weeping, gone mad?
Or is it my voice shouting, 'Steeds, don't hurry!?'

A bit slower, my steeds, a bit slower!
I beg you, don't gallop headlong!
But it looks like my steeds are wayward.
If I didn't live enough, let me finish the song!

I will let my steeds drink,
I will let myself sing,
for a little while longer, I'll stand at the brink . . .

(1972)

Maria Bloshteyn

Joseph Brodsky (1940–96)

Joseph Alexandrovich Brodsky was born into a Jewish family in Leningrad; his father worked as a photographer, his mother as a bookkeeper. Brodsky left school at the age of fifteen. During the next seven years he worked as a milling-machine operator, a hospital attendant, a ship's stoker, in a morgue, in a lighthouse, in a crystallography laboratory and on geological expeditions. Meanwhile, he was learning Polish and English and reading English and American poetry. He was also translating and writing poems, some of which circulated in samizdat.

In 1961 Brodsky met Anna Akhmatova, who befriended him. He became the leading member of a circle of young poets who later, after her death, became known as 'Akhmatova's Orphans'. In 1962 he fell in love with an artist, Marina Basmanova. Their stormy relationship, with its many partings and reconciliations, proved central to Brodsky's life and work. In 'Seven Strophes' (1981) he wrote, 'I was simply blind. / You, appearing, hiding, / gave me sight.' When Brodsky learned in January 1964 that Marina had begun an affair with his friend Dmitry Bobyshev, another protégé of Akhmatova's, he attempted suicide.

In February 1964, after being harassed by the authorities for several months, Brodsky was arrested and tried for 'social parasitism'. When the judge asked, 'Who has recognized you as a poet? Who has enrolled you in the ranks of poets?', he replied, 'Who enrolled me in the ranks of the human race?'[188]

Brodsky was sentenced to five years of exile in the Arkhangelsk region, in the far north of European Russia. Akhmatova commented: 'What a biography they're fashioning for our red-haired friend! [. . .] It's as if he'd hired them to do it on purpose.'[189] Brodsky chopped wood, hauled manure and read Donne, Marvell, Frost and Auden. He was free to think and write. He later spoke of this as one of the best times of his life.[190]

In 1965, after an international campaign in his support, his sentence was commuted, and in September he was able to return to Leningrad. A son, Andrey, was born to him and Marina in October 1967, but Marina then left him.

Brodsky's work from these years is both classical and contemporary; he uses colloquial diction and frequent enjambement, but he keeps to metre and rhyme. The themes include love, liberty and tyranny, and poetry itself. His poems were soon being translated into English, French, German and other languages, but almost nothing was published in the Soviet Union until 1987.

The Soviet authorities decided to expel Brodsky from the Soviet Union, and in June 1972 he was put on a plane for Vienna. There he was met by the American Slavist Carl Proffer. Proffer introduced Brodsky to Auden, who for many years had been spending his summers in a village not far from the city. Proffer then helped Brodsky to settle in the United States. During the next eight years he taught, or was a poet in residence, at several universities. In 1980 he moved to New York.

In 1987 Brodsky won the Nobel Prize for Literature and in 1991 he was appointed Poet Laureate of the United States. In January 1996, aged fifty-five, he died of a heart attack; he had long been in poor health and had undergone heart surgery in 1978 and 1985. He was buried in Venice, a city he loved.

In his Nobel Lecture, Brodsky named five predecessors – Akhmatova, Mandelstam, Tsvetaeva, Frost and Auden – without whom, 'as both a man and a writer, I would amount to much less'. Asked soon after this if he was an American or a Russian, he replied, 'I am Jewish – a Russian poet and an English essayist.' This is accurate. Brodsky's English-language essays – which include studies of Andrey Platonov and many of the most important American, English and Russian poets of the last century – have been widely praised. Many of his best poems, on the other hand, have yet to be well translated. Brodsky's first translators included Anthony Hecht and Richard Wilbur, but over the years Brodsky turned to translating his own work, often distorting English idiom in order to observe the requirements of rhyme and metre. Here we include four of his earlier poems. The first and second are inspired by Marina Basmanova, the third by the son from whom he was separated by exile; the last brings together several of his central themes. We also include a few lines from 'Performance' a 150-line phantasmagorical history of Russian literature. Mikhail Nikolaev, to whom this is dedicated, spent most of his life in different Soviet institutions: a state orphanage during the 1930s, after the arrest of his parents; the Red Army during the war; and around twenty years in labour camps.

Six Years Later

So long had life together been that now
the second of January fell again
on Tuesday, making her astonished brow
lift like a windshield wiper in the rain,
so that her misty sadness cleared, and showed
a cloudless distance waiting up the road.

So long had life together been that once
the snow began to fall, it seemed unending;
that, lest the flakes should make her eyelids wince,
I'd shield them with my hand, and they, pretending
not to believe that cherishing of eyes,
would beat against my palm like butterflies.

So alien had all novelty become
that sleep's entanglements would put to shame
whatever depths the analysts might plumb;
that when my lips blew out the candle flame,
her lips, fluttering from my shoulder, sought
to join my own, without another thought.

So long had life together been that all
that tattered brood of papered roses went,
and a whole birch grove grew upon the wall,
and we had money, by some accident,
and tonguelike on the sea, for thirty days,
the sunset threatened Turkey with its blaze.

So long had life together been without
books, chairs, utensils – only that ancient bed –
that the triangle, before it came about,
had been a perpendicular, the head
of some acquaintance hovering above
two points which had been coalesced by love.

So long had life together been that she
and I, with our joint shadows, had composed
a double door, a door which, even if we
were lost in work or sleep, was always closed:
somehow, it would appear, we drifted right
on through it into the future, into the night.

(1968)
Richard Wilbur

On Love

Twice I woke up tonight and wandered to
the window. And the lights down on the street,
like pale omission points, tried to complete
the fragment of a sentence spoken through
sleep, but diminished darkness, too.
I'd dreamt that you were pregnant, and in spite
of having lived so many years apart
I still felt guilty and my heartened palm
caressed your belly as, by the bedside,
it fumbled for my trousers and the light-
switch on the wall. And with the bulb turned on
I knew that I was leaving you alone
there, in the darkness, in the dream, where calmly
you waited till I might return,
not trying to reproach or scold me
for the unnatural hiatus. For
darkness restores what light cannot repair.
There we are married, blest, we make once more

the two-backed beast and children are the fair
excuse of what we're naked for.
Some future night you will appear again.
You'll come to me, worn out and thin now, after
things in between, and I'll see son or daughter
not named as yet. This time I will restrain
my hand from groping for the switch, afraid
and feeling that I have no right
to leave you both like shadows by that sever-
ing fence of days that bar your sight,
voiceless, negated by the real light
that keeps me unattainable forever.

(1971)
Daniel Weissbort and Joseph Brodsky

Odysseus to Telemachus

My dear Telemachus,
The Trojan War is over now; I don't recall who won it.
The Greeks, no doubt, for only they would leave
so many dead so far from their own homeland.
But still, my homeward way has proved too long.
While we were wasting time there, old Poseidon,
it almost seems, stretched and extended space.
I don't know where I am or what this place can be.
It would appear some filthy island,
with bushes, buildings and great grunting pigs.
A garden choked with weeds; some queen or other.
Grass and huge stones . . . Telemachus, my son!
To a wanderer the faces of all islands
resemble one another. And the mind trips,
numbering waves; eyes, sore from sea horizons,
run; and the flesh of water stuffs the ears.
I can't remember how the war came out;
even how old you are – I can't remember.
Grow up, then, my Telemachus, grow strong.

Only the gods know if we'll see each other again.
You've long since ceased to be that babe
before whom I reined in the plowing bullocks.
Had it not been for Palamedes' trick
we two would still be living in one household.
But maybe he was right; away from me
you are quite safe from all Oedipal passions,
and your dreams, my Telemachus, are blameless.

(1972)
George Kline

A Part of Speech

I was born and grew up in the Baltic marshland
by zinc-grey breakers that always marched on
in twos. Hence all rhymes, hence that wan flat voice
that ripples between them like hair still moist,
if it ripples at all. Propped on a pallid elbow,
the helix picks out of them no sea rumble
but a clap of canvas, of shutters, of hands, a kettle
on the burner, boiling – lastly, the seagull's metal
cry. What keeps the heart from falseness in this flat region
is that there is nowhere to hide and plenty of room for vision.
Only sound needs echo and dreads its lack.
A glance is accustomed to no glance back.

(1975)
Daniel Weissbort

from *Performance*

to Misha Nikolayev[191]

Enter Tolstoy in a nightie, musing over deathless lines.
(Youths with knives prepared for fighting spread the
smell of Komsomól.)[192]
He is swinging on his writing just like Tarzan on his vines;
flying over French entrenchments is a Russian cannonball.
Lev is Russia's veggie lion! High-born, but with dirty feet,
he whose every other scion has no shoes and eats no meat.[193]

Whoops, a count transforms – surprise! –
into bookshelves of some size.

'She got used to oral sex.'
'What a scene – whatever next?'
'He was swearing like a swine.'
''Scuse me, who is last in line?'

(1986)
Alexandra Berlina

6
THREE MORE RECENT POETS

Dmitry Prigov (1940–2007)

Born in Moscow, Dmitry Alexandrovich Prigov began writing poetry as a teenager. A leading figure in the 'Moscow Conceptualist' circle of unofficial artists and writers, he was arrested in 1986 by the KGB. He was sent to a psychiatric institution but freed after protests from important figures. From 1987 he was published and exhibited officially. After receiving many prizes during his last years, he died from a heart attack in 2007.

Hugely prolific, he composed at least 15,000 poems, as well as plays, essays, stories, novels, drawings, textual objects, installations and video art. Much of his work aims to bring out into the open the ideology behind public voices, often by taking clichés to their logical conclusion. Evocations of everyday life are sometimes juxtaposed with the traditional expectation that Russian poetry should offer moral guidance and metaphysical truth.

It is often assumed that the role of an avant-garde is to shatter convention, but there is more than one kind of avant-garde: there are movements such as Cubism and Futurism that shatter norms and there are movements such as Dadaism that are, in essence, responses to a world already shattered. Moscow Conceptualism – and most other avant-gardes of Communist Eastern and Central Europe – were of this second type. Often Prigov seems to have taken on the role of reminding people of the existence of potential behavioural norms, or at least of encouraging them to question how and why these norms have been lost.

Among Prigov's most delightful works are his versions of the

Addresses and Appeals that the Communist Party used to publish on national holidays. Prigov used to write these on placards and attach them to lampposts or tree trunks in parks. It is easy to forget – now that more than twenty years have passed since the collapse of the Soviet Union – what courage this required. Prigov truly was risking his freedom. These addresses continue a tradition that originated with the maxims written by the fictional Kozma Prutkov (see p. 126) and was developed by Kazimir Malevich (who inscribed a 1915 drawing with the words 'You are now being struck on the head by the first word. The End') and then by Vvedensky and Kharms. Here is a brief selection:

Citizens! Don't lose your heads, please!

Citizens! We've never seen such a thing, but then it's never seen us either!

Citizens! The sun has gone behind the clouds but you are already jumping to conclusions!

Citizens! Burdens weighing on your soul are splendid. They increase its load-bearing capacity, don't they!

Citizens! I wouldn't bother you if I didn't believe in you!

Citizens! What can be more historical than a decisive act at a given concrete time!

Citizens! When you enter a dark corridor, you at once want to start running – but don't let yourselves go!

Citizens! There's a dusting of white snow on the fields. Such purity recalls the purity of our soul – can we call this to mind!

Citizens! Only love for you impels me to do this!

Citizens! This is not granted to you alone. Don't be in a hurry – someone more worthy than you may show up!

Citizens! Who taught letters to compose themselves into words? And words into songs? And songs to penetrate into our soul and set it trembling with ineffable delight?

Citizens! I warned you. It's up to you to act according to your own discretion!

Citizens! Honourable behaviour turns out, at the end of the day, to be the most profitable way to proceed!

Citizens! Today is passing – and darkness already clutches at your clothes!

The poem below is about a turning point in Russian history; after the Battle of Kulikovo (1380) the power of the Mongols began to wane. Prigov's irony contrasts with more grandiose treatments of this battle by earlier poets and artists.

from *Battle of Kulikovo*

Now everyone in place I've set
These here on the right I've set
Those there on the left I've set
I haven't touched the others yet
I haven't touched the Polish yet
I haven't touched the Frenchmen yet
I haven't touched the Germans yet
Now all my angels I have set
The ravens high above I've set
All kinds of birds high up I've set
Beneath there is a field I've let
For battle shall this field be set
A field with many trees beset
With oaks and spruces all beset
With bushes here and there beset
With silken grasses overgrown
By tiny crawlies overflown
All things shall run the course I've set!
I shall decide what life they get!
I shall decide what death they get!

So they shall win today, the Russians
They're after all good guys the Russians
The girls aren't bad among the Russians
They've suffered such a lot the Russians
They've suffered horrors from non-Russians
So they shall win today the Russians

[. . .] But then the Tatars do seem nice
To me their names seem rather nice
Their voices too are very nice
Their manners on the whole are nice
Although the Russians have less lice
But still the Tatars are so nice

Now then I'll let the Tatars win
From here the battle I shall see
So there, the Tatars, they shall win
But on the other hand – I'll see.

Alexandra Berlina

Elena Shvarts (1948–2010)

Born in Leningrad, Elena Andreyevna Shvarts attended the University of Tartu in Estonia. She published her first poems in the Tartu University newspaper in 1973, but from then until 1989 – although well known in Russia – she was able to publish only abroad or in samizdat.

The poet and translator Sasha Dugdale writes: 'In Shvarts's poetry, the world about her is transformed into a unique and mystical landscape, half-real, half-Breughelesque fantasy. St Petersburg's streets and enormous tenement blocks are peopled by the souls of the dead, the River Neva is an often malign force, the street where she once lived becomes "my Paradise, my lost Paradise". Her work is full of religious imagery: angels, demons, fools-in-Christ, icons and visions of heaven and hell, but the belief which illuminates the poems is far from orthodox. [. . .] In her writing, poetry itself is the sacred act [. . .] She writes in one poem, "When an angel carries away my soul / all shrouded in fog, folded in flames / I have no body, no tears to weep / just a bag in my heart, full of poems." '[1]

A metaphor running though Shvarts's work is that of bird-song escaping from a cage. The poem 'Birdsong on the Seabed' ends:

> Is it worth singing where no one can hear,
> unrolling trills on the bed?
> I am waiting for you, I lean from the boat –
> bird, ascend to the depths.
>
> (trans. Sasha Dugdale)

The second and third of the poems below are among the last Shvarts wrote.

*

How shameful it is to grow old –
I don't know why,
after all I never made a vow
I wouldn't die
or slip away, my white hairs shining
to the pitch-dark cellar,
nor did I promise myself
I'd stay a child for ever,
but all the same I'm suddenly uneasy –
my withering is plain.
I know why it hurts so much,
but why, oh why, this sense of shame?

(1994)
Sasha Dugdale

On the Street

A mirror's gaze slipped across me
half-mocking, half-severe
and in it, crooked, staring back
some laughable old dear.

Mirrors have often shown me change
yet in them, always, a face I knew –
till now. It would have seemed less strange
to see a beast come leaping through.

(2010)
Sasha Dugdale

Song

The sun once sang of safety
as it rose above
but then the sun knew nothing
of dark destroying love.

Down swept the sky,
slipped purple on the snows
and the blue tit piped:
your life draws to its close.

(2010)

Sasha Dugdale

Marina Boroditskaya (b. 1954)

Marina Yakovlevna Boroditskaya is a brilliant translator of English and American verse. Poets she has translated include Chaucer (the first Russian translation of his *Troilus and Criseyde*), Shakespeare, Donne, Burns, Keats and Kipling. Children's writers she has translated include Hilaire Belloc, Eleanor Farjeon, A. A. Milne and Alan Garner. She has published at least twenty books of poetry for children and five books of poetry for adults, though she does not see children's and adult poetry as essentially different, pointing out that 'they're made of the same stuff'.

Boroditskaya has won prizes for all aspects of her work and, since 1978, has contributed regularly to such journals as *Novy Mir* (New World) and *Inostrannaya Literatura* (Foreign Literature). She presents the Russian equivalent of *Poetry Please!* on Russian radio. Called *The Literary First Aid Box*, it is inspired by her belief that literature is the best medicine.

*

Cordelia, you are a fool! Would it have been
that hard to yield to the old man?
To say to him, 'I, too, O darling Daddy,
love you more than my life.' Piece of cake!
You wanted him to work it out on his own –
who was the best of his daughters. Proud fool!
And now he's dead, you too, everyone's dead.
And Gloucester! Oh the bloody horror –
his eye-sockets – the scene of the blinding –
fingers leafing quickly through the pages
as if through plates of red-hot iron . . . Here,
read it now. I'll turn away. You weren't there
in that Act, were you? Go on, read it,

look what you've done, you stupid little fool!
OK, OK, don't cry. Of course, the author
is quite a character, but next time
make sure to be more stubborn, and resist:
Viola, Rosalinda, Catherine,
they managed – why wouldn't you? Like a puppy,
pull him by the leg of his pants with your teeth
into the game, into comedy! The laws
of the genre will lead us out to light . . . Here,
wipe your nose and give me back the hanky.
I still have to wash and iron and return it
to a certain careless blonde Venetian
in the next volume. Sorry I told you off.
Best regards to your father. Remember: like a puppy!

(*c.* 2003)
Ruth Fainlight

*

And again they'll order a translation,
and a foreign poet, like an alien spaceman,
space-suit on fire, will enter the atmosphere
and land, as literals, on your writing table.

Get to work then, palms pumping chest,
trying to find life in this strange being,
to start the heart's rhythm, the lungs' action,
so he can breathe the harsh local air.

This one will probably live, but some die,
and who can you tell later or explain
how the sacred honey congeals in your breast,
refusing to be poured into strange vessels.

(*c.* 2003)
Ruth Fainlight

7
FOUR POEMS BY NON-RUSSIANS

Blaise Cendrars (1887–1961)

Swiss by birth but naturalized French in 1916, Cendrars was a friend of Apollinaire, Modigliani and Marc Chagall. His 'Prose of the Trans-Siberian', about a journey across Russia shortly before the 1905 Revolution, was printed on folded pages two metres long; it was illustrated by Sonia Delaunay, and Cendrars referred to it as the first 'simultaneous poem'. He also liked to claim that the first printing of 150 copies would, when unfolded, equal the height of the Eiffel Tower.

from *Prose of the Trans-Siberian Railway and of 'Petite Jehanne de France'*

If I were a painter I would expend a lot of red, a lot of
  yellow on this journey's end
For I think we were all of us a little crazy
And that a great delirium bathed the edgy faces of my fellow
  travellers as if in blood
As we neared Mongolia
Which roared like a conflagration.
The train had slowed
And I caught amid the constant squealing of the wheels
The wild tones and sobs

Of a liturgy without end
I saw
I saw the silent trains the black trains returning from
the Far East, passing like ghosts
And my eye, like a tail light, runs on after those
trains still
At Talga a hundred thousand wounded lay dying for want
of care
I visited the hospitals at Krasnoyarsk
And at Khilok we passed a long convoy of soldiers driven mad
In the field hospitals I saw the open wounds pumping blood
like organs
And amputated limbs danced all around or flew off into
the rasping air
The conflagration was on all faces in all hearts
Idiot fingers drummed on every window
And under the pressure of fear gazes burst like
an abscess
Carriages were torched in all the stations
And I saw
I saw trains made up of sixty locomotives fleeing at full
steam pursued by rutting horizons and gangs
of crows winging desperately behind
To disappear
In the direction of Port Arthur. [. . .]
I think I was drunk for more than five hundred kilometres
But I was at the piano and oblivious to everything else
When we travel we should shut our eyes
To sleep
How I wanted to sleep
I recognize all countries with my eyes shut from their smell
And all trains from the noise they make
European trains go at four beats to the bar but Asian ones
five or seven
Others run all quietly are lullabies
And some whose wheels have a monotonous sound
remind me of Maeterlinck's ponderous prose

I deciphered all the confused texts of the wheels and
 gathered the scattered elements of a violent beauty
Which I possess
And which overpowers me.

(1913)

Alan Passes

Nancy Mattson (b. 1947)

Born in Winnipeg and raised in Edmonton, Nancy Mattson spent her childhood summers in Saskatchewan on her Finnish grandparents' homesteads. She began writing poetry in 1977 after completing an MA in English Literature at the University of Alberta. In 1990 she moved to London.

Finns and Amazons, the most recent of her three full-length poetry collections, begins with poems about some Russian women artists of the avant-garde, but moves on to the theme of family history, inspired by her great-aunt Lisi's letters, sent in the 1930s from Soviet Karelia to Saskatchewan.

Learning the Letter Щ

I'm checking the ways to say that Cyrillic letter
shaped like a Roman three with a heelspur
or cricket stumps with a ploughshare
to cut beneath the bottom line of text: Щ

One teacher suggests I pay attention
to the double thistle in the gap
scratched between two words
whose start and finish match: Welsh sheep

Another says, listen to the scrape
of the hinge in a folding pushchair
or the mother's voice when her baby's shout
drowns out the bus's brakes: Hush child, we're nearly home

Another wants me to try the sound of steam released
when you touch the pressure cooker valve,
the cheery whistle of the sealed vessel
shortening the beet time for borsch: БОРЩ

I remember the steam train
screeching to a stop at the station
delivering everyone's grandmothers, flesh-cheeked
babushka-wrapped against December's harsh chill

I remember the shooshch
of my grandma's tongue and teeth
sucking her tea through a sugar cube
telling her stories in Finnish

Hush now, it's the one about her sister
in Soviet Russia, how she barely survived
on watery cabbage soup: ЩИ
but was finally crushed   lost   she

disappeared
the sound is a soft *shchi*
one wave in an ocean of millions
that receded but never returned

(2006)

Robert Chandler (b. 1953)

Robert Chandler first studied Russian at Winchester College at the age of fifteen. He was fortunate to have two outstanding Russian teachers: Count Nicholas Sollohub, whose family had left Russia when he was two; and Gordon Pirie, who later translated both Krylov and La Fontaine. Chandler went on to study Russian and English at Leeds University, spending the academic year 1973–4 as a British Council exchange scholar at the University of Voronezh, the city where Andrey Platonov was born and to which Osip Mandelstam was exiled in the mid-1930s. He is best known for his translations of Platonov and Vasily Grossman.

For Yelena

If your sister mentions your name, what I hear is
always a story you told us that evening,
the story of how, after you had moved to Tashkent –
Russian father, American mother, and you were born in China,
and in 1956 you had all gone back to the USSR, what
with your father suffering *toskà* for the Motherland
and your sister, Nadezhda, meaning 'Hope', dreaming
she could contribute, with her knowledge of languages,

to international understanding – what I hear is how, in
Tashkent, a city your grandfather, General Bitov,
had once conquered for Tsar Nikolay, but where you
yourselves lived in one room, since your holy fool of a father
had entrusted to GosBank all the dollars he had saved
during thirty years reluctantly trading timber,
and where you were trapped, since the USSR, then as
ever, was easier to get into than out of,

and the only blessing was that the Russian Consul in
Tsientsyn had had the grace to dissuade your father,
playing on his worries over baby Misha's asthma, and
the cold, and the journey, from returning before Stalin's death,
in which case you would all have been shot, or scattered
around the Gulag – yes, what I hear is how, in Tashkent,
your mother once boiled some valerian root to tide you
over who knows what upset, and while it was cooling,

the liquid was drunk by the cat, who then slipped into
the cupboard containing precious teacups from China,
your family's last link with a world now lost for ever,
and the cat, crazed by the valerian,
was unable to find its way out of the cupboard and
began to charge round in circles, pulverizing the china
and so aggravating its panic, which made it charge
faster, weaving together this story we always remember you by.

(early 1990s)

Andy Croft (b. 1956)

Andrew Croft is a writer, editor and poet based in the north-east of England. One of the most remarkable recent collections of English poetry is *Three Men on the Metro* (Nottingham: Five Leaves, 2009), the fruit of a ten-day visit to Moscow in 2008 by Andy Croft and two other poets, W. N. Herbert and Paul Summers. The publisher writes of this book: 'The Moscow Metro offers a singular perspective on the Russian psyche. Constructed over thirty years, largely during the Stalinist period, to provide transport, shelter, warmth, and a peculiarly Soviet grandeur, these "People's Palaces" are at once stunning feats of architecture – packed with the minutiae of period iconography to the point of kitsch – and fascinating temples to the quotidian, where all Muscovite life rushes before you. Its stations are named after the central principles and events of Russian society; they are named after its great writers, artists and scientists. They are constructed using marbles and materials from all over the vast hinterland of Mother Russia. The Metro is at once a microcosm of Russia itself, and a symbol of the infernal and purgatorial circles through which the Russian people have passed.'[1] We include Andy Croft's virtuoso epilogue to this collection.

from *Fellow Travellers*

No other railway in the world has ever had so many owners.
Bertolt Brecht

Dem bones, dem bones gonna walk aroun' until the break of day.
Traditional

The system's closing down; it's almost one.
Escaping from the sleepless night above us
we join the usual cast of sleepy lovers,

of night-shift workers, students, porters, punks,
the *bomzh*[2] and bums and shoeless cobbler-drunks,
not counting crows, the blind drunk and the blind,
the Moscow girls who leave the West behind,
pale, fur-lined Olga Kurylenko clones
with chilling Snow Queen eyes and frozen bones
like skeletons beneath their perfect skin.
Their priceless beauty's only rouble-thin.
The Metro graveyard shift is clocking on.

Here myth and magic mix with the mundane.
Before the last train out tonight departs
Sretenskiy Bul'var, the night-shift starts
to sweep the midnight Metro catacombs,
a regiment of witches with their brooms.
A Bilibin-like babushka stands facing
the question, 'Russia, whither art thou racing?'
(*Dead Souls* Part I) inscribed upon the wall.
She gives no answers, though she's heard them all.
She's seen the future and it works long hours.
The present is a bunch of crumpled flowers
and History is a drunk who's missed the train.

Down here among these bruised and bottled boozers
it's said that you can sometimes hear the squeals
of suicides beneath the carriage wheels
of empty, midnight trains that have no drivers;
perhaps it's just the ghosts of crash survivors,
or maybe it's the sound of Metro-2
(the ghostly system built for you know who)
but tales of Metro spirits fill the void
when other kinds of faith have been destroyed,
and maybe when you're heading home to bed
it's hard to tell the dead drunk from the dead,
the legless and the lost from History's losers.

Once caught inside the Metro's spider pattern,
we weave our way round webs of urban myth
re-told by Lukanenko and Cruz-Smith,
Moskva-Petushki[3] meets *The Twilight Zone*.
Some say the Metro's coughing up its bones
(Ezekiel 37) between the tracks –
the soft and matted curses of the *zeks*,[4]
the wet dreams of the Komsomols who drowned,
the cries of orphans buried underground,
the laughter of the architects whose faint
designs still show beneath the fading paint.
October's children swallowed whole by Saturn.

Among the ghosts who've joined us for the ride
is one old Durham miner called George Short.
Blacklisted after '26, George fought
against the Means Test, organized the ban
on Teesside pig-iron destined for Japan
in '38; he led the local fight
against the Blackshirts, won the public's right
to speak at Stockton Cross (for which he spent
three months in gaol); and when the Party sent
him here for cadre-training, volunteered
to dig these Metro tunnels. So I'm cheered
to feel his rebel spirit at our side.

For comrades such as George the age was drawn
in simple black-and-white chiaroscuro.
He was a cartoon Tankie to my Euro,
a hard-line Old Believer, unimpressed
by voices through the smoke of Budapest,
as if the laws of change do not apply
to change itself. And yet I can't deny
that some of those whom I have most admired
themselves admired the will that was required
to change the world and bring to bloody birth
inside these marbled halls beneath the earth
a painful future struggling to be born.

This 'Metro' comes from *metra* (Greek for womb),
the kind of joke that Platonov enjoyed,
and so from *Happy Moscow*[5] straight to Freud:
the rational city blinking in the light
that keeps its deepest secrets out of sight;
the Eloi-Ego who don't want to know
the Morlock-Id who really runs the show[6]
(why else are labour's efforts called the *base*?)
as propaganda is the human face
by which all states declare they will prevail,
so here inside the ribcage of the whale
all questions are reduced to who and whom.

These images of endless cornucopia
suggest the good intentions of the State,
like decorations round an empty plate;
a dream of Holy Rus or old Cockaigne,
from which now only crumbs of hope remain.
The World Turned Upside Down's turned inside out,
belief is just another word for doubt,
and History is a dog that's lost its balls.
The fields of golden wheat-sheaves on the walls
stand like abundant metonyms for famine,
ironic harvest halls which we examine
as if each grain of truth contains dystopia.

The builders of the Metro understood
this railway is a system of belief
confessed in marble, gilt and bas-relief.
It's four fifths engineering, one fifth art,
but where does one part end, the other start?
Down here of course the deepest structure's binary:
utile/dulce, hand/brain, function/finery,
the realms of darkness/light, above/below,
a bread *and* circus horror show, as though
the Base and Superstructure paradigm[7]
goes deeper than geology and time,
like seams of coal contained within the wood.

We mummify the future in the past
and hope that something good will one day grow,
like Russian spuds beneath the winter snow.
Apocalyptic sects go underground
as though the word of God sounds more profound
in amniotic caves of dark and dread.
Like Comrade Mole we crawl among the dead;
like shadows on the wall of Plato's cave;
or like Persephone, whose winter grave
was premised on the faith that it would bring
the pomegranate promise of the spring –
and hope the next one's better than the last.

It's nearly time for us to disappear;
first thing tomorrow morning we're off home,
still clutching our old volumes of Jerome
as if they made a map through History's maze
(cf. the Vernissage on busy days),
a *Rough Guide* to the Metro of the mind.
As if on cue, on our last night we find
they're showing on some Russian TV station
the classic 70s Soviet adaptation
of *Three Men in a Boat* (plus *dance* routines).
Though we were here, don't ask us what it means –
We barely dipped our whiskers in the beer.[8]

(2009)

Further Reading

1. ANTHOLOGIES

Evgeny Bunimovich and J. Kates (eds), *Contemporary Russian Poetry: An Anthology* (Champaign, IL.: Dalkey Archive Press, 2008).

Robert Chandler, Boris Dralyuk and Irina Mashinski (eds), *Cardinal Points Literary Journal*: www.stosvet.net, an important online and print journal where a number of translations in this anthology were first published.

Frances Cornford and Esther Polianowsky Salaman (eds), *Poems from the Russian* (London: Faber, 1943).

Sibelan Forrester and Martha Kelly (eds), *Russian Silver Age Poetry: A Coursebook and Contextbook* (Boston, MA: Academic Studies Press, 2015).

Peter France and Duncan Glen (eds), *European Poetry in Scotland: An Anthology of Translations* (Edinburgh: Edinburgh University Press, 1989).

John High et al. (eds), *Crossing Centuries: The New Generation in Russian Poetry* (Greenfield, MA: Talisman House, 2000).

Yakov Hornstein (trans.), *Poems by Alexander Blok, Nicolai Gumilev, Ilya Ehrenburg and Nina Berberova* (Surrey: Dorking, 1960).

J. Kates (ed.), *In the Grip of Strange Thoughts: Russian Poetry in a New Era* (Newcastle-upon-Tyne: Bloodaxe, 1999).

Catriona Kelly (ed.), *An Anthology of Russian Women's Writing 1777–1992* (Oxford: Oxford University Press, 1994).

Richard McKane, *Poet for Poet* (London: Hearing Eye, 1998).

—— (ed.), *Ten Russian Poets: Surviving the Twentieth Century* (London: Anvil Press, 2003). Especially good for Khlebnikov.

Vladimir Markov and Merrill Sparks (eds), *Modern Russian Poetry: An Anthology with Verse Translations* (London: MacGibbon & Kee, 1966). Russian texts and verse translations on facing pages.

Robin Milner-Gulland and Martin Dewhirst (eds), *Russian Writing Today* (Harmondsworth: Penguin, 1977).

Edwin Morgan, *Collected Translations* (Manchester: Carcanet, 1996).
Alan Myers (trans.), *An Age Ago: A Selection of Nineteenth-Century Russian Poetry* (New York: Farrar, Straus and Giroux, 1988).
Vladimir Nabokov (trans.), *Verses and Versions: Three Centuries of Russian Poetry*, ed. Brian Boyd and Stanislav Shvabrin (New York: Harcourt, 2008).
Dimitri Obolensky (ed.), *The Penguin Book of Russian Verse* (Harmondsworth: Penguin, 1965). Russian text, with good literal translations, republished as *The Heritage of Russian Verse* (Bloomington; London: Indiana University Press, 1976).
Peter Oram (trans.), *The Page and the Fire: A Collection of Poems by Russian Poets on Russian Poets* (Todmorden, Lancs.: Arc, 2007).
Eugene Ostashevsky (ed.), *OBERIU: An Anthology of Russian Absurdism* (Evanston, IL.: Northwestern University Press, 2006).
Valentina Polukhina and Daniel Weissbort (eds), *An Anthology of Contemporary Russian Women Poets* (Manchester: Carcanet, 2005).
Donald Rayfield et al. (eds), *The Garnett Book of Russian Verse* (London: Garnett Press, 2013). Russian text, with good literal translations.
Paul Schmidt (trans.), *The Stray Dog Cabaret: A Book of Russian Poems*, ed. Catherine Ciepiela and Honor Moore (New York: New York Review Books, 2007).
Larissa Shmailo (ed.), *Twenty-first-Century Russian Poetry*: http://tinyurl.com/pz7zr6v.
Maxim Shrayer (ed. and trans.), *An Anthology of Jewish-Russian Literature: Two Centuries of Dual Identity in Prose and Poetry* (Armonk, NY: Sharpe, 2007), vol. 2.
Gerald S. Smith (ed. and trans.), *Contemporary Russian Poetry: A Bilingual Anthology* (Bloomington; London: Indiana University Press, 1993).
Peter Washington (ed.), *Russian Poets* (New York: Everyman, 2009).
Yevgeny Yevtushenko, *Twentieth-Century Russian Poetry*, ed. Albert C. Todd and Max Hayward with Daniel Weissbort (London: Fourth Estate, 1993).

2. SELECTED TRANSLATIONS

Bella Akhmadulina, *The Garden*, ed. and trans. F. D. Reeve (London: Boyars, 1991).
Anna Akhmatova, *Selected Poems*, trans. Richard McKane (Newcastle-upon-Tyne: Bloodaxe, 1989).

Yevgeny Baratynsky, *Half-Light*, trans. Peter France (Todmorden, Lancs.: Arc, 2015).

Alexander Blok, *Selected Poems*, trans. Avril Pyman (Oxford: Pergamon Press, 1972). Bilingual text, excellent notes.

—— *Selected Poems*, trans. Jon Stallworthy and Peter France (Manchester: Carcanet, 2000).

Joseph Brodsky, *Collected Poems in English*, ed. Ann Kjellberg; trans. Anthony Hecht et al. (Manchester: Carcanet, 2001).

G. R. Derzhavin, *Poetic Works: A Bilingual Album*, trans. Alexander Levitsky and Martha T. Kitchen (Providence, RI: Brown Slavic Publications, 2001).

Alexander Galich, *Dress Rehearsal: A Story in Four Acts and Five Chapters*, trans. Maria Bloshteyn (Bloomington, IN: Slavica Publishers, 2008). An interesting memoir, with good versions of sixteen of his songs.

Daniil Kharms, *Incidences*, ed. and trans. Neil Cornwell (London: Serpent's Tail, 1993).

—— *Today I Wrote Nothing: The Selected Writings of Daniil Kharms*, trans. Matvei Yankelevich (London: Duckworth, 2007).

Velimir Khlebnikov, *The King of Time*, trans. Paul Schmidt, ed. Charlotte Douglas (Cambridge, MA: Harvard University Press, 1985).

—— *Collected Works of Velimir Khlebnikov*, trans. Paul Schmidt, vol. 3, *Selected Poems*, ed. Ronald Vroon (Cambridge, MA; London: Harvard University Press, 1997).

Vladislav Khodasevich, *Derzhavin: A Biography*, trans. Angela Brintlinger (Madison, WI: University of Wisconsin Press, 2007).

—— *Selected Poems*, trans. Peter Daniels (London: Angel Books, 2013). Bilingual edition.

Mikhail Kuzmin, *Selected Prose and Poetry*, trans. Michael Green (New York, NY: Ardis, 2013).

Mikhail Lermontov, *Major Poetical Works*, trans. Anatoly Liberman (London: Croom Helm, 1983).

Semyon Lipkin, *After Semyon Izrailevich Lipkin*, trans. Yvonne Green (Huddersfield: Smith|Doorstop, 2011).

Inna Lisnianskaya, *Far from Sodom*, trans. Daniel Weissbort (Todmorden, Lancs.: Arc, 2005).

Osip Mandelstam, *Selected Poems*, trans. James Greene (London: Penguin, 1991).

—— *A Necklace of Bees: Selected Poems*, trans. Maria Enzensberger (London: Menard Press, 1992).

—— *What I Own: Versions of Hölderlin and Mandelshtam*, trans. John Riley and Tim Longville (Manchester: Carcanet, 1998).

—— *The Selected Poems of Osip Mandelstam*, trans. Clarence Brown and W. S. Merwin (New York: New York Review Books, 2004).
—— *Poems of Osip Mandelstam*, trans. Peter France (New York: New Directions, 2014).
—— *Voronezh Notebooks*, trans. Andrew Davis (New York: New York Review Books, 2015).
Samuil Marshak and Vladimir Lebedev, *The Circus and Other Stories*, trans. Stephen Capus (London: Tate Publishing, 2013).
Vladimir Mayakovsky, *Wi the Haill Voice: 25 Poems*, trans. Edwin Morgan (Oxford: Carcanet, 1972).
—— *How are Verses Made?*, trans. George Hyde (Bristol: Bristol Classical Press, 1990).
—— *Listen!: Early Poems 1913–1918*, trans. Maria Enzensberger (San Francisco: City Lights, 1991).
——, *Vladimir Mayakovsky and Other Poems*, trans. James Womack (Manchester: Carcanet, 2015).
Boris Pasternak, Rainer Maria Rilke, Marina Tsvetaeva, *Letters: Summer 1926*, ed. Yevgeny Pasternak, Yelena Pasternak and Konstantin M. Azadovsky (New York: New York Review Books, 2001).
Alexander Pushkin, *Dubrovsky and Egyptian Nights*, trans. Robert Chandler (London: Hesperus, 2003).
—— *The Gypsies and Other Narrative Poems*, trans. Antony Wood (London: Angel Books, 2006).
—— *Eugene Onegin: A Novel in Verse*, trans. Stanley Mitchell (London: Penguin, 2008).
—— *The Captain's Daughter*, trans. Robert and Elizabeth Chandler (New York: New York Review Books, 2014).
Elena Shvarts, *Paradise: Selected Poems*, trans. Michael Molnar and Catriona Kelly (Newcastle-upon-Tyne: Bloodaxe, 1993).
—— *Birdsong on the Seabed*, trans. Sasha Dugdale (Tarset, Northumberland: Bloodaxe, 2008).
Boris Slutsky, *Things that Happened*, trans. G. S. Smith (Moscow; Birmingham: Glas, 1999).
Marina Tsvetaeva, *The Ratcatcher: A Lyrical Satire*, trans. Angela Livingstone (London: Angel Books, 1999).
—— *Bride of Ice: New Selected Poems*, trans. Elaine Feinstein (Manchester: Carcanet, 2009).
—— *Art in the Light of Conscience: Eight Essays on Poetry*, trans. Angela Livingstone (Tarset, Northumberland: Bloodaxe, 2010).
—— *Phaedra: A Drama in Verse, with New Year's Letter and Other Long Poems*, trans. Angela Livingstone (London: Angel Books, 2012).

Fedor Tyutchev, *On the Heights of Creation: The Lyrics of Fedor Tyutchev*, trans. Anatoly Liberman (Greenwich, CT; London: JAI, 1993).

Evgeny Vinokurov, *The War is Over*, trans. Anthony Rudolf and Daniel Weissbort (Cheadle: Carcanet, 1976).

Andrey Voznesensky, *An Arrow in the Wall: Selected Poetry and Prose*, ed. William Jay Smith and F. D. Reeve (London: Secker & Warburg, 1987).

Alexander Vvedensky, *An Invitation for Me to Think*, trans. Eugene Ostashevsky and Matvei Yankelevich (New York: New York Review Books, 2013).

Nikolay Zabolotsky, *Selected Poems*, trans. Daniel Weissbort and Robin Milner-Gulland (Manchester: Carcanet, 1999).

Vagrius (Moscow) publish useful bilingual editions of several poets, including Pushkin, Tyutchev, Lermontov and Mandelstam.

3. BIOGRAPHIES AND CRITICAL WORKS

Christopher Barnes, *Boris Pasternak: A Literary Biography*, 2 vols. (Cambridge: Cambridge University Press, 2004).

David Bethea, *Khodasevich: His Life and Art* (Princeton; Guildford: Princeton University Press, 1983).

Clarence Brown, *Mandelstam* (Cambridge: Cambridge University Press, 1978).

Robert Chandler, *Alexander Pushkin* (London: Hesperus, 2009).

Catherine Ciepiela, *The Same Solitude: Boris Pasternak and Marina Tsvetaeva* (Ithaca, NY: Cornell University Press, 2006).

Neil Cornwell (ed.), *Reference Guide to Russian Literature* (London: Routledge, 1998).

John Dewey, *Mirror of the Soul: A Life of the Poet Fyodor Tyutchev* (Shaftesbury: Brimstone Press, 2010).

Elaine Feinstein, *Anna of All the Russias: The Life of Anna Akhmatova* (London: Weidenfeld & Nicolson, 2005).

Peter France, *Poets of Modern Russia* (Cambridge: Cambridge University Press, 1982).

Marat Grinberg, *'I Am to Be Read Not from Left to Right, But in Jewish: from Right to Left': The Poetics of Boris Slutsky* (Boston, MA: Academic Studies, 2013).

Katharine Hodgson, *Voicing the Soviet Experience: The Poetry of Ol'ga Berggol'ts* (Oxford: Clarendon Press for the British Academy, 2003).

Catriona Kelly, *A History of Russian Women's Writing 1820–1992* (Oxford: Clarendon Press, 1994).
Marianna S. Landa, *Maximilian Voloshin's Poetic Legacy and the Post-Soviet Russian Identity* (New York; London: Palgrave Macmillan, 2015).
Angela Livingstone, *The Marsh of Gold: Pasternak's Writings on Inspiration and Creation* (Boston, MA: Academic Studies Press, 2008).
Lev Loseff, *Joseph Brodsky: A Literary Life* (New Haven, CT; London: Yale University Press, 2011).
John Malmstad and Nikolay Bogomolov, *Mikhail Kuzmin: A Life in Art* (Cambridge, MA: Harvard University Press, 1999).
Nadezhda Mandelstam, *Hope Against Hope* (London: Harvill, 1999).
—— *Hope Abandoned* (London: Harvill, 2011).
Vladimir Markov, *Russian Futurism: A History* (Washington, DC: New Academia Publishing, 2006).
D. S. Mirsky, *A History of Russian Literature*, ed. Francis J. Whitfield (London: Routledge & Kegan Paul, 1968).
Alice Stone Nakhimovsky, *Laughter in the Void: An Introduction to the Writings of Daniil Kharms and Alexander Vvedenskii*, vol. 5 of *Wiener Slawistischer Almanach* (Vienna, 1982) – excellent introduction to Kharms and Vvedensky.
Avril Pyman, *A History of Russian Symbolism* (Cambridge: Cambridge University Press, 2006).
Viktoria Schweitzer, *Tsvetaeva*, trans. Robert Chandler and H. T. Willetts (London: Harvill, 1992).
Victor Terras (ed.), *Handbook of Russian Literature* (New Haven, CT; London: Yale University Press, 1990).
Michael Wachtel, *The Development of Russian Verse: Meter and Its Meanings* (Cambridge: Cambridge University Press, 1998)
—— *The Cambridge Introduction to Russian Poetry* (Cambridge: Cambridge University Press, 2004).

4. OTHER

Andy Croft, W. N. Herbert and Paul Summers, *Three Men on the Metro* (Nottingham: Five Leaves, 2009).
Nancy Mattson, *Finns and Amazons* (Darlington: Arrowhead Press, 2012).

Acknowledgements

1. ORIGINALS

I am grateful for permission to include work by the following poets: Bella Akhmadulina, by permission of Boris Messerer; Anna Akhmatova, by permission of her estate and FTM; Olga Berggolts, by permission of her estate and FTM; Marina Boroditskaya; Joseph Brodsky, by permission of his estate, Farrar Straus and Giroux and Carcanet Press; Ivan Bunin, by permission of the Ivan and Vera Bunin Estate; Andy Croft; Alexander Galich, by permission of Alyona Arkhangelskaya-Galich; Rasul Gamzatov; Vladimir Kornilov, by permission of Larisa Bespalova; Semyon Lipkin and Inna Lisnianskaya, by permission of Inna Lisnianskaya; Alexander Mejirov, by permission of Zoya and Elena Mejirova; Bulat Okudzhava, by permission of Olga Okudzhava; Lev Ozerov, by permission of Anna Ozerova; Boris Pasternak, by permission of his estate and FTM; Dmitry Prigov, by permission of Nadya Bourova; David Samoilov, by permission of Alexander Davydov and Galina Medvedeva; Varlam Shalamov, by permission of his estate and FTM; Elena Shvarts, by permission of Bloodaxe Books; Konstantin Simonov, by permission of his estate and FTM; Boris Slutsky, by permission of Olga Frizen; Arseny Tarkovsky, by permission of Marina Tarkovskaya; Yevgeny Vinokurov, by permission of his estate and FTM; Andrey Voznesensky, by permission of Zoya Boguslavskaya; Vladimir Vysotsky, by permission of his estate and

Editions Le Chant du Monde; Yevgeny Yevtushenko; Nikolay Zabolotsky, by permission of his estate and FTM.

2. TRANSLATIONS

Unless otherwise indicated, translation copyright belongs to the translator. I am grateful to the following or their representatives for permission to include their translations: Alexandra Berlina; Ilya Bernstein; Maria Bloshteyn; Stephen Capus, with acknowledgement of prior publications in *Acumen* and *The London Magazine*; Frances Cornford, reprinted by permission of Tom Cornford; Guy Daniels; Peter Daniels; Andrew Davis; Tom de Waal; Boris Dralyuk, with acknowledgement of prior publication (Gumilyov, Yesenin and Zabolotsky) in *Drunken Boat*; Sasha Dugdale's poem beginning 'How shameful' reprinted by permission of Bloodaxe Books, other poems with her permission and acknowledgement of prior publication in the *Times Literary Supplement*; Ruth Fainlight, with acknowledgement of prior publication in *Modern Poetry in Translation*; Katie Farris; Elaine Feinstein, reprinted by permission of Carcanet Press; A. Z. Foreman; Peter France; Michael Frayn, with especial thanks for his ready generosity; Rawley Grau; James Greene; Yvonne Greene; Marat Grinberg; Eric Hill; Ilya Kaminsky; Catriona Kelly; Alexander Levitsky; Anatoly Liberman, his translations of Tyutchev from *On the Heights of Creation* by permission of Elsevier; Angela Livingstone, three translations of Pasternak reprinted by permission of Academic Studies Press, other translations with her permission; Hugh MacDiarmid, by permission of Carcanet Press; Irina Mashinski, with acknowledgement of prior publication of 'Cranes' in *Cardinal Points* and *The London Magazine*; Richard McKane; Stanley Mitchell, by permission of his estate; Edwin Morgan, by permission of Carcanet Press; Mike Munford, with acknowledgement of prior publication at The Poems and Life of Konstantin Simonov (www.simonov.co.uk/index.htm); Alan Myers, by permission of Farrar, Straus and Giroux; Alice Nakhimovsky; Lev Navrozov; Peter Oram, with acknowledgement of prior publications in *The Page and the Fire*; Eugene Ostashevsky; Alan Passes; Gordon Pirie, by permission of Eva Pirie and acknowledgement of prior publication of all Krylov translations in *Translation and Literature* (Spring 2009);

Judith Pulman; Avril Pyman; James Ragan; Donald Rayfield; Christopher Reid; John Riley, by permission of Carcanet Press; Margo Shohl Rosen; Paul Schmidt, by permission of Margaret Sand and with acknowledgement of prior publication in *The Stray Dog Cabaret*; Alan Shaw; G. S. Smith; Jon Stallworthy; Daniel Weissbort; Richard Wilbur, by permission of Carcanet and Farrar, Straus and Giroux; Steven Willett; James Womack; Antony Wood; Matvei Yankelevich; and Katherine E. Young.

Some of my own translations have appeared in *Adbusters*, *Agenda*, *Brittle Star*, *Cardinal Points, Caravan*, the *Financial Times*, the *Jewish Quarterly*, *London Grip*, *Long Poem Magazine*, *Metre*, *Modern Poetry in Translation*, *New England Review*, *New Humanist*, *The New York Review of Books*, *PN Review*, *Poem Magazine*, *Poetry London*, *Standpoint*, *Stinging Fly*, the *Times Literary Supplement* and The *White Review*. I am grateful to all the following for their help: Michele Berdy, Larisa Bespalova, David Black, Maria Bloshteyn, Olive Classe, Elizabeth Cook, Richard Davies, Xenia Dyakonova, Sibelan Forrester, Milla Fyodorova, Marat Grinberg, Edythe Haber, Ellen Hinsey, Alina Israeli, Sara Jolly, Martha Kapos, Masha Karp, Clare Kitson, Marianna Landa, Josefina Lundblad, Olga Meerson, Larissa Miller, Robin Milner-Gulland, Elena Ostrovskaya, Natasha Perova, Anna Pilkington, Donald Rayfield, Oliver Ready, William Ryan, Sergey Solovyov, Irina Steinberg, Leona Toker and Josephine von Zitzewitz.

R. C.

Notes

INTRODUCTION

1. *It was like a ritual . . . and bitter*: Lidiia Chukovskaia, 'Vmesto predisloviia (1966),' in *Zapiski ob Anne Akhmatovoi*, vol. 1, 1938–41 (Moscow: Vremia, 2013), p. 12.
2. *The shamans . . . seventh sky*: N. I. Gagen-Torn, *Memoria* (Moscow: Vozvrashchenie, 1994), p. 109.
3. *sent a copy by a friend*: Communication channels sometimes functioned remarkably well. In another story, 'The Best Praise', Shalamov mentions hearing a cellmate in Butyrka Prison, Moscow, in 1937, recite recent poems by Khodasevich and Tsvetaeva. The cellmate had lived in Paris, then returned to the Soviet Union (*Sobranie sochinenii v shesti tomakh* (Moscow: Terra, 2013), vol. 1, p. 288).

1. THE EIGHTEENTH CENTURY

1. *the most illustrious . . . Russian writer*: Anna Lisa Crone, 'Derzhavin', in Neil Cornwell (ed.), *Reference Guide to Russian Literature* (London: Routledge, 1998), p. 242.
2. *his genius . . . want of time*: Pushkin, Letter to A. A. Del'vig (Delvig), early June 1825, in *Polnoe sobranie sochinenii v 16 tomakh* (Moscow-Leningrad: Akademiia nauk SSSR, 1937–59), vol. 13, p. 182.
3. *To Rulers and Judges*: The censors did not allow Derzhavin to publish this poem (a paraphrase of Psalm 82) in full until 1808; a version of the same psalm had been sung in Paris during the French Revolution.
4. *On the Death of Prince Meshchersky*: Prince Alexander Meshchersky, famous for his banquets, died in 1779. This ode,

modelled on Edward Young's *Night Thoughts on Life, Death and Immortality* (1742–5), is addressed to General Perfilyev, who, like Derzhavin, was often one of Meshchersky's guests.

5. *The Waterfall*: The opening of one of Derzhavin's grandest odes, written on the death of Prince Potyomkin, a powerful statesman and the lover and lifelong friend of Catherine the Great.
6. *Monument*: A version of Horace's ode *Exegi monumentum* ('I have built a monument'). For a version by Pushkin, see page 101.
7. *Felitsa*: The name of a Tatar princess, but here Derzhavin's name for Catherine the Great.
8. *peasant children . . . a skinflint*: Derzhavin liked to spend time with the peasant children and often acted as arbiter in their arguments. He was, in a way, reliving his last official post – Minister of Justice.
9. *gusli*: A stringed instrument resembling a zither.
10. *On Transience*: Read as an acrostic, the poem takes on another meaning. The first letters of each Russian line form the words 'Ruina chti', either 'Honour the Ruin' or 'Read the Ruin'.

2. AROUND PUSHKIN

1. *Almost everything . . . very own*: Quoted in Michael Pursglove, 'Vasily Andreyevich Zhukovsky', in *The Literary Encyclopedia*: http://www.litencyc.com/php/speople.php?rec=true&UID=4850.
2. *Pushkin Pleiade . . . posthumous reputation*: See Ilya Kutik, *Fulcrum: An Anthology of Poetry and Aesthetics*, no. 7 (2011), pp. 536–8.
3. *No one . . . speech of waves*: Trans. Peter France, *Poems of Osip Mandelstam* (New York: New Directions, 2014), p. 51.
4. *And if my life . . . begins to fall*: Trans. Alan Myers, *An Age Ago* (New York: Farrar, Straus and Giroux, 1988), p. 25.
5. *found . . . moral ills*: Donald Rayfield, 'Viazemskii', in Cornwell (ed.), *Reference Guide*, p. 875.
6. *that's him . . . Russian god*: The Russian for 'that's him' is *vot on* – close to Wotan, the name of the old German god.
7. *a gold mine*: Donald Rayfield, 'Kiukhel'beker', in Cornwell (ed.), *Reference Guide*, p. 454.
8. *a fearsome . . . dream world*: Donald Rayfield, 'Del'vig', in Cornwell (ed.), *Reference Guide*, p. 240.
9. *the first death . . . weep*: Pushkin, Letter to P. A. Pletnyov (21 January 1831), in *Polnoe sobranie*, vol. 14, p. 147.

10. *Baratynsky ranks . . . and deep*: Quoted in *Pushkin on Literature*, ed. and trans. Tatiana Wolff (London: Methuen, 1971), p. 269.
11. *a poet of thought . . . sentiment*: D. S. Mirsky, *A History of Russian Literature* (London: Routledge & Kegan Paul, 1968), p. 102.
12. *I remember . . . I had to do*: Joseph Brodsky, quoted in Lev Loseff, *Joseph Brodsky: A Literary Life* (New Haven, CT; London: Yale University Press, 2011), p. 57.
13. *What if a star . . . rapturous melody!*: While composing this stanza, Baratynsky heard the news of Pushkin's death. He was shocked not only by the news itself, but also by society's apparent lack of concern.
14. *Elizabeth . . . throne*: From 1741 to 1762 Russia was ruled by the Empress Elizabeth.

3. ALEXANDER PUSHKIN

1. *Our desire . . . impending darkness*: Vladislav Khodasevich, 'Koleblemyi trenozhnik', in *Sobranie sochinenii v dvukh tomakh*, ed. John Malmstad and Robert P. Hughes (Ann Arbor, MI: Ardis, 1983–90), vol. 2, p. 312.
2. *Yevgenia Ginzburg . . . found nothing*: See Ekaterina Olitskaia, 'My Reminiscences', in Sheila Fitzpatrick and Yuri Slezkine (eds.), *In the Shadow of Revolution* (Princeton, NJ; Chichester: Princeton University Press, 2000), p. 431.
3. *Pushkin is . . . on his lips*: Andrey Sinyavsky, *Progulki s Pushkinym* (Petersburg: Vsemirnoe slovo, 1993), pp. 69–70.
4. *leshy*: A forest spirit.
5. *Epigram*: This poem is about Count Mikhail Vorontsov (1782–1856), the Governor General of 'New Russia and of Bessarabia', i.e., of most of southern Russia. Vorontsov was Pushkin's boss during much of his southern exile.
6. Addressed to Amalia Riznich, with whom Pushkin had an affair in Odessa. She left Odessa in May 1824 and died in Italy a year later, probably of consumption.
7. *a six-winged seraph*: From Isaiah 6:2, but this poem also alludes to traditions concerning the 'heart-cleansing' of the Prophet Muhammad (Hadiths relating to Sura 94 of the Koran). Pushkin wrote his 'Imitations of the Koran' in the same year as 'The Prophet'. Tsvetaeva's remarkable French translation of 'The Prophet' ends: 'Debout, Prophète! Vois, écoute! / Emplis ton être de ton Dieu! / Que ta demeure soit – la route, / Et que ton verbe soit – du feu.'

8. *To Ivan Pushchin*: Pushchin was one of the conspirators exiled to Siberia after the failed Decembrist rebellion of 1825. Here Pushkin remembers Pushchin being the first of his friends to visit him when he himself was in exile, in Mikhailovskoye.
9. *A Feast in Time of Plague*: One of Pushkin's 'Little Tragedies', an adaptation of part of a play by a Scottish writer, John Wilson (1785–1854). The song from which I have excerpted these lines is Pushkin's original composition.
10. *The Egyptian Nights*: Pushkin worked on this between 1824 and 1835. It probably began as a poem in its own right, but Pushkin then incorporated it in his unpublished story 'The Egyptian Nights'.
11. *Cleopatra e i suoi amanti*: (Italian) Cleopatra and her lovers.
12. *The Bronze Horseman*: The equestrian statue of Peter the Great by Étienne Falconet, long an emblem of Petersburg. Commissioned by Catherine the Great, this was unveiled on 7 August 1782, the official centenary date of Peter's accession to the throne, in a square close to the River Neva.
13. *Nevá*: Stanley Mitchell chose, Russian-style, to stress the last syllable of the river's name. Antony Wood chose to stress the first syllable, English-style. It seemed best to accept this clash as a salutary reminder that translation inevitably entails inconsistencies.
14. Mitchell died before completing his translation of *The Bronze Horseman*. His version of the 'Prologue' is superb, but he would certainly have revised it further. With his family's permission, we have made small changes to six passages we believe Stanley would himself have revised had he lived longer.
15. *the pen of Karamzin*: Nikolay Karamzin's twelve-volume *Istoriia gosudarstva Rossiiskogo* (*History of the Russian State*, 1818–29).
16. *Before it*: A line left unrhymed in the original.
17. *Petropolis . . . Poseidon*: 'Petropolis' is a Greek form of 'Petersburg'. Poseidon is the Greek god of the oceans. Triton is his son and messenger; his emblem is a trident.
18. *the ill work crimson-covered*: Crimson or purple was the ceremonial colour of the Tsar's mantle. This line refers not only to the dawn but also to the Tsar's failure to deal adequately with the flood.
19. *Count Khvostov*: Dmitry Khvostov (1757–1835) was a bad poet generally loved for his good nature. Karamzin once wrote of Khvostov's passion for versifying: 'Here is love that is worthy of a talent. He has none, but he deserves to have it' (*Pis'ma N. M. Karamzina k I. I. Dmitrievu* (Petersburg: Akademiia nauk, 1866), p. 379).

20. *Wedding Song*: Pushkin presents this as a folk song, but it is his own composition.
21. *Exegi monumentum*: A version of *Exegi monumentum* by the Latin poet Horace (65–8 BC). For a version by Derzhavin, see p. 13.
22. *Alexander's Column*: A column erected on Palace Square in Petersburg in honour of Tsar Alexander I (1777–1825).

4. AFTER PUSHKIN

1. *know all of Tyutchev by heart*: Mandelstam is quoted in Shalamov, *Sobranie sochinenii v shesti tomakh*, vol. 3, p. 447.
2. A poem much loved by Russian xenophobes, though it is possible it was intended ironically. In a letter to his wife the following year, Tyutchev wrote, 'dear Russia, a poor and unwelcoming country incomparably easier to love than to live in.' We include two translations: Liberman's is the easier to read ironically. The poet Igor Guberman (b. 1936) has written this retort to Tyutchev:

   High fucking time that someone tried
   to grasp our Russia with their mind.
   (trans. Boris Dralyuk)

3. *as if he were . . . passers-by*: Christopher Barnes, *Boris Pasternak: A Literary Biography*, vol. 1: 1890–1928 (Cambridge: Cambridge University Press, 1989), p. 234.
4. *I replied . . . our soul*: Samuil Marshak, 'Vospitanie slovom', in *Sobranie sochinenii v vos'mi tomakh* (Moscow: Khud. lit-ra, 1971), vol. 7, p. 7.
5. *The Sail*: We include three translations of this famous lyric, each more condensed than the one before it. The first most nearly reproduces the original's external form, but it is the last that best captures its magic – and with no sacrifice of meaning.
6. *Cossack Lullaby*: Partly based on a poem by Sir Walter Scott (1771–1832) called 'Lullaby of an Infant Chief', itself inspired by folk songs, 'Cossack Lullaby' entered the oral tradition and was sung by people who did not know its author. Our translation borrows from an earlier one by Gilbert F. Cunningham. The poem has been set to music at least a hundred times.
7. This poem was not published until 1887, more than forty years after Lermontov's death. He may have written it on receiving

news of his second exile, when he was ordered to leave Petersburg within forty-eight hours. The tsarist police wore blue uniforms.

8. Perhaps Lermontov's most perfect lyric, this was translated into German by Rilke.
9. *the heart's mind*: Tolstoy, Letter to A. A. Fet (28 June 1867), in *Sobranie sochinenii v 22 tomakh* (Moscow: Khud. lit-ra, 1978–85), vol. 18, pp. 665–6.
10. *And whence ... great poet*: Tolstoy, Letter to V. P. Botkin (21 July 1857), ibid., p. 484.
11. *a lyrical poem ... it contains*: Fet, Letter to Konstantin Romanov (27 December 1886), quoted in A. M. Ranchin, *Putevoditel' po poezii A. A. Feta* (Moscow: Izd-vo Moskovskogo Universiteta, 2010), p. 43.
12. *expected ... one's lips*: Fet, Letter to Konstantin Romanov (8 October 1888), in *Sochineniia v dvukh tomakh* (Moscow: Khud. lit-ra, 1982), vol. 2, p. 181.
13. *Without always ... Turgenev's Smoke*: Donald Rayfield, *The Garnett Book of Russian Verse*, ed. Rayfield, J. Hicks, O. Makarova, A. Pilkington (London: Garnett Press, 2013), p. xvi.
14. Here nothing has been lost in translation and much gained. Pirie has edited out some padding; where Fet, for example, writes 'my faithful dog', Pirie writes simply 'my dog'. Many lines (e.g., 'and one day's death become another's dawning') are more memorable than in the original.
15. *A poet ... his poetry*: Annensky, 'A. N. Maikov i pedagogicheskoe znachenie ego poezii' (1898), *Knigi otrazhenii* (Moscow: Nauka, 1979), p. 278.
16. See Kornei Chukovsky, *The Poet and the Hangman: Nekrasov and Muravyov*, trans. R. W. Rotsel (Ann Arbor, MI: Ardis, 1977).
17. *Princess Volkonskaya*: Like most of Nekrasov's work, this poem is grounded in fact. Pushkin spent the summer of 1820 travelling through the Caucasus and the Crimea with the family of General Raevsky. Maria, the general's youngest daughter, is famous for choosing, six years later, to accompany her husband, one of the Decembrist rebels, into exile in Siberia.

5. THE TWENTIETH CENTURY

1. *I don't mean . . . kin to him*: Anna Akhmatova, quoted in *Stikhotvoreniia. Poemy. O poetakh* (Moscow: Kniga, 1989), p. 338.
2. *Bronze Poet*: Annensky has in mind a statue of Pushkin in the Lycée Garden at Tsarskoye Selo. For other takes on the theme of poets and monuments, see Derzhavin (p. 13), Pushkin (p. 101), Khodasevich (p. 246) and Vysotsky (pp. 497–8).
3. *Friend whom . . . eyes of others*: Teffi, *Moia letopis'* (Moscow: Vagrius, 2004), p. 233.
4. *Constituent Assembly*: The All-Russian Constituent Assembly – the first democratically elected legislative body in Russian history – was convened after the October Revolution. It met for thirteen hours on 18–19 January before being dissolved by the Bolshevik Party and their allies. The Bolsheviks had received less than 25 per cent of the popular vote.
5. *another Tamara*: The title role in Fokine's staging of Stravinsky's *The Firebird* was created by the prima ballerina Tamara Karsavina, who left Russia in 1919.
6. *Whether Decadence . . . Yes, me!*: Valery Bryusov, quoted in Cornwell (ed.), *Reference Guide*, p. 188.
7. *Padraic Breslin . . . remembered*: In 1928 Breslin was one of seven Irish Communists invited to Moscow to study in the International Lenin School. After being expelled for 'idealist tendencies', he worked as a translator. As well as socio-political articles, he translated poems by Blok, Korney Chukovsky and Mayakovsky; he also translated poems in praise of Stalin, with verve. In the late 1930s Breslin tried to return to Ireland, but the Irish government revoked his citizenship and he was unable to leave Moscow. He took to drink; on one occasion in 1940, when Britain was at war with Germany and the Nazi–Soviet non-aggression pact was still in force, he began singing 'God Save the King' in a public place. Arrested in December that year, Breslin died in a transit prison camp in 1942.
8. *the False Dmitry*: Grigory (or Grishka) Otrepyev, popularly known as 'The False Dmitry', was a monk who claimed to be Dmitry, the murdered son of Ivan the Terrible. He reigned for eleven months during 1605–6.
9. *his Dostoevskian . . . poetic word*: Marianna Landa, 'Symbolism and Revolution: On Contradictions in Maximilian Voloshin's

Poems on Russia and Terror in the Crimea (1917–1920s)', *SEEJ* (Summer 2014), p. 217. Our thanks to Marianna Landa for her help with this introductory note as a whole.

10. *Alexander Blok and Nikolay Gumilyov*: August 1921 saw not only the death of Blok but also the execution of Gumilyov.
11. *Oprichniki*: The period between 1565 and 1572, during which Ivan the Terrible confiscated land from the old nobility and carried out mass repressions and public executions, is known as the *Oprichnina*. The secret police, the *oprichniki*, used to dress in black and ride black horses; their symbols were a broom and a dog's head – to represent the sweeping away of traitors and themselves snapping at the heels of enemies.
12. *Bakunin*: Mikhail Bakunin, an anarchist philosopher, was imprisoned under Nicholas I. Bakunin criticized Marx for the contradiction between his libertarian goal and his authoritarian means.
13. *Peter's streltsy . . . needed Nikon*: In 1698 the Streltsy regiments rebelled against Peter the Great. More than 1,200 men were tortured and executed. The archpriest Avvakum is the archetypal Russian dissident. His protests against the reform of the Orthodox ritual by the Patriarch Nikon (1605–81) led to his being burnt at the stake.
14. *Blok had spent . . . the last line*: Avril Pyman, 'Blok', in Cornwell (ed.), *Reference Guide*, p. 180.
15. *By the time . . . he calmly agreed*: Lucy Vogel (ed.), *Blok: An Anthology of Essays and Memoirs* (Ann Arbor, MI: Ardis, 1982), p. 173.
16. *So much . . . for us all*: Georgy Ivanov, *Sobranie sochinenii v trekh tomakh* (Moscow: Soglasie, 1994), vol. 3, p. 173.
17. *But great though . . . passionate whirlwind*: Mirsky, *History of Russian Literature*, p. 463. See also the entry on Blok in Victor Terras (ed.), *Handbook of Russian Literature* (New Haven, CT; London: Yale University Press, 1990); Avril Pyman's entries on Blok and 'The Twelve' in Cornwell (ed.), *Reference Guide*; and Pyman's article on Blok in *The Best of Russian Life: Biographies*, ed. Paul E. Richardson (Montpelier, VT: Russian Information Services, 2011).
18. *if he had to choose . . . he would hesitate*: Mirsky, quoted in Alexander Blok, *Selected Poems*, trans. Avril Pyman (Oxford: Pergamon Press, 1972), p. 275.
19. *the tragic tenor of the epoch*: Lidiia Chukovskaia, *Zapiski ob Anne Akhmatovoi*, vol. 2, 1952–62 (Moscow: Vremia, 2013), p. 453.

20. *The Stranger*: Avril Pyman writes: 'She is surely Lilith. By Blok's contemporaries she was taken for a prostitute, and Annenkov even tells us that the Petersburg prostitutes took to dressing exactly like her, even to borrowing her name, so often did they hear tipsy students reciting Blok's tipsy verses' (*Selected Poems*, p. 218).
21. *the earth's bubbles*: 'The earth hath bubbles, as the water has, / And these are of them,' says Banquo to Macbeth when the three witches vanish (I.3.77–8). From 1904 to 1905 Blok wrote a poem-cycle entitled 'Bubbles of the Earth', incorporating motifs from folk magic. In 1907 he wrote of Shakespeare, 'I love him deeply; and perhaps, most deeply of all – in the whole of world literature – *Macbeth*' (*Selected Poems*, p. 232).
22. Pyman writes of the schoolgirl to whom this is addressed: 'Having seen Blok read his poetry at various literary gatherings, she had decided that he would [. . .] be able to help her to resolve her adolescent miseries – loss of faith in God and a corrosive hatred of Petersburg – Blok's Petersburg. [. . .] The man of 27, whose life and poetry were at that time the scandal and delight of literary Petersburg, received the unknown schoolgirl (who had gate-crashed his flat with no introduction) with courteous attention. She left him feeling that he was perhaps more lost even than she, that she was in some way the older. A few days later the poem "When you stand in my path" arrived through the post. The little girl achieved as full a life as Blok could have wished for her. Twice married, the mother of three children, she became a nun in the Paris emigration, helped Jews to hide from the Nazis during the occupation and ended her days [in Ravensbruck] (ibid., p. 233). For more on Mother Maria (E. Kuz'mina – Karavaeva), see Teffi, *Memories* (2016), pp.113 & 258.
23. *Jesus Christ*: In one of several similar notes, Blok wrote, 'I do not like the end of *The Twelve* either. I would like its end to be different. When I finished the poem, I was amazed myself: why Christ? But the more I looked into it, the more clearly I saw Christ. And, then and there, I made an entry: "Unfortunately it has to be Christ"' (*Sobranie sochinenii v vos'mi tomakh* (Moscow-Leningrad: Khud. lit-ra, 1960–65), vol. 3, p. 628).
24. *Once I was sitting . . . writer's inkwell*: Quoted in Raymond Cooke, *Velimir Khlebnikov: A Critical Study* (Cambridge: Cambridge University Press, 1987), p. 160; Velimir Khlebnikov, *Sobranie sochinenii v shesti tomakh* (Moscow: IMLI RAN, 2006), vol. 2, p. 44.

25. *The contact with nature . . . a natural step*: Donald Rayfield, 'Velimir Khlebnikov', Proc. of 10th Congress of Australasian ULLA (Auckland, New Zealand, 1966), pp. 113–35.
26. *Man has taken . . . inside his heart*: Quoted in Yevgeny Kovtun, *The Russian Avant-garde in the 1920s–1930s*, ed. Irina Kharitonova, trans. Robert Goebel and Catherine Philips (Bournemouth: Parkstone, 1996), p. 132.
27. *I announced . . . replaced the Word*: Velimir Khlebnikov, *Collected Works*, ed. Ronald Vroon, trans. Paul Schmidt (Cambridge, MA: Harvard University Press, 1987), vol. 1, pp. 27–8.
28. *Every line . . . icon case*: Mandelstam, 'Buria i natisk' (1923), in *Polnoe sobranie sochinenii v trekh tomakh* (Moscow: Progress-Pleiada, 2010), vol. 2, p. 138.
29. *Laugh Chant*: It was with this riff on the word *smekh* ('laughter') that Khlebnikov made his name; by adding different combinations of the prefixes and suffixes with which the Russian language is so rich, he creates many new words. One of his neologisms – *smekhach* ('laugher') – entered the Russian language; in the 1920s there was even a satirical journal called *Smekhach*. In autumn 1915 Khlebnikov noted, 'A seven-year-old boy, the little son of some people I know, was reading "Laugh away, laughing boys!" He and I chatted together, feeling we were conspirators among the grown-ups' (*Sobranie sochinenii v shesti tomakh*, vol. 1, p. 480).
30. *Vyacheslav Ivanov*: (1866–1949) A Symbolist poet, for several years a mentor to Khlebnikov and many others. 'The Tower', the turreted house where Ivanov lived with his wife Lydia Zinovieva-Annibal, a gifted writer herself, was the most fashionable literary salon of the period between 1905 and 1914. It was there, in spring 1911, that Mandelstam and Akhmatova first met.
31. *the rock of Pavda*: In the Ural Mountains.
32. *Port Arthur*: In the summer of 1904 the Japanese attacked the Russian fleet anchored at Port Arthur. Khlebnikov claimed that his sense of personal humiliation over the eventual Russian defeat led him to devote his life to discovering 'the laws of time'.
33. *the Lay of Igor's Campaign*: The only manuscript of this mediaeval national epic was destroyed during the fire that consumed Moscow in 1812, after Napoleon entered the city.
34. Written shortly before the centenary of Derzhavin's death, this continues the theme of Derzhavin's last poem. See p. 17.
35. *An Appeal by the Chairmen of the Terrestrial Globe*: Khlebnikov was both shy and grandiose. His pseudonym 'Velimir'

means 'world-ruler' and in December 1915 he founded a 'Society of Chairmen of the Terrestrial Globe'. His only real concern, however, seems to have been to recruit enough fellow-chairmen to bring the total up to 317, a key number in his personal system of numerology. Among the other chairmen were Malevich, Prokofiev, the political leader Alexander Kerensky, the Italian poet Filippo Marinetti and many other poets, including Kuzmin, Pasternak, Mayakovsky and Rabindranath Tagore.

36. *By the Grace of Fiji*: Khlebnikov wrongly imagines cannibalism to be widespread in Fiji.
37. *Razin*: Stenka Razin (1630–71), a Cossack who led a major peasant uprising in South Russia.
38. *Love Flight*: This love poem is a greeting to two of Khlebnikov's Futurist comrades. The Russian for 'twisted' is *kruchonykh* (identical to the surname of the poet Alexey Kruchonykh) and the word *nate* (an exclamation not translated here, but which means something like 'There you are!') is the title of an early poem by Mayakovsky.
39. *Samorodov's foot . . . at sea*: Boris Samorodov was an artist and sailor who did indeed instigate a mutiny. We know from Khlebnikov's diary that Samorodov gave him some old clothes and shoes.
40. *Krasnovodsk . . . Red water*: The name Krasnovodsk means 'red water'.
41. *Mahdi*: In Shia Islam the Mahdi is the redeemer who will rule before the Day of Judgement.
42. *Hunger*: Like much of Khlebnikov's work, this poem exists in different versions. We have translated the shortest complete version. A draft includes the lines: 'And their faces are more transparent than windows / so that hunger, like a bearded, self-satisfied landlord, / can look out through a child's face. / The children are melting.'
43. *Hunger*: This is the third section of a longer version of the poem.
44. In an article in the *Communist International* (December 1920) Gorky had written: 'For Lenin, Russia is only the material for an experiment that has been begun on a worldwide, planetary scale' (Khlebnikov, *Collected Works*, vol. 2, p. 581). Khlebnikov evidently sympathized with Gorky's doubts about the ethics of this experiment.
45. *The Solitary Player*: Written after learning of the execution of Nikolay Gumilyov, Akhmatova's former husband. Line 4 evokes Pushkin's 'The Prophet' (p. 72). The 'underground bull' is the

Cretan Minotaur – half-bull, half-man – to which Athenian young men and maidens were sacrificed. Akhmatova may herself be the 'enchantress', i. e., Ariadne, the Cretan princess who gave Theseus the thread that enabled him to find his way out of the labyrinth after killing the Minotaur.

46. *that a sower of eyes must appear*: An allusion to 'Lonely Sower of Freedom' (1823), in which Pushkin doubts the value of his youthful attempts to 'sow freedom' through radical verse; it also alludes to the Parable of the Sower and to the words Jesus speaks immediately after it: 'And in them is fulfilled the prophecy of Esaias, which saith, By hearing ye shall hear, and shall not understand; and seeing ye shall see, and shall not perceive' (Matthew 13:14).
47. *the last swan of Tsarskoye Selo*: In his poem 'To the Memory of Annensky' (1912).
48. *For the Acmeists . . . or whatever else*: Gorodetsky, 'Nekotorye techeniia v sovremennoi russkoi poezii', *Apollon*, no. 1 (1913), p. 48.
49. *the excruciating . . . power of Russia*: In his poem 'Not by a mother, but by a Tula peasant-woman' (1922).
50. *Moscow . . . intensified it*: Khodasevich, *Nekropol'* (Petersburg: Azbuka, 2001), pp. 257–8.
51. *many other Soviet . . . post-Stalin era*: See G. S. Smith, 'Rose and Briar Bush', *Times Literary Supplement*, 17 January 2014, p. 13.
52. *The Monkey*: Influenced by Wordsworth and Southey, Pushkin had experimented with lyric blank verse in his last years. Khodasevich was one of the first Russian poets to follow his example.
53. *Nel mezzo del cammin di nostra vita*: The opening line of Dante's *Divine Comedy*: 'Midway on our life's journey' (Robert Pinsky).
54. *Ode upon Khotín*: The basic rules of Russian versification were established by Mikhail Lomonosov (1711–65). The sonorous iambics of his 'Ode on the Capture of Khotín from the Turks', about a Russian victory in 1739, are considered to be the beginning of modern Russian poetry.
55. *Waterfall*: One of Derzhavin's most famous poems. See p. 12.
56. *Modigliani . . . few have survived*: See R. Eden Martin, 'Collecting Anna Akhmatova' in the *Caxtonian*, vol. 15, no. 4 (April 2007): http://www.caxtonclub.org/reading/2007/apr07.pdf.
57. *a necessary routine*: See Maurice Friedberg, *Literary Translation in Russia: A Cultural History* (University Park, PA: Pennsylvania State University Press, 1997), p. 194.
58. *She recalled later . . . the same train*: See David Wells, *Anna Akhmatova: Her Poetry* (Oxford: Berg, 1996), p. 15.

59. *When ill-wishers . . . Love for Dante*: Irina Sluzhevskaia, 'Dialog o Dante', *Storony Sveta*, no. 10 (2010): http://www.stosvet.net/10/sluzhevski/.
60. *brought into . . . Russian novel*: Mandelstam, 'Pis'mo o russkoi poezii' (1922), in *Polnoe sobranie sochinenii*, vol. 2, p. 58.
61. *All her descriptions . . . flair for details*: Pasternak's review remained unpublished for many years. This translation is from Angela Livingstone, *The Marsh of Gold: Pasternak's Writings on Inspiration and Creation* (Boston, MA: Academic Studies Press, 2008), p. 228.
62. About a well-known portrait of Akhmatova by Nathan Altman (1914).
63. *the window*: i.e., the prison-building window outside which people queued, hoping to be able to hand in letters and parcels to be sent on to relatives who had been imprisoned.
64. *Three Poems*: A homage to Alexander Blok, whose last poem is addressed to Pushkin House in Petersburg.
65. *a blinding illumination . . . and revolution*: Katherine Tiernan O'Connor, 'My Sister – Life', in Cornwell (ed.), *Reference Guide*, p. 620.
66. *Tsvetaeva wrote . . . renovate one's lungs*: Livingstone, *The Marsh of Gold*, p. 212.
67. *I didn't hear this . . . I heard nothing*: Olga Ivinskaya, *A Captive of Time: My Years with Pasternak*, trans. Max Hayward (London: Collins Harvill, 1978), p. 65.
68. *I see . . . a comrade*: ibid., p. 66.
69. *Whenever . . . beliefs about poetry*: ibid., p. 38.
70. *Sleep peacefully . . . know them all*: ibid., pp. 355–6.
71. *Especially hard . . . adapted to your eye*: Angela Livingstone, 'Pasternak', in Olive Classe (ed.), *Encyclopedia of Literary Translation into English* (London: Fitzroy Dearborn, 2000), vol. 2, p. 1044.
72. *Hamlet*: Pasternak first published his translation of *Hamlet* in 1941. It is the best known of his translations and the most popular Russian version of Shakespeare's play. It has been staged many times and Grigory Kozintsev used it for his 1964 film.
73. *Christmas Star*: Pasternak sent this poem to his friend the pianist Maria Yudina in February 1947. She replied, 'Had you written nothing else in your life, this poem would have been enough for your immortality on earth and in the sky'; see Stefano Gardzonio, '"Rozhdestvenskaia zvezda" Borisa Pasternaka: poeziia i zhivopis'', *Vinograd*, no. 1 (2008): http://www.vinograd.su/education/detail.php?id=42833. Zabolotsky praised the

poem almost as highly; see Nikita Zabolotsky, *The Life of Zabolotsky* (Cardiff: University of Wales Press, 1994), p. 308.

74. *Ode to Stalin*: Ilya Bernstein's outstanding translation of this ode is included in Osip Mandelstam, *Poems* (Boston, MA: M-Graphics Publishing, 2014). Bernstein writes: 'The result is "a combination of poetry and untruth", as the poet Vladimir Gandelsman has called it, which is impossible to forget because of the seriousness of the poetry and impossible to like because of the loathsomeness of the untruth.'

75. *Silentium*: A variation on Tyutchev's earlier poem 'Silentium' (see page 105).

76. *Batyushkov's . . . Eternity*: Such an exchange really did take place between Konstantin Batyushkov and his doctor; see Mandelstam, *Polnoe sobranie sochinenii*, vol. 1, p. 533. In 'For the Tombstone of a Little Girl' Batyushkov imagines a dead baby saying to her parents, 'Dear ones, don't cry! / Envy my ephemerality; / I did not know this life, / And know eternity' (trans. Peter France).

77. *The Admiralty*: The Admiralty building beside the Neva is one of Petersburg's landmarks. Its delicate gilded spire is topped by a weathervane in the shape of a frigate.

78. The translator comments: 'This is a hauntingly beautiful lyric, though all the references are wrong: Oliver Twist does not spend a minute in the office, Paul Dombey never deals with his father's clerks, no one cracks jokes in his presence, no debtor hangs himself in that novel, and the Thames is not yellow.'

79. *Solominka*: This poem is addressed to the Georgian princess Salomeya Andronikova. Lenore and Ligeia, who both died young, are from stories by Edgar Allan Poe. Seraphita is the androgynous hero(ine) of a novel by Honoré de Balzac.

80. *honeysuckle*: Peter France writes: 'The word *medunitsa* means both "honeybee" (as in line two of "Heaviness, tenderness . . ."), and the plant "lungwort", as in the twelfth line of "Take from my palms". I don't think "lungwort" means a great deal to non-botanists, and I guess that Mandelstam liked the Russian word because it contains honey (*med*). So I have gone for the more familiar and more evocative "honeysuckle" – may St Jerome forgive me!'

81. Another poem written in response to the news of Gumilyov's execution.

82. *six-winged bull*: The image of a six-winged bull is uncommon. Mandelstam may have taken it from the Book of Revelation 4:8, where a calf is one of four six-winged creatures around a throne set in heaven. The scholar Georgy Kubatian paraphrases these

four lines as follows: 'Labour seems gigantic and awesome, like a bull – yet also six-winged like a seraphim. It is inspired by the idea of the spiritual and crowned with the beauty of roses in blossom' ('Ot slova do slova', in *Vorovannyi vozdukh* (Yerevan: RAU, 2005), p. 10).

83. *bull-like peasant churches*: Many Armenian churches are built on hilltops, on the sites of former Zoroastrian temples. Most are simple and squat constructions, the central cupola resting on an octagon, which in turn rests on four central pillars.

84. *the Mountain*: Present-day Armenia occupies only a tenth of the land once considered Armenian. Mount Ararat, the supposed resting place of Noah's Ark, now stands in Turkey. The loss of this mountain, only thirty miles from Yerevan and a central symbol of Armenian identity, is felt deeply.

85. *a lion who . . . from a box*: Nadezhda Mandelstam remembers her husband, during their time in Armenia, noticing a pencil case with a lion depicted on the lid. And there are carved lions on the walls of several old Armenian churches.

86. *sardars*: i.e., the Persian governors who administered much of Armenia during the seventeenth and eighteenth centuries.

87. *octahedral honeycombs in your hands*: Several medieval Armenian churches have a small model of the church carved high on the outside of the east wall. Typically two human figures (the donors responsible for building the church) stand side by side, holding the model between them.

88. *Soaring forever . . . trumpets of Asia*: Here Mandelstam alludes to a line of Catullus: 'Ad claras Asiae volemus urbes' ('Let us fly towards the bright cities of Asia'). By 'Asia' Catullus meant what was once known as Asia Minor and is now Turkey. Mandelstam's Armenia is soaring not eastwards, but westwards, towards the Hellenistic world to which Mandelstam felt he belonged.

89. This poem evokes the ruins of the great seventh-century cathedral of Zvartnots, a huge three-storey building destroyed in an earthquake. Mandelstam thought of Byzantine culture as sterile.

90. In this poem, as if in a dream, Mandelstam imagines luring Mount Ararat back into Armenian territory.

91. *Kurds run . . . backers of both*: Most Kurds are Muslims, but some are Christians and some practise the Yazid religion, which is often (mistakenly) thought to be dualistic.

92. *who explicitly . . . historical sense*: Catriona Kelly, *A History of Russian Women's Writing 1820–1992* (Oxford: Clarendon Press, 1994), p. 277.

93. *her literary earnings*: Princess Salomeya Andronikova was another source of financial support (see note 79).
94. *NKVD*: The Soviet security service was renamed many times; its main names and acronyms were (in chronological order) the Cheka, the OGPU, the NKVD and the KGB.
95. *Follow after Hitler ... a swastika*: Trans. Moniza Alvi and Veronika Krasnova, in *Modern Poetry in Translation*, no. 1 (2014), p. 12.
96. *Roland's Horn*: This was one of Shalamov's favourite poems. See page 386 and Irina Sirotinskaya, 'The Years We Talked': http://www.shalamov.ru/en/memory/129.
97. *love's boat . . . daily grind*: Trans. Robert Brown, in *Sleepwalking with Mayakovsky* (Kent, OH: Kent State University Press, 1994), p. 12.
98. *As a boy . . . his very character*: Yevgeny Yevtushenko, *Twentieth-Century Russian Poetry*, ed. Albert C. Todd and Max Hayward with Daniel Weissbort (London: Fourth Estate, 1993), p. 241.
99. *This plea . . . central to his work*: See Katherine Lahti, 'The Animal Mayakovsky', in Jane Costlow and Amy Nelson (eds.), *Other Animals: Beyond the Human in Russian Culture and History* (Pittsburgh, PA: University of Pittsburgh Press, 2010), p. 149.
100. *Doronin*: Ivan Doronin (1900–78) was known for his long poem 'Ploughman on a Tractor' (1926).
101. *Angleterre*: The Leningrad hotel where Yesenin committed suicide. See page 342.
102. *Lohengriniches*: The operatic tenor Leonid Sobinov, famous for his performance as Lohengrin (the eponymous hero of an early opera by Wagner), sang settings of Yesenin's poems at a commemorative evening for him at the Moscow Art Theatre.
103. *Kogan*: A critic, then president of the National Academy of Artistic Sciences.
104. *We're ill-equipped . . . to be alive*: The last four lines, a respectful parody of the last lines of Yesenin's suicide poem, are difficult to translate. Capus translates them (*London Magazine*, August–September, 2010, pp. 21–2) as follows:

> On this planet of ours joy is in short supply.
> We must snatch it from the future while we can.
> In this life it's not so difficult to die.
> But it's hard to build a world that's fit for man.

Literally, the last line means: 'To make (or construct) life is significantly more difficult.'

105. *a lamb in wolf's clothing*: Andrei Ar'ev, in conversation with Ivan Tolstoi, 'Veter s Nevy: Zhizn' Georgiia Ivanova', *Radio Svoboda*, 11 October 2009: http://www.svoboda.org/content/transcript/1849756.html; see also Ar'ev's *Zhizn' Georgiia Ivanova* (Petersburg: Zvezda, 2009) and his 'K 50-letiiu so dnia smerti Georgiia Ivanova', *Zvezda*, no. 8 (2008): http://zvezdaspb.ru/index.php?page=8&nput=1025. Émigré writers also showed generosity. In the late 1940s more than a dozen important writers – including Bunin, Remizov, Teffi and Zaitsev – signed an appeal for donations to help Georgy Ivanov, 'whose talent is now at its zenith – except that material need and illness are not only hindering its fullest manifestation but are even threatening the poet's life' (Rene Gerra (Guerra) and Arkadii Vaksberg, *Sem' dnei v Marte* (Petersburg: Russkaia kul'tura, 2010), p. 257).

106. *1933*: Odoevtseva more than once gives 1932 as the year of his death, but there is indisputable archival documentation that he died on 25 September 1933.

107. *An ageing . . . verbal articulation*: G. S. Smith, 'Dust or Fear', *Times Literary Supplement* (9 November 2012).

108. *the teacher of my youth*: Ivanov, Letter to Vladimir Markov, 24 March 1956, in Georgij Ivanov and Irina Odojevceva, *Briefe an Vladimir Markov, 1955–1958*, ed. Hans Rothe (Cologne: Böhlau, 1994), p. 19.

109. *the beginning . . . love of poetry*: See V. P. Kreid, *Georgii Ivanov* (Moscow: Molodaia gvardiia, 2007), p. 12. And see p. 123.

110. *Magadan*: The capital of Kolyma, a vast area in the far north-east of the Soviet Union that was, in effect, a mini-State run by the NKVD. I have translated only the first half of this poem. Ivanov goes on to say that everything else in Russia – from Stalingrad to the 'accursed Kremlin' deserves to be burnt to ashes.

111. *Annensky loved . . . Gumilyov couldn't stand*: Boris Dralyuk writes, 'What lovely Annenskian touches in the first stanza – and then that wonderful twist, calling Annensky's love "greedy", the last word one would associate with such humble objects of affection, and with such a humble subject as Annensky. But it *is* greedy, purely selfish, to love such things – because the love is deeply private, makes nothing happen and crumbles when exposed to daylight'. Ivanov's poem is complex; he admired both poets and was well aware that Gumilyov saw Annensky as his most important teacher.

112. This seemingly simple poem is full of allusions. Lines 3 and 4 are an abridged quote from a poem Ivanov wrote in 1930, 'Pered tem, kak umeret''. Ivanov often revisits earlier poems, sometimes (as here) using words from the earlier work as a springboard for the new one. Line 6 quotes a famous fragment by Pushkin, 'Pora, moi drug, pora' (see p. 85). Line 8 is a distorted quote from '19 October 1828', one of several poems Pushkin wrote to celebrate anniversaries of the official opening of the Imperial Lycée, where he studied and formed many lifelong friendships. Pushkin himself wrote 'Shouting out to the Lycée "Hurrah!"' Ivanov's version literally reads 'Shouting out to Life "Hurrah!"'
113. *your quiet wrestle . . . your tongue round*: Ivanov's wife Odoevtseva suffered from a mild speech defect; she was unable to roll her 'r's.
114. *A large part . . . about animals*: Shalamov, 'Peizazhnaia lirika', in *Sobranie sochinenii v shesti tomakh* (Moscow: Terra, 2013), vol. 5, p. 74.
115. *Samuil Marshak . . . State Publishing House*: Marshak was influential and it was he, above all, who provided his younger colleagues with opportunities to publish and so to survive; it was, however, Oleinikov who first thought of commissioning children's books from Kharms, Vvedensky and Zabolotsky. See Alice Stone Nakhimovsky, *Laughter in the Void: An Introduction to the Writings of Daniil Kharms and Alexander Vvedenskii*, vol. 5 of *Wiener Slawistischer Almanach* (Vienna, 1982), p. 175, note 23.
116. *Marshak Academy . . . camels*: Nakhimovsky, *Laughter in the Void*, p. 19.
117. *Producers of art . . . young readers*: Sarah Suzuki in Marshak, *Baggage* (London: Tate Publishing, 2013).
118. *my friend . . . and abuser*: Yevgeny Shvarts, quoted in Thomas Epstein, 'The Dark and Stingy Muse of Nikolai Oleinikov', *Russian Review*, vol. 60, no. 2 (April 2001), pp. 238–58.
119. *with the special . . . wanted to hear*: Nikolay Zabolotsky, quoted in ibid., p. 241.
120. *Miss, I saw you . . . I can convey*: Trans. Eugene Ostashevsky, *OBERIU: An Anthology of Russian Absurdism* (Evanston, IL: Northwestern University Press, 2006), p. 195.
121. *OBERIU*: A provocative name: 'Ob'edinenie real'nogo iskusstva'. The Russian adjective *real'nyi* is ambiguous. If understood to mean 'real', it implies that the work of other artists might *not* be real art; if it is understood to mean 'realistic', then works by the OBERIU cast doubt on the nature of realism.

122. *an opera ... by Oleinikov*: Nakhimovsky, *Laughter in the Void*, p. 17. Pyotr Sokolov, a gifted artist close to the OBERIU, would have designed the sets and costumes for Shostakovich's opera *Lady Macbeth of the Mtsensk District* – but for his arrest in early 1935.
123. *The poem's human ... instruments of oppression*: Eugene Ostashevsky, *The Poetry Project Newsletter*, no. 197 (New York: The Poetry Project of St Mark's Church, December–January 2003–2004), pp. 9–11.
124. *The poet works ... the poet strives*: Zabolotsky, quoted by Robin Milner-Gulland in 'Zabolotskii', in Cornwell (ed.), *Reference Guide*, p. 900.
125. *babas*: Tall sweet cakes often containing raisins.
126. *pirogs*: A general term for pies.
127. *kulebyaka*: A fish, meat or vegetable pie.
128. Joseph Brodsky considered this the finest of all Russian poems about the camps, saying that Zabolotsky achieves here the simplicity that Pasternak strove towards but seldom achieved; see Solomon Volkov, *Conversations with Joseph Brodsky: A Poet's Journey through the Twentieth Century*, trans. Marian Schwartz (New York; London: The Free Press, 1998), p. 143.
129. *Goodbye sky ... heaven and earth*: P. I. Mel'nikov, *Na gorakh* (Moscow: Khudozhestvennaia literatura, 1979), part 1, p. 303.
130. *The highbrow ... do not die*: Nadezhda Tolokonnikova, quoted in Alexander Vvedensky, *An Invitation for Me to Think*, trans. Eugene Ostashevsky (New York: New York Review Books, 2013), p. xxv.
131. *Conversation about the Absence of Poetry*: From 'A Certain Quantity of Conversations', trans. Alice Stone Nakhimovsky, *Ulbandus: The Slavic Review of Columbia University*, vol. 1, no. 1 (New York: Columbia University, Fall 1977), pp. 114–15.
132. *important artists ... rediscovered*: The Galeev Gallery in Moscow publishes some remarkable books about the lesser-known Soviet artists of the 1920s and 1930s, many of whom collaborated with Kharms and Vvedensky. Two of the finest such artists are Alisa Poret and Pyotr Sokolov.
133. *The world of Kharms's ... reality itself*: Nakhimovsky, *Laughter in the Void*, p. 67.
134. *I trembled ... brother*: Alexander Solzhenitsyn, *Arkhipelag Gulag* (Moscow: Sovetskii pisatel', 1989), vol. 3, p. 106.
135. *Western publishers ... casually*: Shalamov attached great importance to the ordering of his *Kolyma Tales* and to the unity

of the collection. He had expected *Kolyma Tales* to be published in the West in full, as a single book. Instead, the stories appeared two or three at a time, over a period of many years, in issues of *Novy zhurnal*, a Russian-language journal published in the United States. And the selections of stories translated into English, French and German attracted little attention; the German publishers even misspelled Shalamov's name. See Leona Toker, 'Samizdat and the Problem of Authorial Control: The Case of Varlam Shalamov', *Poetics Today*, vol. 29, no. 4 (Winter 2008), pp. 735–58.

136. *Huntington's disease*: In 1957 Shalamov was diagnosed with Ménière's disease; this was confirmed in 1970. In 1979 he was given the still more serious diagnosis of Huntington's disease (also known as Huntington's chorea).

137. *grounded in . . . its truth*: Leona Toker, *Return from the Archipelago: Narratives of Gulag Survivors* (Bloomington: Indiana University Press, 2000), p. 187.

138. *the best of Russian poetry*: Shalamov, *Neskol'ko moikh zhiznei* (Moscow: EKSMO, 2009), p. 31.

139. *The principles of Acmeism . . . aesthetic views*: Shalamov, *Vospominaniia* (Moscow: AST, 2003), p. 313 and http://shalamov.ru/memory/118/.

140. *Old Believers*: See also Voloshin's poem 'Russia' (p. 178). Elsewhere Shalamov wrote, 'In Russian history, it is the Old Believers, the schismatics, who displayed the greatest strength of will, the greatest heroism' (*Sobranie sochinenii v shesti tomakh* (Moscow: Terra, 2013), vol. 3, p. 450).

141. *1950*: The years Shalamov gives for this and most subsequent poems refer not to the date of composition but to the date of incidents that inspired the poems.

142. *Roland's horn*: See Tsvetaeva's 'Roland's Horn' (p. 305), one of Shalamov's favourite poems.

143. *Baratynsky*: This poem records a real incident. Shalamov describes how playing cards were made from paper, saliva, urine, a little chewed bread and a tiny piece of crayon (*Sobranie sochinenii v shesti tomakh* (Moscow: Terra, 2013), vol. 3, p. 447).

144. *wish-granting pike*: A reference to a well-known folk tale, 'Yemelya the Fool'. The lazy and foolish hero saves the life of a pike, which then grants his every wish.

145. *My cross . . . two fingers*: Old Believers make the sign of the cross with two fingers. One of Patriarch Nikon's most controversial

reforms was his decree that the sign of the cross be made with three fingers.

146. *I was young*: Shalamov was himself only twenty-one when he was first arrested as a member of the Left Opposition. See Josefina Lundblad-Janjić, 'Poetry and Politics: An Allegorical Reading of Varlam Shalamov's Poem "Avvakum v Pustozyorske"': http://shalamov.ru/en/research/239.
147. *Nastasia . . . do not despair*: Avvakum's wife Anastasia Markovna accompanied him into exile and remained loyal to him throughout her life.
148. *to knock, as ash . . . human heart*: A reference to *The Legend of Thyl Ulenspiegel*, a novel by Charles de Coster (1827–79) that has long been popular in Russia. Thyl wears round his neck a sachet containing some of the ashes of his father Klaas, who had been burnt as a heretic. As he fights for the freedom of Flanders, Thyl repeats to himself, 'The ashes of Klaas are knocking at my heart.'
149. *The poets . . . to him*: Information from Tarkovsky's daughter Marina Tarkovskaya, by email (20 April 2012).
150. *The poetry . . . central theme*: Arseny Tarkovsky, 'The Opportunities of Translation', in Brian James Baer and Natalia Olshanskaya (eds.), *Russian Writers on Translation* (Manchester: St Jerome Publishing, 2013), p. 119.
151. *an unexpected . . . contemporary reader*: Lidiia Chukovskaia, *Zapiski ob Anne Akhmatovoi*, vol. 2, p. 758.
152. *a keeper of the flame . . . Ivanov*: Larisa Miller, 'A esli byl iiun' i den' rozhden'ia!', *Omiliia* (27 October 2011): http://omiliya.org/article/a-esli-byl-iyun-i-den-rozhdenya-larisa-miller.html.
153. *helping Shalamov . . . Soviet Writers*: Marina Tarkovskaya writes of her joy on learning this in *Oskolki zerkala* (Moscow: Dedalus, 1999), p. 152.
154. *I won't give you up . . . invulnerable*: This represents only the last four lines of a poem that, in the original, is fully rhymed and takes up twenty much longer lines.
155. *Love me . . . pure light*: All of the original is translated here, but using shorter and less regular lines.
156. *March saw . . . wiped from the earth*: This can be read as a sceptical response to the Khrushchev 'Thaw', the at least relatively liberal period following the death of Stalin.
157. *It was as if . . . her own apartment*: Yakov Druskin, quoted in Lev Druskin, *Spasennaia kniga: Vospominaniia leningradskogo*

poeta (London: OPI, 1984): http://www.modernlib.ru/books/druskin_lev/spasennaya_kniga_vospominaniya_leningradskogo_poeta/read.

158. *an article ... Soviet soil*: The increasingly anti-Semitic Soviet authorities eventually forbade publication. A complete Russian text was first published in Israel in 1980, in Kiev in 1991, and in Vilnius in 1993. *The Unknown Black Book* (*Neizvestnaia chernaia kniga*), a separate volume with additional material, was published in Moscow in 1993 and in the United States in 2008.

159. *a long poem ... early 1946*: Maxim Shrayer refers to this poem (reprinted in 1947 and four times between 1966 and 1986) as 'the most historically reliable and extensive treatment of Babi Yar in all of Soviet Poetry', *I Saw It: Ilya Selvinsky and the Legacy of Bearing Witness to the Shoah* (Boston, MA: Academic Studies Press, 2013), p. 238.

160. My translation borrows from that of Vladimir Markov and Merrill Sparks, in their *Modern Russian Poetry* (London: MacGibbon & Kee, 1966), p. 770.

161. *Shmuel Halkin*: (1897–1960) A leading Soviet Yiddish poet and playwright. During the Second World War he wrote powerful poems about the Shoah and was a member of the Jewish Anti-Fascist Committee and of the editorial board of its journal *Eynikayt*. After being arrested in 1949, he suffered a heart attack. This may have saved his life; unlike the other members of the Committee, who were shot in 1952, he was sent to a labour camp. Some of the poems he composed there were included, in 1966, in a Soviet edition of *Mayn Oytser*, but the collection was first published in full only in 1988, in Israel.

162. *Maleyevka*: Once a grand estate, Maleyevka became a Union of Soviet Writers 'House of Creativity' in the 1930s. Among the many writers who stayed there over the years were Anna Akhmatova, Bulat Okudzhava, Mikhail Prishvin and Nikolay Zabolotsky.

163. *Sergey Spassky*: (1898–1956) A poet, translator and prose writer, he was arrested and sent to the Gulag in 1951, but released in 1954, after Stalin's death.

164. *zek*: A prisoner in a Soviet labour camp.

165. *Soldiers cut it out ... killed and wounded*: Konstantin Simonov, *Izbrannaia lirika*, ed. M. Beliaev (Moscow: Molodaia gvardiia, 1964), p. 3. See also: www.simonov.co.uk/biography.htm.

166. *some Jews ... spiritual tradition*: Judith Deutsch Kornblatt, *Doubly Chosen: Jewish Identity, the Soviet Intelligentsia, and the*

Russian Orthodox Church (Madison, WI: University of Wisconsin Press, 2004), p. 143.

167. *Markish . . . saved his life*: Alexander Galich, *Dress Rehearsal: A Story in Four Acts and Five Chapters*, trans. Maria Bloshteyn (Bloomington, IN: Slavica Publishers, 2008), p. xx.
168. *Ivanov writes . . . separate mark*: Galich, *Dress Rehearsal*, p. 189.
169. *CC CPSU*: The Central Committee of the Communist Party of the Soviet Union.
170. *He once explained . . . learn from*: Lev Ozerov, 'Rezkaia liniia', in Petr Gorelik (ed.), *Boris Slutsky: Vospominaniia sovremennikov* (Petersburg: Neva, 2005), p. 342. How much Slutsky knew of other languages remains unclear. It is possible that Slutsky knew T. S. Eliot and Paul Celan in the original; see Marat Grinberg, *'I Am to Be Read Not from Left to Right, But in Jewish: from Right to Left'* (Boston, MA: Academic Studies Press, 2013), pp. 23, 81 n.65, 354 n.56. Grinberg adds, 'He writes about learning English in his unpublished memoir fragment. He knew Eliot through Brodsky and through the translator Andrey Sergeyev, with whom he edited an anthology of modern American poetry in 1975' (email, October 2013). Larisa Bespalova, however, is certain that Slutsky did *not* read English or German; her husband Vladimir Kornilov was a friend of Slutsky's and she knew Slutsky well (in conversation, November 2013).
171. *plain as porridge*: G. S. Smith, 'Rose and Briar Bush', p. 13.
172. *he always . . . borderlands*: ibid., p. 19.
173. *Slutsky almost . . . has survived*: Loseff, *Joseph Brodsky*, p. 54.
174. *moments of extreme banality*: e.g., 'On the pages of classical novels / once studied in school, I find rest; / for their sake I'm able to pardon / the pogroms and the sudden arrests' (unpublished translation by Stephen Capus).
175. *In the 1950s . . . poems he wrote:* Vladimir Kornilov, *Pokuda nad stikhami plachut* (Moscow: Vremia, 2009), p. 498.
176. *Slutsky's poem . . . this incident*: The late Omry Ronen has written about this with insight ('Grust'', in *Zvezda*, no. 9, 2012). See also Semen Lipkin, *Kvadriga* (Moscow: Knizhnyi sad, 1997), pp. 506–13.
177. *his many . . . remembered*: See Grinberg, *I Am to Be Read*, p. 298.
178. *was somehow . . . official world*: ibid., p. 298.
179. *Slutsky . . . typed out*: Email from Grossman's daughter Yekaterina Korotkova-Grossman (8 July 2013).
180. *The life that I lived . . . concise tragedies*: Grinberg, *I Am to Be Read*, p. 154.

181. Slutsky seldom recorded the dates of his poems.
182. *About the Jews*: By 1987 (when it was published in Russia) this poem had become folklore, Slutsky's authorship largely forgotten.
183. *old woman*: Akhmatova. Slutsky's view, as often, is unconventional. Akhmatova was greatly revered and few writers, other than Party hacks, dared to criticize her.
184. *In a talk ... literal version*: Friedberg, *Literary Translation in Russia*, p. 174.
185. *His poems ... convey everything*: Evgeny Vinokurov, *The War is Over*, trans. Anthony Rudolf and Daniel Weissbort (Cheadle: Carcanet New Press, 1976), pp. 12–13.
186. *As he says ... street-cleaner*: 'After a month he was dismissed on the pretext that it was "illegal to employ someone with higher education for such duties"' (email from Bespalova, July 2013).
187. *He writes about ... similar fate*: Vladimir Kornilov, *Pokuda nad stikhami plachut* (Moscow: Vremia, 2009), p. 524, 518.
188. *Who has recognized ... human race*: Loseff, *Joseph Brodsky*, p. 80.
189. *What a biography ... on purpose*: Akhmatova, quoted in David Remnick, 'Gulag Lite: Mikhail Khodorkovsky', in *The New Yorker* (20 December 2010): http://www.newyorker.com/magazine/2010/12/20/gulag-lite.
190. *He later spoke ... of his life*: Loseff, *Joseph Brodsky*, p. 96.
191. *Misha Nikolaev*: Part of Mikhail Nikolaev's remarkable memoir *Orphanage* (trans. Robert Chandler) appears in Natasha Perova (ed.), *Childhood* (Moscow: Glas, 1998).
192. *Komsomól*: A Soviet perfume, named after the Communist youth group, membership of which was all but compulsory in the Soviet Union.
193. *High-born ... eats no meat*: Count Lev Tolstoy liked to dress as a peasant; he also fathered many illegitimate children on his serf girls.

6. THREE MORE RECENT POETS

1. *In Shvarts's poetry ... full of poems*: Obituary in the *Guardian* (6 May 2010): www.theguardian.com/books/2010/may/06/elena-shvarts-obituary.

7. FOUR POEMS BY NON-RUSSIANS

1. *The Moscow Metro . . . have passed*: http://www.fiveleaves.co.uk/poetry.html.
2. *bomzh*: A Russian acronym, meaning a down-and-out.
3. *Moskva-Petushki*: The title of a brilliant short novel by Venedikt Yerofeyev; see the best English translation *Moscow Stations*, trans. Stephen Mulrine (London: Faber, 1997). The novel is told in the first person and the authorial voice is that of an alcoholic on a suburban train.
4. *zeks*: A colloquial Russian term for a prisoner in a forced-labour camp.
5. *Happy Moscow*: Andrey Platonov's novel in which the heroine, an orphan named Moscow Chestnova, has a leg amputated after an accident while working on the construction of the Moscow Metro; see *Happy Moscow*, trans. Robert and Elizabeth Chandler (London: Vintage Books, 2013).
6. *Eloi-Ego . . . the show*: In H. G. Wells's *The Time Machine* the Eloi are the effete descendants of the upper classes, while the Morlocks live underground, tending machinery and providing clothing. At first the hero imagines that the Morlocks are serving the Eloi. He then realizes that the Morlocks feed on the Eloi and are farming them like cattle.
7. *Base and Superstructure paradigm*: Marx saw a society's belief system as a 'superstructure' founded on its economic 'base'; the nature of the 'base' determines that of the religious or philosophical 'superstructure'.
8. *dipped our whiskers in the beer*: Russian folk tales often end: 'I, too, was at the feast, but I barely dipped my whiskers in the mead.'

Index of Titles and First Lines